Bang

BANG,

Shoot

SHOOT!

essays on guns
and popular culture

SECOND EDITION

edited by
Murray Pomerance & John Sakeris

Pearson
Education

Cover image of Christopher Olsen in Alfred Hitchcock's *The Man Who Knew Too Much*
Courtesy of Paramount Pictures Corporation/Corbis.

Published in association with the Media Studies Working Group.

Printed in the United States of America

10 9 8 7 6 5 4 3 2 1

Please visit our website at www.pearsoncustom.com

ISBN 0-536-60344-8

BA 990713

PEARSON EDUCATION
160 Gould Street/Needham Heights, MA 02494
A Pearson Education Company

You just never know when a girl
might need a bullet.

Shelley Winters in *Winchester 73*

Contents

Preface

John Sakeris

We all know about the central gun use in films like *Men in Black, Pulp Fiction* and *Thelma and Louise*; and that our world in general is full of images of guns and gun use. These images and their subsequent social meaning and context interest us, and we believe they will interest readers of this volume. It is now almost impossible to consider pop cultural representations—from a sociological, a political-economic, a psychological, a literary critical, or a cultural point of view—without coming face to face with the image of the loaded gun.

The following twenty papers all deal in one way or another with the issues and questions that arise when we think of so-called mass culture and the mass media, questions that are the focus of a growing number of university courses in communication, pop culture, media criticism, film history, and related fields. For example, what is the connection between gun representation and gender in our society? Indeed, how is social change affecting that depiction? Several of the papers presented here attempt to clarify gun representation in light of that question. Do the "new" images of women—often armed women—in films like *G. I. Jane* and *The Silence of the Lambs* empower women, or do they reinforce traditional patriarchal views? The papers by Carol Dole and Lauren Tucker with Alan Fried open that debate, with a very practical concentration on pop cultural materials; we have perhaps made some progress toward a culture that empowers women, they suggest; yet perhaps not as much progress as might at first seem to be the case.

Even more than gender definition, narrative violence can be about gender liberation, as Robin Wood's careful reflections on *The Doom Generation* show. While Nicole Marie Keating studies the cinematic representation of male and female "gazes" and suggests that in terms of the way they activate gender, the gazes are pointed guns.

Most recent political and cultural analysis operates on the premise that a great percentage of the world's population is a major consumer of American cultural product. As neighbors with a firm economic and linguistic bond with the United States, Canadian viewers constitute a special and unique case. While Canadians do not possess the same number of firearms as Americans per capita, or have the same levels of interpersonal violence, they are nonetheless part of the mix of gunfire and culture, and the Canadian social system and identity are no less affected by gun use and its representation than that of any other country. Around the world one of the most lucrative and global industries is mass media, an industry which, while often centered in the U.S., is run through "branch plant" operations elsewhere. Wondering at the social consequences of this arrangement, Wendy Pearson offers a commentary on *Due South* that examines the cultural clash between Canadians and Americans about guns and gun use, and considers its significance more broadly.

Film and television gun use is of course symbolic and has very real political messages in our increasingly polarized society. Kirby Farrell gives us a provocative look at "aliens" and immigration in his article on *Men in Black* and Grayson Cooke considers guns and technology and the mythology of the American Western, with its distortion of American history. *Top Gun* was a film that could have been made by the military, and Linda Robertson looks at the issue of popular film and war with a keen analysis of the relationship between narrative and propaganda. Three articles consider the direct relationship between film's symbolic power and social and political movements: Anver Saloojee looks at Eisenstein's and Bertolucci's portrayals of gun use as revolutionary forces; Dan Streible considers the films of Verhoeven—in particular, *Starship Troopers*—in light of the fascist aesthetic; and Fred Turner critiques TV shows like *Cops* and their implicit message of police control.

Two challenging papers considers among other things, the issue of gun control: Leslie Fiedler, as always, tweaks conventional wisdom in an incomparably rich and evocative exploration of his own life; and Murray Forman presents an analysis of the representation of gun acquisition in film, contexted by increasing social pressures for legal gun control.

Nor can gun use in pop culture be studied independently of race. Cynthia Fuchs looks at hiphop culture, considering the issue of racism in relationship to mass media depictions of violent postures and behavior.

Film form is interestingly analysed in Steven Woodward's study of the perplexing *Grosse Pointe Blank*. His paper, like all the rest, deals in some way with commerce, with the fact that images of gun use are a form of currency. But two essays in particular stand out. George Gerbner makes the telling point that violence and gun use are easy, cheap and sell readily in a global markets, while Cynthia Walker offers a fascinating history of *The Man From U.N.C.L.E.* and toy manufacturing, showing that marketing through film and TV is not new and that storylines themselves are affected by marketing demands.

But all these papers are in some important way directed to the young. Addressing children specifically, Ellen Seiter presents an innovative formula for the dilemma of parents negotiating with their children on viewing "superheroes."

Considering the diversity and depth of the subjects handled in the papers (and two lectures) of this volume, it's clear that the idea that "violence is bad and we have to stop it" just doesn't go far enough or penetrate deeply below the surface of media images. We wanted to try to get at a serious understanding of the role of violence in popular culture.

Focusing on the image of the gun allows for a rich play of analytical language—from many disciplines—about a central, and too often minimized, element in our cultural life. In fact, as Gerbner said, guns are so pervasive that we no longer notice them: we are like fish who don't perceive the water they swim in.

While we have presented papers here that all in some way deal with the image of the gun in popular culture, they are also, some more explicitly than others, critical of the society and social structure in which these images are created. The media are being blamed increasingly for the more outrageous and tragic shooting incidents that we have witnessed via the news, yet our authors offer explanations deeper and more challenging. As transnationals are concerned only with the bottom line, and sell us more and more inflaming imagery; as the world shrinks in the search for cheaper markets and cheaper labor; as the military infrastructure that protects the interests of those multinationals permeates daily life in North America, our culture changes. We live in a competitive, individualistic, and militaristic world, where racism, sexism, anti-semitism, homophobia and ethnic hatred abound. We are encouraged to become cheerleaders for the police, the military, and war, at one time consulting psychologists to help us over the trauma of Littleton and also feeling humanitarian pride as we drop bombs on civilians in a world that seems so far away and unlike ours. Life is indeed becoming more gun-ridden, nasty and brutal as we compete for the ever-decreasing share of the pie that the multinationals leave us. We are being dehumanized in each others' eyes and dehumanization is one of the most effective ways to get people who might otherwise be happy to live in peace, to kill each other eagerly, be it in war, on the street, in church, in the high school library, or in the family. And as we turn upon each other, the deeper structural causes of our violence are consistently outside the range of our vision.

We welcome to this Second Edition the noted critic of media and popular culture, Mark Crispin Miller, who provides us, in his interview "Bullets in the Entertainment State," with some provocative ideas about the connection between media and societal violence. Further, Judy Hunter's essay on big guns in political culture brings a distinctly political perspective to a challenging discussion of neoconservatism and action heroism. Many of the articles in this book, in addition, have been updated in response to the shocking events that have been capturing headlines since the first edition of this book appeared in January 1999.

We would like to express gratitude for the help we have received in making *Bang Bang, Shoot Shoot!* To Ryerson Polytechnic University, especially the Office of Research Services, we are grateful for generosity beyond the call of duty. Rufus Dickinson of Toronto Court Reporters graciously provided transcription services. Nellie Perret's editorial advice was invaluable. Ariel Pomerance brought his unique vision to the project.

A special thanks is due to our friends and collaborators David Daniels, Lori Bittker, Kristen Kiley, Sarah Hull, Kathy Kourian, Mark Banbury, Andrew Furman, Craig Dunsmuir and Paul Kelly.

Willing to Explode: The American Western as Apocalypse-Machine

Grayson Cooke

I

This paper is about mythography and a myth: the myth of America's progressive past and inevitably technological future, its representation in the Classic Western, and the role of the gun in this system, and I shall begin by outlining the way I see this myth to function.[1] In this paper, I shall be drawing on the works of Gilles Deleuze and Félix Guattari, whose critiques of territorial regimes and theories of machinic assemblages I have found particularly useful for discussing the Western.[2] I shall also make reference to the work of Richard Slotkin, an American historian and Professor of English whose three books, *Regeneration Through Violence* (1973), *The Fatal Environment* (1985) and *Gunfighter Nation* (1992) serve as an eloquent and biting history of American mythography.

Let us look into the heart of the American myth: unlike *tribal* myths, for instance, this myth provides a working model of an *empire*; it begins not with creation but with arrival, and advises domination rather than harmonic coexistence; as with most settler nations, there was never a question of belonging. The American myth does not attempt to explain how Americans came to be humans living on earth (the Puritans already had the answer to this; it was God that did it!), but it does try to come to terms with the position of being in a new land, a New World, some sort of second Eden, as if being new to a land could in some way return you to the pre-lapsarian state of being new to the World—as if innocence comes with a territory, or is a state of being that can be discovered. Indeed, all nations founded on a settler or pilgrim mentality begin with the constitution of territories; with the discovering, claiming, and partitioning of space, the subjugation or destruction of any previous inhabitants of the land as part of the process of making the land one's own, and the institution of sedentary political formations (the *polis*) as a means of governing the land and its new "owners."

This myth is in no way tribal, because it is *Western* and therefore fundamentally technical. We must remember that America has its origin in the age of the printing press, and that its myths stem not from a long and nebulous oral tradition, but from the literary works of hack novelists, travel and adventure writers and others attempting to sell the New World back to the Old one. Derrida was never so American as when he argued for the primacy of writing over orality. In particular, we could mention Delmer Daves' film *Broken Arrow* (1950), in which the hero, Tom (James Stewart) is concerned primarily with convincing the Indians, in all their savage orality, to *let the mail get through*; in other words, to allow the technology of the Word to spread across, and to claim for itself, a territory.

The myth of America is a myth that is real. Or rather, a myth that *must be treated as real*. Myths provide us with a certain awareness of the world and how it might function. Of every myth, we must ask what it facilitates, and what social, technical, biological or rhetorical machines it connects to. Richard Slotkin has consistently called for an examination of the process of myth-making in terms of how myths elide some histories in favor of others, how they re-interpret historical events, and how they feed back into military, political and cultural policy. We can take the myth of America presented in Westerns to be in some senses "true," then, without claiming that it is necessarily historically accurate. Westerns were never about "telling the whole story," and to think that they might ever do such a thing would be profoundly naive.

Rather, myths are true because they bring to the fore the process of myth-making, they expose the dreams of nations. While Westerns may not be historically accurate, they are at least technologically accurate, because they allow us to *see the machines*. They chart the spread of many different technologies (and 'assemblages' or conglomerates of different technologies) across a hitherto open space that can be considered empty because it is inhabited by peoples who are not technical and therefore seem to be going nowhere. John Cawelti notes in *The Six-Gun Mystique* that the Western bounds off and highlights "the image of the isolated town or ranch or fort surrounded by the vast open grandeur of prairie or desert and connected to the rest of the civilized world by a railroad, a stagecoach, or simply a trail."[3] What does this show us but a working model of a territorial machine connected to a technical social machine? A point is laid down in the wilderness and lines are connected between it and other, larger points. If the machine functions correctly, all the points grow and new points proliferate; territories are established, more and more space is captured, time is apportioned according to the demands of production, consumption and technical expansion. Other machines will be needed; guns, the telegraph, mail, and machines of social control—the bounty system, mob rule, puritanical religion. The study of cinematic texts and the myths they propound is important because the cinema sees—simply and directly—machines. And what the Western shows is a program: the assembly instructions for an empire.

II

Let us begin our discussion of the gun with a quick outline of the system, a scene from Anthony Mann's *Man of the West* (1958):

> *. . . a mute holds a gun on a cowardly man while he is made to dig a grave; inside the house the villains are forcing the female captive to strip while the hero is forced to watch; the mute should perhaps be blind as well, seeing only through the barrel of his gun, a form of machinic perception; the coward says he "can't dig no more, with him standing there with that rifle, never says nothing, just keeps looking at you," and we are tempted to believe that he says this of the gun; the mute is just there to direct the gun's attention, focus its gaze . . .*

Guns are omnipresent in the Western, closer to God than any machine could come, the one code that functions when all other codes are gone. Even in their absence—as in depictions of Wyatt Earp's Tombstone, Arizona where all guns must be relinquished upon entering the town—guns continue to signify, to exert a presence. You always know that if a gun is taken away, it is taken away only in order to return. Guns are the perfect Heideggerian technology, because they always "bring forth" a spectacle; a flash of light, an explosion, the sight of the wound and the revelation of sudden death.[4]

One of the stories that has been identified as a founding instance of American mythography, and that is particularly prevalent in the Western, suggests "regeneration through violence," the idea that violent conflict is legitimate because it is potentially redemptive and in this way tied into narratives of progress and "civilization." If we are to talk of the gun as the emblem of this myth of regeneration through violence, we must begin by asking what the gun produces, and what it facilitates, what this production opens up or puts into circulation. I would argue that the gun performs the twofold task of marking bodies,[5] and, as part of this inscription, initiating exchange. Inscription is nothing without exchange, the mark's referral to another mark and the public recognition of this process. The gun functions as a mark before it is even "activated"; like a nuclear weapon, a gun does not need to go off in order to function, for it functions as a sign merely by being attached to, or detached from, a body. In a vital mutation, mechanical becoming is actualized then naturalized—witness the utmost importance of carrying a gun or of being *seen* to carry a gun, and the shock that always accompanies the discovery of a man *without* a gun, or a man who refuses to use one. For instance, as the villains flee the town of Tombstone where their guns were confiscated by Wyatt Earp in Mann's *Winchester 73* (1950), one of them says, "I'm sick and tired of going around naked. We need guns!!"

The first task of the gun is to form an assemblage, an "abstract machine" whose working parts, like those of Cameron's Terminator and other cyborgs of popular culture and much post-modern theory, encompass both the human/biological and the technological. We must note that assemblage is a widespread function of gun use, not in any way limited to the Western; for instance, in Shinya Tsukamoto's underground film *Tetsuo*

II: Body Hammer (1992), a scene in flashback reveals a father teaching his two boys to merge with their guns: "When your will and the will of the gun become one, then you can kill the dog." A similar "entrainment" of wills and hybridization of gun and user occurs in David Cronenberg's *Videodrome* (1982), where a gun emerges from Max Renn's (James Woods) hand (having earlier been deposited in his stomach) when he needs it to constitute "the new flesh." Similarly, in *The Place of Dead Roads*, William Burroughs' foray into the Western, the gun-user is advised to "[i]dentify yourself with your gun. Take it apart and finger every piece of it. Think of the muzzle as a steel eye feeling for your opponent's vitals with a searching movement. Move forward in time and see the bullet hitting the target as an *accomplished fact*."[6] The rhetoric that emerges around gunfighting in the Western strongly attests to this gun-user hybridization, because the idea of the "hired gun" is actually a metonymy, expressing the gunfighter through the gun. There is the suggestion that it is actually the gun itself one hires, with its attendant human "operator," and that the operator has hired it as much as he himself has been hired *as* a gun. Anyone, good or bad, can use a gun and therein lies the most ambiguous virtue of technology as a whole; that—like capitalism, for instance—it is always a *pharmakon*— your poison *and* your cure. You can never know which way it will jump, and it is not until it is connected to social, territorial, despotic, or mystical and spiritual machines that its alignment is actualized or stratified.

But it is only through exchange that assemblages, such as guns, become productive. We could talk first of social exchange—the modes of social interaction the gun facilitates, which are predominantly homosocial. In the Western, men bond under the sign of the gun, the sign of a fetishization of violent acts performed or retributive acts to come. Alliances through the gun are always ephemeral, easily destroyed, and are almost always cruel. Despite the ephemeral nature of the bonds the gun allows for, it is nevertheless a conduit, directing flows of money and blood, racial flows, sexual flows, flows of cattle and land, flows of signs, names and faces: notorious flows.

We can also talk of the bounty and revenge systems, which run on the circulation and exchange of infamy. The hired gun, and the whole system of bounty and reward money that proliferates around it, is the perfect example of the economy of gunplay, because it commodifies one of the most important products of the gun: death. Indeed, killing for money is perhaps one of the purest, coldest and most logical forms of capitalism, in that rather than exchanging alienated commodities and the products of alienated labor, it simply exchanges those things common to all beings: life and death. The bounty system has nothing to do with social justice or lawful retribution, which is its public (and highly duplicitous) face; rather, the whole point of it is the institutionalization of the *desire to produce death*, which allows for the circulation of capital, and it is the gun which allows capital to circulate in this manner. The myth of "regeneration through violence," therefore, comes to equal the movement of capital, the continuation and growth of the system.

Anthony Mann's *The Naked Spur* (1953) expresses this logic well. The film concerns Howie's (James Stewart) supposedly righteous hunt for Ben (Robert Ryan), on the grounds that Ben shot a man in the back. Yet as the film progresses, it becomes clear that Howie's motivations are more economic than altruistic; Howie has lost his wife and his farm, and is in desperate need of cold hard cash rather than any moral reward. Roy (Ralph Meeker), a member of Howie's posse, succinctly expresses Howie's real interest in Ben: "He's not a man, he's a sack of money; why don't you face up to it?"

Death—in the Western always violent and technological—is here subject to an apparatus of capture. There is no such thing as a "natural" death; if a man is to die, he will be shot, or perhaps he will be captured and hanged. Either way, his death will be desired by another, it will be captured, bought and sold; and will become part of the grand flow of symbolic capital. Don Siegel's film *The Shootist* (1976) describes the system well: J.B. Books (John Wayne), an infamous gunman, has cancer; he arrives in Carson City to die. But, in a Western death by something as pathetic as a disease is impossible. Books must cheat *natural* death and go out in a way more "fitting for a gunfighter"; after a gunfight in the saloon, he is shot in the back by the bartender, who in turn is shot by Books' young, and clearly impressionable, disciple Gillom Rogers (Ron Howard). This is technological death, death by the code of revenge.

But what does it mean to build a cinematic genre, or an empire, on a widespread fantasy of violent and technological death? Why build such an elaborate structure in order to disallow—even mythically—the very possibility of such a thing as a private, privately-owned death? "Natural" death is devoid of meaning in the Western because it circumvents the codes of life and death that genre institutes: namely that men live and die by the gun. What is this but a celebration of the God-given right to die at the hands of another, an act that allows blood, money, names, faces and signs to flow? In this sense, the American Constitutional right to *carry* a gun is perhaps more accurately the right to *die* by the gun in a generic, willed death: "Technical, non-natural and therefore *willed* (ultimately by the victim him or herself), death becomes interesting once again, since *willed* death has a meaning."[7] We might wonder exactly what strange techno-Gods the Western, and many other Hollywood genres, propitiate with so many violent, technological and sacrificial deaths.

III

If it were not intrinsically technological and expansionist, an expression of "the American meaning of frontiers: something to go beyond, limits to cross over, flows to set in motion, noncoded spaces to enter,"[8] the Western could be Buddhist in its simplicity, a system which celebrates first the moment before the explosion, as a whole in itself, and the actual explosion only afterward. And it is hard to tell whether we are talking about the myth of the frontier or about guns and gunshots; to a large extent the distinction is meaningless. Because what is the myth of the frontier but a nostalgic celebration of the moment before the explosion, the moment before the frontier was closed and the machine of industrial capital had claimed the earth for its own? The myth of the frontier is certainly a celebration of the *process* of building a machine that explodes, a machine constructed to explode; an apocalypse-machine.

Although I do not have space for a full exploration of the clear relation of the apocalypse-machine to apocalyptic and millenarian thought in America, I should explain what I mean by such a term. Briefly, an apocalypse-machine is any social or technological structure that is designed to reproduce by annihilating either itself or something else. It is this annihilation that is deemed regenerative. In Biblical mythology, the apocalypse is a moment of revelation and judgment, of redemption and purification. The myth of regeneration through violence is an apocalypse-machine, because it is an organized enterprise that will always advise a violent solution to a social problem. Being animals with an awareness of our own deaths, we have used this awareness to encapsulate and commodify the deaths of others, and it is no surprise that such an awareness finds its way into the production of culture; it is also no surprise that this process of taking death hostage is made productive, particularly in a technical culture that desires to make everything productive, everything quantified, everything working and workable. But the myth of the frontier—spaces to fill, endlessly multiplying limits to cross—finds a particular manifestation in a narrative device common to many Westerns, though particularly prevalent in gunfighter films: the exploding limit point, which is gradually approached then finally, cataclysmically crossed, in the hope of instituting something "new."

If the Western is almost Buddhist, it is also almost Taoist and almost Deleuzian, for all of these modes of thought celebrate the idea of process, being in the middle, an eternal *intermezzo,* a lingering preparation for crossing the line, a calm before the storm. Even on an interpersonal level, the logic of anticipation is at work; the hesitation undergone before drawing one's gun, the ruse of hiding the gun arm until the last possible moment, the sparring between gunmen which is more an issue of homosocial foreplay than actual violence. Yet the guns do go off, annulling all the foreplay that has gone before. The explosions do happen, and the terrible truth is that they are desired.

The same can be said of both the representation, and the actual history, of the frontier. From one perspective, the frontier is pure openness, pure potentiality, and it is no surprise that the Western celebrates the moment in American history when such a space not merely existed but could be inhabited, albeit perilously. Witness the stoic, triumphant glory of the tiny house dwarfed by the surrounding plains (in, for example, George Stevens' *Shane* [1953]), and the horror which accompanies shots of this same house burning in the night after an Indian attack (as in John Ford's *The Searchers* [1955]), as if an inconceivable wrong has been done to an innocent people. Yet, as I suggested earlier, this system of the house laid down in the wilderness also includes the promise or threat of explosive growth and expansion. Indeed, the history of America is the history of many kinds of explosions; explosions beyond boundaries, explosions of populations across the land, explosions of guns, light and sound.[9]

The limit point, then, functions as a limit in both space and time; it also functions in order to be broken, or rather, to be *broken down*:

> The social machine's limit is not attrition, but rather its misfirings; it can operate only by fits and starts, by grinding and breaking down, in spasms of minor explosions. The dysfunctions are an essential element of its very ability to func-

tion, which is not the least important aspect of the system of cruelty. The death of a social machine has never been heralded by a disharmony or a dysfunction; on the contrary, social machines make a habit of feeding on the contradictions they give rise to, on the crises they provoke, on the anxieties they engender, and on the infernal operations they regenerate. Capitalism has learned this, and has ceased doubting itself, while even socialists have abandoned belief in the possibility of capitalism's natural death by attrition. No one has ever died from contradictions. And the more it breaks down, the more it schizophrenizes, the better it works, the American way.[10]

The limit point functions by dividing itself equally between deferral and release, silence and explosion; and it is this pattern which makes the limit point an apocalypse-machine; an *ever-present fantasy of the regenerative end*. Although many Westerns revolve around such an idea, it is in films that deal specifically with gunplay and gunfighters that the limit point finds its purest representation; in particular, we can discuss Henry King's film, *The Gunfighter* (1950), which deals with the figure of the gunfighter and the problems of a system which proliferates explosions and limit points in order to function.

The film deals with the fate of Jimmy Ringo (Gregory Peck), a man who is now sick of the tenuous life of the gunfighter and wants to settle down, but is unable to escape his violent past. The opening scene shows Ringo arriving at a saloon and asking for a drink—the bartender recognizes him and greets him by name. The patrons of the saloon also hear the greeting, whereupon a young upstart (Richard Jaeckel) picks a fight with Jimmy, draws (first), and is of course shot. Ringo is then advised to get out of town, as the kid's three brothers (David Clarke, Alan Hale Jr., John Pickard) will undoubtedly seek revenge. He leaves for the town of Cayenne, and is pursued by the brothers. In Cayenne, where Ringo has gone to see his estranged wife and son, he awaits the arrival of the brothers, and tries to fend off the various approaches of Cayenne's resident gun-happy "squirt," Hunt Bromley (Skip Homeier).

The film is driven by the anticipation of two limit points. The first is the expectation of the arrival of the three brothers; Ringo glancing constantly at the clock as he waits in the saloon, and the film cutting between Cayenne and shots of the brothers' approach through the desert. The other limit point is set up by the mounting tension in Cayenne, where all the townsfolk have gathered around the Palace saloon to see the infamous gunfighter Jimmy Ringo either kill or be killed. As in most Westerns, the film revolves around the simple question of who will be killed by whom, and the growing desire for the killing to happen. The children clamor around the bar, trading bets as to who will kill Ringo. The "ladies of Cayenne," led by Miss Pennyfeather (Verna Felton), send a deputation to Marshall Mark Strett (Millard Mitchell), calling for some "law and order"; and "law and order" here is essentially nothing other than the desire to see the town purified by spilling the blood of the outsider. As Miss Pennyfeather says with more irony that she is aware of, "Shoot him down like a dog? That sounds very sensible!" As Richard Slotkin notes, "[a]lthough there will be talk of motives and reasons here, we know that in some sense motives are rationalizations. There is a necessity or fatality at work that cannot be con-

7

trolled by the conventional and historistic rationales of the 'renaissance' Western, and it has something to do with an almost abstract will to violence."[11]

It is this will to violence that feeds the limit points set up by the arrival of the brothers and the mounting tension in Cayenne. Although from one perspective, the film could be said to be "clock-driven" because the film is punctuated by shots of clocks,[12] to see only a clock behind the narrative would be to see only half the picture. It is in actuality a *clock-gun assemblage* which drives the film, the expectation that at a certain time the limit point of anticipation will be crossed at a moment of experience. Then, the guns will go off, and there will be explosions.

I would argue that in *The Gunfighter* the end is both feared and desired, condemned and celebrated. Ringo is now a reluctant gunfighter, in no way enamored of the dubious fame that being the "fastest gun in the West" has brought him. In fact, it has brought him nothing but pain, his life lived beneath the constant promise of violent encounters.

The film ends with Hunt Bromley shooting Ringo in the back as he is leaving town. Not a big explosion, and not a celebration either; nothing more than a trigger-happy upstart doing the only thing he knows how to do; initiating a further cycle in the economic exchange of death. What is significant about this, however, and what makes this film more critical and complex than most classical Westerns, is that the film ends not with a moment of heroism, but a curse. As he dies, rather than condemning Hunt for shooting a man in the back, Ringo states that Hunt outdrew him, condemning him to a life as "the man who shot Jimmy Ringo," eternally prey to anyone willing to buy into the myth of regeneration through violent, technological action. The final shot of the film depicts a lone rider vanishing into a desert sunset. While conventionally this would most likely be a heroic moment, here we know that Ringo, the hero, is dead; and that this moment in which a hero would usually be eternalized is really a moment of parody and critique. Unless we are witnessing some "fantasy" of Ringo's spirit returning to the wilderness, it can only be Hunt disappearing into the sunset, not a hero but the dupe of a technological *pharmakon*, cursed to a life to be lived under the unforgiving sign of the gun and the commodification of death. One can almost see the vultures begin to circle around his head.

What complicates the critique of this mythic system, however, is another of the final scenes of the film, in which Ringo's estranged wife identifies herself as Ringo's widow at his funeral. In taking the *name* of Mrs. Ringo, which she had hitherto kept hidden, she buys into the system of the exchange of names and death as symbolic capital, perpetuating and lending it a heroic aspect at the same time that Ringo explicitly renders such an exchange not heroic, but barbaric. Once again, the laws of the Western and symbolic exchange function as an apparatus of capture; the Western is always hungry for another chance to turn death into symbolic capital, and it can indeed afford to overlook the exact circumstances of this death if it is a hero who has died.

Ultimately, *The Gunfighter* is driven by the tension between its own divided alliances, which are explicitly technological. For Jimmy Ringo, the limit point has been crossed and been condemned, but sadly, more limit points will inevitably proliferate. The Western just builds apocalypse-machines; it sets up explosions. This paper has been an exploration of the idea that the American myth machine has extracted a system of particularly violent and technophilic stories from a history also fraught with violent conflict and technical expansion. The Western is one of the most explicit vessels for these stories. It is certainly not *only* America that has such a history; nor that technical expansion is *only* a trait of the American West. Yet the way in which violent and technological action is justified in American mythography, the inexorable "will to technique" and the nihilistic desire for "baptisms of fire" point through myths of regeneration and the frontier and the commodification of death to an inexorable drive towards the end, which is always, despite it all, construed as a new beginning.

Exactly *what* beginning, however, is another matter. Always through fire are more powerful machines brought into being.

NOTES

1   It should be noted that I am using the term 'America' to refer not to North America in its entirety, nor to the geographical formation known as the United States, but to that mythic America that exists in all cultural and technological production that emanates *from* the United States and places deeply affected by it, and the image of an aggressive technological America that is produced by U.S. foreign policy. This America, then, is essentially an abstract-machine, for it is simultaneously geopolitical, virtual, mythic, and ideological.

2   For an explanation of their ideas of territoriality and machinic assemblages, see Gilles Deleuze and Félix Guattari, *A Thousand Plateaus,* trans. Brian Massumi (Minneapolis: University of Minnesota Press, 1987).

3   John Cawelti, *The Six-Gun Mystique* (Bowling Green, Ohio: Bowling Green University Popular Press, 1984), 40.

4   See Martin Heidegger, *The Question Concerning Technology and Other Essays,* trans. William Lovitt (New York: Harper and Row, 1977).

5   Here I am referring to the way in which technologies of many sorts can be said to "write on the body," in the sense of marking the body with a public record of technology's attachment to, or physical mutation of, the human. For instance, Arthur and Marilouise Kroker frequently make reference to the "tattooed body" of postmodern culture, the human body that has been invaded, marked, or "written on" by a machinic "discourse." (See *Body Invaders—Sexuality and the Postmodern Condition* [London: Macmillan Education, 1988].) Similarly, in *Discipline and Punish,* Foucault describes the way in which torture or similar forms of corporal punishment function by marking the body of the victim with the sign of his or her own infamy; torture "traces around or, rather, on the very body of the condemned man signs that must not be effaced." (Trans. Alan Sheridan [London, Penguin, 1991], 34.)

6   William S. Burroughs, *The Place of Dead Roads* (New York: Holt, Rinehart and Winston, 1983), 67.

7   Jean Baudrillard, *Symbolic Exchange and Death*, trans. Iain Hamilton Grant (London, Thousand Oaks: Sage Publications, 1993), 165.

8   Gilles Deleuze and Félix Guattari, *Anti-Oedipus*, trans. Robert Hurley, Mark Seem and Helen Lane (Minneapolis: University of Minnesota Press, 1983), 151.

9   And this is also the history of the earth under human occupation; the threat of an apocalypse from on high has diminished and we have turned the earth itself into an apocalypse-machine, a cyborg, aching for the moment when it is free to explode us from its back and tear our implants from beneath its skin.

10   Deleuze and Guattari, *Anti-Oedipus*, 151.

11   Richard Slotkin, *Gunfighter Nation* (New York: Atheneum, 1992), 387.

12   Slotkin, *Nation,* 391.

Woman with a Gun: Cinematic Law Enforcers on the Gender Frontier

Carol M. Dole

The last decade has seen the emergence of a new breed of powerful women in film. Unlike the *femmes fatales* who used their sexuality to manipulate men in film noir, or the mother figures who attained moral power in maternal melodrama, these late-twentieth century women appropriate types of power culturally coded as masculine: weaponry and physical prowess. Films such as *Barb Wire* (1996), *The Quick and the Dead* (1994), and *The River Wild* (1994) have featured female leads as sharpshooters, bounty hunters, and white water daredevils, all wielding guns whether for profit or self-defense. At the safe remove offered by science fiction, female fantasy heroes who combine musculature and military skills have scored big box office returns in films like *Terminator 2* (1991) and the *Alien* series (1979-1998). This essay will examine the limits on dramatic representation of women in the world of everyday reality, especially those who wield the most potent combination of physical, moral, and institutional power. The cinematic women I will discuss are those who are triply empowered: by their central position in the narrative; by their association with the physically powerful and symbolically potent gun; and by their socially sanctioned status as officers of the law. What anxieties about gender might be provoked by the licensed woman's assumption of that quintessential masculine totem—the gun, a staple of the cop genre?

Despite widespread support for strong images of women in the media, many mainstream film viewers and academic feminists alike have hesitated to celebrate cinematic women with guns, even those who are upholders of the law. In a controversy summarized by Jeffrey Brown in "Gender and the Action Heroine," academic feminists have sometimes derided action heroines as gender transvestites, or complained of their fetishization.[1] Popular magazines like *Glamour* have debated whether "female shoot-'em-ups help or hurt women": is every strong female movie character "a validation of strength" that helps counter the victimization movies have long modelled for women, or are female action roles just an occasion for women to "sink to the worst of macho men's behavior"?[2]

When women are themselves so divided in their responses to the image of women with guns, one can assume that men will be even more troubled at the reconfiguration of a cultural icon that has so long represented physical power as exclusively masculine. Obsessed with the action film—its biggest moneymaker in the global market—the Hollywood film industry has found it difficult to substitute the troubling figure of the Woman with a Gun for her familiar male counterpart. In its attempt to produce a product palatable to a mainstream audience, the film industry has had to balance the demand for stronger roles for women with the ambivalence of viewers (especially males, who make up so large a percentage of action fans) about the transgressive figure of the Woman with a Gun. In recent years, Hollywood has experimented with various levels of violence, muscularity, and sexualization in women's action films in order to achieve a mix that will produce big profits.

One particular sub-genre, the cop film, undercuts its superficially strong representations of armed women through narrative devices designed to reduce the heroes' power. This essay will demonstrate that earlier women cop films (1987–1991) frequently imitate the excessive violence of male action pictures while counterbalancing masculine power with feminized psychological vulnerabilities, and that later films (1991–1995) tend to privilege intellectual over physical power and to limit the woman's power by splitting strategies. Such splitting strategies, which distribute among multiple personalities or characters the modes of power that would otherwise be concentrated in a single hero, reduce the threat of each individual protagonist who shares in them.

The first wave of films featuring armed female law officers as protagonists, rather than as the hero's partner or love interest, appeared in the late '80s and very early '90s. The more action-oriented titles, replete with big guns and exciting chases, centered on women cops. In *Fatal Beauty* (1987), Whoopi Goldberg played a street-savvy detective with a big gun and a comic edge, and in the darker *Impulse* (1990), hard-shooting Theresa Russell went undercover as a prostitute. In Kathryn Bigelow's *Blue Steel* (1990), Jamie Lee Curtis portrayed a rookie in trouble, subject and object of recurrent violence. In a less violent film, Debra Winger played an FBI agent in danger as she infiltrated a white supremacist group in *Betrayed* (1988).[3] Similar in level of violence to male-centered action films, these films retain for their female heroes both motivations and vulnerabilities associated with traditional notions of femininity. The four films adopt remarkably similar strategies for empowering women without disempowering men.

One strategy for deflecting audience discomfort with the figure of the woman licensed to kill was to ask in the dialogue why she would place herself in a position coded as masculine. Although during the same era cops played by Bruce Willis or Mel Gibson were not expected to justify their career choices, Officer Megan Turner in *Blue Steel* (Curtis) is asked by almost every man she meets why she became a cop; Lottie Mason of *Impulse* (Russell) is forced to examine her motivations in the office of the department psychologist; and Detective Rita Rizzoli of *Fatal Beauty* (Goldberg) must explain how a personal tragedy drives her to cleanse the city of drugs.

In a bow to traditional notions about the propriety of women's arming themselves, in these films the woman's will to (fire)power is constructed as defensive, not aggressive. Women law enforcers are motivated by a desire to protect those weaker than themselves: never men, but always women or children, ideally female children. Rita Rizzoli may blast people to bits every ten minutes, but she does so under cover of the stated maternal aim of protecting other children from the fate of her own young daughter. Megan Turner joins the force to protect women like her mother, who continues to be abused by Megan's father. And though *Betrayed* focuses on her infiltration of an extremist group, the film ends on an unlikely emotional swell as Weaver (Winger) is gratefully embraced by her target's orphaned daughter.

As Jeffrey Brown has shown in his analysis of action cop movies of the '80s and early '90s, male cops often defend their daughters, wives, and girlfriends.[4] But female cops of the same period have no husbands and sons to rescue. The erasure of family structure obviates presentation of the armed woman as stronger than her husband, a potential affront to traditional views of the family. Moreover, the elimination of a family limits women's power through infantilization. Their ability to compete as adults with men is undermined by their status: as daughters (*Blue Steel*), as neurotics lacking the assurance of adulthood (*Impulse*) or as orphans (*Betrayed*).

Another ramification of their unmarried status is that these women are both sexually available and vulnerable through their sexuality. Although male movie cops are only occasionally found sleeping with the enemy, women law enforcers are routinely placed in danger through a sexual relationship, usually with an opponent. This pattern is most obvious in *Blue Steel*, in which Megan Turner is unknowingly dating the very murderer she is tracking. The highly sexualized Lottie Mason is endangered by both the come-ons of her boss and her temptation to prostitute herself to a mobster. In *Fatal Beauty*, Detective Rizzoli makes love with the bodyguard of a prosperous crook only hours before he is ordered to shoot her. And in *Betrayed*, Agent Weaver is assigned to infiltrate an extremist group by attracting one of its leaders, and is further endangered when she falls in love with him.

Although by their ultimate triumph over their antagonists, these women law enforcers fulfill both generic requirements and the desire of some segments of the audience for strong female characters, at the same time the discomfort they may pose to traditionalist viewers is limited by the invocation of feminine ideals—maternal motivations and sexual desirability—and by the elimination of direct competition for power with males other than villains. In spite of these careful limitations, however, the female hero's possession of the phallic gun generates a considerable level of castration anxiety.

The comic *Fatal Beauty* attempts to defuse this anxiety through humor. Rizzoli's dialogue is studded with witticisms on penis size, and the scene in which she persuades a wounded drug dealer to talk by pressing a gun to his testicles is played for comedy. Although the castration threat in *Blue Steel* is less overtly articulated, it is more fundamental. The castration theme is introduced early, when Megan interrupts her male colleagues as they are enjoying a joke about a prostitute who accidentally bit off a client's penis and then sewed it back on upside down. But a more troubling castration story is

Megan's. She has to yield her phallic weapon first to Eugene (Ron Silver), who causes her to be suspended by pocketing the gun of the robber she shot because he was armed; and then to the police authorities. Indeed, Robert Self has found that "the image of castration constitutes the unsettling master trope of the film," which is organized around the desire of male characters to take away Megan's gun and uniform—the signifiers of masculine authority.[5]

Both early reviewers and later analysts have found it difficult to determine whether or not *Blue Steel* constitutes "Progressive Feminism in the '90s?"[6] Megan Turner is a strong and courageous female protagonist; but her violent reprisals against Eugene invite her to be seen as a "Dirty Harriet" who replicates male violence.[7] Discussion is further complicated by the question of how she is gendered within the film, in light of the casting of "androgynous" Jamie Lee Curtis.[8] Curtis's screen history, as the star of *Halloween* and other slasher films, has led her to be identified with the victorious female survivor Carol Clover has dubbed the Final Girl, a character into which "the categories masculine and feminine, traditionally embodied in male and female, are collapsed."[9]

The self-consciousness of *Blue Steel* prevents it from being "a faithful cop thriller," but neither is it a "straightforward feminist revision" of the genre.[10] *Blue Steel* attempts "both to replicate and mock popular genre," exploiting the tactics of the urban thriller even while critiquing them through its awareness of the changes wrought by change of gender.[11] Typical is Bigelow's manipulation of the gun, that icon of the cop-thriller. Rather than using the regulation .38 issued by the New York Police Department, Bigelow planned to arm her female hero with a larger gun; only Curtis's pleas for realism persuaded Bigelow to compromise with a larger, reconfigured .38.[12] The much-discussed credit sequence, with its caressing closeups of a gleaming Smith and Wesson, confirms that *Blue Steel*'s obsession is "not really with guns *per se*, but with their symbolic effects."[13] The gun's eroticization in these lingering closeups "presents this phallic symbol as an object of desire."[14] But the sequence simultaneously recognizes "the disturbing implications of a fetishism surrounding women and guns" and invites us to share it.[15]

In an era when the *Lethal Weapon* and *Die Hard* films were raking in large profits from audiences eager to see male cops in action, these woman-centered films died a quick death at the box office. So too did the action-packed *V.I. Warshawski* (1991), a much-ballyhooed adaptation of the popular Sara Paretsky feminist detective novels, which made it from theater to video store in only six weeks.[16] This failure seems odd in an era in which, as trumpeted in the popular press, "women got tough at the movies,"[17] a claim seemingly validated by the fact that 1991's biggest grossers—*Terminator II*, *Sleeping with the Enemy*, and *Silence of the Lambs*—all featured women with guns. What of the unqualified success of *Sleeping with the Enemy* and *Terminator 2*? The former, which portrays an abused woman resorting to the gun for self defense only when flight and concealment have failed, poses no challenge to gender stereotypes. *Terminator 2* does break new ground in giving its female hero both muscles and munitions, but it also assigns her a traditionally feminine motivation (caring for her child) and surrounds her with cyborgs figured as male who are even stronger and even more relentless than she.

More significant for this study—and, perhaps, for the evolution of women's action films—is the success of *Silence of the Lambs*.

Silence of the Lambs found a way to catch the imagination of a mainstream audience, as is obvious from its impressive grosses and raft of Academy Awards. Jodie Foster, in her acceptance speech for the Best Actress Oscar, expressed her pleasure in having played "such a strong feminist hero." In public discourse, as Janet Staiger has documented, "Women—both straight and lesbian—uniformly defended [Foster] and the movie as a positive, powerful representation of a female."[18] In short, the public was ready to applaud the film's gender politics. How did the female hero of *Silence of the Lambs* manage to be met with such acceptance, when her "sisters" Megan Turner and Rita Rizzoli had been derided even by women critics for acting as a Bronsonesque "one-woman vigilante force" or proving that a woman can be "just as loudly, obnoxiously macho as a man"?[19] *Silence of the Lambs* defuses the threat posed by the female dick through a complex of strategies, showcasing—but simultaneously containing—the female hero's power.

Like her predecessors, Clarice Starling (Foster) is a defender rather than an aggressor, who seeks to hush the bleating of the lambs she failed to rescue in her childhood by rescuing the young women a psychopath, "Buffalo Bill" (Ted Levine), wants to flay. Also like most of them, she is positioned as daughter rather than full adult, subject to not one but three father-figures: her professional mentor Jack Crawford (Scott Glenn), her intellectual mentor Hannibal Lecter (Anthony Hopkins), and the slain father/cop who appears in her flashback memories (Jeffrey Lane).

But the film also erases the female hero's sexual vulnerability. Although some viewers have read her failure to respond to (hetero)sexual invitations as evidence of lesbianism, within the context of other films about female law officers it becomes clear that a more important function of her refusal of sex is to avoid the dangers posed by either sexual desire—which put Lottie Mason, Rita Rizzoli, Cathy Weaver, and Megan Turner at such risk—or sexual desirability. Clarice's refusal to act as sex object, a role in which almost every male character tries to cast her, is a refusal to fall into the limiting categories of womanhood held by the men all around her. This refusal to engage in heterosexual exchange "clearly avoids the castrating threat of the female dick, just as it avoids the clichés of glamorization (consumable sexuality), fetishization, or monstrosity."[20]

Further, Clarice's small stature and lack of physical power are established in the opening scenes of the film, as she pants and struggles through an obstacle course and then rides in an elevator surrounded by towering men. Her power is further undercut by her lack of expertise and experience. Unlike Lottie Mason and Rita Rizzoli, cops with skills and status, Clarice Starling is still a student, and always addresses her (male) superiors as "sir" in a tone of respect. Moreover, in Jonathan Demme's film Clarice lacks the marksmanship and laboratory expertise that she had in Thomas Harris's novel.[21] The female hero's power, and the anxieties surrounding it, are further contained by the use of a different mix of genres than in previous films. Whereas *Fatal Beauty* adds comedy like so many male-centered action-thrillers, *Silence of the Lambs*, as Carol Clover has shown, mixes in the horror genre.[22] Thus, Clarice is cast as potential victim. The horror conventions generate a strong

15

sense of her peril and thus work to curtail her power. Moreover, FBI films such as *Betrayed* and *Silence of the Lambs* are primarily detective thrillers, a genre that requires far less violence than the cop film, with its generic demands for repeated gunplay and dangerous chases. Except in a training sequence so brief that it's hard to catch, *Silence of the Lambs* never shows Clarice assuming the phallic gun except as she herself is being stalked through the killer's lair, appearing through his point of view to be nearly helpless in the dark. Her turning of the gun on a man is thus visually constructed as justifiable self-defense, an action that mainstream audiences have long found acceptable in cinematic heroines (for example in *Sleeping with the Enemy* [1990], or *Jagged Edge* [1985]).

Counterbalancing these many controls on the female hero's power, however, were features that made it easy to read *Silence of the Lambs* as empowering to women: an array of strong female supporting characters; Clarice's own determination and intelligence; and Clarice's ability to capture single-handed the killer that eluded her male superiors.

In the wake of the success of *Silence of the Lambs*, female-centered action films have adopted some of its strategies for dealing with the threatening image of Woman with a Gun. One is dissociating the female hero from excessive violence. While *Silence of the Lambs* easily meets the quota of violence demanded by action and horror genres, its violence is performed almost entirely by two serial killers, not the female hero. Later women-centered action films have tended to be more successful if the woman performs less violence, with *Copycat* (1995) and *Fargo* (1996) eliciting a more positive response than *G.I. Jane* (1997) and *The Long Kiss Goodnight* (1996). Like *Silence*, these films have highlighted the female hero's intellectual rather than physical powers. Even Disney's animated woman warrior film *Mulan* (1998) portrays its hero as winning through cunning and determination rather than through mastery of weaponry or extraordinary skill in martial arts.

Virtually all women-centered action pictures made since 1991 have adopted *Silence of the Lambs*' canny strategy for making a female hero seem both independent and unthreatening: splitting.[23] For many viewers, the most memorable character in Demme's film was Hannibal Lecter, the brilliant and psychopathic psychiatrist whose clues lead Clarice to the murderer. The film's most effective strategy for subtly limiting Clarice's power was to make her dependent on male advice even while using Lecter's incarceration to make her simultaneously appear an independent agent. Earlier films had been troubled by the difficulty of pairing their female heroes with a male partner, as the popularity of "buddy cop" movies seemed to demand: if he was strong, gender stereotypes demanded he rescue her; if he was weaker than she, gender assumptions were overturned and the audience discomfited. In *Silence of the Lambs*, the separation of these intellectual partners—through literal bars and through the demonization of "Hannibal the Cannibal"—provides the female hero independence in the physical world without challenging gender hierarchies.

Jodie Foster's pleased speculation that her film's financial success would spawn numerous "copycat" films with female heroes was literally fulfilled in *Copycat*.[24] This thriller, which reviewers repeatedly compared to *Silence of the Lambs* as a film in which a woman cop tracks a serial killer, adopted the earlier film's splitting strategy with a crucial difference: its incarcerated intellectual is a woman. Dr. Helen Hudson, confined to her apartment by a paralyzing case of agoraphobia triggered by a near-fatal attack, is, like Lecter, an expert on serial killers who is persuaded to assist with a murder investigation spearheaded by Detective M.J. Monahan (Holly Hunter). Helen functions as both hunter and hunted, evoking horror movie conventions both by her position as Final Girl on the serial killer's program and by the casting of the actress famous for playing the first block-buster Final Girl role (in *Alien* [1979]): Sigourney Weaver.

In several ways, *Copycat* gives women more power than does *Silence of the Lambs*. Although this film also emphasizes its female cop's diminutive size, it makes its own strat-egy ironic by inserting a line of dialogue in which M.J. is sarcastically called "the wee inspector." Unlike Clarice, M.J. is experienced and in charge of the case; although she pays lip service to her boss, we know that she never means it when she says, "Absolutely, sir." When she consults an expert for advice, that expert is a female peer rather than a father figure. And the film is not afraid to let M.J. show off what a crack shot she is, in a training scene where she is trainer rather than trainee.

Most importantly, for the first time in an action film two lead women are shown working together in defense of the law, a pairing that not only dares to approach the dou-bled power of the male buddy cops of the 80s, but also fulfills the feminist model of coop-eration rather than individualistic competition. The two women combine their official resources (M.J.) and knowledge base (Helen) to learn the identity of the killer, and when he finally captures Helen they work cooperatively to save each other, Helen allowing her-self to be hanged to distract the killer from the downed M.J., and M.J. shooting him as he is about to reach Helen on the roof. They work as equals, without male rescue.

Although it could not match the extraordinary success of *Silence*, *Copycat* gar-nered some good reviews and made a respectable showing at the box office. Not so for *A Stranger Among Us*. Sidney Lumet's 1992 cop film falls between the tempered films of the mid-'90s, which generally seek to defuse the female hero's threat by reducing violence and restructuring the narrative, and the more excessive films of the late '80s and very early '90s, which either cast women in straightforward macho roles (*Fatal Beauty, Blue Steel*) or combine the macho with hypersexualization (*Impulse, V.I. Warshawski*). *A Stranger Among Us* (1992) struggles to combine the two strategies, by splitting its hero-ine into two almost distinct personalities.

In her first manifestation, New York City detective Emily Eden (Melanie Griffith) is straight out of *Impulse*. Her spike heels and blonde dye-job foreground her sexuality, while the hints of emotional problems show her to be a true sister to Lottie Mason. Like Megan Turner, she is troubled by her relationship with her father, an alcoholic who drove away her mother—and consequently is infantilized like so many of her predecessors. She is also all too willing to use her gun: like Rita Rizzoli and a hundred male movie cops, she is a "cowboy" whom others fear to partner, and whose boss (David Margulies) is always trying to rein her in.

While undercover in the course of a murder investigation, Emily is gradually trans-formed by the lessons she learns in the spiritual community of Hasidic Jews. She falls in love with the rabbinical student Ariel (Eric Thal)—in marked contrast to being "in lust" with her police partner (John Pankow)—and in Ariel's sister Leah (Mia Sara) finds her "first female friend since the third grade." When Emily shows up in the squad room in more modest clothes and her natural hair color, her male colleagues make merry over having momentarily mistaken her for "a lady," a category of womanhood to which she will aspire by film's end.

The film makes little attempt to reconcile these visions of tough and sexual with soft and ladylike womanhood. Its conservative implication that true happiness is only to be found in the latter condition is partly masked by linking each brand of womanhood with a different culture: toughness with the violence of the Brooklyn streets, softness with the peaceful community of the Hasidim.

That being a "lady" is incompatible with the more violent aspects of policework is made clear by the film's climax. After her transformation, Eden remains an insightful investigator, but she is no longer seen shooting "perps" in the back or through the windshields of careening cars. Indeed, she metaphorically renounces the phallic gun, insisting that Ariel take it when the two of them confront Leah's assailant.

Although reviewers largely overlooked the film's representations of gender in their fervor to lambaste its sugarcoating of Hasidism, discomfort with its construction of womanhood emerged in the objections to casting Melanie Griffith, "with her baby-doll-on-helium voice, in the role of a pistol-packing cop."[25] Lumet declared that he chose Griffith based on her "vulnerability and openness," which were appropriate to "the third act of this movie."[26] But reviewers obviously found the tough-cop Emily more credible than her feminized alter ego, since they lamented that Lumet had not cast Jamie Lee Curtis or Sigourney Weaver rather than an actress "who looks more worried about breaking a fingernail than catching lawbreakers."[27]

While the studios still seem to be struggling to find a comfortable position for the armed woman in action cinema, even after the lessons of *Silence of the Lambs*, the most inventive spin on the female cop thus far has come from independent filmmakers Joel and Ethan Coen. *Fargo* (1996) takes the straightforward approach of making its hero an ordinary person who has to deal neither with personal traumas nor with the careening cars and fiery explosions of so many cop films. Like *Silence* and *Copycat*, it leaves most of the violence (and there is plenty in this film) to the criminals; its female hero shoots only once in this film, and then just to wound. Since it relies primarily on the hero's sleuthing skills rather than on displays of physical confrontation, *Fargo* can largely discount gender without ignoring it.

Brainerd, Minnesota police chief Marge Gunderson (Frances McDormand) is "the polar opposite of Frank Serpico, Popeye Doyle, and every other tough-guy cop to have achieved screen immortality."[28] She is also different from the cinematic women officers who preceded her. Glamorization is nowhere evident in this character who favors ruffled blouses and furry earflaps. And none of the strategies for limiting the female hero's power resurfaces here. Neither a rookie like Megan Turner or Clarice Starling, nor a boss-beleaguered veteran like M.J. Monahan, Lottie Mason and Emily Eden, Police Chief

Gunderson answers to no one. Instead of being infantalized as orphan or daughter like so many of her cinematic forebears, Marge carries the signifiers of adulthood: a lined face, a house and husband, and a pregnancy. And rather than being endangered by her sexual relationships like the protagonists of early women cop films, Marge has the ungrudging support of a husband (John Carroll Lynch) who insists on cooking her a hot breakfast when she is called out in the night. Indeed, *Fargo* seems not only to abjure the coping mechanisms of earlier policewoman films, but to parody them. It's even possible to read the film's most infamous scene, a stiff severed leg being forced into a woodchipper, as an outrageous retort to the castration anxieties of films such as *Fatal Beauty* and *Blue Steel*.

Marge's very visible pregnancy serves two essential functions in the film. On one hand, Marge's lone capture of the killer argues that the female body—even in the maternal condition that has so often been cited as evidence that women could not be relied on for physical tasks—need not prevent women from attaining success in endeavors (like law enforcement) that are partly physical. Yet at the same time, Marge's pregnancy is central to the splitting strategy of this film, which enables the female hero to have position, success, firepower, and domestic happiness all at once without threatening anyone. Rather than a split among characters like that in *Copycat* or *Silence of the Lambs, Fargo* relies on a split in tone. Marge's widespread popularity, with reviewers, audiences, and the Academy (surely part of the reason for MacDormand's Best Actress Oscar) is enabled by a presentation that is at once affectionate and satirical. With her ungainly form, singsong speech mannerisms, chirpy demeanor, and relentlessly healthy appetite, Marge is "only a breath away from caricature."[29]

Are film's violent women, then, cause for celebration? Although it is impossible to erase concerns about any glamorization of violence, by male or female, on the whole the answer must be yes. One thing to celebrate is that these characters are a testament to Hollywood's recognition of women's growing economic power and their influence in the industry, both as consumers ("Women are . . . driving the box office," says Fox Chairman William Mechanic[30]) and producers. *Impulse* and *Blue Steel* were directed by women, and *Copycat* was written principally by a woman. The attempt by studios to appeal to the female consumer, of which the proliferation of women's action films is a result, effectively increases the number and diversity of representations of women in popular culture, a change that is likely to erode stereotyped categories of femaleness.

In challenging the exclusive right of the male to the institutional and personal power granted by the gun and the badge, these films, however cautiously, test out the possibilities for women to insert themselves in important arenas from which they have long been excluded. Particularly significant is their questioning and testing of the cultural meaning of the gun, which has been referred to as the "last frontier on the road to equality."[31] If women can be represented as crossing this frontier without becoming crazed or dangerous, and with the societal sanction represented by the badge, gendered boundaries can be fundamentally altered. It is one thing for Ripley to defeat the Aliens or Sarah Connor (Linda Hamilton) to team up with the Terminator (Arnold

Schwarzenegger), but the image of a strong woman restoring order in a world recognizably like our own is a far more important boundary to cross.

NOTES

1   Jeffrey A. Brown, "Gender and the Action Heroine: Hardbodies and the *Point of No Return*," *Cinema Journal* 35, No. 3 (Spring 1996), 52–71.

2   Mandy Johnson, "Women As Action Heroes," *Glamour* (March 1994), 153. Callie Khouri, screenwriter for *Thelma and Louise*, represents the affirmative side of the debate; film scholar Jeanine Basinger represents the negative.

3   Winger also played a justice agent in *Black Widow* (1987), which this essay omits since the Winger character leaves behind her gun when she starts trailing her female quarry, declaring "she's not about guns." However, the film features several of the same mechanisms as the others I will discuss: the female hero is inexperienced (a data analyst rather than a field agent); her status as an adult is in question, partly because she is as insecure as a teenager about her sexual identity; and she becomes vulnerable through her sexual attraction to the villain's fiance.

4   Jeffrey A. Brown, "Bullets, Buddies, and Bad Guys: The 'Action-Cop' Genre," *Journal of Popular Film and Television* 21, No. 2 (Summer 1993), 86.

5   Robert T. Self, "Redressing the Law in Kathryn Bigelow's *Blue Steel*," *Journal of Film and Video* 46, No. 2 (Summer 1994), 33.

6   Harriet Margolis, "*Blue Steel*: Progressive Feminism in the '90s?" *Post Script* 13, No. 1 (Fall 1993), 67.

7   Margolis, "Progressive," 73.

8   Needeya Islam, "'I Wanted to Shoot People': Genre, Gender and Action in the Films of Kathryn Bigelow," in Laleen Jayamanne, ed., *Kiss Me Deadly: Feminism and Cinema for the Moment* (Sydney: Power, 1995), 110.

9   Carol Clover, *Men, Women, and Chain Saws: Gender in the Modern Horror Film* (Princeton: Princeton Univ. Press, 1992), 61.

10 Islam, "I Wanted," 113

11 Cora Kaplan, "Dirty Harriet/*Blue Steel*: Feminist Theory Goes to Hollywood," *Discourse* 16, No. 1 (Fall 1993), 54.

12 Betsy Sharkey, "Kathryn Bigelow Practices the Art of the Kill," *New York Times* (March 11, 1990) 2:17t.

13 Kaplan, "Dirty Harriet," 58.

14 Anna Powell, "Blood on the Borders—*Near Dark* and *Blue Steel*," *Screen* 35, No. 2 (Summer 1994), 146.

15 Yvonne Tasker, *Spectacular Bodies: Gender, Genre and the Action Cinema* (New York: Routledge, 1993), 159.

16   Although *V.I. Warshawski* is not considered in this essay because the female hero lacks the imprimatur of an official position, the film adopts the same softening strategies as the earlier policewomen films. Though the female hero is a tough aikido expert, she is motivated by the desire to save a little girl; and she is placed in danger by her sexual interest in a hockey player she picks up in a bar. Also, this film features as many verbal and physical castration threats as *Fatal Beauty*.

17   Anne Thompson, "What Happened to Warshawski?" *Philadelphia Inquirer* (Aug. 11, 1991), L2.

18   Janet Staiger, "Taboos and Totems: Cultural Meanings of *The Silence of the Lambs*," in Jim Collins, Hilary Radner and Ava Preacher Collins, eds., *Film Theory Goes to the Movies* (New York: Routledge, 1993), 153.

19   Caryn James, "Women Cops Can Be a Cliché in Blue," *New York Times* (Aug. 4, 1991), H17+; Janet Maslin, review of *Fatal Beauty, New York Times* (Oct. 30, 1987), C8.

20   Linda Mizejewski, "Picturing the Female Dick: *The Silence of the Lambs* and *Blue Steel*," *Journal of Film and Video* 45, No. 2 (1993), 18.

21   Joan G. Kotker, "It's Scarier at the Movies: Jonathan Demme's Adaptation of *The Silence of the Lambs*," in William Reynolds and Elizabeth Trembley, eds., *It's a Print!: Detective Fiction from Page to Screen* (Bowling Green: Popular Press, 1994), 199-200.

22   Clover, *Men, Women*, 232-233.

23   Splitting strategies are used not just in policewoman films but in other female-centered action movies as well. In *The Long Kiss Goodnight* (1996) Geena Davis's amnesiac CIA assassin is split into two conflicting personaes: housewifely Samantha, and leaner, meaner, sexier Charly. Naturally the film ends with restoration of the feminine persona, though now informed by some of the toughness of her alter ego.

24   Jodie Foster, quoted in Lawrence Grobel, "Anything is Possible," *Movieline* (October 1991), 32.

25   Stephen Rea, "Lumet Concedes the Boos, Stresses the Cheers for his 'Stranger,'" *Philadelphia Inquirer* (July 19, 1992), N2.

26   Lumet, quoted in Rea, "Lumet," N2.

27   Desmond Ryan, review of *A Stranger Among Us, Philadelphia Inquirer* (July 17, 1992), Weekend 5.

28   Todd McCarthy, review of *Fargo, Premiere* (March 1996), 22.

29   Anthony Lane, "Republicans with Guns," *New Yorker* (March 25, 1996), 99.

30   Mechanic, quoted in Bernard Weinraub, "What Do Women Want? Movies," *New York Times* (Feb. 10, 1997), C11.

31   Susie McKellar, "Guns: the 'last frontier on the road to equality'?" in Pat Kirkham, ed., *The Gendered Object* (New York: Manchester University Press, 1996), 70-71.

Aliens Amok: *Men in Black* Policing Subjectivity in the '90s

Kirby Farrell

Barry Sonnenfeld's comedy *Men in Black* (1997) imagines "about 1500" space aliens living in human guise on earth, mostly in New York City, policed by a shadowy organization known euphemistically as Men in Black. The agency resembles a corporate version of the CIA, FBI, Immigration and Naturalization Service (INS), and the National Security Agency (NSA). According to the veteran agent Kay (Tommy Lee Jones), the aliens are "intergalactic refugees" from persecution and violence, "most of them decent enough, just trying to make a living." The agency is in transition, with two white male agents recruiting replacements so they can retire. They choose a young black New York City policeman (Will Smith) who combines street smarts with the physical superiority stereotypically associated with black athletic celebrities. By the film's end, a plucky, attractive pathologist named Laurel (Linda Fiorentino) has earned the second agent's position.

The movie's villain is an alien called "The Bug" (Vincent D'Onofrio)—"a giant cockroach with unlimited strength, a massive inferiority complex, and a real short temper." The Bug has come to earth to assassinate a refugee prince of the Arquillian Empire, who lives in New York City disguised as a jeweler named Rosenberg (Mike Nussbaum). After a crash landing in upstate New York, The Bug devours a local redneck named Edgar and puts on his skin. Making his way to Manhattan, the alien-redneck murders the elderly jeweler in order to steal a galaxy belonging to the Arquillians that Rosenberg has hidden inside one of his jewels. In reaction, an Arquillian space ship threatens to annihilate the earth if the Men in Black fail to retrieve the lost galaxy.

The film parodies Cold War melodramas such as *The Hunt for Red October* (1990) and *Crimson Tide* (1995) in which heroic agents thwart an apocalyptic nuclear holocaust. With their high-tech arsenal, the Men in Black spoof the already self-parodic James Bond fantasies of Cold War superheroes. On another level, more significant in the post-Soviet era, the plot symbolically turns an American redneck into an alien terrorist who would destroy a global (intergalactic) balance of power mediated by a gentle, urbane Jewish businessman.

In this way *Men in Black* is topically engaged with some crucial fantasies of 1990s America. Although the film is slyly sophisticated about the story it tells, it unwittingly sheds light on anxieties about immigration and economic injustice that look back to the Gilded Age, even as it embodies topical concerns about globalization, an evolving corporate police state, and the effects of technological revolution on subjectivity.

The film uses the extra-terrestrials to satirize conflicted American attitudes toward immigration, as evident in such xenophobic measures as California's Proposition 187, which in 1994 denied health, welfare, and educational benefits to illegal aliens and their children.[1] In the opening scene, Border Patrol agents intercept a van smuggling Mexicans into Texas, unaware that one of the illegals is actually a criminal space alien. When two Men in Black intervene, pretending to work for a special bureau within INS, they quickly detect the impostor and, when he turns menacing, they destroy him. Afterward they calm the astounded, naive Border Patrol agents by "shooting" them with a gun-like "neuralizer" whose blinding flash destroys recent memory and awes the audience. The gun induces amnesia or dissociation, keeping the aliens' existence secret and sanitizing a reality supposedly too disturbing to be public knowledge.

Men in Black jokes about official and everyday use of dissociation to tame reality. Ironically the only inkling of truth about the aliens' presence on earth appears in preposterous tabloids like *The National Enquirer*. The Men in Black not only suppress dangerous aliens, they also use repression to protect ignorant earthlings from terrifying awareness of their cosmic vulnerability. The repression operates on two levels: to manage hostility between newcomers and native humans, and to control the basic existential terror of cosmic alienation and death that the immigrants from space represent to earthlings. With its special guns, including the memory neuralizer, the mysterious police agency keeps the groups and spheres of awareness dissociated.

From time immemorial migration has meant competition for resources and sometimes genocidal displacement. In the Old Testament, for example, God commands Israel to exterminate the Canaanites by killing the men, enslaving the women and children, and seizing their lands and goods.[2] In United States history the Statue of Liberty idealizes tolerance based on a common pursuit of liberty and justice. Ideally, immigrants to America are not competitors but fellow refugees from oppression, disposed to share the fruits of the land. But in practice, newcomers have always been a source of cheap labor and therefore vulnerable to exploitation from above even as they implicitly threaten the nation's working poor. When competition intensifies and assimilation falters, newcomers may be, or seem to be, parasites or predators: the stereotypical Mexican family with too many children, for example, or the ruthless, demonized criminals touted in the media, such as Mariel boatlift Cubans, Latino drug dealers and youth gangs, and Sicilian or Russian "mafia."

Psychologically the newcomers represent dangerous infantile orality: too many mouths to feed and in turn a threat of cannibalistic hunger and survival rage. In "One

Awful Night," a pulp crime story of 1919, detectives descend into "the famous Chinese tunnels" under San Francisco's Chinatown to kill "Chinese crooks gobbling up the girls by the wholesale and shipping them to the Chinese foreign markets."[3] The story appeared during a period of immigrant-bashing after World War I, a time of civil unrest, Red scares, and labor strife. Its maidens are icons of fertility and food "gobbled up" by "slant-eyed," "yellow-skinned devils" associated with rats, snakes, and other vermin. Like the Men in Black, the detectives work for a paramilitary "agency"—presumably Pinkerton—that operates on the edge of the law.

Men in Black winks at this store of pulp imagery. It crystallizes the threat of ravenous immigrants in the cockroach-like assassin called The Bug, who reveals a horrific shark-like maw in the climactic showdown with the agents. The Bug relishes war because "that means more food for my family, all seventy-eight million of them. That's a lot of mouths to feed." Discovering an infestation of bugs in a barn earlier in the film, a human pest-control exterminator (Ken Thorley) could be speaking of immigrants when he quips, "Well, well. Moving in like we own the place." The aliens can usurp someone's skin the way immigrants may take over someone's job and social position. Ultimately, according to this symbolic logic, immigrants compete for nothing less than autonomy and identity itself. The Bug devours the redneck Edgar and appropriates his skin, acting out the immigrants' threat to bring social death to marginal members of society.

This nightmare has revealing antecedents in the tensions aroused by the great surge of immigration from 1890 to 1910. At the turn of the century, as Gail Bederman has shown, imperialistic ideology was sharply ambivalent.[4] It held that the drive to expand economic life and civilize primitive peoples would improve the world. Yet civilization's comforts and ethos of masterful self-restraint also threatened to sap manliness, and when combined with anxiety about the raw energy of colonized people, imperialism could raise alarm, and deep anger, about degeneration and vulnerable effeminacy at home. Projecting aggression onto colonial people, guiltily uneasy about their long-suppressed rage toward their masters, western nations worried about being overrun by savages. In his memoir of 1912 Rider Haggard reports waking dreams about being enslaved by barbarian invaders.[5] "As president, [Teddy Roosevelt] believed his duty was to usher the manly American nation ever closer to the racial preeminence and perfect civilization he had predicted for it."[6] The fearful underside of this compensatory chauvinism came out in Roosevelt's warnings against the specter of "race suicide."

Coined in 1901 by Edward A. Ross, the term "race suicide" was associated with "immigration and women's advancement, as well as the falling birthrate."[7] Teddy Roosevelt maintained, for example, that "civilized but inferior Japanese men were willing to settle for a lower standard of living, and would force down wages, ruining American men's ability to provide for their families. Allowing Japanese men to immigrate ... would thus be, as TR put it, 'race suicide.'"[8] With the closing of the frontiers, distances shrank, competition over colonies increased, and surplus populations now had no room to expand—in Hitler's charged language, no *Lebensraum*. These conditions contributed to the arms races and genocidal warfare of the twentieth century, a history evoked by the ultimatum that drives the plot of *Men in Black* when the Arquillians demand that "their" stolen galaxy be returned or the earth will be annihilated. H. G. Wells anticipated this pressurized atmosphere in *The War of the Worlds* (1898), in which Martians invade Britain with devastating rays that evoke the contemporary industrial arms race and terror of a battlefield Armageddon, but also the anxiety about genocidal colonization that Conrad summed up in Kurtz's dying cry, "Exterminate all the brutes!"[9] Global "others" threaten psychic as well as bodily usurpation, as in western worries about being overrun by the "yellow peril" of faceless Asian hordes.

Men in Black's aliens neatly condense these ambivalent historical attitudes. Their insect-like and squid-like body parts suggest a closeness to nature which can make them both derisively primitive and frighteningly powerful. The aliens arouse human distrust, yet their behavior is virtually indistinguishable from human behavior, and the film satirizes the humans' visceral xenophobia. Much of the aliens' menace lies in their ambiguity. On earth the agency monitors them in a parody of late-twentieth century industrial surveillance technology. But how many aliens finally exist out in the cosmos? If they can adapt so readily to earth and mutate at will, can they be trusted to keep to any reliable form, or are they beyond any sort of psychic or bodily integrity? In this respect they suggest the relativism that has shocked people since modernism began to discover evolution and the range of cultures across the globe.

In this century's fantasies, then, immigration may presage the fall of empires and personal annihilation. Although most of the aliens in *Men in Black* seem benign, the seasoned agent Kay explains that the agency maintains strict secrecy because people would panic if they realized that aliens lived among them, already invisibly—if harmlessly—displacing them. The film maintains a deftly ambivalent attitude toward the newcomers. For one thing, the aliens seem to represent an elite that travels like intergalactic business executives and cooperates with the immigration agency on earth. They resemble the moneyed elites of post-Cold War capitalism, the new breed of global entrepreneurs and financiers who buy citizenship in countries like the United States or Canada when economic home bases such as Hong Kong become untenable. At the same time they can be despotic, as in the Arquillians' peremptory threat to destroy the earth when their disguised emissary Rosenberg is assassinated by The Bug. When the outraged Arquillians send an ultimatum to earth, most of the aliens on earth manage to flee back into space without consulting their official minders, as if they are actually more autonomous than officialdom has admitted. In their superhuman mobility and capacity for bodily transformation, these elite beings more nearly fulfill immortality wishes than their human counterparts.

The Men in Black operate on the margin of conventional awareness. Unlike ordinary people, they confront the cosmic insignificance of humankind, but they also share some of the superhuman capacities of the aliens, thanks to their surveillance technology and high-tech guns. Like St. George opposing the dragon in chivalric romance, the agents belong to an autonomous, professional warrior class and in effect the agents trade the comforts of quotidian life for the warrior-hero's conviction of immortality. "You will sever human contact," Jay is told. But in compensation, "You're no longer part of the system. You're above the system. Over it. Beyond it."

Yet there is an underlying death-anxiety that reveals itself only when age and fatigue impair the heroic dream. In the opening scene, for instance, Kay and his older partner Dee (Richard Hamilton) detect an escaped criminal space alien among some Mexicans being smuggled across the Texas border. Stripped of his disguise the monster turns on them. Dee fumbles his gun and it takes Kay's quick reflexes to blast the monster. Afterward, Dee apologizes: "I'm sorry, Kay. The spirit's willing, but the rest of me . . ." In the context of fin-de-siècle anxiety about manliness, Dee's failure dramatizes the strain of modernism, the debilitating control and vigilance demanded by the preservation of civilization. As Dee's failure to fire his gun illustrates, the role of guardian is exhausting. Dee's middle-aged fatigue signifies encroaching senescence and death-anxiety. Suddenly he is fascinated by the beauty he sees in the stars, reminders of the ultimate framework of life and presumably nature's compensation for old age and death. The scene is comic and rueful, because the human terror of death is displaced onto the criminal monster, who is the grotesque embodiment of predatory greed for life. The stars signify mortal transience to humans, whereas aliens actively travel among the stars as if, like vampires, they can endlessly elude death.

By contrast, the relatively youthful Kay is still absorbed in the warrior-police role. The film draws much of its ironic energy from his style as an agent. His coolness—the sunglasses, business suit, and nonchalance—seems to signify absolute composure. Yet in the larger symbolic context, these qualities are a comic mask for a hypervigilance, numbness, and diminished subjectivity akin to combat trauma. Kay had to abandon his wife to join the agency. He is poised but anaesthetic. By zapping his partner with the memory neuralizer, Kay releases the weary agent from his combat trauma, implicitly equating retirement with a therapy based on repression or dissociation. To protect his own memory from the neuralizer's flash, Kay dons sunglasses, which wittily associate the healer's role with coolness, invisibility, and manipulation.

The symptoms of combat trauma can be divided into depressive and aggressive reactions. Retiring into amnesia and exhaustion, Dee moves toward a depressive position, whereas active agents seem to be continually swept into the berserk state. Confronted by overwhelming terror, a berserker is apt to plunge recklessly into battle, shedding all armor ("baresark" = "without armor" in Old Norse), in a state of beast-like or superhuman rage. No one can be certain why combat trauma immobilizes one soldier and launches another into a murderous rampage. Self-protectively, we assume that a freeze response in the face of death is more logical than a "senseless" rampage. But "when a soldier is trapped, surrounded, or overrun and facing certain death, the berserk state has apparent survival value, because he apparently has nothing to lose and everything to gain from reckless frenzy."[10]

The climactic shootout is a robust convention of twentieth century industrial entertainment. Its epitome is the video game based on the paranoid extermination of dehumanized enemies. But Western, gangster, and war movies also commonly use a fusillade of bullets to represent a convulsion of rage that purges terror and hostility. The fantasy of cathartic fury is as tenacious as it is ancient.[11] It appears in the sacrificial murder of scapegoats, in exorcism of malevolent spirits, and in beliefs about the efficacy of violent purgatives and emetics in Renaissance medicine. These fantasies imagine restoring equilibrium by "fighting off" threat, using violence to expel violence. They conjure up violence by polarizing conflict, concentrating will, selecting a target, and risking all in an act of supreme exertion and release. There is a self-intoxicating or hysterical quality to rage that contributes to fantasies of transcendent or apocalyptic scope. These dynamics play out in millennial imagery and the eschatological fantasy implied in burning witches and heretics in symbolic hellfire to purge demonic forces. In *Frankenstein* (1931) and in vampire films such as *Innocent Blood* (1992) and *Near Dark* (1987), predatory greed for life can be stopped only by annihilation of the demonic criminals in a climactic inferno. In the industrial age that incendiary fury is epitomized in the fire-bombing of Dresden and the nuclear fireball that incinerated Hiroshima, images of rage which drove World War Two to a psychological climax so intense that its aftereffects haunted imaginations through the end of the Cold War.

Seen through this lens, the cinematic "hail" of bullets or "firefight" points to ancient fantasies of demonic exorcism as well as to the psychology of berserk rage. The association of guns with berserking is rooted in deep metaphors. Like gunpowder, rage "blows up," "explodes," or "erupts." Gunpowder's volatility suggests psychic impulsivity, as in a "hair trigger" personality with "a short fuse." The detonation of a cartridge, like the berserk state, is an all-or-nothing phenomenon. "Going" amok, a soldier goes beyond conventional controls, "out" of his mind. Trapped between the enemy and the military command at their backs, facing death on all sides, soldiers may experience a sense of abandonment and cultural betrayal that triggers desperate recklessness.[12] In workplace rampages, a sense of cultural betrayal and social death may goad a "terminated" worker to a suicidal shootout in the conviction that there is no place to go and no way back into his everyday life. As satirized in Oliver Stone's *Natural Born Killers* (1994), say, sensational news coverage of criminal or workplace rampages may fulfill fantasies of transcendence in berserking. Like gambling, gunplay gives the abandonment of inhibitions a magical quality grounded in fantasies about natural instinct, luck, or moralized fate. Films like the *Rambo* series (1985–1988) dramatize survival magic in firestorms of bullets and other munitions in which enemies tend to vanish bloodlessly and the hero emerges unscathed.

Like other tools, guns compensate for the physical limitations of the body. The mind readily imagines transcendence of time and space; it is the body that is deficient. Guns are mechanical, prosthetic enhancements of the body, even as they represent an evolutionary acquisition of improved armor, teeth, claws, and a superhuman phallus. Guns are indestructible fists or teeth, and by extension they are related not only to other projectile weapons such as spears and guided missiles but also to vehicles as different as the ancient war chariot, the tank, the domestic car, the airplane, and the intergalactic battle cruiser.[13] When the human body itself becomes a vehicle and potential weapon for an "alien," then the body too can be a kind of gun. With its robot-like limp and grotesque strength, the redneck's body is charged with explosive force and serves The Bug as a cybernetic weapon. What's more, the gun may serve its master by doing seemingly harmless work, as in surgery with laser "guns" or house construction with pneumatic nail "guns." This is the ambivalence behind robot and cyborg fantasies as different as Ira Levin's *The Stepford Wives* (1975) and James Cameron's film *The Terminator* (1984). In a paranoid universe, radical existential motives such as survival anxiety and striving for heroic power tend to bind self and gun so closely that they fuse.

Like magical practices, firearms have equivocal cognitive effects. They may create a conviction of superhuman power and control, but they can also evoke terrifying irrationality and disrupt culture's conventional immortality guarantees. The media, for example, use imagery of armed children, as in the Jonesboro Arkansas schoolyard killings, or teenagers' drive-by shootings, to signify "senseless" violence that, like berserking, is supposed to exceed or defy all rational social controls. In the hero's hand the gun symbolizes godlike control, yet like Faustian magic, it also threatens to dissolve inhibitions and "possess" the soul, as in so-called impulse killings.

The student gunmen in the Littleton Colorado high school massacre (April 1999), for example, stockpiled small arms and bombs, and planned a do-or-die assault against their "enemies" meant to culminate in the suicidal crash of a hijacked plane into New York City. In the high school library, they interrogated cornered students and impulsively killed some. Eric Harris and Dylan Klebold "laughed triumphantly as they meted out fate," said *Newsweek.* "'They were, like, orgasmic,' says 19-year-old Nicholas Schumann, who heard the worst of it" (May 3, 1999). The news magazine mixed military or sports victory with suggestions of psychopathic coldness ("laughed triumphantly") and godlike, tyrannical authority ("meted out fate"). The student witness interpreted the killers' excitement as sexual frenzy ("orgasmic"). The gunmen, the journalists, and the witness bring together familiar fantasies associated with guns.

Men in Black dramatizes these magical associations in its treatment of guns and the berserk state. Using the memory-zapping gun, an agent transcends ordinary "repressed" life, comprehending it but also initiated into cosmic mysteries beyond it. As in fantasies of "blowing away" a target, the agents' high-tech weapons dissolve alien bodies into harmless, lurid goo. In the final showdown at the World's Fair site in Flushing Meadow, Kay acts out the stages of berserking. When The Bug disarms him by swallowing his assault rifle, Kay taunts the monster into attacking him, then plunges headlong into its fearsome maw to retrieve and fire his weapon, exploding the creature from within. As if reborn, Kay emerges like a newborn infant, thoroughly smeared with the gooey essence of the creature. In the imagery of berserking, conventional categories magically dissolve: killing and sacrifice produce life; the macho enemy becomes perversely maternal; and reincorporation into this devouring parent-figure generates uncanny autonomy. What's more, the rebirth also marks Kay's decision to retire, surrender his memory, and finally accept mortality.

Like the aliens, the idea of berserking assumes many disguises in the film. Despite the agents' professional cool, the agency epitomizes the berserk state. Its agents transcend

29

conventional legal and institutional restraints. Their cryptic letter names neatly evoke their dissociation, as their high-tech car does in rocketing about New York City at speeds too great for personal control, freed from traffic laws. Racing upside down on the roof of the Lincoln Tunnel, "over the heads" of everyone else, the agents' car demonstrates the magical potency of ultimate heedless daring. When Jay accidentally touches a super-charged ball in the agency's terminal, the sphere goes amok. When it ricochets wildly throughout the building, its furious trajectory magically defies the usual laws of physics.

Lest berserking be associated solely with men and men's violence, the film also implicates women in its magic. Although the rookie Jay, for example, covets the hefty assault rifle his mentor Kay requisitions in the final crisis (a "Series IV De-atomizer"), he is issued a little "ladies'" pistol called a "cricket." The screenplay, however, makes the derringer-like pistol capable of a tremendous punch whose recoil invariably knocks Jay over backward. The pistol mocks gender stereotypes and flatters women in the audience by implying that "ladies" pack a concentrated wallop that a man may lack the strength to control. An analogous inversion appears when Jay is dispatched to help an alien mother give birth in the back seat of a car. In the throes of labor the mother reverts to her under-lying alien form, and her tentacles pick up and violently whirl the helpless agent about. Childbirth is akin to going amok. The woman's body that gives life is also capable of over-whelming violence. In a flattering gesture toward blacks, the screenplay insists that despite this shock, Jay has soul. Although his partner Kay is impassive, Jay can still feel, cooing over the newborn alien.

Magical berserking is of course ideologically charged. Since The Bug's berserking is depicted as atrocious, and the agency rescues humanity, we are kept from recognizing that at bottom the agency is a corporate police state with a lawless program of surveil-lance and enforcement. The film's ideological implications are evident in the bodies of the aliens. The disguised alien Rosenberg is a gentle, avuncular shopkeeper who is rescuing part of his "homeland"—the disputed galaxy—from the rapacious Bug. He is "Daddy" to his pet cat Orion. During the autopsy after his assassination, Rosenberg's face swings open on hinges to reveal an infantile ET-like creature inside the head who is operating the body like a machine. Innocents, the film argues, use cybernetics and illusion to compen-sate for their inherent vulnerability.

By contrast, the alien assassin assumes the form of a hostile if bumbling redneck, a type regularly vilified in Hollywood films. He is uncouth and abusive to his wife (Siobhan Fallon). But as the climax of the film argues, inside this skin or form of a man is a more primitive evil, the cockroach-like Bug. The monster is as intrinsically evil as Rosenberg is "really" a childlike, elderly incarnation of ET. The film's symbolic logic makes Rosenberg the admirable old man that retiring agents like Dee and Kay would become, while pro-jecting onto the redneck monster all their darker motives as agents. After all, in his sur-vival rage and lust for the Arquillians' galaxy, The Bug acts out a lawless greed for life that is only too human. By destroying the monster, the agents tame death-anxiety and greed for life in themselves. In emerging from the grave-like crater, animating a grotesque male body, the rampaging assassin resembles the Frankenstein monster. As in Mary Shelley's novel, the ungainly body parts evoke proletarian incoherence, in this instance not the revolutionary mob of Nineteenth-Century Europe,[14] but the marginalized white men associated today with neo-Nazi and militia terrorism. One such figure is Buford O'Neal Furrow, who was apparently acting out fantasies associated with Christian identity and white supremacist groups in the northwest when he assaulted a Jewish day care center in Los Angeles on August 10, 1999. In effect, The Bug is a caricatured redneck gone amok, and the intergalactic war threatened by the stolen galaxy actually euphemizes a more disturbing prospect of class violence suppressed by agents of the corporate state recruited from the anxious middle class.

As Teddy Roosevelt's concerns show, at the beginning of the Twentieth Century middle- and lower-class men felt their traditional status endangered, under pressure from industrialism, urbanization, immigration, and nascent feminism. *Men in Black* projects an ambivalent solution to this continuing distress. It envisions a radical gap between an invisible elite and ordinary people. It imagines a corporate state whose unseen executives manage the affairs of an even more dissociated alien elite, editing reality for everyone else. Select, gun-toting recruits from the lower ranks serve the corporate state and preserve the "galaxies" of an alien elite from brutish enemies. A liberated woman such as Laurel or a young black cop like James can "be somebody" by becoming a Praetorian security force. Teaming up against enemies, the rookie agents create a romantic bond and a potential family, humanizing the corporate state even as they free weary middle-aged managers such as Dee and Kay to enjoy the fruits of their labors. But the heroic rookies are still finally servants. Their first assignment, for instance, is to scare up luxury sports tickets for a visiting alien diplomat.

Those at the bottom of society are epitomized by the redneck monster Edgar and in turn associated with immigrant stereotypes of a century ago. As scapegoats, greedy and aggressive, they draw off guilt the corporate insiders might otherwise feel. The monstrous redneck Edgar is abusive to "his" wife, behaving like the immigrant in Alice Guy Blache's didactic, pseudo-documentary film of 1912 called *Making of an American Citizen*.[15] In the film an immigrant husband named Ivan mistreats his wife as he did in the old world, until his new American neighbors reeducate him through chivalrous exhortation and, as a last resort, a prison term. In *Men in Black,* that despised, uncouth barbarian once again invades America's genteel shores. After debriefing Edgar's wife, preparing to zap her memory, the young black agent Jay wants to give the woman a new feisty identity to remember instead of the usual banal formula. He tells her that she "kicked out" her boorish husband and should now "hire a decorator" and get a new wardrobe. But this is Hollywood feminism, deflecting attention to personal style when the deeper problem is the woman's poverty and the ownership of "galaxies" by an armed and inaccessible global elite.

But there is also another way that immigration lore serves the film's fantasies about the present. If The Bug represents white trash subculture, his opposite is his victim, the jeweler "Gentle Rosenberg." The grandfatherly Rosenberg is an expression of a privileged business class that in the 1990s feels older and vulnerable to ruthless rivals, afraid of losing its wealth and real estate—the prized galaxy. The jeweler belongs to an "alien"

Arquillian royal family, but he can also be seen as a representation of the new corporate elite, disguising its acquisitiveness and *arriviste* insecurity. Rosenberg possesses a "galaxy" that suggests the immense wealth—the business "empire"—controlled by this financial elite, just as the redneck monster embodies the rage of the underclass in an era that has been compared to the Gilded Age. This is an "alien" elite insofar as it has cut itself off from the poor. The galaxy-in-a-bauble is in fact an invaluable "sub-atomic energy source," even as the mild jeweler puts a harmless face on military-industrial aggression.

In an era of identity politics, the manipulation of ethnicity and class markers makes for especially good box office. Like the film's black and female superheroes and its de-monized redneck, Rosenberg is part of an ideological formula. Hollywood commonly ide-alizes "Jewishness," as, for example, Steven Spielberg has done in *Schindler's List* (1993) and Barbra Streisand does in *The Prince of Tides* (1991).[16] But in the post-Reagan world Jews are more likely to be suburban, affluent, and politically conservative than the inse-cure urban immigrants once well-known for liberal, working class loyalties. Rosenberg's "Jewishness" expresses Hollywood ambivalence about these conflicted changes. The film makes him a figure of commanding, vindictive power and yet also a childlike victim, in a fantasy that combines self-aggrandizement and self-effacement. Rosenberg's "Jewishness" is an honorific, sentimental marker that celebrates ethnic pride yet also leaves out the real struggles of past Jewish immigrants chronicled by Henry Roth and others.

These fantasies are also a projection of Hollywood's own situation. In their reliance on disguise and their ability to get inside ordinary humans, the aliens resemble the "galax-ies" of movie "stars" who also thrive by impersonating others. And like the Arquillians, financial elites around the world and in Hollywood struggle over galaxies—"entertain-ment empires" such as Disney. In fact, when the agents finally discover the contested galaxy, it shimmers inside Rosenberg's bauble like an image on a television screen. But Hollywood equivocally identifies with ordinary folks as well. In making the lowly New York cop James (Jay) and the young pathologist Laurel heroic initiates to the real story of the 1990s, *Men in Black* flatters minorities and women.

Guns and the transforming magic of berserking support this equivocal stance. The selected agents can be happy serving their human and alien overlords because the agency allows them an illusion of professional autonomy signified by their high-tech guns and surveillance devices. Tacitly the guns make the Men in Black not servants but free agents, not only morally superior to the elite they rescue, but also capable of policing and if nec-essary even killing them. Just this rebellious potential makes it necessary to have de-monized enemies like The Bug to deflect anger away from the social world. Guns and berserking keep the agents in a state of hypervigilance that separates them from awkward questions about status and social justice, while the memory-zapping neuralizer can instantly switch them into amnesiac bliss.

In their doomsday ultimatum, the Arquillians dramatize the old American wish for both exterminatory supremacy (as in the genocidal "taming" of the American frontier or General LeMay's exhortation to bomb Vietnam "back to the stone age") and innocence worthy of "the new Jerusalem." In euphemizing the Arquillians the film unwittingly reveals its fears that even in the prosperous, post Cold War 1990s, far removed from mid-century horrors, the drive for status is grounded in dog-eat-dog survival rage.

These fantasies call into question the nature of subjectivity. The idea of aliens dramatizes anxiety that the core of self is foreign and manipulative. It personifies the Freudian unconscious, making it to some extent controllable through surveillance and guns. As in some fashionable psychological therapies, the film wishes for a frenzied, purgative abreaction through berserking. In plunging down The Bug's throat in the climactic confrontation, Kay dispels the threats of the primitive unconscious. He magically undoes the terror of cannibalism associated with the man-eating insect, hungry immigrants, and aliens who can devour humans' innards and wear their skins. In plunging into the belly of the beast, shedding all inhibitions, going out of his conventional self, the berserker puts himself in the grip of a deeper will analogous to the alien inside a human. The berserker, that is, implicitly participates in the aliens' cosmic reality.

And yet this pseudo-religious transcendence is eerily equivocal. An autopsy discovers inside Rosenberg's head a diminutive alien being something like the philosopher's "ghost in the machine." What agency moves the ghost? The question has long haunted modern cultures. Industrial technology produces tremendous power by anatomizing things, reducing them to manipulable components. It can overcome death by replacing body parts in organ transplants. The factory can reproduce useful things in infinite abundance and even clone living beings. Yet these same processes also arouse fears that we are nothing more than bio-mechanical gizmos, even in mental life—that reality is always virtual and intelligence ultimately artificial. They invite us to look for a ground of being that can never be seen, if it's there at all. Though industrial democracies deny it by appeals to national identity, patriotism, and community, societies are also assemblages of competing individuals, subgroups, and classes, each manipulated by powerful external forces, from the time clock to headline news, themselves manipulated by even more remote agencies. *Men in Black* closes with a vision of galaxies being knocked about like croquet balls in an absurd game played by agents as capricious as the ancient gods.

Like disproportions in wealth and freedom as the century closes, the disproportions of scale in this absurd cosmology resist practical thinking. With an executive elite ever more removed and invisible, ordinary people understandably appreciate fantasies about aliens stealthily taking control of their minds. To some extent this is in fact what media monopoly does by determining the vocabulary and arguments available to the dominant culture. But there is another problem of scale no less dusturbing. At least some of the aliens are refugees from life-or-death territorial disputes, perhaps a small elite escaping from overpopulated home planets.

This scenario resonates with Richard L. Rubenstein's thesis that the "demographic explosion that began in Europe during the eighteenth century" initiated "the modern, worldwide phenomenon of mass surplus population" and an "age of triage."[17] Rubenstein contends that technological, economic, and demographic pressures have been making whole groups of people expendable, resulting in mass migrations and genocidal horrors. His examples range from the enclosures that eliminated entire villages in seventeenth-

33

century England, to the Holocaust. In the late twentieth century anxiety about triage has intensified—or resurfaced—with increasing globalization, and the economic quakes and new waves of immigration brought about by the collapse of Cold War empires. As the frontiers have closed off outlets for emigration and the great powers have lost their former empires, imperialistic rhetoric has claimed space as the last frontier. Intergalactic fantasies such as *Star Trek* (1965 and onward) routinely envision the future in terms of expanding empires and dangerous competition over colonies. Closer to home, and symptomatic of the 1980s and '90s, Michael Moore's film *Roger and Me* (1989) documents General Motors' triage of its workforce, which desolated Flint, Michigan and scattered its "surplus" population to the winds in rental trucks. As in the Social Darwinist nightmare of the Gilded Age, the haunting question remains: Is there nothing but insane competition at the core of experience?

Men in Black implicitly worries this question. When the fleeing alien couple gives birth to a baby in the back seat of a car, the scene evokes—even spoofs—documentaries about refugee flight and social collapse. The refugees face a twofold threat, from political mayhem and from inexorable nature. In her birth throes the alien wife is helplessly violent. Ultimately both threats are manifestations of survival drives. Similarly, an alien elite and paramilitary agents are joined by their shared survival dread. This is one implication of the association of the loss of identity in berserking with the sense of an alien will "taking over" personality. *Men in Black* imagines urbane wit, technology, and daring precariously keeping order on an imperilled planet. But behind this cool demeanor, like an alien inside a humdrum human body, is a darker fantasy that the stress of globalization, immigration, and the emergence of a corporate police state are pressuring human populations toward the berserk state, psychically disembedded, open to hair-trigger rage over life-threatening shortages: of vital energy, autonomy, and even subjectivity itself.

NOTES

[1] In *New Strangers in Paradise* (Lexington: University Press of Kentucky, 1999) Gilbert H. Muller eloquently sums up his survey of "the immigrant experience and contemporary American experience" using a rhetoric that invokes globalism, tectonic shocks, and historic conflict. His metaphors unwittingly resonate with the cosmic immigration scheme in *Men in Black*, as when he refers to "The galaxy of immigrant women and men who populate today's fiction [and] signify the 'ex-centricity' of the nation" and to "a new nation emerging from global catastrophe, diasporic wandering, racial and ethnic resurgence, and vast cultural change." (236)

[2] "As he announces his plans for the ethnic cleansing of Canaan," says Jack Miles, "the Lord does not, to repeat, seem angry with the Canaanites, but the effect is genocidal all the same, and there is no escaping it." See Jack Miles, *God: a Biography* (New York, 1995, rpt. 1996), 117.

[3] *True Confessions: Sixty Years of Suffering and Sorrow*, ed. Florence Moriarty (New York, 1979), 2-5. For a more detailed reading, see my *Post-Traumatic Culture:*

Injury and Interpretation in the Nineties (Baltimore and London: Johns Hopkins University Press, 1998), 169–70.

4   Gail Bederman, *Manliness and Civilization* (Chicago: Univ. of Chicago Press, 1995).

5   H. Rider Haggard, *The Days of My Life* (London, 1926), II, 169–72.

6   Bederman, 196.

7   Bederman, 200–01.

8   Bederman, 199. For Roosevelt's attitude toward "race suicide," see 199–206.

9   Joseph Conrad, *Heart of Darkness*, ed. Robert Kimbrough (New York, 1963), 51.

10   Jonathan Shay, *Achilles in Vietnam: Combat Trauma and the Undoing of Character* (New York, 1994), 79.

11   Daniel Goleman calls it "the ventilation fallacy." See *Emotional Intelligence* (New York: Bantam, 1995), 64. See also *Handbook of Mental Control*, ed. Daniel Wegner and James Pennebaker (Englewood Cliffs: Prentice-Hall, 1993).

12   See Shay, *Achilles*, ch. 1, "Betrayal of 'What's Right.'"

13   Cf. the World War Two B-17 bomber dubbed *"the flying fortress."*

14   See "The Politics of Monstrosity" in Chris Baldick's *In Frankenstein's Shadow* (Oxford: Clarendon Press, 1987), esp. pp. 14–21.

15   See *The Movies Begin*, Vol. 5 (VCR cassette), from Film Preservation Associates, 1994.

16   See my further discussion of these two films in *Post-Traumatic Culture*.

17   Richard L. Rubenstein, *The Age of Triage* (Boston: Beacon Press, 1983), 1.

Who's the Cowboy? Who's the Indian?: The Slowest Gun in the West

Leslie A. Fiedler

As we approach the end of the century in the second decade of which I myself was born, I find myself intrigued and perplexed by the contradictory changes which have occurred during that relatively brief time in the behavior condoned by society and permitted by law. Concentrating on the most passionately debated and widely publicized of these changes—the legalization of abortion and euthanasia—it is possible to think of our age as one of ever-expanding freedoms.

But in a larger context this seems only half true; since though by and large liberals rather than conservatives have played the key role in determining what has been condoned and permitted, for every opening up in the traditional moral code they have sponsored there has been a matching or sometimes overmatching closing down. So, for instance, the consumption of alcohol is no longer prohibited as it was when, at age fifteen, I choked down my first shot of bootleg booze (I really did; I may be the only one in this room who can boast that he had a drink during prohibition in the United States), and the pressure mounts for a similar decriminalization of pot. But opiates like laudanum, once sold freely over the counter, now cannot be bought without a prescription.

In some quarters, moreover, benign stimulants like coffee and tea have also become taboo; and fanatic new prohibitionists have even sought to ban from the family dinner table beverages and foods like milk, cream, butter, eggs, and good red meat, once urged on them as children by their solicitous mothers. So, too, some left-wing puritans forbid their children ice cream, chocolate cake and other classic desserts with which their mothers rewarded them for having eaten up the more nutritious entrées.

To be sure, the only one of such newly nominated forbidden foods which has been accepted as taboo by more than a few of their fellow fanatics is meat—the scare campaign against which has been so successful that it is almost impossible these days to find a cafeteria or school lunchroom in which a diner gnawing a hamburger does not feel himself being stared at contemptuously by a group of self-righteous vegetarians, usually teenage girls.

Moreover, if he is moved to smoke at his meal's ending and is lucky enough to be in one of the rare places where this is still permitted, he is even more likely to attract the cold gaze of pious disapproval, along with, perhaps, a stage-whispered insult or two from a coven of equally self-righteous anti-tobacconists—most of them probably only recently delivered from an addiction to what was once America's favorite drug and now has become its favorite bugaboo.

The anti-nicotine crusade, moreover, shows no signs of letting up. It seems likely, indeed, that long after I am dead and gone—and perhaps the youngest among you as well—politicians will still be finding the noxious weed an occasion for speechifying and the press a source of headlines. Recently, however, another subject has been competing for top place on the agenda of both. This is, as you are of course aware, the uses and abuses of sex, a very old subject, indeed, since like smoking tobacco making love is rooted in a primal human appetite. But two newsworthy events have caused our interest in it to peak: the cosmic tragedy of the AIDS epidemic and the domestic comedy of Bill Clinton's erotic misadventures. Between them they have moved us to re-examine traditional notions of how, how often, and with whom we should ideally consummate that drive.

Since those I have been rather snidely calling the New Puritans were pioneers in this area, it has seemed to me useful to begin by evaluating the code of sexual behavior with which they have proposed to replace the traditional one. As an unreconstructed libertarian, I rejoice in their subversion of the Judaeo-Christian ban on pre- and extra-marital intercourse between consenting heterosexual adults and all intercourse between homosexuals of any age. But I am dismayed by their redefinition of formerly acceptable kinds of flirtation between men and women—the casual slap and tickle or erotic badinage—as "sexual harassment": a crime punishable under the law.

It does not excuse so blatant an infringement of First Amendment rights to argue that it was intended to end the humiliation of women; and no more does it justify the concomitant banning from polite discourse of pejorative names for women. Once started, such lexical cleansing is hard to stop; and indeed, the prohibition of palpably offensive epithets like "bitch" or "bimbo" has led to the banning of apparently neutral ones like "girl" or "lady" for reasons I find it hard to understand and impossible to accept.

Nor did such politically correct euphemizing end here. It has been extended to other beleaguered minorities like the sexually deviant and the physically disabled, as well as stigmatized ethnic groups, especially those of color. As a result, the ruder colloquial epithets by which their stigmatizers formerly identified them have been banned from use not just in books and on the screen, but in academic discourse and polite conversation, quite like what the generations before us called "dirty words"—meaning the once infamous Anglo-Saxon monosyllables, erotic and scatalogical, which in my own childhood appeared only in hard core pornography and the graffiti scrawled by naughty boys on backyard fences and the walls of men's rooms.

Indeed, well into the early years of my adolescence, prissy females still referred to the more horrific of these tabooed epithets coyly as the "F" word and the "S" word. But now, of course, they are spelled out in full in otherwise quite respectable journals and books, and have become, as it were, not just permissible but almost required in the dialogue of pop films and TV shows. Finally, they have made it into the classroom and the lecture hall; so that even aging, tenured professors like me do not hesitate to say, when this seems necessary to make the point, "fuck" and "shit."

It seems to me only mildly ironic (in a realm of discourse where for every zig there is a zag) that delivering the relatively few old dirty words from the censors' limbo was the work of those who at the same moment were consigning a much larger number of new ones to the realm of the forbidden. This turns out not to be the fair swap it might seem at first glance; since while, in the presumably "Bad Old Days," the disciplining of an academic for improperly using a tabooed word was kept strictly in house, in the presumably Better New Ones, the forces of Law and Order are called in from the outside to help. Formerly, the worst that could befall a student found guilty of using such then forbidden words as "ass" or "sonofabitch" or "condom" was the loss of his scholarship or suspension from school, while an instructor accused of a similar offense faced only a delay in promotion or tenure. But nowadays any academic who uses one of the newly forbidden ones like "crip" or "gimp," "fairy" or "faggot," "kike" or (God forbid!) "nigger," may be charged with the felony of infringing on someone's "civil rights"—and if convicted, be sentenced to a whopping fine or a long stay in the slammer.

Much more ironic, it seems to me, is the fact that in order thus to enforce the New Morality, the New Leftists have entered into an alliance with the cops and the courts, whom the Old Leftists hated and feared as understrappers of the oppressive state. Such an alliance, moreover, and the criminalization of all disapproved behavior moves us ever closer to becoming a truly totalitarian state, in which everything that is not forbidden is required and whatever is not required is forbidden. To be sure, though some of these attempts at criminalization have succeeded, sometimes even spectacularly as in the case of tobacco, others have failed. Such failures, however, have impelled those who failed to turn to strategies even more distasteful and dangerous, like guerrilla actions or downright terrorism.

A prime example of the latter is the campaign launched by the self-appointed champions of "animal rights" against the manufacture, sale and wearing of fur and leather garments. As far as I know, no law prohibiting these has ever actually been passed. But perhaps for this very reason, frustrated advocates of such legislation have attacked the wearers of the skins of dead animals, slashing to ribbons the minks or sables they proudly sport. So, too, the pro-animal activists have blocked the entryways to, and broken the show-windows of, shops that sell such wares, and smashed open the pens to free the beasts bred for their pelts.

Nor has the campaign of terror stopped there. Eventually, in fact, any place where creatures thought of as lower on the evolutionary scale are confined, exploited, tortured or killed by others who deem themselves higher up on that scale, is considered fair game. This includes not just zoos and experimental laboratories but slaughterhouses and butcher shops—and even those pastoral sites where hunters gather together to prepare for tracking down their prey. Predictably enough, then, the defenders of animal rights have also supported the banning of the weapons used in hunting, thus becoming, as it were, the fathers (and mothers) of gun control: a movement in which they have been subsequently joined by some who, though untroubled by the killing of pheasants or antelopes, are uneasily aware that those who wield those guns will eventually—both accidentally and on purpose—turn them not just on each other but on some who have never shot at, much less killed, anybody or anything.

With this, I have come at long last to the subject we have supposedly gathered here to discuss, but which I have felt it necessary to approach slowly and circuitously in order to make clear not just who it is that have been trying to classify the possession of guns as a crime, but why they have had so much trouble doing so. It is, I am convinced, because, unlike other problematical activities, like smoking tobacco or shooting dope or eating meat, the legitimacy of owning guns is written into the Law of the Land. That is to say, the right of all Americans to bear arms is guaranteed—presumably forever—by the Second Amendment to the Constitution of the United States, or so it is possible to read that Amendment. To be sure, it is phrased there so ambiguously that more litigious advocates of gun control have felt it possible to argue it really does no such thing. But anyone familiar with the long struggle of the rising bourgeoisie for equality, which climaxed in the French and American Revolutions, cannot doubt for a moment that this key passage in our Bill of Rights, like earlier revolutionary manifestoes, unequivocally demanded that along with such other privileges as the rights to vote and to learn to read, once reserved for the ruling class, the formerly oppressed classes should be granted the right to carry guns, which, appropriately enough, to this very day are called in the vernacular, "equalizers."

That egalitarian right, however, which they finally won and have long enjoyed, some Americans (chiefly though not exclusively lower class, politically conservative white males) fear is now threatened by the liberal sponsors of gun controls; and that, to make bad matters even worse, the government of the U.S.A., which they have supported loyally in peace and war (many of them are veterans) is doing little or nothing to protect that right. Consequently the more militant and hopeless of these malcontents—some actually neo-Nazis—have begun to organize themselves into quasi-military bands—marching in protest down hostile city streets; or withdrawing to more peaceful wilderness retreats where they have previously stockpiled weapons to prepare in secret for an inevitable Final Conflict and for survival in the ravished world it will leave behind. That ultimate conflict has not, of course, come and never will; but brushfire combats have already begun to break out, when state or federal troops—scared kids, really, not knowing what it's all about—have been ordered to silence or disarm them.

Reading lurid accounts of such shoot-outs in the press or watching even more lurid shots on TV, the advocates of gun control were not merely outraged but terrified as well, though, of course, they are sitting safely at home and, in any case, they are confirmed in the belief that they are beleaguered and threatened victims rather than heartless victimizers. In a sense, this is a paranoiac fantasy, but in another it is quite true; though, confusingly enough, the same can be said of their opponents' equal and opposite belief. Consequently, so that its own half-truth might prevail, each side has sought to convince some constituency with prestige and clout that their half is truer than the other's. Understandably, both sides turned first in this quest to their elected legislators, though in this area the anti-gun-controllers seemed to have an initial advantage since the well-heeled NRA had long been lobbying Congress on their behalf.

Finally, however, their edge proved to be only marginal, because by and large most lawmakers sided automatically along party lines: the Democrats supporting the purportedly liberal cause, the Republicans the one considered conservative. To escape that ideological stalemate, advisors for both sides seem to have urged that an attempt should be made to appeal more directly to the people, the shortest way to whose heads and hearts was the mass media. However, most of the movers and shakers of Show Biz, no matter how notoriously conservative in the past, are now, ostensibly at least, liberals—on all public occasions, for instance, deploring the anti-leftist black listings of radicals in the '50s, and in the '80s and '90s sporting red ribbons to show their solidarity with the bleeding-heart cause of the moment. I was not surprised, therefore, when just as I was writing this (it was Prime Time in the midst of the last Sweeps before the Summer Lull), the most highly publicized show of the evening, a semi-documentary called *Incident on Long Island* (one of whose producers and chief financial backers was Barbra Streisand), turned out to be a piece of flagrant pro-gun control propaganda.

I had not realized before watching it that it would treat that subject at all; though I recognized that the incident to which its title referred was the messy attempt at mass slaughter perpetrated on a Long Island commuter train by a paranoid black racist all of whose intended victims were white. One of those he actually killed was in fact the husband, and one of the seriously wounded the son of Carolyn McCarthy, a white woman who eventually wrote the first person account from which the film was made.

What interested and disturbed me about that atrocity, however, had nothing to do with gun control. What it triggered in me was a meditation on the historical and psycho-social roots of the vicious circle of hatred and incomprehension, violence and counter-violence, in which black and white Americans have been trapped for so long—and from which it sometimes seems we may never manage to escape. It did not occur to me that the event had happened because a particular man had found it so easy to buy a particular weapon on a particular day; and that consequently it and other such catastrophes could have been avoided by the passage of stricter gun control laws.

So blithe a faith in preventive legislation seems to me incredibly naive, since we have long since learned that though prohibition may jack up the price of forbidden goods, it does not necessarily lessen their availability. But even more so, I found disturbing the blindness of the makers of this film to the role played by race not just in this but in many violent crimes. As a matter of fact, that subject is never raised at all in the TV script except in one short intruded film clip of William Kunstler speaking of "black rage," in an apparent attempt to exculpate the African-American assassin.

41

In context, however, that radical do-gooder lawyer is made to seem a minor villain and his comment irrelevant if not actually downright malicious. He is, in any case, like its other villains, major and minor, male in a book whose only true hero is female: a kind of superwoman, in fact, who meets the criteria of female virtue in both the traditional old and the revolutionary new moral codes. On the one hand, she is "An angel in the house," a good Christian wife and mother, competent housekeeper and nurse. On the other, she is a formidable presence in the public arena (eventually elected to congress on the Democratic ticket) who fights the good fight for what is deemed politically correct, like "freedom of choice" and gun control, and against that which is not, like capital punishment, negative political campaigning and poverty.

That I ended up hating her cordially will surprise none of you already aware that I prize ambivalence more than self-righteous certainty, believing, like Melville before me, that all who say yes—especially to what is considered gospel in their own little world—lie! And, like William Burroughs, convinced that the world would be a better place if a toxin could be invented that would kill only those who think they are right. Still, I am occasionally moved to say, "Yes, but . . .," as I am about to do to the argument that no matter what its cost in terms of personal freedom, some measure of gun control is at this moment urgently, desperately needed to save the children. There has always been deep in my psyche a longing not just to snatch deadly weapons from the hands of kids—but also to calumniate self-righteously those who put them there.

So, for instance, I reacted back in 1970, when I visited Odessa in what was still the Soviet Union, and my patriotic guide proudly watched with me an array of twelve-year-old boys and girls marching in uniform and with guns on their shoulders past a monument dedicated to the sailors who had died in the second World War. "Is it not beautiful," she asked, "to see these youngsters honoring the fallen Naval Heroes of the Great Patriotic War?" To this I replied, "Though not yet fallen, I am also a 'Naval Hero,' but I think kids like these would be better off at home playing games or reading books with no guns in sight." At this she wept and I, I am ashamed to admit, smugly smirked—forgetting what surely I already knew, that given free choice the books they would have read would be heroic accounts of bloody combat, and the games they played would be Russian versions of "Cops and Robbers" or "Cowboys and Indians." Certainly these were the choices I had made as a child and later watched my own children making. Unlike my more righteous friends and neighbors at the time, however, I did not lecture them for wasting time on such trash; instead, I sometimes joined them in acting out their gun-centered fantasies—and even on some rare occasions, I would bring out as an additional prop a forty-five caliber automatic pistol—a real gun I had acquired in a real war.

AND HERE IT IS!

At this point I had originally intended to bring out for you that forty-five and bang it down like a gavel to signal my coming out of the closet as a gun lover—or rather out of the sock and handkerchief drawer in which my wife had persuaded me to hide that weapon, which finally, of course, I was not brave or foolish enough to try to smuggle across an international border. You will therefore have to take my word for it that I have it still in my possession after more than half a century—having resisted all offers to trade it in for cash, and snatching it from the smoldering ashes of a fire that almost totally destroyed my home. So, too, you will have to accept on faith the fact that, after being so loved for so long, that gun is still virgin, which is to say, I have never fired it. Indeed, even though I have hundreds of times in the playground and in the back yard blasted imaginary enemies with toy revolvers, cap pistols, water guns, sticks, twigs and, when nothing else was available, my naked index finger (*"Bang Bang,* you're dead," my child's voice still cries in my remembering head and "the hell I am," the boy next door—in fact long dead—replies), I have never pulled the trigger of any honest-to-god firearm.

Before I grew too old to play out such masturbatory fantasies in the waking world, I had begun to live them in the world of dreams, in which we seem never to grow old. Quite soon, moreover, I discovered that for the price of admission to the local movie theater (in those days only a dime) I could attain what Thoreau called the most blessed of states, "to be in dreams awake"; that is, I could while booing and cheering and munching jujubes in my grubby native city also be riding and shooting in the mythological West of *The Virginian* (1929) or *Riders of the Purple Sage* (1931). Only much later did I learn that these classic films were based on novels by Owen Wister and Zane Grey; in which the simpleminded plot of the shoot-out between the hero and the villain, both males, had been complicated and enriched by the addition of a female third character.

Beloved by the former, who eventually saves and marries her and threatened by the latter, who seeks to murder or rape her, she had not made it into the sexless games we played as pre-pubescent kids. But she had already become a standard feature of "adult" Western pulp stories, paperback books and radio and TV shows. In these she continued to play a major role well into the late 1960s—typically portrayed as a church-going schoolmarm skeptical about the macho code of the West: an advocate *ante lettera*, as it were, of what we have come to call "gun control." It is of course not in the name of liberal "political correctness" but of pacifist Christianity and bourgeois gentility that she pleads with her would-be protector not to shoot it out with the villain but to turn the other cheek.

Realizing, however, at the last possible moment that this ill-advised strategy would mean the destruction of them both, she abjectly apologizes to her beloved for her female weakness and, by implication at least, disavows Christian morality. "Master, be merciful," she cries out, "you are a man. When you buckled on your guns I loved you then." At that point, not only is the doom of the villain sealed—but the ultimate establishment of lasting peace and security for a well-armed America is assured.

Equally popular during the same period is another kind of Western (about which I have written at considerable length elsewhere) set in a frontier wilderness where even the schoolmarm and the prostitute have not yet arrived. In that world without white women, the lonely white male is compelled to seek for an alternative "helpmeet unto him," and finally he finds one—improbably enough—in a redskin warrior; a refugee from the tents of his enemy, as the pale face himself is from the settlements of his people.

Before the novels of Owen Wister and Zane Grey had appeared, James Fenimore Cooper had already described such an interethnic, homoerotic union in his *Leatherstocking Tales,* in which the white refugee from civilization abandons along with

43

much else his white man's name. Though baptized "Natty Bumppo" he is re-named in Indian fashion at each critical stage of his life with descriptive names like Deer Slayer, Hawkeye and *La longue Carabine* or Long Rifle.

Of all these the last seems to me the most mythologically resonant, suggesting that Natty and the long line of uniquely American heroes created in his image not merely carry them but in some sense are one with their weapons, which seem finally as vital a part of their essential selves as their maleness or their American-ness.

It is, in any case, only on that weapon and themselves that such uniquely American heroes can depend, when, at the moment of their final showdown with the overwhelming forces of evil, they find themselves absolutely alone: the Community they defend having turned its back on them out of fear or indifference; and their few true friends being—for one reason or another—simply not there. Whenever, therefore, we come upon characters in this plight, we recognize them as authentic re-embodiments of Natty-Long Rifle, however much their superficial appearance has changed. Though they sometimes these days still come on as woodsmen or cowboys, they are more likely to assume the guise of undercover Narcs, street cops, private eyes, spies, mercenaries or Marines. Even more confusingly they often wear the immediately recognizable faces of the actors who play them; macho favorites of the moment like Clark Gable and Gary Cooper, John Wayne or Clint Eastwood.

Consequently, such latter-day avatars of Natty are typically found in such not-quite-respectable pop genres as the Detective Story, the Horror Novel, the Tale of Wilderness Adventure and the War Story—as well as much Fantasy and Science Fiction—and, of course, as always the Western. All these genres are aimed at the male audience, in order to lure whom away from watching sports they are set in a world of bloodshed and mayhem, with a constant rat-a-tat-tat of guns on the sound track loud enough to drown out all polite conversation. Occasionally a work glorifying the Killer with a Gun makes it—in drag, so to speak—into Female pop, too; most notably in that best known and most loved of Ladies' Romances, Margaret Mitchell's *Gone With the Wind* (1939). In it, her heroine, Scarlett O'Hara, experiences the full orgasm which she had apparently never achieved in bed, when she shoots to death a Yankee Soldier.

Mitchell's all time best-seller was, however, ignored or savaged by some elitist critics and self-righteous moralists. Nor was this, as they claimed, but because like all pop it was slick and shallow—less a work of art than a commodity packaged and hyped for quick sale on the cultural supermarket. They seem also to have been turned off by Mitchell's sado-masochistic portrayal of Scarlett as a Justified Killer. Certainly they have similarly vilified other works which similarly glorified violence and its practitioners, even when they were clearly high art, intended from the start not for instant commercial success but for preservation in the libraries of the future. Their authors include such troubled and troubling but gifted writers as Hemingway and Faulkner, Stephen Crane and Jack London, John Steinbeck and Norman Mailer.

Despite the critics, these highbrows live on not just in libraries, as they desired, but disconcertingly also in the hearts of the mass audience side by side with equally troubling but less gifted lowbrows like Rex Stout and John D. MacDonald, Louis Lamour and

Margaret Mitchell. Indeed, joined in this improbable alliance, such highbrows and low-brows have created a mythic grid through which certain key figures of our history have come to be perceived—or even have come to perceive themselves—as "Justified Killers," no matter how ambiguous their motives and equivocal their achievements. Included in their ranks are figures otherwise as different from each other as Davy Crockett and Daniel Boone, Generals Custer and MacArthur, John Brown and Nat Turner, Theodore Roosevelt and Buffalo Bill, Wyatt Earp and Malcolm X.

Most Americans find it possible to identify only with some of these, few with none or all. But the composite archetype of the Righteous Gunslinger, to which they add up, lurks somewhere in the deep psyche of everyone of us—influencing at a level below that of full consciousness our political attitudes, whether we are liberals or conservatives.

This is particularly true in the case of gun control. And realizing this, its more ardent advocates have sought to prevent the circulation of all new works glorifying the Hero with a Gun. Being as contemptuous of First Amendment rights as of those protected by the Second Amendment, such would-be censors do not hesitate to call for their total banning particularly on the air. Failing this, they advocate attaching to such presumably dangerous matter warning labels—and providing anxious parents with the technological means for blocking their children's access to material thus labelled. Unwilling to confess that they despise freedom of speech, the gun controllers contend that their censorship is directed not against what they themselves consider "politically incorrect" but at what everyone finds intolerably "violent."

To be sure, everyone does so because it is in fact violent; but so also are the plays of Sophocles and Shakespeare—and, for that matter, much of the Old Testament. I must confess that I have a special fondness for works of art which, like them, are intended to move us to "pity and fear"; so that, for instance, I do not willingly watch on television any program rated higher than "R." Why then have I not taken advantage of this opportunity to condemn without reservation or qualification the holier-than-thou censors of violence and advocates of gun control? After all, in addition to everything else that inclines me to do so, is my long term opposition to any attempt to prohibit for any reason any previously permissible form of human behavior. Despite all this, I have continued to equivocate—in large part I fear, because I find the defenders of the Second Amendment often as smug and sometimes even more obtuse than those who seek to repeal it. This is, however, mere snobbery—and does little to explain why on the subject of gun control I am not just ambivalent, as I am about almost everything, but ambivalent about my ambivalence. A clue to why this is so is to be found, I am convinced, in the fact that while, on the one hand, I have treasured my deadly beautiful .45, on the other, I have not only never fired it, but never stripped, cleaned, or loaded it as well. The first part of this paradox is easily explicable in light of my long exposure to the archetype of the Lonely Hero with the Gun, but the second part is harder to explain. It is tempting to try to do so by talking a little about the kind of community in which I lived during the first twenty years of that exposure: its inhabitants petty-bourgeois, second generation East European Jews, all of whom could have boasted that like me they have never fired—and certainly never owned—a lethal firearm. Moreover, they did their best to continue that pacifist tradition—gifting their sons when they came of age, not with beebee guns or even Swiss pen knives, but fountain pens. To be sure there were tales of bloody combat told in those environs—some by my own grandfather; but in them the killers were not portrayed as Heroes but as Villains: Cossacks and *pogromchiks,* whose victims were, of course, Jews.

Tempting as it is to attribute my encrypted desire to silence all guns to my upbringing in Newark, New Jersey, I find it a theory hard to sustain in light of the fact that my only brother, who grew up in the same milieu, became a decorated war hero and a life-long covert agent for the C.I.A. Moreover, I, as soon as I could, fled westward ending up finally in Missoula, Montana, a goyish town in which no activities were suspended on Yom Kippur, but everything shut down on opening day of the hunting season—and there was no household without a well-filled gun rack. Yet though I finally did not leave Montana for twenty-three years, I never in all that time picked up a gun—in order perhaps to bug those of my neighbors whom I thought of as "the Cowboys"; since they wore the faces which I had encountered before only in my dreams: faces not made for sociability but only for gazing toward some distant horizon out of which an enemy would come. But this is also, of course, the face of Gary Cooper gazing down the railroad tracks, prepared for the final shoot-out in *High Noon* (1952), which triggered those dreams to begin with. Those cowboys were, in fact, descendants of the pure white pioneers who had stolen that beautiful land from the Indians, and my refusal to play cowboy with them did bug them, since occasionally one of them would take time enough from buying and selling and suing another to drop me an anonymous note, reading "JEW COMMIE FAGGOT GO HOME!!!"

The response of the actual Indians, however, was quite different. Perhaps because they recognized me as a fellow outsider, or realized that I had smoked without shame or apology the Holy Weed they had given to the world, they took me in. The Blackfeet, indeed, finally adopted me, giving me the name of Heavy Runner: one of their most admired warrior-chiefs, who had, they informed me, "gone East and come back with the weapons of his enemy." *Go thou and do like we,* they seemed to imply. And this almost made me giggle; since I was about to spend a year's leave teaching at Princeton and could not help speculating about which venerable Ivy League academic I would despoil and what weapon I would strip him of. I never decided on my victim but knew immediately that what I robbed him of would be the PMLA, an unreadable scholarly journal called in our house "the deadliest of weapons" since we used it only for swatting flies.

For some reason it did not occur to me until much later that the implied Blackfoot prophecy had already been fulfilled; since on an earlier, longer leave taken after I had surprised everyone, including myself, by joining the Navy, I had gone east as far as China, and returned with a trophy weapon. It is hard, however, to think of any sense in which those from whom I took it could be considered my enemy. The official enemy in that war in the East was, of course, the Japanese, from whom I took nothing. Indeed, as a Japanese interpreter and interrogator of prisoners of war I was forbidden to loot or harm them—much less to slaughter them or suffer them to be slaughtered. Even when I found myself on the bloody beaches of Iwo Jima, where the order of the day on both sides was kill or be killed, I invested all my time and effort in keeping those on our side from killing those on theirs. Ostensibly, my intervention was intended only to keep those prisoners alive long enough for a proper interrogation, but neither side appears to have believed this. The Japanese saw me as a heroic savior who had rescued them from their cruel captors, bonding ever closer with me in the ensuing interrogation and crying out, when the time came for us to part, "I love you. Take me home with you."

To play my part properly in this scenario I actually felt it incumbent upon me *not* to carry a gun; but this, of course, only further exacerbated the distrust and hostility of those on our side who already believed I was a double agent, which—like all interrogators—I was.

When fighting on Iwo which it seemed would never end, finally did, I was shipped off to Guam, the last stage, we were told, before the invasion of Japan and for which we prepared by drinking ourselves insensible day after day, night after night. I therefore felt no pain when I was for the first time actually issued a gun and ordered to wear it, as I led a platoon of equally sodden enlisted men into the dark heart of a woods where a last hold-out Japanese soldier was reputed to be hiding. Fortunately for all of us, we never found him, and so this gun, too, remained unfired.

On the very next day, in any case, the Bomb was dropped, ending the war, and in the ensuing hubbub that gun was lost or stolen. But that scarcely mattered since though also a classic forty-five, it was not destined to be the one I have for so long preserved. That prize awaited me in China where we were routed now instead of to Japan. Though at first we were welcomed there like liberators, the cheers soon stopped: and the curious crowds that gathered still to gawk at us instead of shouting, "Hubba, hubba, Joe," yelled, "Yankee go home." At that point our cautious commanding officer decreed that none of us should walk alone in the street but in pairs, at least one of whom should be armed. Happily, my favorite partner at that time, a dapper and articulate marine, turned out to be an expert procurer who procured for us a brand new forty-five. But fearing the unsightly bulge it would cause in his tailor-made uniform, he urged me to carry it, since in my ill-fitting jacket, he assured me, one more bulge would scarcely be noted. And I complied, not realizing, of course, that once I had stowed away that weapon I would never part with it. Occasionally, I have been moved to thank that dapper donor for his condescending gift—but have had no opportunity.

I did in fact see him once in the ensuing years. But that was on TV which had caught him—a veteran congressman by then (and dapper still) in the midst of a speech in which he was contending that a fellow marine, adored by many as a hero, was in fact an arrant villain. But I am unable any longer to stand immersion in a realm of discourse where it is difficult to tell a hero from a villain, an ally from an enemy—even good from bad. So very quickly I switched him off and went channel hopping in search of an old-fashioned Western—preferably one starring John Wayne or Gary Cooper—in which a gunslinger whom everyone knows is good shoots it out with one everyone knows is bad and the Good Guy wins, as everyone knows he will in the long lost land of Let's Pretend.

Getting the Gun: The Cinematic Representation of Handgun Acquisition

Murray Forman

There is a scene early in James Cameron's *The Terminator* (1984) where Arnold Schwarzenegger, portraying the deadly T-800 cyborg unit, enters a gun shop that prominently displays a sign reading "store-wide clearance sale." When he asks to inspect a range of handguns and rifles—in one humorous instance inquiring about an as-yet uninvented firearm from the future—the salesman offers brief reviews of each piece pulled down, remarking admiringly, "You know your weapons, buddy. Any one of these is ideal for home defense." He momentarily turns his back on the T-800, stating that, "There's a fifteen day wait on the handguns but the rifles you can take right now." When he wheels around to see his customer methodically loading shotgun shells into the 12-gauge auto-loader he pauses and says, "You can't do that," to which the T-800 responds, "Wrong," before pulling the trigger.

This scene is compelling for several reasons, not least of which is the depiction of the cyborg itself as a calibrated weapon of destruction devoid of any ethical or moral content. My focus here, however, is only marginally related to the theme of cinematic aggression. Of greater interest is the scripted attention to the contextual frames within which gun acquisition is located. The vast majority of films involving guns and their uses tends to emphasize instances of violent eruption and their eventual consequences; as rather blunt props, therefore, guns tend to serve a primarily catalytic function. In their prevalence, guns mobilize the narrative flow of films, often either directly or indirectly mediating the central tensions among characters. There is considerably less narrative—and very little critical—attention granted to the processes by which guns arrive in a given situation. The means by which they are acquired are frequently overlooked or ignored in the script. *Getting the gun* subsequently constitutes a de-emphasized aspect of the cinematic representation of guns and gun violence.

In exploring the issue, I will examine the cinematic representation of handgun acquisition in five contemporary films: *Thelma and Louise* (1991); *Falling Down* (1992); *Juice* (1992); *Strapped* (1993) and the aforementioned *The Terminator*. These generically diverse films have been isolated as examples in which the act of getting the gun is explicitly portrayed and, moreover, portrayed in different ways. These films also speak subtly to prevailing social conditions that warrant scrutiny. Methods of gun acquisition (in both film scripts and daily life) are always related to patterns of social interaction, one's station and status in life, and one's attitudes or relationship to the law. Furthermore, the larger issues of public health and safety resonate throughout any representation of firearms and their use.

The films isolated for discussion here are also historically engaged, therefore, accommodating prevailing social perceptions and, in some cases, minimally depicting the legalities involved in handgun acquisition. I refer here to the ongoing public debates about handguns, their availability and circulation, and, in the U.S., the powerful influence of constitutional Second Amendment rights. The highly contestatory discourses around guns and their regulation or "control" that have accelerated over the past twenty years emerged with new force in early 1998 after a spate of murderous teen outbursts in the schoolyards of the nation. These incidents have intensified public analysis, focusing on the relative ease with which the young aggressors were able to acquire firearms.[1] The trend, which reached its apex with the April, 1999 massacre of twelve high school students and a teacher by two students at Columbine High School in Littleton, Colorado, has triggered intense discussions about the media portrayals of violence as well as about gun laws and the question of access and use, especially among youths. While these incidents have resulted in enhanced school security measures, there has been a comparative inability to enact more stringent measures of surveillance of gun purchases and an apparent refusal to plug loopholes in the existing system. Since the Littleton shootings, only a few states (including California) have intensified their state gun laws. Others, including Tennessee, Nevada, Louisiana, Maine, and Texas—home of presidential hopeful George W. Bush—actually eased their existing gun laws or squelched bills that would constrain gun access and instate more aggressive safety measures such as enforced gun storage.[2] And since Littleton the sense of crisis has been reinforced. An enraged individual went on a shooting rampage in Atlanta, Georgia in July, killing nine; and in mid-September another man targeted a group of teenagers attending a prayer group in Fort Worth, Texas, causing seven deaths. In October 1999 there were two more shootings nationally reported, in Honolulu and Seattle. The issues raised by these examples promise to be an important facet of U.S. political debate during the upcoming elections in 2000 and beyond.

Gun acquisition (as well as the acquisition of ammunition) is a necessary precursor to gun violence. In analyzing the representation of handgun acquisition it is my intent to isolate this crucial cinematic narrative requirement and to link it more closely with several of the prevailing public discourses concerning handguns and violence in contemporary society.

OUTLAW AGGRESSION AND PUBLIC POLICY: *THE TERMINATOR*

The issue of handguns in North America has generated considerable debate since at least the early 1980s, and has polarized forces along gender, class, and racial lines as well as producing radical regional polarities as states and provinces respond to federally imposed legal policy initiatives. These distinctions are pertinent, since they also indicate the ways in which gun violence is distributed across the social spectrum. For instance, men constitute the majority of gun owners in North America by far; the poor are more likely than the wealthy to be victims of violent aggression involving firearms; blacks have a higher *per capita* homicide rate involving handguns than do other ethnic or racial groups; and Southern states tend to have more lenient gun purchase restrictions than do Northern states.[3]

The murder of John Lennon, the assassination attempt on President Ronald Reagan, and sky-rocketing numbers of accidental and intentional handgun deaths through the 1980s galvanized gun control lobbyists, setting the social stage for an all-out discursive fire-fight engaging individuals and activist groups which occupy fiercely divergent, even polarized, positions. The result in the U.S. was the 1993 Brady Handgun Control Act (known as The Brady Act, it was written into law in February, 1994) which instated a nation-wide system requiring prospective handgun purchasers to submit to an intensive background check with a mandatory five-day waiting period.[3] Prior to the Brady Act, the background checking system for handgun purchases was sporadically applied and was not mandatory in every state. Some states already adhered to similar regulatory practices and, in several cases, these have proven to be even more extensive and rigorous than those eventually proposed by the federal government.

Returning to the example of the gun shop scene in James Cameron's *The Terminator*, the salesman's reference to a waiting period explicitly acknowledges the widely circulating discourse of gun control and the accompanying law and order structures that are intended to monitor and contain the purchase of handguns. It resonates with actually existing laws in California (the locale of the film story) where, since 1975, a fifteen-day waiting period for the purchase of handguns has been imposed by the state to enable law enforcement agents to conduct more thorough consumer background checks. In its revelatory capacity, this brief scene provides a preliminary insight into government policy distinctions between handguns and rifles or shotguns, implying a hierarchy of public concern and legal enforcement that places handguns in a different category than long-barrel weaponry.

As Kleck explains,[4] this distinction is related to the fact that of all American gun owners, the majority by far are in possession of non-military style shoulder weapons (i.e. hunting rifles or shotguns). Within the distinction between short- and long-barrel weaponry, however, is a further policy initiative that seeks to separate the "good" guns (such as rifles and shotguns or single shot handguns) from the "bad" guns, which include semi- or fully automatic weapons of any kind as well as many kinds of military assault weapon. Kleck notes that although there is widespread public concern about a perceived prevalence of military assault weapons, in reality they comprise approximately 1 to 2 percent of all illegal guns confiscated by the authorities. The presence of automatic weaponry in films is considerably higher than this, undoubtedly fueling public misperceptions about the prevalence and implementation of these guns in violent confrontations.

The T-800's brazen response to the sales clerk's feeble invocation of legal purchase procedures also has a script function that narratively reinforces the outlaw status of the

Schwarzenegger character. It implicitly suggests a stance of resistance against government gun controls that has similarities with modern conservative forces, especially those associated with either the survivalist movement (which is further referenced at the end of the film) or, more recently, armed militias. Each of these factions demonstrates a propensity for acquiring mini-arsenals, and the factions are often aligned by a fierce opposition to government tracking strategies that permit the documentation of not only registered guns but also licensed gun owners.

Yet there is a subtle, double-edged irony in the scene as well. Because the T-800 has no record of residence in the state, "he" is already forbidden from purchasing handguns. He has no constitutional "right to bear arms" because he is, ultimately, an illegal alien unprotected by the provisions of the Constitution. Here is an acknowledgment of a growing social problem in Southern California at the time the movie was made. Both those with a "record" (i.e. convicted felons) and those without (undocumented "foreigners") were then—and still are—legally ineligible for gun licenses and disallowed from registering a handgun, a state of affairs that forces them toward either the underground gun trade or gun theft if they seek a weapon.

MASCULINE RAGE AND HANDGUN ACQUISITION: *FALLING DOWN*

The conservative themes saturating *The Terminator* get articulated somewhat differently in Joel Schumacher's *Falling Down*. This film offers a display of contemporary white male angst, anger, paranoia, and resentment that, once personified, runs amok across the multi-cultural landscapes of Los Angeles. More *Terminator* than *E.T.* (1982), Michael Douglas as the bigoted and xenophobic character "D-Fens" seems cybernetically guided as he tries to "go home" to his estranged wife and daughter. As with both E.T. and the T-800, however, D-Fens is also constructed as an alien, the Other in his own middle-class cultural environment. Doubly displaced by the unforgiving fluctuations of the late-twentieth century market economy and by his capable wife whose protective maternal instincts warn her that her husband is beginning to unravel, D-Fens emerges as an archetypal figure of emasculation, reduced to living in his childhood room in his mother's house.

The film's interesting depiction of the decline of white masculine control is more pointedly emphasized by the portrayal of the shifting urban cultural composition, especially due to the massive influx of immigrants and, concomitantly, the subsequent squeeze between the interests of impoverished and wealthy social classes. As Cameron McCarthy *et al* write:

> Armed with more socio-normative fire power than any gangbanger could ever muster, D-Fens is ready to explode the seams as at everyday provocateurs make him seethe to boiling point.[5]

The ambiguous ideological leanings of the film—is this a critique or is it sympathetic to D-Fens's white plight?—complicate the representations of gun acquisition. There is an element of innocence overlaid on the character who seems incapable of processing a world in which he himself has become simultaneously foreign and redundant. Perceiving threat at every turn, D-Fens's trajectory across the city is literally mapped by the police by monitoring his use of weapons. His trek leads him into a series of aggressive confrontations that provide him with an accumulation of ever more dangerous and sophisticated weaponry: graduating from a club (obtained from a bewildered Korean shop owner) to a butterfly knife, he finally obtains a small array of automatic and semi-automatic hand-held firearms that he confiscates from threatening young Chicano thugs.

It is in a racially charged encounter with several Chicano gang members that D-Fens's gun acquisition is depicted, with D-Fens cast as the naive boundary transgressor who unknowingly crosses into gang territory without the proper cultural affiliations or credentials. The stereotypes of emotional and eruptive young Chicano men are reinforced through their associations with guns and violence. This is an important structural detail of the narrative because it exemplifies the many ways in which race is traced upon the characters of *Falling Down* through a series of symbolic representations.

By working within and through a widely circulating system of media images and conservative discourses, the representation of gun-toting minority youth is sustained as a facet of the public cache of common-sense knowledge. In this protracted scene, the association of violence and urban minorities is solidly framed within the prevailing hegemonic ideologies relating to the "law and order" society and the importance of coercively containing threat or ruptures within the dominant social structure. Conflating youth with violence and minority identities intensifies the dynamics portrayed, reproducing an image-idea of the violent potentials harbored by minority youth. As a final extension of this structuring element, the notion that urban youth are *always already* armed and dangerous is firmly imbued in the public imagination. Thus, *Falling Down* does not simply operate within the aforementioned system of negative images and discourses pertaining to youth, ethnicity, class, and gun acquisition, but it amplifies the racist logic upon which such a representational system is founded.

Chicano youth are narratively constructed here as social marginals. Their incapacity to publicly articulate themselves is resolved through another form of public articulation; that of gunfire. Statistically, however, the likelihood of Chicano youth acquiring such an intense and impressive array of weapons is minimal. As Joseph Sheley and James Wright have illustrated, while there is a notable relationship between gang membership, gun acquisition, and gun use, there is a relatively low likelihood that the guns involved will be automatic or semi-automatic, hand-held assault weapons.[6] Therefore the weaponry is exaggerated to extremes as a means of reproducing a powerful, but ultimately flawed and inaccurate, image of minority youth. In the portrayal of youth in *Falling Down*, the guns they have acquired consequently serve as *loaded signifiers* that give meaning to the idea of a desperate and dangerous social subset.

The gangsters' firearms come into the hands of D-Fens quite by accident, after a drive-by murder attempt by this rag-tag group of homeboys. As they lie amidst the wreckage of their crashed car immediately following this murderous spree, D-Fens picks up their guns and chastises one boy for his sad ineptitude. The inability to hit their target (res-

53

onant with the notion of *The Gang That Couldn't Shoot Straight* [1971]) seems to reinforce the conservative themes that lace the film, portraying the aggressors as being profoundly unskilled and ignorant as well as dangerous. Their failure to annihilate D-Fens seems to confirm his—and, by extension, conservative society's—negative assessments of immigrants. In this scene, the guns have ultimately been made available to D-Fens as a result of the boys' grievous error. This transfer of weaponry functions as a mobile signifier of power, but not simply a masculine phallic power. In this transfer, the power that is maintained pertains to the "proper" social order of white adult authority which D-Fens momentarily relishes when he smugly shoots a round into the leg of his already inert assailant. His gun acquisition is framed as a patronizing, paternalistic right, and when he absconds with the duffel bag full of guns it is as if he has done nothing more than take dangerous toys from the hands of children.

Like the youth he has vanquished, D-Fens, too, is an outlaw. As the film suggests in several instances, however, he is not like the self-serving, aggressive, and offensive Others he encounters; he is not like "them." However, the discursive construction of the identity of "the Other" entails the internalization of an element of the very otherness which is being denied. For D-Fens to deny the validity of the ethnic and class-based Others that he confronts, he must also become other—*their Other*. By fixating obsessively on those who are different than himself, he has completely lost sight of his shifting role in the "new America" in which he lives.

As his name suggests, D-Fens's purpose is to halt the erosion of white patriarchal dominance by adopting a defensive stance. His line of defense is drawn internally and domestically at precisely the time that the U.S. has relinquished its major Cold War posturing and is in search of new enemies, creating the imagined threat of "the enemy within." D-Fens is identifiable as a problematic defender of so-called "traditional" middle-American values (concerning the family institution, work, property, etc.) in a broadly conceived ideological sense while also demonstrating a capacity to stand and resist the wildly hyped threat of America's folk devils: urban teen minorities. Not coincidentally, these are common sentiments in the self-righteous and frequently racist discourses of anti-gun control lobbyists and American "free men." From this perspective, then, his illegal acquisition of handguns is scripted as a justifiable reflex in a drastically unstable nation.

OVERCOMING (GUN) SHYNESS: *THELMA AND LOUISE*

Ridley Scott's *Thelma and Louise* explores gender themes and issues of power and authority with a particular emphasis on handguns and their acquisition. Janice Hocker-Rushing and Thomas Frentz refer to "the unwitting patriarchalization of Thelma and Louise, who reject men in their lives but choose men's outlaw, gun-toting methods to declare their independence and fight their enemies."[7] Rather than through this limited assessment which assumes a sustained patriarchal centrality, *Thelma and Louise* can be approached within a more progressive feminist ideal that involves creative innovation and the development of new skills in order to meet new or prevailing social demands. Whereas the D-Fens character in *Falling Down* demonstrates an incapacity to adjust to new conditions, Thelma and Louise display a will and ability to make necessary personal changes.

From this perspective, Thelma and Louise's transformative evolution from gun-shy homebodies to gun-savvy, pistol-packing mommas is consistent with women's capacity to adjust to new options, opportunities and circumstances as they ascend the social ladder. For example, the film explicitly conveys the detail that Thelma and Louise have never before gone fishing without men. Their gal-pal fishing expedition is a symbolic adventure expressing a readiness to learn on their own. As the narrative unfolds, it is Louise (Susan Sarandon) who evidently has prior gun experience, who handles the gun confidently, and who fires the first fatal shot. Yet Thelma's (Geena Davis) transformation as an individual and as a woman is more radical, symbolized by her development of skill and proficiency with the weapon. A more explicitly feminist reading of the film that expansively accommodates such aspects as skill and learning might mitigate the all-too-frequent fixation on symbolic phallic authority which purportedly resides in the gun.

Cinematically, the presence of the gun prefigures its use in a manner that is consistent with incidences of deliberate and accidental shootings in the U.S. *The Journal of the American Medical Association* reports that almost 40,000 citizens died by gunfire in 1994 and that "handguns . . . are disproportionately involved in firearm violence."[8] Both factually and cinematically, then, the "meaning" of a handgun is structured within an associative framework in which guns can be equated quite easily with their violent potential. In *Thelma and Louise* this serves a narrative priming function that activates an expectation in the audience, preparing us for the gun's eventual use.

The gun is introduced early in the film, while Thelma packs her luggage in a wild and wanton manner (accompanied by a version of Van Morrison's "Wild Nights" on the soundtrack). As she hurls clothing and accessories into her luggage, she encounters her husband's pistol in the bedside table. In this portrayal of handgun acquisition, the gun is rendered as a banal object, devoid of noticeable significance. Contrary to Hocker-Rushing and Frentz's interpretation, it is not a symbol of patriarchal authority as much as a curiosity, for although Thelma does not register a fear of guns, she does seem to display a certain discomfort, an apparent shyness with the weapon. This is conveyed as she picks it up gingerly between thumb and forefinger and drops it into her purse with a shrug.

Shortly afterward, as she and Louise embark on their weekend "getaway" (a subtly embedded *double entendre* that produces an intelligent foreshadowing effect), Thelma nonchalantly says, "Oh, Louise, will you take care of this gun?" She pulls it out, again handling it as a neophyte, gripping it loosely by its barrel rather than holding it tightly in her palm. Louise asks with irritation, "What in hell did you bring that for?" to which Thelma replies, "Oh come on—psycho killers, bears, and snakes. I just don't know how to use it. Will you take care of it?" Louise, looking perturbed, instructs her to place it in her purse and after a momentary pause, it is apparently forgotten. The initial sense of gun-shyness is conflated with a relative indifference to the idea of carrying the gun in a concealed fashion and transporting it. At the point that they get the gun, the women have no discernible sense of gun laws and regulations. Indeed, it is only later that we learn the gun is, in fact, loaded, complicating the legalities of gun transport. As they embark on their adventure, their limited interests in guns do not accommodate the issue of whether or not Thelma's husband owns a premise license or a carry license.[9]

The casual tone in which the women speak communicates a relative familiarity with handguns in the home. Thelma's shyness is embellished here as she reveals that her discomfort is related not to the mere presence of the gun, but to the handling of it—she has never held a gun before. Her obvious lack of concern about finding the weapon is intentionally disarming on Scott's part; her complacent attitude normalizes the object, ultimately deflecting attention from it.

To my mind, this is the sinister factor in this scene, since the normalization of handguns in the home and throughout the public sphere is precisely at the root of a major American crisis. It has been estimated by the National Opinion Research Center that one out of every four homes in the U.S. contains at least one handgun. In this regard, the narrative retains a certain fidelity to the current social setting in which handguns are a standard part of daily life for millions of Americans and their families.

COLD STEEL IN THE CITY STREETS: *JUICE* AND *STRAPPED*

Ernest Dickerson's *Juice* and Forest Whitaker's *Strapped* are both examples of the 'Hood film genre,[10] centering on the gritty urban environment that is home to a broad swath of Black and Latino youth as well as to poor families of various ethnic and racial backgrounds. The genre, fueled by the accompanying cultural phenomenon of Rap and Hiphop, ostensibly taps into the "real," loosely deploying a discourse of authenticity while recreating the socio-spatial landscape of drugs, gangs, and violence.[11] There is some accuracy in the general portrayals of a 'hood-oriented social milieu, but the discursive reproduction of black cultural crisis, the erosion of the black family unit, and the labeling of certain spaces as *no-go zones* all demand careful critical interrogation. Indeed, many of these 'hood films, including those by empathetic black directors, continue to disseminate stereotypical images and constraining discourses in their representation of minority youth.

And what is the reality to which these films respond? Speculating on the knowledge base from which urban minority youth draws, Sheley and Wright note:

> It is a sobering possibility that many teenagers in today's cities know more about the technology and operation of a semiautomatic handgun than they know about personal computers or even automobiles. More disturbing still is the likelihood that their knowledge of firearms will prove more useful, at least as they see it.[12]

In 1995, the Centers for Disease Control announced that roughly 2 in 25 high school students (or 7.9%) reported having carried a gun in the last 30 days, and numerous studies corroborate the findings that guns cause approximately 1 in 4 deaths of teenagers ages 14 to 19. It is worth reiterating the sobering statistic that, for black males between the ages of 15 and 34, homicide by gunfire remains among the leading causes of death, leading some observers to speculate on the "epidemic" scale of the crisis in the nation's black communities.[13]

In *Juice*, the closing of opportunities among the four central characters and the compression of hope are matched by an intensification of stress and, often, fear. The young members of the clique represent cinematic composites of a range of ghetto-centered identities. Among them, Q (Omar Epps) emerges as the character with foresight, energy, and a latent optimism for self-achievement and uplift. As a group, however, their options are reduced and out of near-desperation they turn to a local gun dealer, who provides them with a cheap *burner*. This particular gun deal is not shown, although it is referred to, providing the context for the following events in which the gun is crucially implicated. The boys' strategy is entirely hinged on the acquisition of a gun, for the gun in this context provides a tool by which intimidation and threat can be made economically empowering.

Deployed in a robbery that goes awry, the gun effectively produces the film's catalytic moment, which is the murder of a neighborhood Asian store owner. In the aftermath of the shooting, the incendiary Bishop (Tupac Shakur) becomes intoxicated with the power of the gun and quickly succumbs to a deep paranoia that begins a process of unfocused elimination of friends and enemies alike. Within the narrative, Bishop's homeboy Q must now arm himself defensively as well, leading to the key scene where we see the source of the boys' guns.

Dickerson sets the gun deal in a small subterranean social club, literally locating it underground, behind walls and down narrow alleys. Q enters, asking for "Sweets," who turns out to be a matronly, 50-ish woman (Jacqui Dickerson) whose image defies the tough, masculine exteriors which are commonly associated with images of underworld activities in 'hood films. She is all business, and when Q tells her "he needs some protection," his youthfulness is doubly exposed. He exudes a virginal quality and it is precisely this inexperience with such activities that has been his character's dominant positive feature to this point. Passing him a .38 caliber pistol, she asks politely to be remembered to his mother as he stands in awe at what he now holds in his hand.

Sweets's social gestures arise as an interesting component in Dickerson's representation of gun acquisition, amplifying a social element that articulates an essential facet of the "reality" factor. Her social graces defy the standard gangster posturing that is commonly associated with scenes of this nature. Rather than seeming incongruent, however, the scene punctuates a theme that has been subtly embedded throughout the film. Sweets attests to the importance of the 'hood's profoundly tight-knit community relations, the foundation of ghetto life, whether they be in relation to the underworld or the legitimate terrains of commerce and familial interaction. In this moment, *Juice* conveys an often unexplored facet of urban existence, drawing out an important element of social interaction within depressed urban environments. It is entirely relevant to foreground the fact that handguns are exchanged, legally and illegally, within communities that also feature characteristics of trust, respect, and support, even when handgun use might fracture these very forces. In stepping beyond the official authoritarian legal structures and the mainstream social code, Q enters into a new, unfamiliar terrain where guns and gun violence are accommodated—though not necessarily accepted—according to an alternative social code.

Of the films discussed here, *Strapped* perhaps features the most literal focus on issues of gun acquisition and gun control as it revolves entirely around the issue of illegal gun distribution and street-level handgun purchase. *Strapped* remains true to many of the generic codes of the 'hood film, but it also explores in closer detail the actual circumstances concerning handgun registration and the various laws concerning dealer licensing and bulk weapon purchasing. The central scene that shifts the tensions among the various characters develops as Diquan (Bokeem Woodbine) and Bamboo (Fredro), two young illegal gun dealers, decide to circumvent their supplier by going to Georgia themselves to acquire low-cost handguns for resale in New York. Prior to this, they functioned as middle-men, selling guns onto the streets (in one instance selling a handgun to an eleven-year-old) for a white, middle-class gun runner.

According to gun control lobbyists and government officials, the gun-running practice in the U.S. has become a major source of crime weaponry in the larger urban centers along the east coast. For instance, Florida state officials have been able to trace 1,243 guns that were purchased in their state in 1996 and used in crimes in New York, New Jersey, and Washington D.C. Gun-running is one of the major targets of the Brady Act and other proposals before the U.S. Senate, including the "One-Gun-a-Month Act"[14] which seeks to stall interstate gun-trafficking along what has been dubbed "*the iron pipeline*" between lenient southern states and the northeast. *Strapped* attempts to critically portray the processes through which guns move through this iron pipeline onto the street and into the hands of ghetto youth by exposing the ridiculously loose southern licensing and purchase procedures.

The quick explanation offered to Diquan and Bamboo by their locally-based "straw purchaser" is this: "If you wanna buy a gun, boom. Buy one. Need another one? No problem. As long as you got two things: cash and proper ID." Recalling aspects of *The Terminator*, proper ID locates the buyer in the state and, generally, identifies him as a law-abiding citizen. Initiatives such as the Brady Act weed out felons but they are not intended to discriminate against legitimate gun consumers. The young men gaze in fascination at the cornucopia of handguns in the display cases before selecting three Glocks—a popular brand of handgun known for their accuracy and reliability—for purchase. The salesman then goes through the obviously perfunctory list of questions about the buyer's background, saying "I'm going to have to see some ID; formalities, you see." He asks the straw purchaser, "Are you under indictment in any court for any crime punishable by imprisonment for a term exceeding one year? Have you ever been convicted in any court of a crime? Are you a fugitive? Are you an unlawful user of or addicted to marijuana, any depressant or stimulant?" With the last question the buyer and the salesman are chuckling, evidently sharing a laugh at the sheer absurdity of the questions. Diquan, Bamboo, and their buyer leave the store and when the New Yorkers are displaying their nervousness at carrying the guns with them, their local connection tells them, "Chill, man. It's not like we committed no crime or nothing . . . it's good New York laws are so tight, otherwise we wouldn't be in business together."

By maintaining this fidelity to actually existing laws and regulatory procedures, portraying the detailed, mundane, and unsensational aspects of legal handgun acquisition, and carefully profiling the mandatory questions required with a gun purchase, director Forest Whitaker accentuates his critical agenda. That he does so while also maintaining the 'hood film's firm commitment to representing "the real" sets this film apart from most films in the genre and, in fact, from most films that feature handguns and handgun acquisition. *Strapped* therefore surpasses films that obliquely allude to handgun acquisition or simply frame it as a necessary narrative hinge between scenes. Foregrounding the act of handgun acquisition within a clearly critical gaze, the film effectively portrays a key facet of contemporary social policy and public debate without sacrificing the film to pedantic message-making.

CONCLUSION

In their ubiquity in contemporary American cinema, guns can almost be described as banal objects that are aimed and fired in order to move the story along in some way. This is pointedly evident in the hyper-violent cinema popularized by Quentin Tarantino or in the more choreographed gun play of John Woo's work.[15] Yet, as I write these words, one youth is dead and another lies in critical condition as a result of a gun fight in the streets of Boston just last evening. This is no mere representational violence. The guns and the bullets they fire are not remotely banal; real steel with real consequences ended a young man's story even as it generates new images and new narratives in the media.

As anyone who is even partially engaged with contemporary social issues can attest, gun control and the regulation of handguns have emerged as crucial agenda items that span the political ideological spectrum and encompass numerous debates concerning public health or constitutionally guaranteed rights and freedoms. New and evolving legislative initiatives in both Canada and the United States have also generated considerable scrutiny. Despite their centrality in the media and in the lived experience of millions of citizens, the laws and discourses surrounding handguns as well as the important social contexts in which they are acquired remain underrepresented in most films. With greater critical attention to the cinematic representation of handgun acquisition and the procedures involved in getting the gun, we can more easily trace the circulating social discourses onto contemporary films. Films can then be opened to new meanings that connect more directly with the social actualities that shape our perceptions of gun violence in everyday life.

NOTES

[1]   Rising rapidly as a "moral panic" on an epic scale, the media coverage of the 1998 school shootings fluctuated between critical assessments of contemporary gun regulations and ease of access and the problem with youth, which is, as Charles Acland suggests, already often publicly conceived as "that internal Other defined as a threat

to the stability of the social order." *Youth, Murder, Spectacle: The Cultural Politics of "Youth in Crisis"* (Boulder: Westview Press, 1995).

2   Arlene Levinson, "States' call for more gun laws grow quiet," *The Boston Globe,* July 16, 1999, A-11.

3   For a broad and balanced analysis of the gun control debate in the early 1990s, see Charles Cozic, ed., *Gun Control* (San Diego: Greenhaven Press, Inc., 1992).

4   In June, 1997, the portion of the Act requiring state, county, and municipal officials to conduct the background checks on behalf of the federal government was ruled unconstitutional by the Supreme Court, reflecting traditional contestatory struggles concerning federal and state jurisdictions. The ruling exempts non-federal officials from this duty until November, 1998, "at which time the National Instacheck System (NICS) will become effective" (official press release, Office of the Attorney General, Washington D.C., June 27, 1997).

5   G. Kleck, *Point Blank: Guns and Violence in America* (Hawthorne NY: Aldine de Gruyter, 1991).

6   Cameron McCarthy, Alicia Rodriguez, Ed Buendia, Shuaib Meacham, Stephen David, Heriberto Godina, K.E. Supriya, and Carrie Wilson-Brown, "Danger in the Safety Zone: Notes on Race, Resentment, and the Discourse of Crime, Violence, and Suburban Security," *Cultural Studies* 11:2 (1997), 284.

7   Joseph Sheley and James Wright, *In the Line of Fire: Youth, Guns, and Violence in Urban America* (New York: Aldine de Gruyter, 1995).

8   Janice Hocker-Rushing and Thomas Frentz, *Projecting the Shadow: The Cyborg Hero in American Film* (Chicago: University of Chicago Press, 1995), 174.

9   Garen Wintemute, "The Relationship Between Firearm Design and Firearm Violence," *The Journal of the American Medical Association.* Special Communication (June 12, 1996), 1.

10   Additionally, as the primary handgun market (comprised of white males) has reached its saturation point, handgun manufacturers have begun to aggressively pursue new female markets. One gun dealer advertises the "Diana Handbag Holster" for which the ad copy reads: "The Diana handbag from Feminine Protection is as regal as the person it was named for and allows wide side strips to allow for expansion."

11   For a discussion of the 'hood genre, see Murray Forman, "*The 'Hood Took Me Under*: Urban Geographies of Danger in New Black Cinema," in Murray Pomerance and John Sakeris, eds., *Pictures of a Generation on Hold: Selected Papers* (Toronto: Media Studies Working Group, 1996).

12   See Forman in Pomerance and Sakeris, *Pictures,* and *"The 'Hood Comes First": Race, Space, and Place in Rap Music and Hiphop,* forthcoming, Wesleyan University Press.

13   Sheley and Wright, *Line,* 1.

14   Robert Berkley Harper, "Gun Control Would Reduce Crime Against Blacks," in Charles Cozic, ed., *Gun Control* (San Diego: Greenhaven Press, 1992).

15   The Anti-Gun Trafficking Act was proposed in 1997 by Senator Frank Lautenberg to reduce gun-running by prohibiting bulk purchases of handguns.

16   This is especially true of Quentin Tarantino's *Pulp Fiction* (1994) in the sequence where Vincent (John Travolta) inadvertently splatters the unfortunate Marvin's (Phil Lamarr) head inside the Chevrolet.

While my pen blow lines ferocious: Hiphop Politics and Gangsta Rap's New Bad Rep

Cynthia Fuchs

> Hiphop, particularly gangsta rap . . . attracts listeners for whom the "ghetto" is a place of adventure, unbridled violence, erotic fantasy, and/or imaginary alternative to suburban boredom.
>
> Robin D. G. Kelly, *Yo' Mama's DisFunkTional! Fighting the Culture Wars in Urban America*

Gangsta rap has always had a bad rep. But that's been to its advantage, in the sense that much of its considerable popularity and profits have been based on this bad rep; this despite and because of the fact that, initially, gangsta set itself at odds with the white-dominated commercial culture that to this day reviles and craves it. Asserting a realness that would not quit, an urgency that all but forced its listeners to pay attention, early gangsta portrayed the violence of inner-city "thug life." Back in the eighties—when West Coast gangsta style erupted on the pop scene via N.W.A.—gangsta had political currency and potential. Today's gangsta rap is struggling to maintain this adversarial relationship, to be, as Tricia Rose puts it, "fundamentally linked to larger social constructions of black culture as an internal threat to dominant American culture and social order."[1] But the terms of this threat, like the times, have changed.

It wasn't so long ago that critics were proclaiming the death of gangsta rap. With the murders of Tupac Shakur in 1996 and Biggie Smalls in 1997, it seemed that gangsta rap's violence had become too spectacular and immediate for its moneyed, suburban audiences. Its goals to lay bare injustice, corruption, and frustration and to give voice to real life concerns about police brutality, drug abuse, and familial disintegration were suddenly overshadowed by the bloody images on TV and in newspapers. Gangsta's bad rep had apparently caught up with it.

But rather than killing gangsta rap, these very public tragedies seemed to readjust its commercial and political courses. Gangsta's alarming black-men-with-guns image has not driven consumers away, but has led to an unexpected success within and in relation to that "dominant American culture and social order." Now, gangsta's bad rep is even worse, for its hardcore proponents and for those fans who want to combine gangsta style with hiphop politics. As Robin Kelly observes,[2] gangsta rap's new bad rep is a function of its being absorbed into the very culture and system it once purported to oppose. But this selling-out narrative misses some crucial details, in that the business interests that have absorbed and spit out hiphop and gangsta in a variety of ways have themselves changed in at least two significant ways. First, what were once perceived as distinct components of the "entertainment industry"—music, movies, television—cannot be viewed separately today. Will Smith, Master P, Queen Latifah, Brandy, the Beastie Boys, Ice Cube: these are only the most famous hiphop or hiphop-affiliated artists who have expanded their influences to include movies, television, sports, and other media production, as well as political causes. Secondly, the music industry, such as it is, has undergone a simultaneous consolidation of corporate structures at the top levels and dispersion at lower levels, resulting in a proliferation of independent labels, film production companies, and marketing venues. Small music labels, for example, are no longer made up of only hip (or not so hip), white producers and distributors.

What's more, the selling-out process has not been easy or straight-ahead. Rather, it has been difficult and erratic, marked by classism, racism, and sexism, shaped by its shifting political and social environments. And still, the outcome remains far from a done deal. It's plain enough that gangsta rap sells records, to black, white, and other kids who feel disenfranchised—and many kids do feel that they are, as Mike Males puts it, "scapegoated" by their elders and the powers that be for any and all recent social ills. It's less clear how violent, gun-oriented rap works—for its makers and its fans—on a long-term basis.

According to Ronin Ro, gangsta music from its inception "equated guns with masculinity, depicted them as 'problem solvers,' and stressed that, since other kids probably owned guns of their own, why shouldn't we all be strapped?"[3] He argues that, though "gun homicide has been the leading cause of death for black teens since 1969," gangsta culture promoted "casual attitudes that somehow made homicide acceptable."[4] True enough. But this view also omits other, ongoing and escalating reasons for "black teen" violence, such as other (white) media imagery, poverty, or educational and penal system failures. Perhaps the most salient effects of Tupac and Biggie's still-unsolved murders are the diverse rearticulations of gangsta's meanings for mainstream culture (where violence sells for Arnold Schwarzenegger or Bruce Willis as well as or better than it does for Ice Cube or Snoop Dogg) and, even more significantly, its meanings for and in relation to hiphop culture.

The connection between hiphop and gangsta is continually mutating, with gangsta generally thought of as a more violent subset of hiphop concentrating on gang life. The current versions of gangsta only reinforce the complexities of this connection: if some new gangsta rap is, admittedly, *wack* (trivial, posturing, evacuated of its promise or threat), much of it is also combining hiphop politics with gangsta experience, working toward the survival of those primary victims of inner city violence, young black men. In what follows, I'm examining the intricate relations among current hiphop, gangsta, and commercial cultures, as these are depicted in *The Players Club* (1998) and *Bulworth* (1998), as well as Master P's No Limit ventures (films, albums, soundtrack collaborations, fast food, clothing, and sports management) and the Wu-Tang Clan's projects (albums, music videos, live shows, movie soundtrack collaborations, associated artists like Sunz of Man and Deadly Venoms, and their clothing line, Wu-Wear). As the line in my title, from the Wu Tang Clan's "Triumph," suggests, I'm exploring the ways that these hiphop acts take up gun and violence metaphors in order to resist and accommodate commercial forces; as well, I consider the ways that authenticity and performance can work not as oppositional concepts, but as a representational continuum, to contest the stereotypical coupling of gangsta rap and guns.

This coupling paradoxically underlies the often repeated generalization to the effect that gangsta culture has sold out. This charge relies heavily on images of Snoop, Dr. Dre, DMX, or some other famous young black male in handcuffs and it goes like this: gangsta artists are inextricably immersed in gang culture, such that they kill each other over turf and reputations. And the story of Death Row Records (which includes chapters on CEO Suge Knight, producer Dr. Dre, and rappers Tupac and Snoop, among others) is perhaps the most notorious example.[5]

As Andrew Ross points out, the circumstances of the discursive collapse of violence and gangsta culture are more than a little troubling, though hardly surprising, given U.S. social and political history. Noting that "black male youth are quite systematically being driven toward social obsolescence," Ross argues that "those who reduced rap to a discussion of its most disturbing misogynistic or antisocial lyrics ignore how this context merely exacerbates, rather than creates, forms of social prejudice long rife in white, patriarchal America."[6] The 'hood movies of the early 1990s remain powerful examples of the ways that the context works, the ways that black youth resistance and aggression are exploited by white corporate and political powers as well as confused by gang-banger characters and their audiences. In these films—for instance, *Boyz N the Hood* (1991), *Juice* (1992), *Menace II Society* (1993), *Strapped* (made for HBO in 1994), and *Clockers* (1996)—guns (Glocks, AK47s, 9mms) are emphatically signs of power and respect for young men and boys, and as much as the films might argue against the gunplay and drive-bys they depict ("Increase the peace" was Singleton's final epigraph in *Hood*), viewers typically get off on the bloody imagery and identify with protagonists whose violent acts were forced on them. No surprise: these viewers are coming up in a culture that continues to celebrate masculine violence.

Ice Cube's *The Players Club* addresses the forms of prejudice that Ross cites, head-on. Taking seriously the complaint that gangsta culture focuses on black male anger and violence, the film offers a female protagonist, Diana Armstrong, a.k.a. Diamond (LisaRaye, once a dancer in Tupac's "Toss It Up" video). A single mother and aspiring journalist working as a shoe store clerk in Atlanta, Diana takes the advice of a particularly skeezy-looking customer, and starts dancing at a local "exotic" club. While Diana can handle the crude clients who frequent the club (including Luke [Campbell] and Ice Cube), not to mention her equally vulgar employers and co-workers, her young cousin Ebony (Monica Calhoun) cannot. Almost as soon as she starts dancing, Ebony falls in with a bad crowd, and is eventually beaten and gang-raped. With the help of the club's DJ, Blue (Jamie Foxx), Diana takes revenge on the villains, as well as on the "evil lesbian" dancers, Ronnie (Chrystale Wilson) and Tricks (Adele Givens), who set up Ebony.

Diana enacts her revenge with fisticuffs and guns, in an extended climactic struggle which shows her to be as potent a "player" as the men around her. The soundtrack—including Ice Cube's "We Be Clubbing,'" as well as songs by Mia X, Scarface, Crucial Conflict, and Master P—asserts the film's appeal to a young, urban (read "black") audience. Using familiar gangsta images (guns, tits and ass, black male crews), the movie simultaneously challenges the meanings routinely associated with such images, in part by simple gender inversion (Diana enacts the violence, and Blue plays the [unnecessary] girl's role as backup) and in part by showing Diana's revulsion for her actions. She's too intelligent for what she's doing, the film implies, to the point that she returns to her shoe store job and takes Ebony with her. Both women are physically and economically bruised, but morally intact.

This "return" at film's end suggests the film's investment in conventional values (easy money is never really easy). But more interestingly, the return allows Diana a measure of emotional complexity, in having to deal with her ostensible regression while not demanding that she die for her social and moral transgressions. Moreover, the film is clever about its representation of its female protagonist: Diana is beautiful, to be sure (and spends much of her screen time in her stage costumes), but more importantly, she's strong and intelligent. By emphasizing her point of view and challenging those of her ignoble male employers and scuzzy customers, the film critiques rather than celebrates the violence and sexism in gangsta/playa culture, representing that culture as a business aimed at a target demographic, young males. This is a keen strategy, no doubt, as it delivers strip club imagery to that target audience, but also challenges its assumptions and expectations, offering a more emotionally insightful and politically progressive understanding of young women who work in the sex industry than is typically available in most youth-oriented movies, black, white, or other.

Ironically, today, the savviest hiphop marketing tactics assume a range of consumers by asserting in part that the "realness" of a product can be fathomed only by those who are seriously committed to hiphop politics and world views. *Bulworth* is a recent example of a white man finally "getting" and then proclaiming all this. Desperately disillusioned, the liberal California Senator Jay Bulworth (Warren Beatty) hires someone to assassinate him, then—miraculously—finds a kind of religion in the street culture he accidentally taps when he reveals himself to a black church audience. Several black girls in the audience start following him around to his campaign stops, and they in turn inspire him to tell the truth, in rhyme. Bulworth is transformed in particular by his unbelievable connection with Nina (Halle Berry, miscast as a hardcore girl), who is, unbeknownst to

Bulworth, his would-be assassin; she ends up stalking him with a gun, until she is also converted by his charismatic naivete and vision.

Taking his inspiration from Nina (who gives him a mini-speech on the reasons for the "loss" of black leadership, including the decimation of an urban manufacturing and economic infrastructure due to the "shift to Sunbelt and third world" labor and the nefarious collaboration among politicians, megacorporations, and mass media), Bulworth begins rapping to any media outlet that will have him (which is all of them, as a famous politician's melt-down in public is the second best kind of scandal that passes for news) about the conditions that produce violence. Bulworth is so "moving" during cornball escapades that he changes the practices of a local thug, L.D. (Don Cheadle), who stops training his "little soldiers" to shoot down his enemies—this despite the fact that he and Bulworth seem to agree that the current educational and employment systems offer very little to these boys, aged about 8 to 16. That Bulworth is eventually shot down not by any "ghetto" inhabitant but by an insurance lobbyist underscores the film's point that it's the big-money white folks who cause real violence. The murder also provides for a hugely cinematic moment—Bulworth downed in the street, illuminated by a chopper searchlight—that allows Beatty to restage Bobby Kennedy's martyrdom. The point of all this seems to be the death of liberalism, the loss of ideals and practical ways to implement them, the triumph of small-minded profiteers.

Despite the soundtrack's plain appeal to hiphoppers, *Bulworth* does introduce a white, middle-class, and middle-aged audience (the normal turnout for a Beatty movie) to the inner city via stereotypes like the constant sound of police choppers, the common sights of bombed-out and graffitied buildings, the standard wariness that attends stepping out the door when a drive-by might occur anytime. The film was rightly chastised by critics for leaning so heavily on such stock 'hood movie images, but its insertion of Bulworth/Beatty into these scenes, looking as if he's from Mars in his hiphop outfit (knit cap, long shorts, big old t-shirt, sunglasses in the dead of night—all borrowed from Nina's brother), is quite ingenious, capturing as it does the simultaneous alienation and alienness of gangsta culture, in relation to the white culture that Bulworth/Beatty incarnates.

A similar narrative of dislocation is evoked in the video for Pras' "Ghetto Supastar," from the *Bulworth* soundtrack. Cast as the quintessential "angry black man" the dreadlocked and glowering Pras steps out of the opened jaws of Beatty's whiteguy senator (who, in the film, appreciates hiphop and black urban cultures for having access to political and economic truths long ignored by DC politicians). The video's insights are acute: as would-be assassin Nina stalks Bulworth from within the crowd that's cheering his blah-blah-blah campaign speech, the scene is set for a powerful critique of media hyperbole and the violence of so-called political culture (the bodyguards, the ready-to-rumble boxer that Pras becomes). Moreover, the video uses a huge U.S. flag as backdrop for Pras and Ol' Dirty Bastard's raps, and showcases the ingenue artist Mya's seductive and somewhat unnerving performance by dressing her in red, white, and blue, so that she becomes a walking and singing personification of the promise made by the flag and withheld by those in power. The video's critique of the political system—making speeches, telling people what they want to hear, adhering hard and fast to a status quo—is tight; and the most prominent target is the blinding whiteness of the players in this high-stakes club.

In both *Players Club* and *Bulworth*, gangsta rap and style are refashioned through hiphop politics: the gangsta look is apparent in Ice Cube, L.D., or even Nina, but the films are working a different nerve, using the look to compel viewers' attention. That is, both films understand gangsta as a youth-oriented business, in particular, one that incorporates youth resistance as a means to make money and, in its more idealistic forms, to inspire social transformation; they use such potential resistance to sell ideas and habits to young people and to represent the anxieties and desires reproduced by such a system.

Even more pointed critiques of this system are leveled by music artists and performers. (In large part, these critiques can be fresher and more acute, because of the relatively lower costs in producing music and music videos, compared with full-scale films.) Recent hiphop and gangsta-hybrid artists and proponents are demonstrating an increasing range of concerns and approaches to specific problems, from literal-minded and lyrical to postmodern-deconstructionist. Master P is a good example of the gangsta as hyper-performer: he uses every possible gangsta and gangster cliché, thrilling his loyal fans by wresting the images of standard white power for black political and—importantly—financial purposes. His most recent theatrical release, *I Got the Hook Up* (1998), is premised on the belief that moral as well as financial good can come of scamming "the man." In it, local bad boys Black (Master P) and Blue (A. J. Johnson) stumble upon an irresistible opportunity when they offer to help a white delivery man who shows up in their New Orleans neighborhood. On learning that the boxes in the van are to be delivered to a "Mr. Goldstein," Black claims the name. Fine, says the driver, relieved to be getting the hell out of there. Fine, say Black and Blue, delighted to have an easy con drop into their laps.

The boxes, it turns out, contain stacks of cell phones. And soon after, Black and Blue have figured out the scam details. Assisted by a male hacker friend (Anthony Boswell) and a female cellular fraud investigator (Gretchen Palmer), who agrees to exchange regular dates with Black for her services, they hook up everyone in the vicinity. Eventually, they run into trouble, ruining a gangster's deal by a faulty connection (his instruction to pick up a bundle of money is broadcast over the hiphop radio station, leading to a stampede on all nearby lockers, in gyms, train and bus stations). This being a comedy and Black and Blue being quick thinkers, they beat the heat coming from the gangster's scary strong arm (Tiny Lister), a crowd of dissatisfied customers, some inept fraud investigators, and a couple of sketchy federal agents.

At one level, this is a basic 'hood comedy, wherein homeboys, while trying to get by, encounter trouble and too many stereotypes: loud women with gold teeth, ridiculous thugs with ski masks, a has-been pimp-addict with a white feather boa, and a foul-mouthed old lady (Helen Martin) who sits on her porch and smokes reefer while overseeing everyone's activities. But at another level, the running joke about the phones becomes multiply layered, even insightful. The cellulars are apt metaphors for the boys' clever manipulations of communication systems and standard versions of upward mobility. And though this particular scam falls through, Black and Blue prove themselves to be successful players, fast with smart answers, ladies, big ideas, cash, and cons. They're appealing, aggressive, ambitious. Some would call them obnoxious. But they see themselves as keeping it real and giving back to the community.

And this, according to Master P, is the short version of the No Limit story. At 26, Master P (a.k.a. Percy Miller) is legendary, a rapper-entrepreneur come up from the streets. He's a multi-millionaire and CEO of No Limit Records and the state-of the-art facility, No Limit Studios. These days, he rarely appears in public without his soldiers, as well as assorted suits and bikini-wearing groupies. But it wasn't so long ago that he was just another aspiring rapper. In 1990, P moved from New Orleans, where he was born and raised, to Richmond, California, where he opened his first No Limit venture, a record store that catered to the tastes of his friends and other Bay Area hiphoppers. Soon after, he ventured into production and distribution, with *The Ghetto's Trying to Kill Me* (500,000 copies sold so far) and *99 Ways to Die*. P then signed a distribution deal with Priority for his next solo effort, *Ice Cream Man* (over 800,000 copies sold). Since then, the success has been non-stop. P's *Ghetto D*, released in early 1998, went double platinum. P and his brothers Silkk and C-Murder, as TRU, released two albums (which, according to P, have sold some 2 million copies), and he's produced singles and albums for Mia X, Steady Mobb'n, Concentration Camp, Mystikal, Mr. Serv-On, Skull Dugrey, Soulja Slim, and an R&B band called Sons of Funk.

Today, the business is in perpetual expansion mode, with holdings including a real-estate company, a Foot Locker outlet, a gas station, a No Limit clothing line, a phone-sex company, and No Limit Sports Management, representing football and basketball players and draft picks. And then there's No Limit Films, which made *I Got the Hook Up* (distributed by Dimension Films) and 1996's straight-to-video hit, *I'm Bout It*, an autobiographical film portraying his dealing and gangbanging roots. P disliked the distribution schemes offered him by New Line and Paramount—not enough screens—so he decided to go to video with the seductive advertising hook, "Banned from theaters." The video quickly went to the top of music video charts (the only measure SoundScan had for it) and both the video and CD went platinum (the CD being the first soundtrack in history to hit charts without a theatrically distributed film attached).

A friend of mine calls Master P and crew "country," meaning that they're retro and simple, stubbornly dedicated to outmoded styles and ideals (for instance, referring to women as "bitches" and "ho's"), and consuming conspicuously. At the same time, it's plain that Master P has found an eager and expanding audience. On that tip, No Limit calls itself a "revolution." According to SoundScan, the label's many releases (the goal is now something like one release per month) last year accounted for 10.3 percent of all black music sales. Increasingly, P is everywhere, wearing designer sunglasses, diamond-encrusted rings, and—always—his No Limit logo-pendant, a distinctly ornate tank, made of gold and diamonds. The No Limit soldiers are exponentially more visible with each contract signed. A case in point: after months of negotiation, P bought out Snoop's contract from the near-death Death Row. This signing is a big deal, signaling loudly the revitalization of gangsta style. Other rappers have followed P's lead, asserting street credibility, posing for photos with guns and weapons, reclaiming their gangsta IDs in splashy rather than covert ways. Jay-Z, for instance, released his CD *Streets Is Watching* (1998) with an accompanying movie-as-video, featuring gang-banging, pole dancing, and homeboys chilling. That this kind of familiar and much-repeated imagery still passes for keeping it real has as much to do with industry dictates and desire for sure things as it does with any experience which might be represented. Gangsta rap remains a disturbing paradox, turning the reality of street violence into a commercial product and resisting mainstream conformity while catering to mainstream consumers.

This paradox might help to explain Master P's speedy rise to super-stardom. The No Limit empire emerges in the wake of two specific models, and one-ups them both. First, No Limit borrows from the Wu-Tang Clan, who exploded hard in 1997 with the much-hyped release of the double CD *Wu-Tang Forever*. Mixing images and ideas from kung fu movies, their own street experiences, numerology, and other sources mysterious and mundane, the Shaolin conquer-the-world strategy involves a multi-pronged attack, with members signed to their own (Wu-Tang and Razor Sharp) labels, ad campaigns (for St. Ides beverages, for example), and their clothing line, Wu-Wear. Master P can also be compared to the early incarnation of Puffy Combs' Bad Boy Records in their similarly combative declarations of gang-like allegiances. Recently, Puffy and his Bad Boy Family (now including Mase, the Lox, and 'Lil Kim) have been dubbed "designer rap," a dis that Puffy nowadays embraces: after Biggie Smalls's murder, Puffy, who had been instrumental in building his career, swore his own business was to entertain, to make people smile and dance. And to be fair, his success (which might in large part be attributed to his control of a considerable Biggie track and sample storehouse) has so far outlasted criticism that his work is prefab, lite or sell-out, even winning establishment prizes, like Grammys and MTV Video and Music Awards.

On his good days, Master P might be considered the anti-Puffy, true to his streets background. But P is also very much like Puffy, buying into consumer capitalism whole-hog, and in love with lavish displays of wealth. Both have been accused of turning out too much repetitive, unimaginative, or otherwise derivative product, and yet both reach enthusiastic audiences. However, unlike Puffy, Master P is not about to win a Grammy. His persona is rough, his posse is rougher. He remains impassioned about his authentic persona, which is gigantically performative. The video that accompanies and illustrates his last CD as a solo artist, 1998's *MP: Da Last Don*, is a perfect example of his method. He plays Nino Corleone, a reluctant gangster and enthusiastic player, surrounded by mafia stereotypes, black and white. When his pregnant wife is gunned down in her shower (mistaken by thugs for Nino), he tracks them down and kills them all in a bloody shoot-out (he also knifes some and breaks one guy's neck, demonstrating that he's also capable of extremely intimate violence). Captured by the cops and convicted, Nino is on his way to serve four life sentences when he escapes (according to a final epigraph). A coda scene shows Nino reappearing just long enough to shoot one of the corrupt white cops in a men's room, blood all over the mirror and his hands slowly trailing down the drain as the stone killer attempts to wash it off. We might assume that for all his violence, Nino pays a price, even as his audience might cheer his revenge. Or, more to the point, his audience cheers his tremendous ability as producer to turn anything, even this tired plot, into money and expansion possibilities for No Limit.

The Wu-Tang Clan's work, by contrast, exemplifies the ways that hiphop can make money without so loudly declaring this as its central objective. The Wu Tang are in it to change the world. Led by the producing genius RZA, they reframe popular and familiar imagery and sound samples in specific, politically significant ways. Their cinema-perforated album, *Wu-Tang Killer Bees: The Swarm, Volume 1* (Wu-Tang Records, 1998), is a collection of previously unreleased singles linked on the album through sampled dialogue from *The Swarm* (1978), in which Michael Caine frets repeatedly about horrifying "African killer bees" traveling as a "black mass" toward "civilization" with destructive intentions. In the video for "Triumph," from the album *Wu-Tang Forever* (1997), the collective appears as a group of individual but like-minded superheroes, each with his own power and gimmick: Method Man blasts through a wall of flames on his motorcycle, Ol' Dirty Bastard oversees the action from atop an urban roof, other members hang batlike from trees, offer sight to a blind man on the street, and, in the end, take the form of a swarm of killer bees literally bursting through a prison wall, through a white guard's open mouth, and out again, to free all the brothers inside. I'm not saying that this video offers a singular plan of resistance to the police state rappers envision, or even that it imagines a particular and long-term social change strictly speaking. Some crew members continue to run afoul of the law, neglecting to pay child support or getting busted for stealing sneakers, despite their obvious financial success. "Triumph" does, however, stage a series of struggles with commodification and assimilation, at the same time displaying keen self-consciousness with regard to the Wu-Tang Clan's own positioning within marketing apparati, as both cultural products and conscientious artists.

Such conscientiousness becomes public, a kind of persuasive politics and consciousness-raising, through the increasingly visible formats for hiphop and gangsta rap, including MTV, BET, the Internet, and extensive touring. It's no longer possible—if it ever was—to posit a purity of music and performance apart from visual media. While all of the artists I've discussed are enormously successful, their audiences and paychecks expanding daily, they are difficult to impeach as sell-outs, in part because (along with bands that might be considered more overtly political, like Rage Against the Machine, Poor Righteous Teachers, Rakim, or Public Enemy) they advance and effect changes less in the ways that the music is and does business than in its political possibilities. In particular, they are using images of guns and violence in increasingly sophisticated ways, not only to titillate audiences but also to critique the violence that pervades popular white culture and to investigate their own "street" experiences. As they trouble generic categories and star conventions (which rely on fixed and recognizable identities), they theorize the risks of popularity, pluralism, coalitional activism and social transformation, reframing what Will Straw calls a "politics of cultural bricolage," so that temporal and spatial connections become contingent and disruptive, and productive and deconstructive.[7]

The new gangsta rap artists have introduced an urgent kind of bricolage, drawing from hiphop politics as well as from the gun cultures, white and black, from which they emerge. They illustrate something that Andrew Ross has observed more generally of gangsta (authentic and performative) culture: that "while socially denied people do not express rage just as they please, or under circumstances of their own choosing, they do tend to opt for vehicles that are least likely to be culturally influenced by the powerful."[8] The predominant vehicle for gangsta at this point remains music, in the form of albums, radio play and live shows. However, as Wu-Tang and No Limit are proving, the trajectories of influence and exploitation are hardly one-way. These businesses are booming. And their expressions of rage are at once aggressive and intelligent, progressive and retrograde, local and universal. In all cases they are increasingly difficult to ignore, often especially in their efforts to reach a crossover audience. It's worth noting in this respect that both Ice Cube and Warren Beatty focus their expressions on black women with guns. Perhaps these seem more readily sympathetic characters for crossover audiences than black men with guns, even though initially militant Nina's seduction by white Senator Bulworth is more a white man's projection than a black woman's reality. While the Wu-Tang Clan occasionally falls back on some tired and offensive sexist rhymes, they also express hope for collaborative progress.

What is most striking in any of these acts—from Ice Cube to Master P to Ol' Dirty Bastard—is their understanding of the importance of appropriating familiar imagery, of finding ever more inventive ways to use gun imagery in place of guns themselves. Their pens—not their weapons—are "blowing lines ferocious." In appearing belligerent or violent, they are delivering to expectations. I have seen Ol' Dirty Bastard, for example, be extremely ornery in his live show, warning his audience that he and his crew are "the cockroaches that invade your home." In their efforts to sell you something—their ideas, their ideals, and their clothing line—these artists use what they know, including gun imagery and macho posturing. But at the same time some of them, especially the Wu-Tang Clan, push the possibilities of rap's internal threat, inviting their listeners to rethink their own positions and responsibilities.

NOTES

1   Tricia Rose, *Black Noise: Rap Music and Black Culture in Contemporary America* (Hanover NH: Wesleyan University Press, 1994), 144.

2   Robin D. G. Kelly, *Yo' Mama's DisFunkTional! Fighting the Culture Wars in Urban America* (Boston: Beacon Press, 1997), 39.

3   Ronin Ro, *Gangsta: Merchandising the Rhymes of Violence* (New York: St. Martin's Press, 1996), 7.

4   Ro, *Gangsta*, 7.

5   See Ronin Ro, *Have Gun Will Travel: The Spectacular Rise and Violent Fall of Death Row Records* (New York: Doubleday, 1998).

6   Andrew Ross, *Real Love: In pursuit of cultural justice* (New York: New York University Press, 1998), 73.

7   Will Straw, "Pop and Postmodernism in the 1980s," in Simon Frith, Andrew Goodwin and Lawrence Grossberg, eds., *Sound & Vision: The Music Video Reader* (New York: Routledge, 1993), 19.

8   Ross, *Love,* 76.

Who Is Shooting Whom?: The Content and Context of Media Violence

George Gerbner

I cannot resist the temptation to tell you the story of the teacher who asked her class, "Children, who can tell me what our century owes Mr. Thomas Edison?" One child spoke up, and she said: "Teacher, I can tell you. Without Mr. Edison, we would still be watching television by candlelight." Children, if not most of us, cannot imagine the time B.T.—Before Television.

Television represents a major transformation in the way our children are socialized. It is a major transformation in the way we are being humanized: a shift in the way in which stories are told.

Most of what we know or think we know, we have never personally experienced. We know the world, and, in a way, we know ourselves, by the stories we're told by others; the stories that we see, read and write. We live in a world that is directed by these stories, and a major change in the way in which they are told is represented by the shift from the time stories came from parents, schools, churches, communities and even nations, to our time when stories are being told not by anyone who really has anything to tell, but essentially by big major global conglomerates that have something to sell. That huge shift in human socialization has far-reaching and profound consequences.

In a cultural environment that is driven essentially by marketing—by the imperative need to produce mostly stories that sell—there are certain things that are privileged and there are certain things that are relatively neglected. These commissions and omissions explain many of the distortions of what I call "casting" and the fate of the cultural environment into which our children are born and in which we all live.

A few highlights of that casting and fate will be sufficient to give you some indications of what the Cultural Indicators Project has been trying to track on an annual basis now for over thirty years.[1]

Perhaps the overwhelming discovery is that on almost any kind of program—drama, news, public affairs—men outnumber women three to one. Now, how can anything reflect reality when you put a cast on the stage that is as skewed as that? Sometimes, when I discuss this in an interview situation, the interviewer wants to trump me, and says, "Well, if you were the czar of all media, what would you do?" I simply say, "Cast more women!" The interviewer's reaction is usually a kind of surprise and shock. Cast more women and the world will begin to change.

There are only so many kinds of stories that you can tell with a predominantly male cast. Most of them are stories about power, and the easiest and cheapest of those stories are stories of violence, many of which glamorize the use of guns. These stories also travel best around the world, since they entertain in the easiest and cheapest way.

We have also studied the question of age. Young people under eighteen on TV are about one third of their real proportion in the population in the casts of prime-time major American produced network drama. The only group that is vastly over-represented, with more than 150% of their true proportion in the population, is white males in the so-called prime of life. An interesting contrast is the elderly: older people, sixty-five and above, are underrepresented. As characters, they are one fifth of their true proportion of the population.

The result is that you have essentially a distorted cast in which white males are over-represented, and it is the context of male power that explains violence. The fastest and cheapest dramatic resolution of mostly male conflict is the exercise of male violence, often with the use of more powerful and "sophisticated" guns and weaponry.

These stories are globally transportable without writing extensive dialogue or providing sophisticated explanations. They are driven by global marketing, not by popularity. You can overcome unpopular programs, unpopular assembly-line ingredients, if you can extend the market sufficiently to more than overcome what you lose domestically in every country. This, then, is the global marketing formula, with its power-driven and largely distorted ingredients, imposed on the creative people in Hollywood and foisted on the children of the world.

I'm often in touch with those Hollywood creative people and they *don't* like the global marketing formula any more than I do. They say, "Don't talk to me about censorship from Washington, I've never heard of it. I get censorship every *day*. The producers tell me, 'Put in more action.' (*Action*, of course, is a code word for violence in the American media trade.) That means I should have more men, I should have more action, I have to provide the ingredients for a global marketing formula. That is *my* censorship. I am under that kind of marketing iron censorship every *day*."

There is indeed a de facto censorship which is driven by the monopolization of media, in which there are no alternative perspectives, there are no alternative major productions, and there are no alternative major distribution outlets. We are faced with a very large and powerful global monopoly in the cultural field, for which there are no alternatives other than citizen action. That is what prompted us to start the Cultural Environment Movement, which you are, of course, most welcome to join.[2]

76

The analysis that I am presenting explains the context within which violence and gun use become ingredients in a global marketing formula that is enormously effective and enormously productive of profits, even though it is destructive of essential integrity and equity in every sphere of life.

There is a scene of violence on the average of five times per hour in prime-time major network American programming, and an average of twenty five times per hour in cartoons—which basically saturate Saturday morning children's viewing times. Apologists say this cartoon violence is humorous, not to be taken seriously. But, on the contrary, humor is the sugar-coating that makes the pill easier to swallow. And the pill is power, with violence and guns as its chief ingredient.

Beyond the issue of violence is the total cultural environment into which our children are born and in which they learn much of what they know. A ten-year-old child recognizes Joe Camel (the symbol of an industry that advertises the only legally addictive product that is guaranteed to kill if used as directed) as easily as she or he recognizes Mickey Mouse. A ten-year-old child is as ready to recognize the names of brands of beer as the names of American presidents—in fact *more so*.

An even more troubling part of our cultural environment driven by marketing imperatives is that it has no room for poor people. In our analysis, the bottom fifth of the income distribution, low-income people, are represented by only 1.3 percent of characters. I walked around the city last night and saw homeless people all over the place, but you never see them on television. They're out of sight, out of mind.

If poor people are invisible, how can we, as citizens, connect with the great crisis of our times? How can we connect with a virtual, although undeclared, civil war that is going on in North American cities whose inner cores are under occupation by police? Those of us middle-class whites who live in the suburbs know only that we don't like to go into the inner city: we are told that it is a fearsome place, it is a threatening place, and if we go, we make sure that we park in a well-lighted parking lot and get as many escorts as possible. We're taught to look at the lower-income one-fifth of the population as a threat, not as a great and grave social problem in the two richest countries in the world. The richest country, the United States, is plagued by the largest inequalities, the largest polarization between rich and poor, in which the top one percent of the income distribution has ninety percent of the wealth. We're never told that on television.

So, the great commissions and omissions in our cultural environment damage all of us as citizens and, in many ways, present a world that is not suitable for all of us as citizens. It is a world that is suitable only for purposes of marketing commodities. We are up against a global system to which there seem to be no clearly visible mainstream alternatives. Of course, there are alternative perspectives on the margin, and as long as they *are* on the margin we can be told that we live in a free culture. After all, if you look in the libraries and the reference sections, or go on the Internet, it is true that you can find other points of view. But the marginalization of other perspectives *itself* is a part of the formula that integrates us into a mainstream view, one in which we are dimly aware of some marginal opinions that relatively few people—as long as it's a safe few—select.

* * *

Q: In Canada and the United States, there is a myth perpetuated by the media that there is an increase in youth violence these days. I am wondering if you can respond to that.

GG: Well yes, there is an increase in what I call kid-bashing. There is an increase in blaming kids for committing violence, while ignoring the fact that the most highly victimized group of our society are young boys.

Q: Can we consider the impact of the Telecommunications Act Reform? It seems that the principal impact is that since we're already at a point of corporate monopoly in media, with that Act, a company like CBS, which was previously limited to owning a handful of radio stations, now can own hundreds and hundreds, and, in fact, within a year, most of these major corporations did go out and buy hundreds and hundreds of stations. Has this legislation just made it harder to fight this fight?

GG: The Telecommunications Act of 1996 was a disaster. It has put the stamp of official approval on a monopoly situation. The problem, of course, is that the true government of our societies is the media, or are the media (I am still old-fashioned enough to consider media a plural noun, but I guess I won't hold out much longer). Most politicians are beholden to the media for support for election or for re-election. If you cross the media in the United States, you are dead as a politician. Media monopoly, in effect cultural monopoly, is political monopoly. We simply cannot speak of a democratic society in the United States anymore. Not until citizens recognize what we have difficulty recognizing (because we have not had enough real information): it is difficult for fish in the ocean to know that they are swimming in salt water. We have not had enough alternatives, because public television in the United States is virtually non-existent. I am delighted to see the public television here, although it is under siege in Canada, too. American public television has been so intimidated and so reduced in financing that it does not have the resources to put on dramatic programs; and if you don't have dramatic programs, you don't have the audience. Ultimately, the system of advertising-driven media is a system of ideological monopoly.

The question in any democratic country is how to get adequate resources to produce a press or media (and by press, I mean broadcasting as well as the printed press) that can illuminate life, and from which people can select from different perspectives. There is information diversity in countries in which there is a socialist party and press, a communist party and press, a fascist party, a religious party, and whatever ideological spectrum there happens to be historically and traditionally in that country.

Q: Hollywood is basically self-regulated, and has been so since the 30s, with the Hays Code serving as a reaction to potential state censorship. Is the alternative to put it back into the hands of the state? If so, given that certain states have passed rather punitive laws against minority groups such as homosexuals, and, here in Ontario, poor people, how can we trust them to do the job that Hollywood is not prepared to do?

GG: North Americans have forgotten that the airwaves are not the property of the networks and of the broadcasters. The airwaves are a public resource. Broadcasters are tenants in public space. That tenancy is limited. The terms of that license depend on the government, and what the government is depends on the citizens. If government is beholden to a media monopoly, then the terms of the license will be simply financial ability: if you can finance it, you can have it.

If you have a country in which the diversity of points of view is of value, then licenses will be given to make sure that there is a choice; that there is ideological and regional and ethnic and gender and other demographically-based distribution of this public resource, so that every significant major group and perspective has a voice on the airwaves. We are far from that, and, of course, things are going in a regressive direction right now. What we have to do is to turn the tide.

Q: Some people claim that it is difficult to prove the connection between TV violence and violence in real life. Can you comment on that?

GG: Absolutely. You see, this claim is ironic, because for 30 years we have been trying to publicize the evidence. The reason the question comes up in this form is itself a media ploy. The media say, "Well, prove to us that there is a relationship between the violence we provide and violence in society." For 30 years, we have been saying that is not the point.

When you see violence and when you are exposed to the scenario of violence, the major and most pervasive consequence of violence is not incitation. Using violence has several inhibiting factors: number one, it is stupid; number two, it doesn't work; number three, they hit back. The major contribution of a cultural environment saturated with violence is what we call the "mean world syndrome." If you grow up in an environment of violence, you feel at risk; you feel this is a very mean and dangerous world much more so than it really is. You are afraid to go into the streets at night; you are afraid to go into the inner cities; you are mistrustful of strangers; you are exemplifying all of the exacerbated suspicions and misanthropy that destroy the veneer of civilization. So the ultimate fallout of violence is a sense of insecurity, a sense of vulnerability.

Q: Can you comment on the amount of gun usage in the media?

GG: Most media violence involves firearms and cultivates a misplaced sense of insecurity that leads to buying, owning, and carrying guns. A poll conducted by the National Institute of Justice in 1998 estimates that 35 to 50 percent of American households have at least one gun at home (which is where most homicides take place), and about one third of gun owners carry a firearm presumably for protection at least once a year.

Q: Could you to comment on V-chip technology?

GG: The V-Chip is a band-aid on a big, gaping wound. When you are polluting the airwaves, it doesn't really address the cause of the problem to say "Don't worry; I am going to sell you a gas mask." You have got to clean it up. Cleaning up the airwaves means making them more diverse.

Q: Could you comment on the impact of globalization, and its threat to cultural sovereignty?

GG: The globalization of U.S. television is essentially global colonialization with its violence and gun culture; cultural colonialization is basically the prerequisite for imposing trade agreements that are inequitable.

Q: I have been thinking about how well you have succeeded in your career in being a public intellectual and how, in many ways, the Cultural Indicators Project allowed you access to a public discourse about the media. You provide empirical findings that both reporters and politicians like, because they feel they are concrete—there's something there. In fact, you have been talking about ideology for all of these years and it is a brilliant kind of strategy.

There is a crisis in cultural studies and film studies where among intellectuals there is a growing sense of having abrogated responsibility to the public by dealing with arcane theories and perhaps centering too much on issues of text and interpretation. I myself was thinking about what television shows meant and what viewer activity meant when one day, I was watching TV on a Friday night—Disney on ABC—and the characters were all going to Disneyland on the show, and I thought that there was absolutely no difference between the commercials and the program anymore. Monopolization has really accelerated: those issues are what a lot of media scholars are worrying about now—whether we have been looking in the right places, and have been talking in a language that is accessible to the public.

When I read your work or hear you speak, there is such a clear-cut political edge to what you are saying, yet a lot of the time when you are cited or when you are reported on in the press, that political edge is lost. I was wondering if you could talk a little bit about your strategies for communicating your research, and how you can keep that political edge in the kind of work that you do once you lose control.

GG: This is a complex question, and it calls for some self-reflection. The first and most important thing is to live long enough and stick to the same thing until you get on everybody's Rolodex. After a while, you find that you are an authority, because they call upon you. An authority is somebody who is called upon to speak as an authority.

The other issue here is grantsmanship. I have been very fortunate in finding foundations and organizations; for the last 40 years or so, I have never been without a research grant, partly, of course, because my institutional affiliations have granted me a certain credibility. It is important to have that kind of institutional setting and institutional title, and to process grants through institutions so that things are neutralized, but in another sense, it gives you the so-called academic freedom which too few people take advantage of; if you don't use it, you lose it.

Media reporting of my findings is a trade-off. You have to recognize that media usually cite what fits *their* story, not yours. So you trade that for spelling your name correctly, giving some contact information, and gaining some visibility. That should reach some of those who may be interested and will contact you directly for more information.

NOTES

1   The Cultural Indicators Project has been directed by the author since 1967. It analyzes the way in which the mass media depict the American cultural environment, using a database on over 3,000 television programs and 35,000 characters.

2   The Cultural Environment Movement is an international coalition of over 150 groups in some twelve or thirteen countries around the world. CEM is working for gender

equity and general diversity in mass media employment, ownership, and representation. Readers can reach CEM by writing to PO Box 31847, Philadelphia PA 19104; fax (215) 204-5823; e-mail: cem@libertynet.org.

Action Heroes and Strong Leadership: Big Guns in Political Culture

Judy Hunter

The big gun heroes of popular action films speak to our impotence and desires. In the face of fearsomely threatening crises, they accomplish admirable deeds with supreme competence. They inhabit dangerously exciting worlds, where they always vanquish the evil forces. Their worlds contrast to our everyday Canadian and American lives, which are filled more with routine responsibilities than with danger and gun play; our moral paths are much less clear than those in the film worlds. Rarely do we experience clear-cut crises; rather we often feel impotent to understand or affect the ambiguous pressures on our lives.

Despite the obvious gap between our real life worlds and the worlds of action film, I would like to argue that the neoliberal political discourse has captured the images of media action heroes, and that these images are responsible for a substantial component of popular support for the agenda of the right—albeit not a primary source of the popularity but a significant one. Successful new right leaders are "big guns." They present themselves and are presented in the news media as strong, decisive leaders, who operate in a world of clearly defined crises and never fear strong action. At the same time, they draw moralistically on the values of family, individual freedom, and meritocracy.

How are these real and virtual heroic identities constructed to reflect and shape our desires? How might film heroes articulate what resonates in the appeal of many popular leaders? In answer to these questions, I'll look first at the concept of heroic identity, illustrate how it's embodied in action films, and then examine how audiences might find it personally desirable. I will show how the discourses involving these media identities are reflected in popular tastes, how I see them as translated into our political culture, and particularly how they contribute to hegemonic support for the new neoliberal political voices. Finally, I'd like to argue for the important place of academic and social analysis in the current North American socio-political climate.

BIG GUN HEROES OF *THE PEACEMAKER*

A close look at one recent action film, Mimi Leder's *The Peacemaker* (1997), can help us understand how the appeal of heroic identities is constructed. A pivotal scene in the film plays off Lt. Col. Tom Devoe (George Cluny), the canny field-experienced hero, against Dr. Julia Kelly (Nicole Kidman), his foil and supervisor, and a Washington-based Ph.D. The pair have located a truckload of stolen nuclear arms being driven through the Ural Mountains. Because the Russians have failed to intercept the smugglers, Devoe, the decisive hawk, wants to enter Russian territory with helicopter gunships and take out the truck. He tells Kelly, "We have to act now." She forbids him to take action without proper authorization, provoking him to ask: "Who do you think I am—some gung-ho stupid son of a bitch?" With an attempt at clear-headed, condescending analysis, Kelly retorts, "I don't think you're stupid. I think you're a talented soldier with sloppy impulse control and I don't want you provoking an international incident for a personal agenda." But she's missed the point, and Devoe has to set her straight: "Right now you're not in Washington. You are in the real world now, and in the real world there are nuclear arms heading for Iran." Devoe and his men head for their gunships, and Kelly phones Washington to call for the attack. Devoe and the gunships vanquish the arms smugglers, of course, and with Kelly now onside, the two team up for the rest of the movie to hunt down the one missing nuclear warhead that had been taken off the truck at an earlier point. Thus, in the end there are two heroes who save the world, or at least New York City, from nuclear terrorism.

How can we better make sense of this scene as a demonstration of the development of heroic identities? The question of identities, particularly social identities, has recently interested scholars from a number of social science and humanities disciplines, and their work has established several commonalities in various post-modern concepts of identities and the processes of creating and maintaining them.[1] As well, some have examined the ways that audience members take up desirable media identities to shape and articulate their personal identities.[2] Current theory generally considers identity as self in relation to others, rather than as a discrete label with fixed properties.[3] Identity is culturally and contextually situated; and therefore multiple, for relationships with others vary across settings, times, and institutions.[4] Gee defines such a context or culture as a "socio-culturally distinctive and integrated way of thinking, acting, interacting, talking, and valuing connected with a particular social identity or role, with its own unique history, and often with its own distinctive 'props' (buildings, objects, spaces, schedules, books, etc.)."[5] Moreover, identity is not statically determined by social categories, such as gender, race, or age. Rather it is dynamically established, displayed, and sustained through social practices and interpersonal interactions, notably language,[6] and through associations with particular histories and props.[7] This theoretical framework can provide a means for understanding the underlying elements of identity both in *The Peacemaker* and in our society.

The Peacemaker's context is the world of international intrigue, involving governments, Mafias, terrorists, and heroes. What's more, it's a world in crisis—first with a sudden, mysterious nuclear explosion in a remote part of Russia, next with a desperate hunt for the arms smugglers and terrorists who may unleash further nuclear destruction. In this dramatic context we perceive the protagonists' identities through the actions they take and the language they use when they interact with others and initiate or respond to events. We see them positioned as heroes in juxtaposition to other characters in the film.

We are introduced first to Julia Kelly, an earnest, but graceless, intellectual, an *Acting* Director in her department. She is often situated physically at the margins of men's discussions, hanging about while they chat in the hallway. She briefs her team from behind a table, her presentation dependent on documents. As we are introduced to Tom Devoe, on the other hand, he is in the midst of an apparent disciplinary review; unabashed, defending himself as one who enlightens the uninformed. Subsequently, when he reports as Kelly's military assistant, he interrupts her briefing about a mysterious nuclear explosion, takes the floor, and proceeds to reassess the situation. In her office, he again takes control, giving orders, telephoning, grabbing documents from the hands of others. His speedy success at accurately uncovering the reasons behind the explosion is enhanced relative to Kelly's passivity and ineptitude. His language is direct and colloquial, his expertise based on practical experience as opposed to her academic talk and reliance on print-based knowledge. In the remainder of the film—the hunt for the stolen arms—we see two other sides of Devoe, the main protagonist: the violently aggressive gunfighter and the moral, sensitive man.

As gunfighter, Devoe's identity is accentuated in several ways by weaponry. Guns make him feared, for his armed power extends into the space beyond his physical self. Carrying a gun shows that he is unafraid of participating in the world of killing. His use of guns also attests to the strength of his moral stand, for as a good guy he must not kill for frivolous reasons, and it's a physically easy feat to shoot a gun. For example, the assassination of his friend and colleague Dimitri (Armin Mueller-Stahl) by ambush seems to him to call for slaughter of the murderers, and after a suspenseful car chase scene in which he and Kelly are also intended victims, Devoe walks up to the murderers' smashed car, shoots them coolly as they lie injured, and walks away.

In the next scene, we see Devoe's moral and emotional sensitivity: he holds his head in his hands, mourning Dimitri's death and lamenting for the man's family. Later on in the gunship scene, we see his altruistic concern for world safety when he reminds Kelly that the arms are headed for Iran. In other words, the need to act, to put aside the formality of authority and regulation, is imperative, for in the stereotyped view we find in the film world, nuclear weapons in Iranian hands would endanger us all. And we see him as a thoughtful, respectful man when he listens to Kelly's analysis of the arms theft—but only after she has been transformed into a woman of action. The other players in Devoe's world are either good or bad (or props to highlight his heroism), and there is no remorse in violence against the bad.

How do these screen identities relate to us as viewers? How could this obnoxious masculine character and awkward female be admirable? First, like most desirable media models, they are youthful, vital, physically adept, and attractive. What's more, Devoe is successful: he makes the right decisions, he makes them quickly, he is fearless and undeterred by danger, he does not get nervous and flustered; others respect his decisions and acquiesce to him. He shoots when it's practically and morally necessary. Devoe's victims disappear cleanly from the scene; there are no negative consequences for his violence. His world is suspenseful and exciting. There is no drudgery of arranging his moves, getting along with co-workers, or managing his daily life. Most of us have none of these qualities or these choices. So in relation to others in the movie Devoe is heroic, and in relation to us he is outstanding.

Secondly, although Kelly is the female hero, she does not represent a fixed female identity. Rather her character is fluid, only inhabiting the physical form of a woman; she is more an antithesis to the male hero. In addition to being a woman, she's a character derived from a stereotyped world of academia, and a weak indecisive dove who must learn the importance of decisive action. Her intellectual abilities do contribute to success, but until the point when she realizes the urgent need for armed, decisive action, she is an inept character. Only then can she participate intellectually with Devoe in saving the world. Once she has transformed herself into the vital new woman, the enlightened academic, and the reformed ex-pacifist, she becomes finally what we might all apparently strive to be. Interestingly, it is the female here who transforms to adopt the more traditionally masculine heroic characteristics. The cultural link of heroism and masculinity is too strong for Leder to reshape, but it is important to point out that while the hero image is "masculine," it is not only a physical man's image. Indeed, the fluidity and disembodiment of masculinity and femininity in the film allow the audience to transcend the physical self and adopt a masculine heroic identity. As we will see, heroic roles in 90s action films are taken up not just by strong, youthful, attractive white men, but also by many others.

The Peacemaker was neither a blockbuster nor a critical success. But the elements of heroic identity in this film are typical of many others in the late 90s. Often action heroes begin as unassuming, "ordinary," middle class characters who develop heroic identities as a threatening crisis unfolds. Typically they must muster a strong personal response that calls for, and morally justifies, urgent, decisive action. In these films, the critical moral imperative is propelled by threats from the "other"—outsiders who jeopardize the safety and security of innocents in the American world. Family security figures as a strong supporting moral theme. The heroes must take up guns—which show them as both feared and fearless—to overcome the threat, a challenge they meet in the end with glory and without remorse. Their guns demonstrate and enhance their power, affirm their fearless readiness to engage with danger, and show the sureness of their moral position. In achieving their goals, they have become decisive, cool, detached, and morally righteous. In sum, hero identities develop dynamically as a crisis unfolds. It is a crisis that calls for violent, brave action in defence of a clear moral imperative, often protection of threatened innocents. The existence of crisis is a precondition for the birth of heroic goodness, to such a degree that crisis will be produced if necessary so that "goodness" can exist in heroic figures that audiences may come to love.

For example, in *The Rock* (Michael Bay, 1996), two heroes, an aging prisoner who loves his daughter (Sean Connery) and a young government biochemist (Nicholas Cage), reluctantly team up to save America from evil terrorists who have stolen biochemical weapons. The US President as gun-toting hero (Harrison Ford) in Wolfgang Peterson's *Air Force One* (1997) overcomes another cadre of foreign terrorists. In some films the hero must save the world from alien destruction. Will Smith in *Independence Day* (Roland Emmerich, 1996) and *Men in Black* (Barry Sonnenfeld, 1997) begins as an "ordinary" reserve soldier/police officer who initially fears danger, but learns to be cool, and with the help of big guns empowers himself to save the world. In *Conspiracy Theory* (Richard Donner, 1997) the female hero (Julia Roberts), as in *The Peacemaker*, moves from resistance against the violent discourse to enlightened recognition of the crisis and the apparent need for violent action, thence to aggressive participation: she shoots the villain. Renny Harlin's *The Long Kiss Goodnight* (1996) features a suburban school teacher suffering from amnesia (Geena Davis), who recovers to realize she was once a government-trained assassin and must now team up with a private detective to defend herself and her family against killers from the past. In other films, male heroes live out identity reversals. In Michael Caton-Jones' *The Jackal* (1997) an imprisoned foreign (IRA) terrorist, Duclan Mulqueen (Richard Gere), is released under joint FBI and KGB supervision to help capture an elusive international assassin (Bruce Willis) before he strikes in America. Yet the hero is only permitted to pick up a gun when he sees his personal mission no longer as escape but as avenging the past and protecting the intended female victims of the Jackal. In other words, he's adopted an acceptable moral mission, and has a right to shoot. And at a crucial point, a woman's gun saves him. He shoots in turn, to save the woman. Overall, however, these powerful Hollywood heroes with big guns are not new identities. They have been the heroes of Westerns, police and vigilante movies, and many other action genres.

While they tend to share distinctive core elements, the heroes of these films represent multiple social identities. Their initial identities as "ordinary" people, or at least as family members with "loved ones," enable us to identify with them; they seem plausible characters, one of us. As well, they are males and females, whites and blacks, young and old, prisoners and law enforcers, professionals and government leaders. As Miller notes, such a variety of social identities further allows a wide range of audiences to identify with them.[8] Once we can identify with them morally and emotionally, we can engage vicariously with their power and the violence they perpetrate. Moreover, many researchers on popular culture consider that media images like these shape and articulate what we see as desirable styles, tastes, and identities.[9] In Miller's view, for example, the cool, powerful, unaccountable hero of the 90s media culture has become a desirable identity among young people. And Kellner, from an American point of view, analyses content in similar Hollywood movies as providing favorable imagery for US military adventures.[10]

BIG GUNS IN ONTARIO POLITICAL CULTURE

The appeal of powerful, brave, decisive action heroes has been successfully appropriated in the imagery of the new right political discourse. In fact it's not surprising that political leaders would look for an image with broad popular appeal to voters. Indeed, support for the new right socio-political ideology is widespread across North America. In the words of critical educator Michael Apple, the new right derives from a "hegemonic alliance ... [with] a wide umbrella."[11] It includes not just the corporate elites who benefit most from the right agenda, but also working and middle class people who see their traditional values under threat, feel powerless to maintain them, and buy into a populist authoritarianism. Such authoritarianism is articulated in promising and exciting ways through the films we have discussed. Here in our lives, the heroes' guns of action films translate into the bold, authoritarian exercise of political powers.

While the desirability of action men is traditional for American political leaders, it has not been for Canadians. But even for Americans, the masculinity of this imagery has powerful and ironic appeal. Lois Weis writes in a study of American working class white high school males, "It is likely that the New Right will be able to rearticulate smoothly the profamily rhetoric and racism expressed in the voices of the young men."[12] This political imagery has redirected the historically worker-oriented Democratic Party far to the right. According to Michelle Fine, the images that traditionally inhabited the discourse of the male working class have been used by the American neoliberal movement to exploit them.[13] To my mind, the action hero image embodies this exploitation, for it is the working class—and increasingly the middle class—men and women depicted as heroic in the films I have been discussing who will be the major victims of the new socio-political agenda. In my view, not only do the powerful media images emulated in Ontario politics appeal to these segments of the population, they also attract the business and corporate elite, who have long been saddled with an image of overly comfortable stodginess. Indeed, Linda McQuaig[14] quotes two bank heads celebrating their upcoming mega-merger with "talk of their desire to 'kick ass', 'grow like hell', and stop 'dicking around on the beach.'"[15] She also cites a "high-level Finance official" who claimed that Gordon Thiessen, head of the Bank of Canada, had to take brash action so that the financial community wouldn't view him as a "wimp."[16]

There are strong and direct parallels between the new conservative political discourse and the action films discussed above. The first is a context of crisis. The debt and deficit "crisis" exists globally, nationally, and locally, along with the view that there are no other choices than to drastically restructure the economy and society (in a heroic frenzy). Murray Dobbin traces the "deficit hysteria campaign" in Canada to 1988, when the CBC proclaimed the "crisis" immediately after the free-trade election.[17] McQuaig's 1995 analysis of the debt crisis, entitled *They Shoot Hippos, Don't They? Death by Deficit and Other Canadian Myths*, illustrates the parallels between the political and the film contexts succinctly.[18] Her book opens with reference to an episode of *W5*—the Canadian television documentary—in support of New Zealand's conservative restructuring. The show led with a news story about a public zoo that was forced to shoot its baby hippo because the government could not afford to support it. McQuaig reports on the show:

> [Eric] Malling, the consummate TV host, makes it all sound necessary, even reasonable. What choice is there but to shoot the baby hippo? The government is in debt. What other possible solution could there be? ... Hippos, line up. Bam, bam, bam.[19]

The construction of a crisis, of the need for drastic action, indeed shooting, is again on the screen, but this time as a representation of reality (a documentary) rather than as escapist fiction. And significantly, it is a discourse constructed by neoliberal voices.

The provincial government's recognition of the value of crisis to position itself is clear in the infamous 1995 leaked speech by John Snobelen, then Minister of Education and Training. In claiming the need for radical changes in the Ministry, at one point he explains the failure of organizational change at Chrysler: "They were late with the[ir] declared crisis in a different way than we do with a "real" one. A real crisis for an organization is when it is threatened from without."[20] Snobelen goes on to invoke the need for boldness; he defines his agenda as "very brave work. It requires an enormous amount of courage."[21] He continues: "Creating a useful 'crisis' is what part of this will be about . . . we probably need to move fairly quickly in that area . . . yeah, we need to invent a crisis."[22]

Within this context of crisis, neoliberal leaders, particularly in Ontario, are easily positioned to display themselves as action heroes. From the beginning, the Ontario Tories have eschewed politician identities. They define themselves not as government but as "fixers" of government, and what they do, not as politics but as "common sense." This "common sense" label allows them to spell out simplistic answers to complex social and economic questions without debate, because these are considered matters of common sense, i.e. what everyone should naturally know. Like action heroes, operating under dangerous crisis conditions, they have moved quickly and decisively to enact their agendas, using their legislative powers as weaponry. Toronto's Metro Network for Social Justice describes them as a "'blitz' of changes."[23] Bezanson and Valentine find, in interview research done through the Caledon Institute, that the provincial government's "speed of change" was striking to a majority of participants.[24]

Moreover, the Tories have also redefined relationships in their socio-political context as "us versus them," the latter often labelled as "special interest groups." They tend to demonize those who suffer from their social program cuts and other policy changes, just as Devoe demonizes foreigners in *The Peacemaker*, and they show no remorse for their actions, like Devoe, remorseless as his pursuers lay dying in their car. Cuts to welfare mothers' food allowances, for example, were justified by claims that the extra money women on welfare were receiving was just spent on beer. Not only welfare recipients, but civil servants, teachers, unions, protesters (Native protesters have been shot, in fact), criminals, street people, and political critics have been placed in the role of threatening villains to facilitate the government's tough hero image. They are generally presented as selfish and undeserving, and the role appeals to conservative supporters because it allows them to place blame for many dissatisfactions in their own lives. At the same time the vilification of the "other" deflects attention from those who benefit most from the new right agenda—big business, financial institutions, transnational corporations, to name but three. In *The Peacemaker*, it was the "foreign" arms smugglers and gangs who were demonized.

Conservative Ontario neoliberals stand in contrast to their predecessors, particularly former Premier Bob Rae, who played the piano and sang cute songs for the Christmas audience at CBC Radio. At the same time, they are careful to maintain the image of being moral beneath the surface, for without such an image they might be seen as callously brutal—as Devoe might have, without the scene where he mourned Dimitri's assassination. When Premier Mike Harris's marriage break-up briefly became public in August 1999, potentially jeopardizing his family-man image, subsequent news reports framed him as initiating attempts to save the marriage. This same motivation partly underpins the Premier's reversals shortly before his re-election campaign, for example his decisions to generously compensate both the Dionne quintuplets, who were exploited as spectacles during their childhood, and all the Hepatitis C victims for having received tainted blood transfusions from the Ontario Red Cross in the late 80s and early 90s.

In June, 1999, the Ontario Conservatives were re-elected. Certainly they were dramatically helped by the buoyant economy, but their campaign style attested to their faith in the action hero imagery of their first term. For example, the party retreat held in March 1999, before the election announcement, opened with the theme music[25] and "ready to rumble" chant of the World Wrestling Federation. Much of the news media publicized the imagery extensively. For instance, Harris was quoted as lauding his own "courage to stare [the unions] down"[26] and as adopting the buzz phrase, "the debate is over."[27] Harris was described by his campaign Chair and reported in the news as offering "real . . . determined leadership," as "unafraid to administer the 'strong medicine' necessary."[28] The same story quoted Harris's description of the Chair as "a very caring father." The Chair's attack on the Liberal contender for being "uncertain, indecisive, vague, unsteady, vacillating, . . . wishy-washy, waffling and just plain weak" was also quoted.[29] On many campaign stops, Harris was televised and photographed in an open-necked, blue denim-coloured shirt with rolled up sleeves, in order to appeal to hard-working, working class voters as, in what the pollster Ekos labelled him, a "populist anti-intellectual kind of guy."[30]

BIG GUNS AROUND THE WORLD

Although we have looked most closely at the big gun imagery in the Ontario political culture, similarities exist across North America and beyond. One example is the 1998 election victory of Jesse Ventura as Minnesota State Governor. Ventura, a wrestling celebrity, ran an anti-government, populist campaign and split the traditional democratic vote, roundly defeating the favored candidate Hubert Humphrey III, descendant of the late Vice-President. Micah Sifry describes the contrast between the two: "Where Humphrey was bland and uninspiring, Ventura was all edge,"[31] and according to Sifry, the bulk of his support was found among young, working-class men. Although Ventura may not embrace the new right ideology unequivocally, he ran on the conservative Reform Party ticket. His image mirrors the action hero of popular film.

On the national scale, we need look for examples only at the aggressive foreign affairs records of the past three American Presidents, Bill Clinton, George Bush, and Ronald Reagan. During their collective terms in office, they have ordered the bombings and invasions of several small developing countries like Grenada, Iraq, Libya, Panama, Serbia, and Sudan, all to strong popular support. In fact, despite criticism that Clinton bombed Sudan and Iraq to distract the public from the sex scandal in his private life, his popularity was high. And despite his officially "liberal" face, Clinton instigated work-for-welfare in 1996, a neoliberal system based at least partly on the vilification of the poor. Today he remains a popular leader.

Beyond North America, we may recall the reactions to the May 1998 nuclear bomb tests conducted by India and Pakistan, ostensibly for defensive purposes. While outside world opinion was critical, North Americans watched televised in-the-street interviews with cheering supporters of their governments' moves to empower their national image and bolster their new stance as a world-class threatening force. As Americanized cultural images begin to dominate the world, we should not be surprised to find reflections of the big gun image of leadership.

CONCLUSION

In summary, a strong component of the new right's appeal lies in their successful appropriation of action hero identities. They have redefined and simplified the socio-political context. They have reshaped relationships with others, and identified themselves as big guns through their actions, language, and style of presentation. In this discussion we have drawn primarily on the example of the Ontario Conservatives, but as we can see, the big gun imagery of the new right ideology can be found in other Canadian provincial governments, in various American states, in both federal governments, and in much of the business and corporate elite. In addition, it's embraced by many of their supporters across race and class.

On the whole, social activists have tended to identify reasons for the popularity of the conservative agenda in economic and social terms (e.g. Toronto's Metro Network for Social Justice). They point out the new right's appeal to racism and xenophobia in their promises to eliminate employment equity; the appeal to fears for personal security in their promises to create jobs, to attack the debt and deficit, and to reduce personal income taxes. In the American context, Weiss and Apple, cited earlier, have argued similarly. Toronto activists counter the neoliberal agenda with factual and social justice arguments and appeals to public sympathy for the unfortunate. Such approaches are crucially important to informing the public, promoting debate, examining moral values, and encouraging civic participation. However, unless the left also confronts the strong popular appeal of gun-carrying media heroes, I don't believe factual arguments alone will win over the minds and hearts of the working and middle class supporters of the new neoliberal world order. In 1999 the new right resoundingly won a re-election victory in Ontario, a sign of successful entrenchment similar to that in Alberta, in many American states, and in both the Canadian and American federal governments.

I'd like to close with reference to our place as academics in the public sphere, and recall the scene in *The Peacemaker* in which Dr. Kelly telephones Washington to argue for the helicopter gunship attack. Her superior cuts her off, saying, "I'm not asking for an analysis. I'm asking for an answer." Now that I've given an analysis, I'd like to ask if there is a place for academics and intellectuals in the discourse of the new world order. There's certainly pressure for us to join the new discourse and act decisively, working primarily as teachers: teach the stuff, test the students, and dump the failures. Otherwise we're labelled inept wimps. Or we could analyse popular texts instead of just the classical literary works. We could escape to early retirement or a summer home by the lake. But I think we need to join the new discourse as a contrary voice, to add a participatory debate. We can use analysis to redefine our socio-political context—to refute the framing of the "crisis," expose whose interests it serves and whose interests it exploits. Most of all we need to become public intellectuals and speak out about the social and political relevance of our analyses. We can work to expose the duplicity behind neoliberalism, as Linda McQuaig has begun to do. Through the dramatic tensions in our everyday lives, we can work as men and women to reposition ourselves with energy, power, vitality in thinking, and civic participation.

NOTES

1   James Gee, "Socio-cultural Approaches to Literacy (Literacies)" in W. Grabe, ed., *Annual Review of Applied Linguistics*, 12 (1992), 31-48; E. Graham McKinley, "In the Back of Your Head: *Beverly Hills, 90210, Friends* and the Discursive Construction of Identity," in Murray Pomerance and John Sakeris, eds., *Pictures of a Generation on Hold: Selected Papers* (Toronto: Media Studies Working Group, 1996), 115-130; D. Schiffren, "Narrative as Self-portrait: Sociolinguistic Constructions of Identity," *Language in Society* 25 (1996), 167-203; Valerie Walkerdine, "Video Replay: Families, Film and Fantasy," in V. Walkerdine, *Schoolgirl Fictions* (London: Verso, 1990), 173-204; Chris Weedon, *Feminist Practice and Poststructuralist Theory* (New York: Basil Blackwell, 1987); Lois Weis, *Working Class without Work. High School Students in a De-industrializing Economy* (New York: Routledge, 1990).

2   Judy Hunter, "Power and Gendered Discourses: Girls Learning School Writing," in J. Addison and S. McGee, eds., *Feminism and Empirical Writing Research: Emerging Perspectives* (Portsmouth NH: Heinemann Boyton/Cook, 1999), 72-86; McKinley; Henry Giroux and Roger Simon, "Popular Culture as Pedagogy of Pleasure and Meaning," in H. Giroux, R. Simon et al., eds., *Popular Culture, Schooling, and Everyday Life* (Toronto: OISE Press 1989), 1-30; Walkerdine.

3   Kenneth Gergen, *The Saturated Self: Dilemmas of Identity in Contemporary Life.* (NY: Basic Books, 1991); Weis.

4   Gee; Gergen; Weedon.

5   Gee, 33.

6   Gee; McKinley; Schiffren.

7   Gee.

8   Mark Crispin Miller, "North American Youth and the Entertainment State: A Talk," in Pomerance and Sakeris, eds., 131-146.

9   Stanley Aronowitz, "Working-class Identity and Celluloid Fantasies in the Electronic Age," Giroux, Simon, et al., 197–218; Giroux and Simon; Miller.

10 Douglas Kellner, *Media Culture* (London: Routledge, 1995).

11 Michael Apple, *Cultural Politics and Education* (New York: Teachers College Press, 1996), 6.

12 Lois Weis, "White Male Working Class Youth: An Exploration of Relative Privilege and Loss," in L. Weis and M. Fine, eds., *Class, Race, and Gender in United States Schools* (Albany: SUNY Press, 1993), 256.

13 Michelle Fine, paper presented at the 16th Annual Ethnography in Education Research Forum. Centre for Urban Ethnography, University of Pennsylvania, Philadelphia, 1995.

14 Linda McQuaig, Smoke and Mirrors, *The Toronto Star* (February 1, 1998), D1, D6.

15 McQuaig, D1.

16 Linda McQuaig, *The Cult of Impotence* (Toronto: Viking, 1998), 118.

17 Murray Dobbin, *The Myth of the Good Corporate Citizen* (Toronto: Stoddart, 1998), 219.

18 Linda McQuaig, *They Shoot Hippos, Don't They? Death by Deficit and Other Canadian Myths* (Toronto: Penguin Books Canada, 1995).

19 McQuaig, *They Shoot Hippos*, 1.

20 John Snobelen, untitled speech [Transcription] (Toronto: Graham Verbatim Reporting, July 6, 1995), 21.

21 Snobelen, 24.

22 Snobelen, 36–38.

23 Metro Network for Social Justice, *An Economic and Political Literacy Primer* (Toronto: MNSJ, 1996), 45.

24 K. Bezanson, and F. Valentine, "Act in Haste . . . The Style, Scope and Speed of Change in Ontario," Speaking Out Project: Periodic Report No. 2 (Toronto: Caledon Institute of Social Policy, 1998)

25 Joel Ruimy, "Harris Opens Fire on Rival Liberals," *Toronto Star* (March 11, 1999).

26 Ruimy.

27 Jim Coyle, "The Fangs Behind Those Tory Smiles," *Toronto Star* (May 27, 1999).

28 Joel Ruimy, "Key Tory Lashes Out at 'Weak' McGuinty," *Toronto Star* (March 13, 1999).

29 Ruimy, "Key Tory."

30 Joel Ruimy, "Three For All. Harris: Preparing to Star in New Role," *Toronto Star* (May 9, 1999).

31 Micah Sifry, "Power to the Populists," *The Nation* (May 3, 1999), 22.

If Looks Could Kill: Female Gazes as Guns in *Thelma and Louise*

Nicole Marie Keating

As the climax approaches in *Thelma and Louise* (1991), a virtual army of police officers chases the two main characters across a desert landscape. Louise (Susan Sarandon), dumbfounded, turns to Thelma (Geena Davis) and faintly utters: "All this . . . for us?"

This line of dialogue foreshadowed the enormous public controversy generated by this "small" Hollywood film. In this paper, I argue that the contradictory deployment of female and male gazes in the film triggered wildly divergent judgments in the reactions of viewers, ranging from "shockingly sexist" to "blatantly feminist." This internal contradiction paved the way for the widespread debates about the film, revolving around Thelma and Louise's "violent behavior" evidenced mainly by their use of guns. Through an analysis of public discourse about the film in popular media—in conjunction with reference to the film itself—I argue that Thelma and Louise's gun-related transgressions were consistently associated with their gaze-related transgressions. In this sense, Thelma and Louise can be seen to have been presented as twin Medusas, and the active female gaze became a metaphor for violent instruments of destruction. Still, the film's comment upon this gaze/gun association is less clear: in some ways, it celebrates female rage; in other ways, it punishes it. Either way, the gun toting violence within the film generated a different kind of mayhem beyond the screen: widespread public controversy.

In response to this widespread public debate, for example, in January of 1992 *Cineaste* quickly published "Should We Go Along for the Ride? A Critical Symposium on *Thelma and Louise.*" In the introduction to the piece, Toni Kamins and Cynthia Lucia refer to the intensity of the public discourse surrounding this film:

> The continuing controversy over *Thelma and Louise,* a mildly revisionist Hollywood genre item which nevertheless proved to be the summer's most provocative release, has less to do with the film's modest artistic achievements

than with its success in stimulating widespread public debate over the relationships between men and women.[1]

The contributors to this symposium—Pat Dowell, Elayne Rapping, Alice Cross, Sarah Schulman, and Roy Grundmann—each offer various perspectives on what Sarah Schulman calls "the public outcry about the film," Elayne Rapping "the furor surrounding this movie," and Alice Cross "the ruckus *Thelma and Louise* caused in the media." Roy Grundmann observes that "*Thelma and Louise* is a good example of the fact that films don't exist in a void. If the evidence lies in the issues the film raises . . . it also lies in the critical and public response to the film." It is this public response that I examine in this paper. As Elayne Rapping comments, this response is interesting in its own right:

> The most important things about *Thelma and Louise* are to be found in the media hullabaloo that followed its release—the fascinating, passionate public discourse it engendered—rather than in the merits or meanings of the film itself.[2]

On June 24, 1991, the cover of *Time* announced "Gender Bender: A White-Hot Debate Rages Over Whether *Thelma and Louise* Celebrates Liberated Females, Male Bashers—or Outlaws." On June 10, John Leo of *U.S. News and World Report* called *Thelma and Louise* "Toxic Feminism on the Big Screen," and *Newsweek's* June 17 headline read "Women Who Kill Too Much: Is *Thelma and Louise* Feminism, or Fascism?" One reason for this outrage can be traced back to the gun/gaze association, which is the theme of this study.

Thelma and Louise centers around two female characters: Thelma, a bored, repressed, and vaguely glamorous housewife, with movie star good looks partially hidden by her disheveled, frazzled appearance; and Louise, a world-weary, restless, chain-smoking waitress. These two are both "buddies" and an "odd couple," for Thelma is scattered yet charming in an infantile sort of way, and Louise is mothering and authoritative; decisive and tidy, yet sensitive. Louise takes care of Thelma and tries to compensate for her flightiness, and Thelma helps Louise to relax. The two of them are opposites, yet they complement each other in a way that inspires a deep connection and a natural friendship. The film begins as the two of them are planning a weekend trip to a cabin in the mountains, but as the narrative progresses their plotting takes on a new twist. Thelma decides to pack three or four suitcases for the trip, bringing along most of her wardrobe, a few home appliances, and her husband's gun ("In case of psycho killers, bears or snakes"). On the road, Thelma and Louise make a pit stop at the Silver Bullet where Thelma's encounter with a hulking hard-core womanizer, Harlan Puckett (Timothy Carhart), becomes menacing when he sexually assaults her in the parking lot. Louise comes to Thelma's rescue and threatens Puckett with the gun; the would-be rapist backs off, but not without retaliating with offensive language. Though his cruelty and lack of respect shock Louise, his coarse and flippant remarks—"Bitch, I shoulda gone ahead and fucked her" and "Suck my cock"—push her past tolerance. Her finger hits the trigger, and suddenly Harlan Puckett is dead.

The gunshot signals the beginning of a new phase of life for Thelma and Louise. Two relatively routine-bound women are suddenly outlaws, on the run from the police and headed for Mexico. En route to the Mexican border they become progressively rebellious and subversive; they blow up trucks, commit adultery, armed robbery, kidnapping of a law enforcement officer, and assault with a deadly weapon (assaulting a police officer, no less, and then "kidnapping" him by locking him in the trunk of his car). They also blow up an oil truck after the lecherous driver makes obscene gestures. The rig explodes into flames as the trucker falls to his knees, howling, "YOU BITCHES FROM HELL!!" Most of these crimes are motivated by Thelma and Louise's pent-up anger against a patriarchy that has oppressed them with sexual violence and demeaning treatment; and the ubiquity of towering Mack trucks, loudly honking traffic, police sirens, lumbering freight trains, clanking industrial machinery, roads jammed with bulls, lurking hoses and deafening crop-dusting planes suggests the claustrophobia induced by the male-oriented world that pushes them out onto the edge of a cliff—and beyond.

Are they relentless male-bashers, radical feminists who will stop at nothing short of mass murder and destruction? Or are they operating in service of the patriarchal project by emulating the stereotypical image of the hysterical woman who is unable to control her own life? Is this film feminist? Sexist? Fascist? Or all three and more?

In this paper I argue that the film is in fact, and simultaneously, *all* of these things. The contradictory deployment of the gaze within and toward the film paved the way for the ensuing controversies, since the paradoxical nature of the text facilitated such diverse interpretations. As I hope to show, the paradoxical deployment of the gaze within the film heightened viewer awareness of the mechanics of production and generated widespread public wrangling, particularly with respect to the ironically consistent portrayal of a female gaze/gun association. Although this association is prevalent throughout the film, the film's perspective on it is complex and contradictory. The film glorifies female gun use, but also condemns it; the film revels in female liberation, and then undermines it.

The narrative content of the film (women on a violent rampage) clearly provides one explanation for the "media hullabaloo," but an examination of the film's signifying practices (the female gaze in particular) illuminates a number of important insights concerning the anatomy of this controversy. For analytical and organizational purposes, I have placed my own examination of these signifying practices within the framework of Laura Mulvey's three looks associated with the cinema. Although this breakdown provides a useful framework for my own analysis, it is important to note that Mulvey's "Visual Pleasure and Narrative Cinema"—albeit a groundbreaking essay—is hardly the last word on the subject; the essay provoked waves of response throughout the community of film scholars. Still, her breakdown of the three cinematic looks is valuable: (1) the look of the camera as it films the event (i.e. the perspective of the filmmaker's camera); (2) the look of the viewer toward the screen (i.e. the perspective of the audience members); and (3) the look of the characters at each other within the screen illusion (e.g. the "looks" between Thelma and Louise, or between J.D. [Brad Pitt] and Thelma, etc.).[3]

Mulvey argues that the filmmaker's and viewer's perspectives must be sublimated to the character's in order to ensure that the viewer is affected by the "binding-in" effect of suture (voyeurism) in the realistic Hollywood narrative. In other words, the viewer must become so absorbed in the looks between the characters as to temporarily lose sight of the fact that this apparent "window on reality" is actually a filmmaker's construction involving a "look of the camera." Devices which provoke awareness of either the cinematic apparatus or the presence of the gazing audience (such as distancing devices or obvious editing techniques) are therefore avoided in service of the viewer's total identification with the *male* gaze within the narrative. According to Mulvey, this identification is generally with male characters since males tend to be the "bearers of the gaze" and females tend to possess "to-be-looked-at-ness."[4] So it is a male active gaze which is directed towards the feminine spectacle, denying—in fear of castration—an active gaze to the female.[5]

But as we shall see, it is insufficient to concentrate on the gazes of male characters alone when females are shown onscreen to open and focus their eyes as active weapons. What happens when female characters become the "bearers of the look" *within the narrative?*

I believe that the presence of the female gaze "within the narrative" provokes the viewer's awareness of viewing, destroying the "binding-in" effect of suture (voyeurism) which is dependent upon the sublimation of the "look of the viewer" to the "look of the characters within the narrative." The female gaze thus emerges as something explosive—not unlike a gunshot—which is violent, transgressive, and disorderly. In the case of *Thelma and Louise*, these active female gazes, so associated with diegetic "gunshots," also led to an explosive public conversation.

In this film, the constant association between active female gazes and guns reinforces what Eisenstein called cinematic "shocks." Since an emphasis on the female gaze is a departure from the norm—and a "loaded" departure at that—viewers become conscious of (and perhaps uneasy regarding) the look as female, and therefore ultimately conscious of "the look" itself. The presence of these three elements (awareness of the look, awareness of the look as female, and the treatment of the female look as provocative) paved the way for the controversies surrounding this film. Using the three looks as an organizing principle, I elaborate on this analysis below.

THE CHARACTERS' PERSPECTIVE

Because *Thelma and Louise* focuses on two female protagonists, we tend to look at the filmic events through their eyes, and critics have argued that the film thus conveys a female perspective with an honesty and forthrightness that very few mainstream Hollywood films have accomplished. Certain moments in the film support this thesis—the fact that we see Thelma's husband Darryl's (Christopher McDonald) chauvinism from her perspective, for example, or the image of Thelma gazing lasciviously at J.D.'s ass while sighing, "Did you see his butt?"[6]—but there are equally compelling moments in which the film undermines its focus on the female gaze, sabotaging an otherwise celebratory account of female subjectivity.

Thelma and Louise are in a constant state of looking throughout the course of the film, and their looking is consistently associated with gun-bearing destruction. On one level they are searching for an escape route to Mexico, but on another they are searching for themselves, trying to find out who they are as female subjects rather than as mere objects capable of only "to-be-looked-at-ness." There are a number of prominent signs of this "search for subjectivity" at the outset of the film. In one scene, Louise and Thelma have just finished packing their vacation luggage into Louise's green Thunderbird when they decide to take a picture of themselves, a moment which highlights the act of looking and suggests clearly that they are beginning a journey of self-discovery.[7] This scene is key to the project of the narrative because as Thelma and Louise take the snapshot of themselves, they simultaneously become "objects" and "bearers" of the camera's gaze. Interestingly, it is directly following this snapshot scene that we first see Thelma's gun; this timing sets up the association between active female gazing and female gun use.

The importance of the female gaze is continually emphasized in the early stages of the journey. At one point, Thelma and Louise are in the Thunderbird driving towards the mountain cabin when Thelma glances into the rear-view mirror, poses in a playful fashion, puts a cigarette into her mouth and jokes "I'm Louise." This moment presages the significance of mirrors as agencies of intentional self-regard—an indication that identity formation is a crucial theme:

> Pictures and mirrors abound in romance as symbols of the state of the protagonist's identity. Northrop Frye associates this symbolism with the archetypal structure of the romance—its pattern of descent and re-ascent in which the hero loses his or her identity and enters a world of chaos, only to achieve a renewed identity at the end in a state of heightened order and meaning. Frye notes that the initial loss of identity, which freezes or paralyzes the hero, is often rendered by his merging into a work of art or into a mirror image.[8]

There are a number of striking parallels between the above description and the narrative structure of *Thelma and Louise*. When Thelma gazes into the mirror searching for an identity,[9] she enters a world of chaos characterized by guns, rape, murder, armed robbery, and so on. The crucial point is that Thelma is gazing at her own image, and that, as in the snapshot scene described above, she is the object as well as the bearer of her gaze. This gaze bearing is soon associated with gun toting as Thelma and Louise take their pit stop at the Silver Bullet and Thelma practices her newfound liberation by visibly "eyeing" Puckett. A series of shot/reverse shot combinations at the nightclub reveals the implied connections between Thelma's active gaze and the ensuing attempted rape and consequential gun use. Thelma glances off-screen right and waves twice while sitting in the jam-packed honky-tonk with Louise, and each time the object of her gaze is Puckett, who smiles flirtatiously and salutes her with his beer bottle. In the moments between these awkward flitting hand waves, Thelma consistently glances self-consciously towards Puckett. After the final playful peek in his direction, Puckett responds by asking Thelma to dance, and despite Louise's protests, Thelma decides to "have a little fun." They dance and Puckett follows Thelma out to the parking lot where he attempts rape. After Louise arrives on the scene and hits the trigger, both she and Thelma are forever transformed into outlaws.

The structure of the film suggests that this transformation occurred before the fatal gunshot, however. The chain of events leading up to the killing—beginning with Thelma and Louise's "active gaze" through the eye of the Polaroid and Thelma's "active gaze" upon Harlan Puckett—once again implies an association between the female gaze and female gun use. One could read this association in a number of ways. It could be argued that the film endorses female agency in the sense that the active female gaze is presented as an equivalent to gun use for self-protection; from this perspective, Thelma and Louise become increasingly assertive, aggressive, and powerful throughout the film, therefore capable of expressing their rage and demanding retribution. A close cousin of this interpretation—the argument that the film advocates female gun use as a form of liberation—is commonly considered to be the source of the public frenzy surrounding the film. On the other hand, it is the deployment of the active gaze in association with gun bearing that ultimately leads to Thelma and Louise's demise, as they are forced off a cliff at the end of the film. This ending implies a sort of parable in which Thelma and Louise are punished for both bearing and baring both the gaze and their guns. To complicate matters, Thelma and Louise's active gazing is often undermined by the look of the camera (see below), which fragments their body parts and turns them into Hollywood "buddies." Ultimately, however, it is the contradictory deployment of the gaze (particularly with respect to the way the female characters actively look, as compared to the way the camera tends to look at them) within the film that causes viewers to become aware of the film as a message about—rather than merely a mirror of—society. This awareness, I argue, ultimately triggered the controversy associated with the film.

The gaze/gun association does not stop with the killing of Harlan Puckett. Down the road, Thelma finds another object worthy of her gaze. She literally bumps into a hitchhiker, J.D., after leaving a phone booth in a scene where the inconsistent nature of the film's presentation of "active gazing" becomes evident. She gazes at him in a rather conspicuous fashion, aiming her sight through the rear-view mirror of her car (therefore watching herself watch him rather than watching him directly). Although J.D. is the focal object of her gaze, she dominates the visual frame. Because the narrative focused on self-discovery until this point, we can only read this glance at J.D. as a looking away from herself and towards him for a sense of identity and self-worth. The object of her gaze derives a certain power from her attentions: "The act of gazing turns people into works of art, and artworks, by gazing back on us as 'speaking subjects,' create us in their image."[10] But the J.D. who is the object of Thelma's rapt attention will soon be her teacher, providing an example she can mimic of how to use a gun to rob a store. Thelma's active gaze therefore leads back directly to her use of the gun: she pulls off a stick-up at a local convenience store in an effort to compensate for the money stolen from Louise by J.D. (this stick-up eventually leading to their capture due to the hidden camera in the store). Her gazing/gunning behavior seems obviously borrowed from standard male practices.

The initial active female gaze into the eye of the instant camera triggers a series of events including the murder and armed robbery, along with kidnapping, explosions, and the instigation of a full-fledged, gun-rich Hollywood chase scene. Thelma and Louise began their journey as a search for self-discovery; by the end of the film they are simply being chased off the edge of a cliff. As their options slowly diminish, the film frames this oppression as an "awakening," with the result that towards the end of the film, while Thelma and Louise are embroiled in an action-packed car chase sequence, their gazes are focused on each other. The rear-view mirror on the side of Louise's Thunderbird is torn off by one of the charging police cars. It is significant that this mirror, the site of female looking and self-reflection throughout the film—Thelma's glance into the rear-view mirror with a cigarette as she pretends to be Louise; Louise's inspection as she touches up her lipstick just before she abandons the cause of "to-be-looked-at-ness" and tosses the lipstick out of the car; Thelma's lusty gawking at J.D.; her "awakening" as she takes in the sights of the Western landscape through the rear-view mirror; Louise gazing into the mirror in a women's restroom when she sees the reflection of a tiny spot of blood on her cheek and anxiously scrubs it off—is lost just before the two of them expire.[11] Thelma and Louise are punished for their active female gazing (although purportedly for their gun use), but rather than being killed for their "transgressions," they choose to kill themselves.[12] As Thelma and Louise head towards the cliff in the Thunderbird, Louise wears J.D.'s hat and the accosted policeman's sunglasses, and Thelma wears the truck driver's baseball cap: it is no mistake that as Thelma and Louise head towards their deaths they are wearing the clothes of their oppressors. Interestingly, however, just before they fall into the Grand Canyon these clothes are swept away by the momentum of the chase.

Although the ending of the film suggests an endorsement of the status quo rather than a revolution, I do believe that one could make a strong case for either argument. My thesis, in fact, is that it is precisely these internal conflicts within the text that engendered the controversy surrounding *Thelma and Louise*. Active gazing is presented as a metaphor for gun use, and while in some ways this association is presented as empowering, in other ways it is presented as a sign of fanaticism, surrender or co-optation. While the "look of the characters within the narrative" promotes active female gazing, perhaps ambivalently, the "look of the camera," equally ambivalently, rehearses standard practices. These contradictions triggered vehement public argumentation perhaps because so many shards of this ruptured text seem to be there for the taking.

THE FILMMAKER'S PERSPECTIVE

The look of the camera in *Thelma and Louise* provides further evidence of the film's contradictory presentation of female subjectivity. Although both of these women do demonstrate their right to "bear the look," the camera frequently treats them as spectacle. One primary trace of this tendency is the scene in which Thelma sunbathes by a hotel swimming pool in her bikini. Neither the sunbathing nor the bikini wearing is necessary to the storyline, and yet the camera leeringly scrutinizes Thelma's bared thighs.

On the other hand, J.D.'s body is also closely ogled by the eye of the camera in the lovemaking scene with Thelma. Thelma's body is presented for inspection in this scene as well, but for the most part, J.D.'s ass, shoulders, pelvis, and thighs are the center of attention. Although male bodies are often displayed in Hollywood films, in *Thelma and Louise* J.D. is occasionally treated as spectacle, which is far more pronounced and unusual a treatment, one typically reserved for females. In one scene Thelma gazes at J.D. while she drives away in the Thunderbird. Staring at his ass as the camera lingers upon it, Thelma comments: "Watch him go . . . I luuuv to watch him go!" Clearly, there are moments in the film in which the female gaze cultivates "to-be-looked-at-ness" in the opposite sex; whether or not these patterns of looking are borrowed from typically male practices is yet another question.

There are other ways in which the look of the camera as it records the event undermines the seemingly feminist orientation of the film. The "buddy movie" structure and the glorification of guns and violence (in the final scene especially) seem to counteract any efforts to focus on the rather circumscribed goals of female empowerment and self-protection. In the standard Hollywood climax, the guns *per se* seem to be the *cause célèbre* (along with helicopters, ammunition, and hordes of lawmen), changing the tone of a film beginning innocently enough with a snapshot of two vacationing women taking pictures of themselves. Some of this inconsistency could be attributed to the fact that film is a collaborative art form, in which many personalities (with perhaps conflicting agendas) work together on a single product (Khouri and Scott, for example). Regardless, the inconsistency generated by the formulaic, mainstream "look of the camera" in *Thelma and Louise*— compounded by the jarring and repeated deployment of the female gaze—results in heightened viewer awareness and a greater degree of ensuing critical strife.

THE VIEWER'S PERSPECTIVE

Because the signifying practices in *Thelma and Louise* structure a paradoxical representation of both female objectivity (women as objects of the gaze) and subjectivity (the female gaze), viewers are provoked out of absorption by these contradictions and develop an awareness concerning the constructed nature of the film itself. In general, once filmic apparatuses are exposed, viewers are more likely to believe that the film may have a causal impact on the "real world"—the film is considered a statement about the world rather than merely a mirror of some "objective reality"—and are therefore more likely to identify the film as ideology and perhaps challenge its messages.[13]

Thelma and Louise, intentionally or unintentionally, cultivates this awareness in a number of ways. Importantly, the prominent depiction of the female gaze in association with female gun bearing (discussed previously) disrupts the typically Hollywood-style viewing patterns for most audiences. Viewers accustomed to classical Hollywood fare (men and women alike) often hope that identification with protagonists (usually male) will result in two hours of pleasurable escapism. When these traditional looking patterns are disrupted, as in *Thelma and Louise*, viewers are jolted out of their absorption and catapulted—or "shot"—into an awareness of the filmic apparatus. The mere act of female gun bearing is perhaps not enough to create these "shots," but the guns in combination with the active female gazing is a killer combination.

An active female gaze, however, is not always foregrounded in *Thelma and Louise*. As outlined in the previous sections, a number of techniques in this film undermine the power of the female gaze: Thelma and Louise often gaze through mirrors rather than looking directly, and Thelma (and Louise, to a certain extent) often looks in order to be looked at. Both women are treated as spectacle (Thelma in particular), and ultimately the film conveys the message that for women, looking/gunning means trouble. Thelma and Louise's options slowly diminish as they face the continual repercussions of active female gazing, usually followed or compounded by gun toting.

In summary, it is important to emphasize that these internal contradictions within *Thelma and Louise* provide ammunition or evidence for a wide variety of conflicting interpretations. In other words, textual evidence potentially supports wildly divergent claims with respect to this film, since the text itself is so paradoxical and contradictory that it almost begs to be both accepted and rejected by everyone. Crucial to the purposes of this paper is the fact that these constantly shifting perspectives cultivate viewer awareness of the seams underlying filmic representation—an awareness that inevitably plants the seeds of disputation. Viewers who manage to identify with the female gaze are shocked out of this identification (when the camera objectifies women in the next scene, perhaps), while viewers attempting to identify with a male perspective also meet with resistance (when they encounter the active female gaze). As a result, viewers are provoked out of absorption and are therefore more likely to acknowledge the filmmaker's presence, to consider the film a potent comment on "real world" violence and sexual arrangements, and to "talk back" or debate about the film's messages.

THE RIGHT TO BEAR GAZES?

Through *Thelma and Louise,* female gun use is both celebrated and punished due to the contradictory deployment of gazes. The "three looks" in *Thelma and Louise* combine to create a filmic mixed message. The female protagonists in the film gaze defiantly into the eyes of the camera and the eyes of other characters. These female protagonists commit murder and suicide; they are also "murdered," sexually abused, objectified, and tortured and scarred psychologically. The implications of this correlation (i.e. that the active female gaze leads to destruction) are devastating, and yet the question remains: does this film endorse, condemn, or merely express these associations? Certainly some members of the public view this film as an endorsement of female violence; mere "expression" is far too benign to ignite controversy, debate, intolerance and dissension. But the crux of my argument has been that as viewers become aware of the constructed nature of filmic worlds, they are more likely to engage in debate since they therefore read the film as a perspectival endorsement of a particular point-of-view, rather than as an objectively grounded fictional display of "real-world" sexual dynamics and social arrangements. Because the three looks Mulvey associates with the cinema are deployed in such contradictory terms in *Thelma and Louise*, the Hollywood spell is broken, leaving a ruptured text. These contradictions suggest deep cultural ambivalence concerning the female right to bear arms (or gazes).

Either way, it seems that by solving one problem, filmmakers have created another. The invisible style of classical Hollywood cinema was used to communicate ideological messages in a subtle and insidious fashion. When filmmakers disrupt this invisible style, however, or violate the restraints on the activity of a female character's gaze, they run the risk of being censored, picketed, pummeled, castigated or shunned, even while winning an Academy Award.

NOTES

1   "Should We Go Along for the Ride? A Critical Symposium on *Thelma and Louise*," *Cineaste* Vol. 18, No. 4 (January 1992), 28ff.

2   "Feminism Gets the Hollywood Treatment," in "Ride," 30.

3   Laura Mulvey, "Visual Pleasure and Narrative Cinema," *Screen* Vol. 16, No. 3 (Autumn, 1975).

4   In Mulvey's words (from "Visual Pleasure and Narrative Cinema"): "In a world ordered by sexual imbalance, pleasure in looking has been split between active/male and passive/female. The determining male gaze projects phantasy on to the female figure which is styled accordingly."

5   Mulvey's essay was roundly criticized by subsequent theorists who responded that her account ignored the presence of the female spectator. Much of this theoretical response focused on the "look of the viewer onto the screen" rather than the "look of the characters within the narrative." See Janet Bergstrom and Mary Ann Doane, "The Female Spectator: Contexts and Directions," *Camera Obscura* 20-21 (May-September, 1989).

6   Whether or not Thelma's focus on fragmented male body parts represents a specifically female gaze is yet another question.

7   In the final scene of the film, it is this snapshot—which is also the film's logo—that is swept up and out of the doomed Thunderbird just before Thelma and Louise fall to their deaths in the canyon below.

8   Wendy Steiner, *Pictures of Romance* (Chicago: University of Chicago Press, 1988), 49.

9   Thelma and Louise do merge with one another—in a cinematographic sense—in a scene much later in which slow dissolves symbolize the joining of the two women. This moment occurs after Thelma's "awakening." She says, "I feel awake. . . . I don't remember ever feeling this awake . . . everything LOOKS different."

10   Steiner, *Pictures*, 137.

11   Some could argue that the destroyed mirror (site of the *indirect* female gaze) suggests that Thelma and Louise are now able to gaze directly and forthrightly.

12   It is interesting to consider a comparison to the film *Butch Cassidy and the Sundance Kid* (1969), which *Thelma and Louise* resembles. The final scenes of the two films are practically identical, but in the former, Butch and Sundance fight until the end, storming into a blast of gunfire. If this is the male response, then is suicide somehow female?

13   See, for example, Robert Ray, *A Certain Tendency of the Hollywood Cinema, 1930-1980* (Princeton: Princeton University Press, 1985).

Bullets in the Entertainment State: An Interview

Mark Crispin Miller

JOHN SAKERIS: Mark, what do you think is the link between media violence and societal violence, if any?

MARK CRISPIN MILLER: There is no single link, nor does the question really lend itself to any simple answer either way—although there are two over-simple answers that we hear quite often. Those two answers are opposed, yet also fundamentally alike, as is the case with all such warring propaganda arguments.

On the one hand, there's the neo-Prohibitionist position, which casts the whole complex relationship between the spectacle and its mass audience as a simple one of stimulus/response—or, to put it in Judaeo-Christian terms, of temptation-and-sin. Those two languages—the biblical and the behavioristic—indicate the two main blocs of neo-Prohibitionist opinion. The emphasis on sin comes, of course, from the likes of Jerry Falwell and the Rev. Donald Wildmon, as well as many right-wing politicos like William Bennett, Alan Keyes and Pat Buchanan—the crowd that sees "the media" as a vast cabal of evil Jews, seducing our young innocents. Of those who misbehave because of this or that CD or movie, that crowd tell us—and this is really no exaggeration—that "the Devil made them do it!" It's what Ted Bundy said the night before they executed him—that he became the serial killer that he was because of dirty magazines.

On the other hand, there are also certain media reformers, health activists and others (including anti-porn feminists) who, although better-educated and more well-intentioned than the Bible-thumping types, still tend to share with those fanatics a marked censorious impulse. As they see it, "the media" churns out anti-social messages which many people, mostly kids, will just unthinkingly obey. Now in some cases—as with certain kinds of advertising—there's a lot of merit to that general view. For example, cigarette advertising is often pitched at children, and does frequently help get them hooked on cigarettes; and so there's no excuse for, say, filling inner-city neighborhoods with Kool and Salem billboards pitched at kids. But that's a form of outright propaganda, which is meant to sell a certain toxic product. It's a clear-cut public health concern.

The problem is more complicated—and far larger—when it comes to violence overall and the media products that extol it, or that appear to do so. An effort to abolish all such fare would never work, at this late date—nor would it be a good (much less a Constitutional) idea to try it. But there are some activists who would prefer to see that happen, just as there were once a lot of people who believed sincerely that you could cure the lower classes of all dissolute behavior just by making booze illegal. Of course, it only made the situation worse—and so, in its way, would such an effort now.

So there are those believers, whether public-spirited or pious, who see the media's influence as clear and strong and absolute, and wholly deleterious. On the other side are those who either will admit no influence at all, or who deem it unimportant. In this crowd we find, predictably, the likes of Jack Valenti, Steve Bochco and Oliver Stone—i.e., spokespersons for those corporations that so hugely profit from the sale of homicidal fantasy. Then there are those whom we might call the corporate liberals—Nat Hentoff, Martin Garbus, and other such ACLU-type purists, who often find themselves indignantly defending big-time corporate sleaze on First Amendment grounds. This is, as far as I'm concerned, a grotesque misapplication of the doctrine of free speech, inasmuch as it equates the likes of, say, Rupert Murdoch's News Corporation, and its product, with any individual American and his/her personal views. That confusion has been catastrophic, cloaking corporate irresponsibility in the inviolable mantle of such early freedom fighters as Tom Paine. So we now have local TV stations arguing that they enjoy the sacred freedom to bombard their viewers with alarmist crime-scene "news" night after night, and insisting that nobody has the right to ask them to observe a higher journalistic standard, and cover things like local politics and health and education. There's the same kind of bad faith in movies like *The People vs. Larry Flynt* (1996), in which the Bill of Rights functions merely as a great excuse to glamorize a money-hungry bottom-feeder as a martyr to the cause of free expression—as if Larry Flynt were Upton Sinclair, or Lenny Bruce.

Now, that movie brings to mind another major sector of pro-corporate ideology. Aside from the media industries' own flacks and the cadre of corporate liberals, there are an awful lot of people—in journalism, business and the arts—whose animus against the Prohibitionist position is based on a reflexive adolescent tendency to jeer "authority"— as long as that "authority" looks stereotypically uptight, unhip, puritanical: "dead-white." This tendency entails an automatic approbation of whatever might gross out the likes of Liddy Dole, or Tipper Gore, or Jesse Helms, or Rudy Giuliani, or any such notorious public parent-figure. It is, indeed, an oedipal reflex, probably the more pronounced among those activists or critics who have had big problems with their Moms and Dads. It's also culturally determined, by which I mean that it is, by and large, an urban (or suburban), upper-middle-class, post-Sixties stance—and therefore consciously, and necessarily, at odds with all that seems provincial, earnest, credulous, rural and/or petit-bourgeois.

Although perverse, that posture isn't critical. After all, the snickering "subversion" of the crabby high school teacher, or the prissy Goody-Two-Shoes ("Isn't that special?"), the harrumphing moralist or the ill-dressed square, is a familiar staple of mass advertising, and the premise of a million music videos. Therefore, to groove on movie violence, or sadistic porn, or the snot jokes of a Butt-head just because such stuff offends the neo-cons and evangelicals is a very mainstream move, however "on the edge" the groover likes to think he is.

Now, finally, to your question—which neither of those sides has answered. There is certainly a link between media violence and the real thing. Countless studies prove as much—that is, that kids exposed to violent fare are likelier to get aggressive than kids who don't watch stuff like that. Of course, that scholarly consensus has not gotten any mainstream coverage. Indeed, as Martin Lee and Norman Solomon have pointed out, the only study that did get any play was one that NBC commissioned, and that seemed to prove, not surprisingly, that there is no connection between what kids watch and how they act. (That study, it turned out, was badly flawed.) Today the media tunes out that inconvenient mass of scientific evidence—just as, until fairly recently, it tuned out all the evidence that smoking isn't good for you. Now, as then, it's the big money that dictates such suppression of the evidence about violence, since violence turns a mighty profit, just as cigarettes used to do.

That analogy does have its limits, though. The carcinogenicity of cigarettes is a physical reality that hasn't much to do with social, cultural, psychological or economic factors. You smoke too much, you get real sick, no matter how or where you're raised, or who your parents are, or what you're taught to think. The influence of violent media fare is not so cut-and-dried. While too many Marlboros will disable nearly anybody, "The Mighty Morphin' Power Rangers" may not move all children everywhere to try to kick each other in the throat. While there's no doubt that such explicit fictions of aggression do invite their viewers to imitate them, there's more at work than just the invitation. The entire system must be, as it were, hospitable to that sort of acting-out, or else it would be just a few loose nuts who do so. These days the number of such nuts has risen exponentially, with a dozen cases every year of mass murders like Charles Whitman's, which stood out as a gross anomaly in 1966. We therefore ought to take a good look not only at the stuff that's on TV and in the movies, and not just at the broad availability of high-tech weapons, but also at the whole machine we're living in.

Thus far, both sides in the debate (if we can call it that) have failed to take an honest look at what has been going on, preferring to ride hard on their respective hobbyhorses and score points off one another. The right-wing Prohibitionists refuse to go beyond their ritual attacks on "Hollywood," which they see, of course, as absolutely separate from America. Thus they turn a blind eye to the very soil from which the weeds have grown, preferring, naturally, to blame them on some alien source. In their view, only inculcation of the right "core values" in the young will stop the violence: love of God and home and country and free enterprise. But the violence is itself, in part, a consequence of those same values—a fact that you would think is so well-known by now that no one needs to point it out, and yet it still strikes many people not as a banality but as pure blasphemy, and so we have to make the case again, and yet again.

If we compare our own society with Japan's, we're struck by the tremendous difference between our explosive ways and that well-ordered and non-violent system—which is just as saturated as our own with images of graphic violence and sadomasochistic porn. If we regard Japan as a control group, we have to grant that violent spectacle *per se* does not necessitate an increase in mass murders. We have our own peculiar history, in other words, and our own institutions, customs, mores. Here, for one thing, you can get your hands on guns of marvelous sophistication, which makes a major difference in the scale of common violence, whatever Charlton Heston has to say about it. Sure, "guns don't kill people—people kill people," but Eric Harris and Dylan Klebold were people who would be alive today, as would all their classmates, if they had gone to Columbine that day with baseball bats.

But guns too tell us only part of this depressing story. Ours is a society with quite an awesome heritage of violence—and it has been particularly violent throughout the last half-century, since the start of the Cold War. That conflict entailed the political and cultural exaltation, unprecedented in our history, of the US military—"Violence Central," as Alexander Cockburn has called it. The history of our most spectacular mass murders is inextricable from the post-war upsurge of that military influence. For every mere civilian drifter like Charles Starkweather, there's been an ex-Marine like Whitman (or Lee Harvey Oswald), or a gung-ho veteran like Timothy McVeigh; and in the years to come there surely will be other killers from the ultra-right, men trained to kill "mud people" in good conscience, with God on their side. Now that there is no more Evil Empire against which the state can send those able murderers, we're faced with an enormous blowback problem that will pose a graver threat to us by far than all the assets of the Kremlin ever did.

The rightist patriotic impulse, then, can hardly be an antidote to this epidemic of domestic carnage—and neither is Judaeo-Christian piety at its most militant, although the Prohibitionist right has been insisting that the problem is the banishment of God from public classrooms. ("Guns don't kill people—the separation of Church and State kills people!") After those young Baptists were gunned down in Texas, Jerry Falwell spoke the right-wing Prohibitionist line by claiming that those murders, like the murders of those Christian girls at Columbine, were the consequence of "the media bias against people of faith." This view was so ridiculous that even Fox's dishy anchorwoman had to take exception to it, mentioning shows like "Touched by an Angel" (1994).

Of course, there is no such "media bias" against Christians (which is what Falwell really meant) as we can see from the high mawkishness with which the entertainment state invariably treats all Christian piety that doesn't rock the boat—as in the case of Mother Teresa, who was sanctified not only by the Vatican but also by the mainstream press. And if there's anything that can be said to "cause" those indiscriminate shootings, it is that very militant religiosity which Falwell and his brethren see as our salvation from such danger. The most dangerous mass murderers are not the odd Satanists, like Charles Manson, but the true believers—men like Baruch Goldstein, or the Hamas or Taliban com-

110

mandos, or Tim McVeigh, resolved to take revenge for those saints slaughtered in the Waco compound. Several of the recent mass murderers had been devout church-goers, and some had even been choirboys, but such formal membership is not a necessary feature of the sort of cracked religiosity that leads to murder. Whether he's a well-schooled neo-Nazi or a wandering schizophrenic, the man who takes his gun and ventures forth to wipe the devils out is usually convinced, somewhere inside, and maybe only on and off, of his own special rectitude, or of the providential animus of his own grievance. His violence has the same religious cast as did the violence of the Crusaders, or of those Anabaptists who ran wild in sixteenth-century Germany, or of the Bolsheviks, and so on. It therefore follows that this latest wave of murders should be taking place just at the threshhold of the new millennium, since such temporal turning points are likely to arouse the chiliastic impulse in those lone believers.

Finally, the right-wing Prohibitionists also refuse to see the link between the sort of images they hate and the economy that they revere, although it is this great "Free Market"—that is, corporate power freed from all restraint—that is now overwhelming us with dreck. Like the Nazis, the US rightists would absolve the economic system by imputing all its ill effects to a highly visible minority of hateful aliens. Thus we have Dan Quayle—himself the scion of the Pulliam family, a very wealthy media dynasty—hinting darkly at a foul conspiracy of "the elites" snickering away in "newsrooms, movie studios and faculty lounges"; and William Bennett—much enriched by publishing with Viacom—railing at "the Bronfmans and the Levins" for the media's crimes against society (and pointedly not mentioning Rupert Murdoch, who gives even more to the Republicans than he gives to the government of China). That list could go on and on. The point here is that the right-wing media "critique" conveniently ignores the crucial fact that, in this ever-tightening corporate oligopoly, it is the drive for ever higher profits from the culture industries that has degraded all our arts and journalism. It is that inhuman force—and not an alien conspiracy of "unbelievers"—that has overfilled our entertainments with euphoric scenes of gunplay, and what passes for hot sex. (The rightists actually don't mind the gunplay, but that's another matter.)

For their part, the corporate liberals and their allies in the industry and audience are just as blind to the big picture. While the rightists' anger is reactionary, the corporate liberals' attitude is *laissez-faire*. Like so many Phillip Morris spokesmen, c. 1965, they often simply will deny that the contested product poses any danger whatsoever. Or they will minimize that danger, claiming that the homicidal influence of current movies and TV and video games strikes only now and then, and only through a few unbalanced types who would have run amok in any case. Whichever their position, the apologists rely heavily on a pseudo-scholarly perspective that appears to get the media corporations off the hook.

It's a blasé historicism that we hear *ad nauseam*: "But it's always been that way!" they'll yawn, or, more invidiously: "Critics have been screaming gloom-and-doom for years/decades/centuries! Why, they thought that dime novels/billboards/comic books/radio shows/movies/television would drive you crazy/stunt your growth/destroy society!" And so on. Then there's the knowing reference back to some earlier genre, with

111

its peculiar violence: the revenge tragedy, the Gothic novel, Grand Guignol. That sort of journalistic long view is supposed to make the critic realize that he or she is just another Chicken Little, furiously clucking in the infamous tradition of Savanarola, Anthony Comstock and Allan Bloom.

So let's get real. Of course it's true that violent spectacle is nothing new. It is also the case that readers have always been as likely as spectators to succumb to the allurements of the text, and live vicariously within their own book-addled heads. The consequences of such strenuous fantasizing have long since been evoked and analyzed by many artists, who have seen it as pathetic (as in *Don Quixote*), funny (as in *Northanger Abbey*)—or destructive (as in *The Red and the Black, The Possessed, The Secret Agent,* among many others). Just because it's nothing new, however, doesn't mean that such vulnerability to fiction isn't, let's say, highly problematic. Plato had good reason to ban poetic "imitation" from his Republic, since poets are inclined to imitate the bad; and "things unbecoming the free man [our guardians] should neither do nor be clever at imitating, nor yet any other shameful thing, lest from the imitation they imbibe the reality."

To travel so far back in time in search of prior examples is not entirely relevant, however; for there's a great qualitative difference between literary and/or theatrical effects, however vivid, on the one hand, and the ultra-sophisticated high-tech spectacle surrounding us today. Because of its explicitness and visceral power, a cinematic rendering of pleasurable violence—even one that's mediocre—will tend to pack a greater wallop than the smartest literary evocation. For that matter, it is likely to be more compelling than an actual murder taking place in front of you, since real murders aren't as clean as those in movies, where, by and large, the gunshot victims don't lie shivering and screaming for their mothers.

More important, the media's scenes of violence now gratify their viewers with an illusion of vicarious agency that is not available to readers or playgoers. The media sells us all a fantasy of vast empowerment. This has been noteworthy in the horror films, which, since the emergence of the slasher genre in the late Seventies, have tended more and more to put *you* in the position of the murderer. The socioeconomic context for that weird subjectivizing move—which became a common cinematic feature in the Reagan era—has yet to be explored [See the essay by Fred Turner in this volume.—eds.]. Likewise, the more atrocious video games are predicated on the deep appeal of that "empowerment" which is available to the well-accoutered modern soldier. Like a Ranger on the prowl in some rebellious Third World country, the gamester has the weapons and the ammo, and feels as if he has the skill, to keep on picking off the bad guys, one after another, at little risk to himself.

Banning all such games, or policing Hollywood, would not itself eliminate the danger here, which is as much ideological as it is recreational. (Of course, such efforts also wouldn't work.) This does not mean, however, that such spectatorship is not sociopathic, or that it does not in its way contribute to the rise of violence in real life. As Lt. Col. Dave Grossman has argued (in *On Killing: The Psychological Cost of Learning to Kill in War and Society*), there are very troubling similarities between such "violence enabling" recreations and a certain kind of military training. Others have made similar arguments. Such speculative warnings (Grossman's book came out in 1995) anticipated some of what has happened lately. The kid who shot those people in Paducah, for example, had done little actual shooting, but had learned the necessary self-control by playing video games for hours and hours.

I've only scratched the surface answering your question; and I don't pretend to any wisdom on the subject. The basic problem is the same today as it was when Kubrick came out with *A Clockwork Orange* in 1971. It's not a problem of prevention (athough that one is serious enough, God knows), but of something deeper: Is it possible for us to "cure" ourselves of violence, or of the will to violence, without becoming something neither animal nor really human?

JS: I'd like to hear more of your thoughts about A Clockwork Orange, *which seems an especially germane film these days, with Stanley Kubrick's recent death.*

MCM: It would take us hours and hours—days, in fact—to start doing justice to that film. Let me say first, though, that the best artistic treatment of the "blowback" problem that I mentioned earlier is probably *Full Metal Jacket* (1996).

A Clockwork Orange is still just as vexing as it was when it came out. It is an excellent example of a work of art that deals directly, and brilliantly, with the peculiar charm of violence in mass society—and that itself became horrifically entangled in the very jungle that it would illuminate. It seems to have inspired some heinous copycat crimes in Britain, finally leading Kubrick to withdraw the film from circulation in his own adopted country. There's a certain dreadful poignancy to the whole episode. It reminds us that, however subtle and profound a work of art may be, out in the mass arena there are many who will simply miss the subtleties and the profundities, and get a big charge out of "the old ultra-violence," just as Alec (Malcolm McDowell) does. The story helps us understand the limits of irony—which countless third-rate artists use as a sort of prophylaxis, to shield themselves against the charge of tasteless exploitation (which is what they're really doing). "Oh, but it's tongue-in-cheek!" is what we're supposed to tell ourselves, as if that makes it okay. While *A Clockwork Orange* is a masterpiece, there are many 90s movies, critical successes all, that don't have that excuse. They're as shallow as they are sadistic, but encased in that protective irony. If they weren't ironic, no one would go near them. I'm thinking here of *Fargo*, and *Pulp Fiction*, but there are many others.

But, to get back to *A Clockwork Orange*, and speaking now as a film critic, I'll say only that one must remember that it's a subjective work throughout. That is, it's Alec's story, told from first to last from Alec's point-of-view. The first half, with its wild colors and frenetic pace, with Alec represented as the emperor of his own little world, is Alec's view before they tame him with the Lodovico Technique. The second half, with its drab daylight and claustrophobic rooms, is Alec's view once they've conditioned him. I'd better stop before I break into a lecture.

I'm thinking, though: It's hard now to imagine any movie starting a big ruckus as *A Clockwork Orange* did. Or *The Wild Bunch* (1969). Or, on the sexual front, *Last Tango in Paris* (1973). That sort of controversy seems kind of quaint today, now that shock *per se* is not an avant-gardist act of boldness but a commercial obligation. "Grow or die" has always been the watchword of corporate capitalism. In today's entertainment state, there's also this corollary rule: "Gross out or die."

JS: That particular corollary rule makes me think instantly of a recent film that is both exceptionally violent and, to my mind, exceptionally noxious. I'm speaking of The Matrix *(1999).*

MCM: Well, yes, that *is* a good example. Not that it sparked the sort of outcry that we heard back in the early 70s, because the din around us now has made a fresh response of any kind impossible. But *The Matrix* is a good example of a number of the trends we've been discussing.

As far as I can see, the movie gives us little more than a romantic vision of chic out-lawry, with this platoon of really cool "outsiders" flitting cybernetically about, trying to Smash the State, which is under the control of some extremely creepy white guys dressed up like Jack Webb in "Dragnet" (1951). The good platoon is just a modish, p.c. update of the good platoons in countless World War II movies. There, the group was ethnically diverse—"O'Reilly!" "Tonelli!" "Kowalski!", and so on. Here, the group is culturally diverse, with a lesbian, a motherly black Dad, his mixed-race son, and so on—all of them led by a towering and supremely competent sage (Laurence Fishburne), who speaks that pidgin Zen made popular by Obi-Wan Kenobi. He's also like the Pat Morita character in the *Karate Kid* movies (1984–1994), since what he mainly teaches is the martial arts; and he too is non-white. For all his size and wisdom, this black man ends up having to be saved from "Jack Webb's" clutches by the film's two leads, a pair of lithe, impassive Gen-X acrobats in Ray-Bans and black leather (Keanu Reeves and Carrie-Anne Moss). They do a lot of otherworldly fighting, and there's a lot of retro-futuristic techno-gimmickery that seems to have been borrowed from the sets of Ridley Scott.

Now, what makes this film a good example is the way it mounts its lavish scenes of violence—which is its main appeal. That fact is handily obscured by the story's vast pre-tentiousness. I've had some over-enthusiastic students—all males—who think *The Matrix* is a work of genius because of its packed subtext of mythical and Biblical allusions, and the seeming depth of Laurence Fishburne's endless riffs about Appearance and Reality. (On that score, the story makes no sense at all, but that's another matter.) There is, of course, also the usual overlay of 90s irony, with the heroes looking lean and beautiful and very, very *now*, while the bad guys look like old TV.

So here's another film whose nihilistic nastiness comes packaged in protective irony ("It's tongue-in-cheek!")—and also in a dense pseudo-profundity, fraught as it is with seeming Christian and apocalyptic symbolism. But what you have here, basically, is just one more teen fantasy of macho invulnerability (she's just as macho as he is, since they are one in any case). And for all its "stylishness" and many hints of Heavy Meaning, what most viewers—maybe all viewers—must mainly take away from it is lots of exhilarating violence, with whose perpetrators we are clearly meant to empathize. Think of that big shoot-out in the lobby of the Man's headquarters, or wherever it is. The two of them have such big, sophisticated guns—and so many of them!—and they're invulnerable, Keanu and Carrie-Anne, and they look great. Those multitudes of cops, on the other hand, are tubby, aging, and they look lower-middle-class. Oh, sure, they're agents in disguise—but what we see is two cool young movie stars, blasting the bejeezus out of an entire police force. For all the movie's Wired-type metaphysics, it's a fantasy that Gordon Liddy might have written, and that he probably enjoyed.

It's a bad film—incoherent, over-reliant on f/x, and finally celebrating only narcissism. (When Carrie-Anne kisses Keanu at the end there, she might as well be kissing herself.) There can certainly be, and have been, first-rate movies on the subject of the young violently clashing with the system, but this isn't one of them.

JS: As compared to Lindsay Anderson's If . . . *(1968), for example.*

MCM: Yes. *If . . .* is a film that deals with a genuinely repressive system—the English public schools—whereas the social order in *The Matrix* is pure Sega fantasy. The violence that breaks out at the end, moreover, is so surrealistic that it seems unlikely anyone would be inclined to emulate it. (Certainly I could be wrong about that.) If I remember right, nobody in the audiences I saw it with broke into cheers of empathy—the way that people did at certain moments in *The Battle of Algiers* (1965), to name another movie of that era.

Ultimately, though, a film's artistic value doesn't bear any clear relation to the audience's readiness to cheer wrong-headedly at certain moments. Bad or good, a violent film will often bring out the beast in some of us—unless it's trying consciously to deglamorize violence, which is of course a worthy goal, but not artistically essential. George Will has written lots about this problem—for instance, condemning *Boyz 'N the Hood* (1991) because of violent outbursts in its audiences, while praising *Menace II Society* (1993) for its more dispiriting effect. I see what he means, but that's no way to judge a movie. They're both powerful and interesting films.

But back to the general problem: As with the pretensions of *The Matrix*, so with the nuances and ambiguities, and the telling ironies, of great films like *A Clockwork Orange* and *The Godfather* (1972). All such superficies will be lost on certain viewers, who only see the vicious parts. When Kubrick's film came out in Britain, among other crimes there was a seventeen-year-old Dutch girl who was gang-raped by a pack of yobs who were shouting "Singin' in the Rain" throughout.

Finally, you can't tell how an audience will respond to a good movie—or, for that matter, to any rousing work of art (as Alec's tale reminds us). With TV and cinema, however, it's even riskier to deal with violence than it is for writers, because those visual media are empathically advantaged, more viscerally moving than the written word. The whole thing is particularly problematic now that viewers are so jaded, and it takes so much to rouse them. All we can say with certainty is that many filmmakers do try, generally under market pressure, to do nothing more than titillate. There's no excuse for it, but there's no solution, either—other than to make some space for different kinds of work.

You know, I don't think we're getting to the heart of the matter. Maybe it's our focus, thus far, only on those works in which the violent act is pointedly and broadly celebrated. Such explicit pandering does not tell the whole story.

What is it that makes people give way to that temptation to explode on others? What is it that finally sparks such atrocious emulation of fictitious violence? I don't pretend to know the answer to that question, but can only make a suggestion: that it has to do with somehow trying to fulfill an infantile fantasy of total, hostile "empowerment." To be parked behind a massive and unfailing automatic weapon, to be unassailable, invulnerable as you mow down your enemies—there's something about it that is dangerously appealing. Although that stance seems rigorous—tense, vigilant and ready!—it also promises the utter ease of absolute command. It's therefore not unrelated to the fantasy of high-life, of perfect luxury/convenience, that comes at us from countless ads. Thus it's not only a macho thing, but has to do as well with class frustration. You want to blow your enemies away—that is, blast to nothingness whomever might stand in your way—just as you want to have all green lights on that highway stretching out before you, so you can gun your Bimmer all the way to the horizon, and beyond.

I think it's safe to say, in short, that this is an appeal that works especially effectively on those who feel most powerless.

JS: And of course, it's not just the poor who are feeling powerless. There's all this current middle-class violence.

MCM: Well, it's not just the outgroups, not only the poor, who are disempowered. It is also kids, who tend to feel quite powerless, because kids *are* relatively powerless—even the privileged ones, who make up the majority of rap fans. Basically, what the entertainment state—the advertising agencies included—do the most consistently is sell the powerless a fantasy of power; and such empowerment is usually aggressive, often homicidal, always individualistic, and also always technologically dependent. "Without it, you are nothing. With it, you are everything."

JS: Ultimately, then, it's not real power.

MCM: Not at all. First of all, because it isn't economic power. But I don't want to wax economistic here, because, God knows—maybe only God knows—there are also other, finer kinds of power. There is the power that comes from capability, from being competent, and more than competent, at certain things; from mastering certain kinds of labor. There is the power that one would have, and should have, over one's work. It is a creative kind of power that takes the sort of time and training, and respect for both the task and the trainee, that's just about impossible here in the entertainment state. Instead, the media keeps selling its crass, empty "power" to the powerless, who are no more powerful or any happier for buying it.

Now this bogus sale of "power" isn't just a matter of enacting giant scenes of violence that invite you to enjoy a safe vicarious experience of the carnage. In other words, you needn't be invited only to pick up an imaginary handgun—although that's the usual way in which the fantasy is "realized." If you want to capture the attention of frustrated people, kids especially, you might as well show your hero with an Uzi or a Magnum in his hand, if not in either hand. But this invitation need not have to do with violence *per se*. Rather, it entails an entire frame of mind—a frame of mind essential to the maintenance of a system based on advertising.

What we might call mass spectatorship consistently encourages the view that *you come first*, that *you should be unstoppable*, that *you deserve it all*, should *have it all*, should *take it now*, that *it should all be yours*—and not only should it all be yours but you should take it all from others, those contemptible, oppressive others: would-be parent-figures, cops, doctors, social workers, politicians. People like that—the people who claim to have authority over you, when the advertisers ought to be the only ones that tell you what to do. Thus there is a sociopathic message that the advertisers and the media corporations keep impressing on us all, and especially on the young and disadvantaged. It is a resentful message—utterly destructive, and, of course, completely apolitical. Because of that enormous volume of solicitations, and the unprecedented sway and cleverness of the technologies that channel them, there seems now to be an ever-present voice in everybody's head, urging all of us to "go for it"—even though we can't afford to, and even though "it" may not be what anybody really wants.

I'd suggest that it is out of this that violence comes, albeit indirectly: out of this endless propaganda on behalf of violent desublimation, and out of the frustration that inevitably comes from trying to do what's impossible.

JS: So, in the movies, does the image of the gun itself invite us to consume?

MCM: Well, yes. The gun has always figured in our entertainments as a daunting means to a consumeristic end. Especially in the gangster films, the gun is the immediate way out of poverty and insignificance. And that really hasn't changed. The great gleaming automatic weapon functions in the music videos much as the tommy gun did in the gangster movies of the 30s; only I don't see much moralizing in the videos. Some, but not much, whereas such films as *Scarface* (1932) and *Little Caesar* (1931) did try, to some extent, to have it both ways, by drawing back at the finale and deploring the career of crime they had just spent some ninety minutes glamorizing. The videos are franker in their celebration of the great big gun, the Maseratis, the voluptuous babes, and so on. These are desublimated times we're living in—just as the advertisers always wanted, whether they knew it or not.

But, again, it's not only the guns *per se* that matter. What matters is the entire gangsterist world-view of advertising. Whichever demographic bloc it aims at, it always offers the assurance that *you* are all-important, your every whim is sacrosanct and has to be fulfilled. The rhetoric in most political propaganda does exactly the same thing. A culture like ours, which is utterly suffused with propaganda—commercial or political—is one where everybody has to think him- or herself extraordinarily and especially deserving. Needless to say, it's not a vision that's conducive to a decent, liveable society. It's not a vision that's at all hospitable to democracy, or, indeed, to any social contract. One can deplore the likes of Oliver Stone and Rupert Murdoch all one wants, but such selective criticism of a few flagrant examples of media violence will not help solve the problem, which is far too pervasive. It has to do not only with this or that movie, but with the overall vision of the world, and of humanity, that the whole spectacle has been so heavily propagating now for decades.

JS:. Is there any connection between the ongoing concentration of media owner-ship and the type of material that we are seeing as media product?

MCM:There is indeed.Violence sells—especially in a world of thwarted people.And as the entities that own the media become ever fewer and larger, and still more competitive with one another (although they also do a lot of business with each other), they inexorably show less and less restraint in trying to rouse as many people as they can.Violence is one sure way to do just that.This explains in part why the spectacle has become so graphically violent and, often, salacious, too. And of course it isn't just the spectacle, either, because we're talking here not just about the movies and TV but also about radio, and magazines, and newspapers,and books. No longer separate sectors,all the culture industries today keep stooping lower and lower,because the pressure on them all for ever higher profits is relentless. It is axiomatic that the stronger that pressure to raise profits, the fewer scruples media workers can afford to show as they package their "content" for mass consumption.

Let's look at a specific case. Local TV news in the United States is an international scandal. It offers next to nothing in the way of journalism, relying mainly on reports of violent crime, and, whenever possible, rich footage of the aftermath. My non-profit research group, the Project on Media Ownership, did a study of Baltimore's local TV news in 1998, and what we found was typical of local newscasts all over the country.We found that 38 percent of each night's news relates to violent crimes. Often those crimes hadn't even been committed in the City of Baltimore but, you know, if the show's "crime hole" hasn't been filled up with local stories, they'll go elsewhere to find whatever they might need.

JS:That's a lot of violent stories, thinking over the span of the year.

MCM:They do this to hook younger viewers—the most desirable, most lucrative, of demographic blocs.As people sit there watching the last bits of their favorite prime-time shows, just before the end there'll be a tease from that station's upcoming newscast, and it almost always has to do with something violent that happened, or that supposedly happened, in or near the city. It's meant to grab a younger audience than generally tunes in. The news has long since come to be a favorite with older viewers,and they're not the ones the choicest advertisers want.

Now, why has local TV news become so bad—so lurid and alarmist? Well, in most cases the local TV stations belong to huge station groups that are headquartered somewhere out of town, and whose news directors are obligated to please the advertisers and keep the revenues rolling in.And this, you know, points in one direction: toward ever more crime news.This is why any local TV newscast, if it were transcribed and published as a newspaper, would look like a police gazette.The over-emphasis on crime has everything to do with the pressure for ratings, and not much at all to do with actual crime rates, which are generally declining. If TV stations were locally owned they wouldn't be under so much pressure from headquarters, and, also, they would be staffed by people with roots in the community. It would, of course, be better still—ideal, in fact—if there were not just genuine competition between several local entities, but a real public alternative. There needs to be a non-commercial choice.

Anyway, this degradation of the local TV news is only one example of how concentrated ownership, and excessive commercialism, have made the daily fare more violent.

JS: Let's talk about the Columbine phenomenon. Some people think this sort of crime is peculiar to the United States, although we have seen some of these things happen in other countries like Scotland and Canada.

Nonetheless it seems to be seen as a kind of American problem and a lot of the critics, even in the United States, will point to the gun culture. Is there really a gun culture?

MCM: Of course the US gun culture has much to do with the upsurge of such crimes in this country. This kind of thing just couldn't happen with more primitive weapons. That seems so obvious as to preclude all argument.

It's also true, however, that as time goes on, and as the consumerist ideology spreads ever further over all the world—and as the chasm between the haves and have-nots grows ever wider and more flagrant—this kind of crime will surely cease to seem peculiarly American.

Why wouldn't it? We already accept the fact that the incidence of gangsterism rises steeply wherever capitalism rules the roost. We've seen it in US history, and we see it the world over, especially since the fall of Communism (whose own gangsterism tended to be more predictable). As with gangsterism, so does it seem to be the case that a particular kind of sociopathology accompanies the entertainment state. Only certain strong indigenous social institutions can inhibit that development, as, evidently, in Japan. But as the ideology of advertising becomes culturally paramount, with more and more wealth falling into ever fewer hands, there is no doubt that we will see the spread, even into the unlikeliest places, of this explosive sort of criminality.

There's something irresistible about the gun. That's why the movies, and the movie ads, are full of them. If you were dropped down from another planet, and took a look at the movie ads in any major newspaper, you'd think that that is all the movies are about. It's probably to be expected in a system worshipful of that completely mediated individual "empowerment" that we were just discussing. To have and hold a gun—especially a big, expensive gun—is to be at once promoted from non-entity to heroism—although "heroism" isn't quite the word, because the stance that's glamorized is now largely anti-social, destructive rather than creative. Compare Shane, for example, with the tortured mercenary killers in *The Wild Bunch*—and then with "the Professional," "la femme Nikita," and all those other able hit-persons routinely celebrated in the entertainment state. Somehow, the figure of the lone assassin, or of that wandering, hip "psychopath" whom Norman Mailer once romanticized back in the 50s, has now become a cultural ideal: the gun, the shades, the perfectly impassive face, the utter nihilism. It's rather like those Special Forces soldiers who come home and join the far-right underground. It's like the ultimate blowback—all our chickens coming home to roost.

JS: That's pretty grim.

MCM: Let's just keep our eyes open.

"Have You Considered a Gun?": Reading *Due South* as Ironic Commentary on the American Cop Hero

Wendy Pearson

> MRS. VECCHIO: He's very nice, so polite!
> RAY VECCHIO: He's Canadian, ma.
> MRS. VECCHIO: Oh, I thought he was sick or something.
>
> *Due South* (Pilot)

An interesting conversation between a gun-toting criminal and the "hero," Royal Canadian Mounted Police Constable Benton Fraser (Paul Gross), marks the defining moment of the cultural commentary on the relationship between guns and nationality in the pilot movie for *Due South:*[1]

> Would it be asking too much to show us your gun?
> No, not at all. I carry a standard .38-caliber Smith and Wesson service revolver. But without a local license, I am not permitted to use it and that is why it is empty.[2]

Fraser pulls his handgun in a bar full of heavily armed criminals and proceeds to demonstrate, with some care, that it is unloaded. Action heroes are not, of course, supposed to wander unarmed through the streets of Chicago, fighting crime with a combination of quick wits, fisticuffs and Inuit stories. The scene in the bar, with an unloaded official-issue RCMP handgun, is so typical of the ironic and rather camp atmosphere that the show seems to strive for, that it occurs repeatedly in television commercials for the program. The unloaded handgun—or, at times, the empty holster—that Fraser carries comes to serve symbolically for all of the serious and humorous distinctions between Canadians and Americans that lie at the very heart of the show.

This particular scene also functions to differentiate Constable Fraser from his Chicago P.D. buddy, Ray Vecchio (David Marciano), who is, at least according to the show's press releases, "the antithesis of Fraser." This apparent antithesis in character serves not only to create an "opposites attract" form of buddy-bond between the two protagonists, but also to further the show's consistent delight in satirizing the relationships between Americans and Canadians. To the Mountie, the handgun is a symbol of law and order, a symbol which need not be mobilized in order to induce respect for the law; to the cynical Chicago cop, the loaded gun is a necessity, a symbol of the impotence of the law that he disregards almost as often as do the criminals he pursues. In the chaos created between the tavern's denizens and the murderer in the scene described above, a man who shoots his way out indiscriminately, Vecchio attempts to fire Fraser's empty gun (foreshadowing a similarly unsuccessful attempt by the murderer in a later scene). Tossing it aside in disgust, he asks, "What do they shoot people with in Canada? Serviettes?"

Americans, we are told repeatedly, are the ones with the guns. Early in the movie, before he flies to Chicago, Fraser is searching for his father's (Gordon Pinsent) killers. He seeks out a local pilot in the hopes of tracking down six American hunters who may have been implicated in the murder. The pilot asks, "You're sure they were Americans, eh?"; Fraser replies, with heavy irony, "They were all wearing big boots, they were driving a Jeep Wrangler, and they carried big guns." "Americans it is," replies the pilot sardonically. All through this particular narrative, the only Canadians who both possess and shoot guns are villains. At the end of the episode, when Fraser and Vecchio are holed up in Fraser's father's cabin, waiting for the bad guys to pounce on them, and with no cavalry in sight, they discuss the probable ending of their plight in a scene which caps the distinction the show has already created not only between the two men, but also between the two cultures.

The scene begins with Fraser moving supplies around the cabin while Vecchio, in a neck brace, struggles to put on his socks:

VECCHIO: So, we've got some fishing rods, a rifle last used by Chuck Connors, and a bag of rice. So what's your plan?

FRASER: We wait for them to come.

VECCHIO: Yeah, and . . . ?

FRASER: And then we arrest them.

VECCHIO: You see: that's such a simple plan that the American mind automatically tends to discount it, so let me run it back to you. We wait here; Gerrard and God knows who else comes, some time when, we're not sure, and then, when we least expect it, they shoot us dead with automatic weapons. Any part I left out?

FRASER: Yes; I need Gerrard alive to testify, so we can't kill him.

VECCHIO: Oh, I don't think we're in any danger of doing that.

Vecchio's humorous response suggests at least two possibilities to the audience: first, that the heavily armed villains will indeed shoot the two protagonists; but, secondly, that he's too cheerful and his ironic tone too light for the audience to doubt that Vecchio, at the very least, expects Fraser to have a plan more likely to be successful than the one he has just outlined. Fraser goes on to elaborate, "If you're going to take on a man, you'd better know more than he does. Our strength is, I know this area better than anyone. Their weakness is they think they have an advantage," to which Vecchio replies, "Let me see that bag; being an American, I also know where my strength lies, and that's in being as heavily armed as possible at all times." He then proceeds to dump out a variety of handguns, grenades and other explosive devices before the eyes of the dumbfounded Fraser. The eventual "hmm . . ." with which Fraser responds to Vecchio's protestations about the weapons' legality indicates that he puts more faith in his wits and his knowledge of the environment than in possessing enough weaponry for a small militia.

Repeated moments throughout the first and second seasons of *Due South* recapitulate the pilot film's emphasis on the possession of guns as one of the most important markers of nationality. It is not, of course, that Fraser doesn't have a gun—although Canadians in the show, as in real life, have far fewer guns than do Americans—but that he is not licensed to use it in the United States. Vecchio, by contrast, does not show an equal respect for Canadian firearms regulations; he is furious when he is made in the episode "North" to give up his handgun upon entering Canada.

Although Vecchio is replaced in the third season by Stanley Ray Kowalski (Callum Keith Rennie), *Due South* continues to play with guns as national and personal markers of identity. When Fraser invites the Americans into the Canadian consulate, where Kowalski has sought sanctuary, in the episode "Asylum," he forces them to check their weapons at the door—and every single person, whether male or female, whether police officer, journalist, criminal or politician, adds at least one gun to the growing heap, thus confirming the somewhat *cliché* Canadian perception that Americans are obsessed with guns and are all, always, armed. In Kowalski's case, the show's humor focuses around the irony that, although he does have a gun and is perfectly willing to use it, he refuses to wear his glasses and therefore can't hit the criminals at whom he's shooting. In "Seeing is Believing," both Kowalski and Fraser are crouched behind a car, being shot at by the villain of the piece, while Kowalski fumbles with his glasses:

FRASER: Ray, have you considered contacts?

KOWALSKI: Too much fuss. Have you considered a gun?

FRASER: Too many legalities.

The villain is captured when he runs out of bullets. While Kowalski fumbles to reload his handgun, Fraser faces down first the villain's empty gun, then his knife-throwing skills. At least for that moment, Fraser is framed as morally invincible, standing in his red uniform and protected by his belief that the villain's actions, using what Fraser thinks of as a sacred *inuksuk* (a stone figure built to resemble an Inuit person with outstretched arms) as cover for a murder, will haunt him. Guns are, momentarily at least, characterized as impotent against the true power of Fraser's morality, which is emblematized both by the red full-dress uniform in which he confronts the villain and by his dedication to his heritage as a northern Canadian, someone who has spent virtually his entire life in the Yukon and Northwest Territories.[3] Not unusually, the North becomes a metonym for what is most "naturally" Canadian. Fraser's pristine northern wilderness is once again contrasted to the urban landscape of Chicago, which is characterized as both literally and morally dirty.

Ownership of guns is not the only difference between the citizens of the two countries. The show thrives on the ironic comparison of our two cultures: where American cops shoot the bad guys, Fraser uses words or fists to subdue them; where American cop heroes thrive on car chases, Fraser runs the bad guys down on foot, or in a dog-sled; where American police dramas, both in film and on television, frequently depend on the hypermasculinity of the hero, *Due South's* attribution to Fraser of a peculiar and somewhat androgynous masculinity seems to be based in character rather than ideology. His androgyny is further complicated by his possession of a number of rather "feminine" traits and by his near-complete incapacity with women. The whole construction is exacerbated in the pilot film when neither Fraser nor Gerrard (Ken Pogue), the corrupt Mountie responsible for sending a hired killer out for Fraser's father, prove capable of killing each other. When he has Fraser at the end of a gun, Gerrard shoots Drake (Page Fletcher), the hired killer, rather than Fraser, even though he must know that he's given himself away. When Fraser, back in Canada, points his now-loaded handgun at Gerrard, there's no implication that he intends more than to arrest the other man, and he cannot, in the end, stop him from walking away. In a second season episode, "Bird in the Hand," when Fraser has to recapture Gerrard, he is still unable to kill him, despite the urgings of his father's ghost[4] and the explicit permission of his partner.

Both the first and third season press releases for *Due South* identify the show's style as satirical; they also make it clear that the primary object of the satire is "the constant interplay between Canadian and American cultures," an interplay apparently explored through "fanciful flights of adventure hallmarked by revelations of character and the not-quite-camp." Part of this interplay, I will argue, involves satirizing both the television cop show and the idea of the masculine cop-hero, not to mention masculinity itself. Fraser is sometimes painfully human, sometimes almost cartoonishly superhuman, but he's a Canadian Crash Test Dummy superhero—indeed, the Dummies' "Superman's Song"[5] plays in the background of the pilot, at a time when Fraser seems most alone in the strange city in which he has failed to find his father's killer. *Due South* also plays with superhero conventions, along the lines that John Bell, curator of the "Canadian Superheroes" exhibit at the National Archives in 1992, noted is typical of Canadian versions of comic book superheroes:

> Typifying Canadian reticence in so many things, some of these [Canadian] heroes possess no actual superpowers, relying rather on superior physical and intellectual skills to enable them to combat their enemies.[6]

Supremely fit, with senses honed by a lifetime spent in the far North, and equipped with police training provided by the RCMP, the tracking and observation skills of the First Nations, and an eccentric but exceptionally thorough education given by his grandparents, Fraser fits the Canadian superhero mold.

In *Television and the Drama of Crime*, Richard Sparks notes that, in general, "[c]rime fiction on television does for the most part address us as fearful 'privatists' rather than contented social beings.... It does routinely register a level of social anxiety about crime and law enforcement, and in so doing tends to reproduce its cultural salience."[7] The many examples of crime dramas and cop shows that Sparks examines are almost entirely British or American; they are also, on the whole, serious dramas. The notion of the cop show as comedic, at least as much as dramatic, is apt to strike critics as quirky. In this regard, *Due South* has more in common with the UK's *Hamish Macbeth* (1995) than it does with its American contemporaries, like *Law and Order* (1990), *Brooklyn South* (1997) or the almost hyper-realist *Homicide: Life on the Street* (1993). Self-conscious irony, a main register in which the show operates, is not a common device of the usual crime drama, regardless of how self-conscious it may appear in its use of generic and media effects (for example, in *Hill Street Blues [1981]*).

In *As Canadian as ... Possible ... Under the Circumstances*, Linda Hutcheon argues that irony is itself a peculiarity of the Canadian approach to identity:

> What then is the basis of the relationship I am positing between irony and Canadian culture? I would not want to say all Canadian culture is bathed in what someone once called the cold douches of irony; that would manifestly be wrong. Nor would I want to say that only Canadian culture has dipped its toes into those ironic waters; that too is patently false. I merely want to suggest that irony is one mode of self-defining discourse used by English Canadians....[8]

One might suggest that irony is one of the preferred modes of discourse used by *Due South* precisely because this show, for all its comedic intent, repeatedly returns to contentious issues—the use of guns, environmental concerns, masculinity, justice, poverty, the rule of law, and Canadian-American relations. As Hutcheon points out, one of the many possible uses of irony for Canadians is in some sense political, "the critique of ideology operative in the ironic treatment by Canadian artists of what is now the dominant culture against and within which Canada operates: that of the United States of America."[9] At the same time, as Hutcheon, Northrop Frye, Wayne Booth and others have noted, uses of irony by Canadians are often distinctly self-deprecating.

One example should suffice: in "Perfect Strangers," Fraser and Kowalski are in Chicago P.D. Lieutenant Welsh's (Beau Starr) office, watching a black and white video set to religious music. Kowalski is bemused to learn that the video is an "RCMP re-creation of a crime." Fraser responds by saying, "It's interesting, isn't it? The government funding of the arts in Canada produced a glut of filmmakers at the same time as American domination of Canadian cinemas left these enthusiastic young artists with very few arenas in which to ply their crafts." It's the kind of lecture that only Fraser could get away with; one of the many double-edged jokes about him is his tendency to pedantry—based on a near-encyclopaedic knowledge. On the one hand, it's clear that Fraser's disquisition is a little dig at Americans for what Canadians often perceive as their cultural imperialism; on the other hand, it's also a self-reflexive joke at the quirkiness of Canadians themselves. Would any police force, really, no matter how many frustrated filmmakers they had on call, turn their crime re-creations into art films? The humor works both ways as the show creates much of its impact through its ability to aim at targets on both sides of the border.

Leaving aside for the moment the question of Canadian versus American identities, I want to consider the ways in which *Due South* can be read specifically as an ironic commentary on the American cop show, its iconic gun-toting hero, and his weapon itself. Linda Hutcheon notes that

> the works of . . . [Canadian] artists and writers offer examples of the liminal spaces in between, the double meanings that double-talking ironies are making room for. The tactics used to bring these spaces into being . . . are common enough: those familiar rhetorical devices of understatement, hyperbole, anticlimax, and repetition, as well as those modes of strategic positioning that provide counter-expectation—incongruity, recontextualizing, defamiliarizing clichés, or parody. Whatever the medium and whatever the function, irony seems to be at least one of the ways so-called English-Canadians have chosen to articulate their problematic identities.[10]

In fact, *Due South* uses almost all of these techniques to produce its ironic effect. We've already considered repetition as a method of creating ironies around both the stereotypes and the truths of the differences between American and Canadian attitudes toward guns. In the pilot, anticlimax functions to ironize the apparent initial conflation of guilt with nationality: while it seems that it is the evil American, Drake, who has murdered the innocent Canadian Mountie, it is precisely at the moment when Fraser captures Drake and the story appears to be over that the storyline twists—Gerrard kills Drake to prevent him from talking and thus reveals the complicity of not only Canadians, but some members of the RCMP, in Fraser Sr.'s murder. Americans are not, after all, the only bad guys, and Canadians are not purely good.

James Inciardi and Juliet Dee have argued that the central image in even the most cynically-updated American police drama is still that of the sheriff, Colt in hand, facing off against the bad guy in the dusty main-street of some two-bit town in the West. It goes without saying that in this, as in his more modern incarnations, the image of the cop as hero in American popular culture is hard, masculine and aggressive: the cop, like the gangster, has his image, his woman, and his gun. He shoots, he swears, and he fucks. While many contemporary television crime dramas are more realistic in both setting and flavor, they invariably resonate for the viewer with the central image, or icon, of the gun-slinging sheriff. The quintessential modern image of the sheriff at work in an urban setting is, perhaps, Clint Eastwood in *Dirty Harry* and its sequels (1971–1988). In these films, Harry is so masculine and the law so feminized that he must act outside the law in order to fulfill his function. As Dennis Bingham notes, in *Acting Male*, "Harry is the primal man who discards an overly civilized, refined, and intellectualized system because it does not recognize and reward male virtues."[11] These are precisely the virtues which, by both generic and societal conventions, should also be "cop virtues," yet they are markedly not those of either gun-toting Vecchio or gunless Fraser in *Due South*. While Vecchio's position is the more ambivalent—he must appear to fit the "Dirty Harry" mold, if only on the level of rhetoric—Fraser's position is diametrically opposed to Harry's. Fraser believes in the rule of law, and his repeated assertion of that belief, although often played for comic effect, is the moral axis around which the episodes revolve. While that belief is marked as one of the apparent differences between Americans and Canadians, it is also a refusal of both the gun and the gun-as-phallus. Fraser's indifference to women and rejection of phallic power, made particularly obvious by his attractiveness to women, recapitulates on the psychoanalytic level his refusal to carry a handgun.

Bingham's discussion of the conflict between masculine hero and feminized law is significant here, particularly in regard to the central role of the gun in maintaining the phallic authority of the male. Bingham notes that in *Dirty Harry*, "The law, cast in the role of the withholding mother, threatens Harry's ruin ... Authority deprives him of the phallus—his 457 Magnum, 'the most powerful handgun in the world.' It renders him impotent, unable to kill the villain when he presumably has him dead to rights."[12] The *Dirty Harry* movies rehearse over and over the lengths to which Harry must go in order to protect the endangered phallus. In *The Dead Pool* (1988), the last of the *Dirty Harry* movies, when Harry is forced in the final battle to give up the oversized handgun with which he has already killed a dozen or so criminals, he finally dispatches the main villain, a schizophrenic murderer (David Hunt), by shooting him with a harpoon: the already excessively phallic handgun has metamorphosed into what should seem a parody of itself, yet the film plays the killing entirely without self-consciousness. The somewhat effete villain, already associated with drugs, Satanism, madness and a marked but unspoken assumption of homosexuality, meets an end that the film portrays as a proper reappropriation of the phallus when his body is penetrated by the new and even larger weapon of the hypermasculine hero.[13]

Due South plays off both sides of the image of the lone cowboy, the cop fighting a corrupt system and the man entrapped in an incapacitatingly feminized society. The American cop, Ray Vecchio, works to parody the Dirty Harrys of pop culture: "He's a kid who grew up on the mean streets of Chicago, a city that teems with life and corruption, and who manages to make a new Armani suit look slept-in ... Vecchio [has] learned to get ahead by careful carelessness and avoiding paperwork, ... [and he] didn't get his shield by volunteering and hasn't stayed alive this long by trusting in his fellow man." All of these descriptions from the official press release for the first season serve to show the way in which the show sets up the antithesis between the Chicago cop and the Mountie and the ways in which it plays off our cultural preconceptions about the protagonists of American cop shows.

And yet, Vecchio's Armani suits aren't that crumpled, at least until Fraser gets hold of him; he takes his newfound best friend home to a cacophonous but obviously loving family; he can be sweet-talked by Fraser into doing almost anything; and, at one point, he gives away several thousand dollars and his dream of replacing his beloved Buick Riviera in order to help save Fraser's shabby tenement building and his lowlife neighbours.[14] Virtually the only person he shoots, throughout the entire series, is Fraser himself—and he's aiming at someone else.[15] At almost every point where he seems to fit the stereotype which contrasts him with Fraser, something happens to complicate, deconstruct or, at the very least, ironize Vecchio's image as the tough, rule-bending, gun-toting American cop. This ironic deconstruction begins from the very first moment when the two protagonists meet, and is inevitable as the growing relationship between the two men erodes both of their positions as outcasts and loners. Not only does Vecchio seek out Fraser at the Canadian consulate in order to assist him in tracking down his father's killers, he also hunts Fraser down when he's alone in a diner, takes him home to dinner with his large Italian family, defies orders to continue to help him, comes close to getting himself killed in a bomb blast, and finally follows Fraser all the way back to the Yukon. The strong homo-erotic subtext of the show, reinforced by dialogue, situations, the framing of certain shots, further serves to ironize the coding of Vecchio as a masculine *Dirty Harry* type of cop.

In fact, one might argue that the subtext of the relationship between Vecchio and Fraser reverses the largely unacknowledged sexual subtext, which is both misogynist and homophobic, of the *Dirty Harry* movies. If one reads the final killing at the end of *The Dead Pool* as a symbolic penetration of the feminized male villain by the masculine hero, *Due South*'s refusal both of the phallic gun and its particular subtext suggests a larger refusal to see the world as consisting only of binarisms. It would seem not only that *Due South*'s version of the hero does not need to assert his position in the world through the use of guns, whether taken literally or as symbols of the phallus, but also that the true strength of the pair as law officers comes from their bond of partnership, rather than from the weapons they carry.

The construction of Fraser as the problematic Canadian near-superhero, the moral centre around whom the program seems to circulate, is as much a doubling as is the character of Vecchio. He appears to fit a specific kind of mold: the pilot show names him "the last of a breed," and he is set apart both from the urban landscape of Chicago and what should be the more familiar environs of the Yukon RCMP post to which he is assigned when the pilot begins. In his reluctance to use his weapon, he is reminiscent of the RCMP's real historical icon, Sam Steele, who is said never to have needed to fire his gun throughout a long and illustrious career. In addition, Fraser is super-competent: the viewer first sees him as he drives a dog-sled through a blizzard to bring in "his man." The duplicitousness of *Due South*'s parody of its own protagonist is evident in the viewer's initial reading that this madman has just risked his life to catch a fisherman who has gone over the limit; this reading is immediately upset, however, when it turns out that the "fisherman" has dynamited four and a half tons of salmon—not an insignificant offence.[16]

Another difference between Fraser and Vecchio that is consistently underscored in the show revolves around their very different attitudes towards women. The relationships between masculine heroes and women have always been somewhat strained.

Constrained by the absolute requirement of heterosexuality, the hero, whether of Western or of police drama, is required to express an appropriate desire for women and to illustrate a certain degree of sexual prowess. In *Due South*, the heterosexual proficiency of the American cop is demonstrated rhetorically, in Vecchio's repeated characterization of himself as a ladies' man, but there is very little onscreen evidence for his success with women. In fact, most of the time, his interactions with women are notably unsuccessful: his ex-wife, while friendly, doubts his probity; the prosecuting attorney he pursues would like to see him, and Fraser, jailed. With Fraser, however, the cop hero's masculine attraction *for* women is there in force—but there is very little evidence of an attraction *to* women on his part. In fact, he rarely seems to know what to do with women, except when he is able to treat them on a purely professional level. He even addresses his female superior, Inspector Thatcher (Camilla Scott), as "Sir." Women, in general, and Ray's sister Frannie (Ramona Milano), in particular, tend to leave Fraser flustered and incompetent or to make him run like hell. The psychoanalytically-minded can read Fraser's empty holster as symbolic either of a complete lack of libido or of a lack of the expected heterosexual, but misogynist, interest of a 'Dirty Harry.'

The ironic treatment of Fraser's sexuality is underscored both by the homoeroticism of the relationship with his unofficial police partner, a subtext common to virtually all police dramas of the "buddy" variety, and by the continual move towards and retreat from camp in the character's actions and dialogue. The campiness of the character develops in part from the conventions of the superhero genre, whose protagonist is rarely "good" with women, who wears silly clothing, and who operates on the far side of "normal" masculinity.[17] The superhero is able to risk being identified with camp because, like Fraser and unlike the Harry Callahans of the world, the superhero relies upon his (or even her) own innate abilities, rather than on external weaponry, for his identity; Superman doesn't need a gun. Fraser's flirtation with camp is further emphasized later in the series when, to help Vecchio out with a case that requires a woman to go undercover in a girls' school, he turns up in remarkably good drag in "Some Like it Red."

The American cop, as we have come to understand him through his image in popular culture, derives from an imaginary history of the West, mediated by both the cultural transition that replaced westerns on television with police procedurals and a darkened vision of law and order infused by a sense of real world crisis.[18] As a result, Clint Eastwood's *Dirty Harry* has become emblematic of the police officer who can function properly only on the far edge of the law and whose gun is not merely a useful tool but essential to his very identity as a man. Despite the relatively problematic history of the RCMP in the last few decades, outside of Canada, at least, they remain symbols of integrity, courage, and success: the Mountie always gets his man, as every tourist knows. The invariably unarmed Fraser is positioned by the show as both the "ideal Mountie" and the perfect antithesis to the real Dirty Harry. Again, this is played out in both personal and national terms: Fraser contrasted to Vecchio, Canadian to American. Identity has become irony and Canadians and Americans are revealed as both more and less distinct, more and less interwoven, and more and less affectionate than our cultural stereotypes suggest. The doubled proliferation of layers of meaning that circulate through *Due South* suggests a ludic, post-modernist approach to the ideologies that, by popular conception, proliferate around and between weapons (particularly guns), masculinity, and national identity.

NOTES

1   *Due South* is a Canadian show, produced by Alliance, which focuses on the adventures, both dramatic and comedic, of the peculiar partnership between an idiosyncratic Mountie and a Chicago cop. It has just finished its third season, in Canada, after a one-year hiatus; in the United States, all but four of the completed episodes have been shown. The last thirteen episodes will constitute a fourth season in Canada.

2   All quotations from *Due South* are taken directly from either the pilot movie or the individual episodes. I will be making a number of references to the pilot movie for this series, which is simply called *Due South,* and, to avoid confusion, I will be referring to the series as *Due South* and to the pilot movie as "the pilot"; individual episodes will be identified by their titles.

3   Here I am giving an idealized reading of this episode.

4   The ghosts of both Fraser's and Vecchio's fathers turn up for the first time midway through the first season, in an episode about father and son relations ("The Gift of the Wheelman"). Fraser's father, Bob Fraser, pops up fairly regularly in episodes throughout the series; early in the third season, he even builds himself a cabin in Fraser's closet.

5   Brad Roberts, "Superman's Song," *Crash Test Dummies* (BMG Music, 1991). The song is quite clearly used both as irony—it's played at a point when Fraser's investigation seems to be going nowhere and he has no home to go to and no work that isn't trivial (addressing envelopes and standing guard at the Consulate)—and as foreshadowing, since Fraser is 'exiled' to Chicago after he brings a fellow RCMP officer to justice for his father's killing.

6   John Bell, *Guardians of the North: The National Superhero in Canadian Comic-Book Art* (Ottawa: National Archives of Canada, 1992), v.

7   Richard Sparks, *Television and the Drama of Crime: Moral Tales and the Place of Crime in Public Life* (Buckingham: Open University Press, 1992), 156.

8   Linda Hutcheon, *As Canadian as ... Possible ... Under the Circumstances* (Toronto: ECW Press & York University, 1990), 10–11.

9   Hutcheon, *Canadian,* 41.

10   Linda Hutcheon, *Splitting Images: Contemporary Canadian Ironies* (Toronto: Oxford University Press, 1991), 39.

11   Dennis Bingham, *Acting Male: Masculinities in the Films of James Stewart, Jack Nicholson, and Clint Eastwood* (New Brunswick, NJ: Rutgers University Press, 1994), 186.

12   Bingham, *Acting,* 191.

13   When the villain's body is struck by the harpoon, the force of the penetration lifts him from his feet and pins him to the door behind him. He is left dangling there, like a big game hunter's trophy.

14   *One Good Man,* a.k.a. *Thank You Kindly, Mr. Capra.*

15   *Victoria's Secret, Pt. II.*

16   The initial set-up in the pilot is repeated at the beginning of the third season, where Fraser chases a man for seven days and several thousand kilometres for "littering." The littering turns out, in fact, to be the dumping of illegal toxic waste.

17   Think, for example, of the very obvious campiness of Batman, a campiness that led one American psychiatrist, in 1953, to issue a warning, in all seriousness, to parents of boys, in which "he detailed the 'factually proven' method by which comic books turned innocent children into homosexually and pederastically inclined 'deviants and perverts.'" (Freya Johnson, "Holy Homosexuality Batman!: Camp and Corporate Capitalism in *Batman Forever*," *Bad Subjects* [December, 1995])

18   See, for example, Richard Sparks' work in *Television and the Drama of Crime: Moral Tales and the Place of Crime in Public Life* (Buckingham: Open University Press, 1992).

Air Wars: Lone Wolves and Civilized Violence at the Movies and Live from Baghdad

Linda Robertson

At 3:00 a.m. local time in Baghdad on January 17, 1991 a Stealth fighter dropped the first bomb, laser-guided to dead-center of the International Telephone and Telegraph Center. Within a moment, at 7:00 p.m. EST, television screens in America carried live CNN pictures of the bombing of Baghdad. George Bush, watching the coverage from the Oval Office, commented: "This is just the way it was scheduled." During the phased deployment of forces in the Middle East, known as Operation Desert Shield, polls had shown the American public was highly reluctant at the prospect of a ground war. With the advent of the air war, the mood was transformed into what President Bush termed "euphoria" at his press conference of January 18. A Gallup poll conducted minutes after the President's speech to the public the night the war began found a 19% point jump in approval for his handling of the crisis.[1] The favorable public response, which continued to show in the polls throughout the air war, was widely attributed to the television coverage, a conclusion supported by a study to correlate the amount of television watched with knowledge about and support for the Persian Gulf War. It showed that the greater the viewing time, the lower the relative knowledge about the war, and the higher the relative support. The study also showed that the more knowledgeable an individual was about the Middle East and factors relevant to the war, the less support he or she was likely to give to it.[2]

Jean Baudrillard, who is regarded as one of the most important current neo-Marxist critics, commented on a public "amnesia" about the Persian Gulf War that set in shortly after it was over, calling the mental state a "confirmation of the unreality of this war. Overexposed to the media, underexposed to memory.... Forgetting is built into the event itself in the profusion of information and details," a consequence, he argues, of the technology of mass communication.[3]

The focus on the technology and sheer bulk of the televised coverage overlooks the content and style—and who controlled them. The military producers of "The Persian Gulf Air War" showed considerable skill in anticipating both what the American public would not want to see and what would seem believable and even admirable in the conduct of an air war.

Far from disliking television press coverage, the military relied upon it, and resented it only when the pictures were not those the military would have liked to have conveyed. Television coverage gave an aura of authority and authenticity to the highly selective pictures and information chosen by the military for public consumption, because journalists and expert commentators seemed to be the ones presenting them.

The influence of the military on press coverage in general but on television coverage in particular has important consequences. For one thing, some military experts assume the Persian Gulf War ended "one day too soon" because President Bush was sensitive to the public's outcry over the pictures of the carnage caused when planes attacked the routed Iraqi Army fleeing Kuwait City. What the public imagines an "air war" ought to be, and what the accepted limits for the use of air power are thought to be in the public's mind, will be important factors in future decisions to take the United States to war.

We cannot really estimate the consequences of information control for the formation of public opinion about the Persian Gulf air war by attending solely to the project of ferreting out what was censored or by condemning the influence of television technology as a visual medium. Attention must also be directed to the signifying practices which traditionally have been used, evolved, and recombined to create the public's conception of "air wars" and of "combat pilots."

What follows considers briefly significant misinformation and censorship in order to shed light on what the military thought the American public or others throughout the world would object to in the conduct of the war. This selectivity of images and information is provides a clearer context when examined in light of the cultural significance of air combat, including how pilots now understand their historical legacy. The most serious consideration must be given to the role played by Hollywood films in shaping popular conceptions of air wars, an important factor given that films about the air force cannot be made without the cooperation of the United States Air Force—for the obvious reason that they have all the planes.

THE PERSIAN GULF WAR: TELEVISION AND THE MILITARY

The suppressed information about the air war indicates what the military assumed would be unacceptable, both in the United States and around the world, while what we saw on television screens is a rather clear indication of the opposite. The televised coverage left the impression that the majority of the bombs dropped in the war zone were "smart bombs" targeted at inanimate objects—such as buildings, hangars, or runways—and that they rarely missed. However, "smart weapons" accounted for only about 8% of the total tonnage dropped, an amount which exceeded that used in all of World War II.[4] The majority were "dumb" (unguided) iron bombs ranging from 500 to 1000 pounds of explosives, or containing incendiary chemicals, land mines, or the like. The surrender of the majority of the Iraqi army was credited to the psychological and physical effects of protracted saturation bombing of men trapped in bunkers, much of it attributable to B-52s. Yet, the military imposed absolute censorship on images of B-52s, their crews, or information about their missions. There were no pictures of the planes taking off from their bases, no interviews with the crews, no pictures taken from the planes of the havoc they wrought on the ground below, no visual reference to them at all except brief file clips when military experts for the major networks or CNN mentioned they were being used in the air war.[5]

Americans were left with the dramatic impression that the air war was conducted and won primarily by resolute fighters flying alone or in small groups of two or three; yet, modern air wars are conducted by large flying armadas, a "strike package" stretching in some cases for forty miles and comprised of highly specialized planes, each having a specific function. War conducted from the air is as complex as ground maneuvering.[6]

Why was it not only permissible but highly desirable to broadcast into American homes pictures of a modern city at night defending itself against aerial bombardment by American planes, but not permissible to show high-level saturation bombing over the theatre of war? Why were pictures repeatedly shown of single planes taking off or landing, but none of large, multiple-squadron armadas?

The B-52 carries the nuclear arsenal of the United States and was used for saturation bombing of Vietnam and Cambodia. So potent and negative are the images of the B-52s that there were protests in India at the news that B-52s would use bases there to refuel. Saudi Arabia and Egypt refused to allow the use of air bases for B-52s. Even granting that the United States military might not want to draw attention to the use of B-52s, why portray the air war as conducted primarily by individual planes? Why is that image more pertinent not simply for controlling public opinion, but for sustaining a sense of public "euphoria" instead of depicting the complex interdependence of an air armada?

MECHANIZED WARFARE AND THE SOLDIER AS A SYMBOL OF NATIONAL CHARACTER

Part of the answer resides in the traditional connection between the combat pilot and an idealized national character. The propaganda campaign developed by Great Britain during World War I stressed that British and Commonwealth soldiers showed individuality and initiative, while their Prussian counterparts could only follow orders blindly. This testimony to the superiority of the liberal nations at character formation was picked up by the United States and repeated in World War II and in the build-up to the Persian Gulf War.

Note, for instance, the centrality of "character" in a "prolegomenon" to a peace note written by Woodrow Wilson in November, 1916 as a response to the mechanized, stalemated slaughter along the Western Front that destroyed the capacity to regard warfare as a proof of manhood:

Deprived of glory, war loses all its charm. . . . The mechanical slaughter of today has not the same fascination as the zest of intimate combat of former days; and trench warfare and poisonous gases are elements which detract alike from the excitement and the tolerance of modern conflict. With maneuver almost a thing of the past, any given point can admittedly be carried by the sacrifice of enough men and ammunition. Where is any longer the glory commensurate with the sacrifice of the millions of men required in modern warfare to carry and defend Verdun?[7]

But the image of the air warrior offered a tonic to this disappointed imagination of how war should be fought. To him were transferred the values of individual initiative which, at the beginning of the war, had been ascribed to the ground soldier.

World War I saw the advent of every kind of air combat that later developed, including strategic bombing. But it was the combat pilot, and particularly the "lone wolf" who was played up for the public and who remains the central icon of that war in the public imagination. He was portrayed as an exemplar of hyper-individualism, the member of an exclusive fraternity of "aces," each one dependent entirely upon his own will to combat and innate skill. The iconographic conventions associated with the lone wolf established him as an independent hero, not as the team member of a wing or squadron. Hilda Beatrice Hewlett, writing of her visit to the front in *Our Flying Men*, echoed the propaganda message: "In flying, more than in any science of war, the man is alone, and on his skill and nerve depends the result."[8] In the popular imagination, war for the lone wolf was personal—he was known to his enemy either by name or by the distinctive designs painted on his plane.

Yet even as American college men were being recruited into the air service, when the United States entered the war, by images of "aces" on "lone wolf" patrols, emerging combat tactics made the role of the "lone wolf" and self-assigned missions increasingly obsolete, because contrary to the aim of co-ordinated air support for military objectives on the ground. At the end of the war, the military addressed the problem created by the publicity they themselves had fostered. In the "lessons learned" reports, the recommendation was that ways be found to temper the image of the combat pilot.[9] It was no longer useful to portray him as either a chivalric knight on a personal quest or as an entrepeneurial loner interested primarily in accruing personal glory.

The relationship of man and machine, and hence, man and weapon, also changed as the technology of the plane developed. The most important attribute of the World War I combat pilot was his cybernetic relationship to the plane he flew and its weaponry. With the advent of synchronized, forward-firing machine guns, the combat pilot uniquely among the soldiers of World War I used mechanized weaponry as an extension of his skill and courage.

The weaponry of the ground war enforced a sense that one was either serving the machine as a cog-in-the-wheel, or, if on the receiving end of its thrust, merely a paralyzed victim of it. The advent of long-range artillery meant that men loaded shells into large barrels, stood back while it was fired, and began again. The targets were so far away that often they could not be seen by those loading the weapon. The same was the case with sub-marine torpedoes. Crews in the early tanks could see little besides the poor individual who was assigned to stand on the ground in front of them and guide them with flags. The most lethal weaponry, in addition to the long-range artillery, was gas, which required none of the martial skills either to use or to avoid. The weaponry of the ground war in World War I was at a far remove from either the skilled, highly trained maneuver of cavalry forces, or the eye-to-eye combat that was part of the romanticism associated with warfare as a test of personal strength. This reality explains much of the psychological appeal of the combat pilot. On the ground, the machine mastered the man; in the air, the man and the machine merged.

The traditional role of the warrior was nevertheless maintained, because combat pilots saw their opponents; the engagement was personalized. But by the advent of the war in Vietnam, air combat had become as highly mechanized as ground weaponry. The cockpit radar picked out enemy aircraft well before the pilot could see it; guidance systems locked on the target, so that with the squeeze of a finger a missile could be launched at the invisible opponent. Air-to-air combat and especially maneuver were assumed to have been rendered obsolete by advanced technology, until the unanticipated losses in the skies over Vietnam led the air force to revive air-to-air combat training—and with it the glamorized iconography of the combat pilot—as depicted in *Top Gun* (1986).

AIR WARS ON FILM

The values the combat pilot has been used to represent in Hollywood films have undergone a moral devolution when it comes to his accepting responsibility for causing death, either to the enemy or to those under the same command. The change can be traced from *Wings*, the 1927 silent film about a World War I "knight of the air" who is tempered by a moral code of guilt and restraint, through to the *Top Gun* stick jockey indifferent to a faceless "enemy" and concerned primarily with personal performance. It is a journey from a version—albeit diluted—of the tragic self-consciousness of Achilles to a Nintendo game that proves the "prowess" of the kid who puts the slugs in the slot. "Accepting responsibility" changes from meaning that the pilot confronts his guilt as a warrior to meaning that he learns to follow orders, tempering his sizable, competitive ego just enough to meet the needs of his command unit while showing a callous indifference to destroying the enemy in a ball of fire.

Films about air combat made prior to World War II were predicated on the pre-World War I desire to conceptualize warfare, properly fought, as enhancing rather than diminishing the humanity of the man. Seeing one's enemy called forth pity and fear, or shame and guilt; having to rely upon skill, maneuver, and courage tested the refinements of civilization on primitive instinct. Ultimately, war required accepting personal responsibility for the death of others.

Two films by John Monk Saunders, who had flown with the United States air service over the Western Front, invited a traditional catharsis by demonstrating not only the thrill of flight and combat, but also the consequences of it; not only the loss of life, but the moral costs to those who survived. *Wings* won the first academy award; *Dawn Patrol* was essentially an anti-war film made in two versions, one in 1930 (for which Saunders won the Academy Award for best screenplay) and the second in 1938. In both films, the preferred narrative is that the enemy is just like us, only he wears a different uniform. This point is made in a disturbing way in *Wings*, where the hero Jack Powell (Charles Rogers) shoots down his best friend David Armstrong (Richard Arlen). David is flying a German plane which he stole after he was shot down behind enemy lines. As Jack fires at him with a machine gun, David screams helplessly, "Don't you know me?" and is of course unable to return fire because he does not want to kill Jack. Jack relentlessly pursues him in a private vendetta to kill Germans because he thinks they have killed David.

Dawn Patrol is another "buddy" movie about flyers in World War I, this time serving in the Royal Flying Corps. Scotty (David Niven) is brought down and presumed to be dead. The German pilot who shot him down is captured and brought to the rustic officer's club, where he meets Courtney, Scotty's best friend (Errol Flynn). Courtney greets him courteously, and they spend the evening together drinking and singing. Scotty shows up bedraggled, a bump on his head, and carrying six bottles of champagne. He is delighted to meet the German who shot him down, and invites him out for a night on the town; unfortunately, the German officer cannot go because he is a prisoner of war.

In *Wings* and *Dawn Patrol*, the enemy is the war itself, which divides men from men who would otherwise be friends; in *Dawn Patrol*, the enemy is also a murderously stupid command that insists upon sending untrained pilots in inferior planes on offensive patrols. In *Wings*, Jack is absolved of his guilt by David's mother, who says she has tried to hate him, but cannot, because ultimately the cause of her son's death was the war. While this may seem too glib, the point is that the film requires Jack to face the question of his moral responsibility for his role in killing "the enemy"—symbolically displaced—during war, and to seek absolution for it. Similarly, in *Dawn Patrol*, the recognition of the enemy's humanity makes the war all the more senseless—which is the point of the film. *Dawn Patrol* is an early example of what came to be called the "pressure of command film," of which *Twelve O'Clock High* (1949) is a good example from World War II. *Dawn Patrol* depicts the successive mental breakdowns of the commanders who are ordered day after day to send young, unskilled, poorly trained pilots into the air to their certain deaths. It is an oddly pacifist film, in the sense that it argues against the senselessness of war while demonstrating that men did not shirk their duty, even while they recognized the pointless waste of life caused by a murderously misguided command whose orders they were bound to obey. This doubly potent message of waste, guilt, and disillusionment is driven home by the sense that the film reflects the experience of those who fought the war.

WORLD WAR II: "FRIED JAP GOIN' DOWN!"

In *Air Force* (1942), the enemy is the treacherous and cowardly "Japs" who are never humanized as the German pilots were in the earlier films about World War I; and the internal threat is the motive to "be a hero," acting on one's own rather than being part of a larger team. *Air Force* was made by Warner Brothers, a $2 million "A" feature directed by Howard Hawks and produced by Hal Wallis. Leading men included Gig Young, Arthur Kennedy, Harry Carey, and John Garfield. The studio enjoyed the full co-operation of the commanding general of the U.S. Army Air Force, H. H. "Hap" Arnold, who had also served as a commanding officer in Washington during World War I, overseeing the birth of the air force. He was a personal friend of Jack Warner. *Air Force* reflects a number of propaganda messages important to the air force at the time. Some were congruent with the messages typically advocated by the domestic Office of War Information; however, it is a testimony to the influence of the air force that the essentially racist anti-Japanese content of the film remains a central feature despite the energetic opposition of the O.W.I.[10]

Air Force tells the story of the crew of a B-17 named "Mary Ann," a Flying Fortress that takes off on a routine flight from San Francisco to Hickham Field, the airbase at Pearl Harbor (Honolulu), on the evening of December 6, 1941. Diverted to Maui by the attack on Pearl Harbor, the fliers are shot at on the ground by what are called "fifth column" snipers, or Japanese living in Honolulu. They fly over Hickham Field, circling it briefly before landing, so that the base is seen from the air, burning. After refueling, they are ordered to the Philippines. Shortly after they land, the base at Manila is attacked, and the "Mary Ann" takes off to confront the enemy. One of the "Mary Ann's" gunners hits a Japanese plane and shouts exultantly, "Fried Jap goin' down!"—the first of several shots in the film of Japanese pilots burning to death. The plane returns to base damaged by the attack of enemy aircraft. The entire crew works together to repair the plane and take off just before the Japanese overrun the island. En route to Australia, they spot the Japanese fleet, call in reinforcements, and successfully sink it, a sequence that splices in actual battle footage. The film closes on a base in Australia with a briefing sometime in the future when everyone's dream comes true: they are sent to bomb Tokyo.

Air Force breaks with the representation of air combat offered in the earlier films in two important ways. One is that it repeatedly invites the viewer to respond with glee at seeing the death of Japanese flyers.[11] The second is that it openly displays World War II in the air as not being about individual heroics or the finesse of air-to-air combat. The aim is to bomb the enemy into submission. The bomber is not an extension of the fighter's skill; it is a warehouse loaded with deadly weapons carrying the war to the enemy.

Tex Raider's (James Brown) conversion from a combat pilot to a bomber pilot exemplifies this change in focus. At the beginning of his journey, he states categorically that he prefers being a fighter pilot because it means that he does not have to be responsible for anyone but himself, and that he relies upon his own skills. He makes a long, derogatory speech about modern bombers which are so highly technical that the planes rather than the men who fly them "seem to be doing the thinking," and says that the B-17 is flown by the equivalent of "mechanized brains." Tex prefers the role of a fighter pilot because it means he can be a "one-man army." Unable to fly a fighter plane for various reasons, he ultimately assumes command of the "Mary Ann" when the original pilot is killed. The imperative to "accept responsibility" is reduced to learning to fit into the larger command structure of the military.

TOP GUN

The same message is conveyed in *Top Gun*. The time is the Cold War, when there is an enemy but no shooting war—more's the pity, the film seems to say—until the very end, an explosive battle between U.S. Navy planes and planes from an unnamed nation (which later denies that the battle took place). The opening sequence is an encounter with an unnamed enemy, flying what are supposed to be MiGs. Lt. Pete Mitchell (Tom Cruise), tellingly nicknamed Maverick, stunt-flies his plane so that his canopy is inverted over the canopy of the "enemy." In *Wings* and *Dawn Patrol*, flyers throw military salutes to those they shoot down out of respect for the man. In *Top Gun*, Maverick flips his counterpart "the bird" and takes his picture with a flash camera. Maverick has "counted coup" without firing a shot; he has "shown off" and humiliated the enemy, although to no particular purpose beyond proving that he has the skill to do it. In the final battle scene, where Maverick blows three planes apart with missiles, enemy pilots are not discernable in the cockpits; nor is the opposing nation—which for some reason has an overwhelming desire to risk war with the United States by attacking an American freighter that has drifted into "hostile water" somewhere in the Indian Ocean—even named.

Some faint echo of former glory is restored to air-to-air combat because of the marriage of man and machine and the encounter with hostile enemy aircraft requiring skill and courage to survive; but it is a thin veneer painted over what is essentially vainglory. Facing the enemy does not have a tempering influence, invoking the humanizing sentiments of pity, shame and guilt. The lesson of learning responsibility is worked out through the death of Maverick's radio and weapons operator Lt. Nick "Goose" Bradshaw (Anthony Edwards), who rides behind him in the F-14 Tomcat. Overly eager in a competitive maneuver, Maverick loses control of his plane because of backwash from another plane. Goose is killed during the attempted ejection when his head hits the canopy. Maverick learns from the sobering event to control his impulses and to stay in formation rather than be a maverick flier. In *Top Gun*, being responsible is reduced to the simple requirement to follow orders; the death of a comrade entails no moral encounter for the pilot because it resulted from equipment failure.

PERSIAN GULF WAR: THE MOVIE

Given the number of movies about air combat that have been made since the end of World War I, it is not an exaggeration to say that The United States Air Force has been in the business of making movies for the better part of the century. It does not stretch reality very far to say that the use of the broadcast press during the Persian Gulf War provides another example of the military "producing" a movie using commercial venues to promote its own message. With the real war in the Persian Gulf, the challenge was how to portray as both interesting and admirable the use of overwhelming force to bomb an undefended enemy into submission in a lopsided war. To the extent that the representation was successful, as it evidently was, the result can be seen as arising from a number of factors in addition to the suppression of information. For one thing, it was easy for the viewer to be involved, particularly young male viewers. Because the complex interdependency of "strike packages" was not explained, and the key role of the high-altitude bombing by B-52s was suppressed, the representation gratified childhood fantasies of lone-wolf heroism and adventure in air combat. The "fighter plane" as a weapon has morphed into a bomber, but conveys the romantic iconography of personalized combat, perhaps a hint of the former glory of the "knights of the air," and most certainly the contemporary narcissistic glamor of being a "Top Gun."

The air war was represented as being about individuals taking off into the darkened sky or flying into the sun, prevailing over an opponent who could not fight well because he was the product of an autocratic regime. It was a '90s kind of war, where individuals performed feats for which they were especially trained, using technology that reflected the intellectual and economic superiority of the west. The warrior and his plane symbolized *laissez-faire* liberalism giving rise to a highly-coordinated and successful undertaking. The efforts by the Office of War Information to promote films that represented the war effort as socially balanced—an infantry unit, for example, would have to have included a minority soldier, an urban and immigrant youth from The Bronx, a boy from the midwest, and usually somebody with a college degree—are well documented. Because this emphasis smacked of "New Deal" collectivism, conservative members of Congress reacted against the O.W.I. The representation of the Persian Gulf War, on the other hand, emphasized a predatory, elite Individualism.[12] Images that reinforced the romance of the "lone wolf" were reiterated. Americans were repeatedly shown stunningly beautiful depictions of the F-17 "Stealth" bomber taking off into the fading light of the evening sky; or a lone Intruder launched with breathtaking force from the decks of a U.S. carrier. Handsome young pilots were interviewed to reveal how they "felt," rather than to explain to the public complicated tactics requiring cooperative interdependence.

The referent for the televised coverage was not the real war, but celluloid air wars, what Walter Lippman would call the "images in our head" of wars.[13] As with Hollywood movies about modern air combat, the air war over the Persian Gulf did not invite a cathartic response in the traditional sense. The effort was to discharge the fear of a ground war—and the unwelcome resonance with Vietnam—by offering the air war instead. There was no invitation to guilt or shame—particularly on the ticklish matter of bombing cities—because the images were highly sanitized, the strikes "surgical." There was a profound unwillingness to invoke the moral imagination of the public, to suggest that the war would require of the average citizen anything even approaching sacrifice, never mind a sense of oneself as a responsible, historical agent for the nation's use of massive destruction. The war re-enacted on a different stage what Woodrow Wilson lamented about the advent of mechanized warfare: the Persian Gulf War had no glory to it, and hence no proof of manhood in the oldest military sense, which is why the luster so quickly faded from the Commander in Chief, and the public's "amnesia" set in so soon. The war was presented as a Saturday-matinee "summer-guy flick," such as the blockbuster *Independence Day* (1996), timed to open on July 4, hence the shortened title, *ID4*. This film broke all opening day records and was about single-pilot combat planes saving earth from very large, squishy aliens. Both the Persian Gulf War and *ID4* seem aimed at the same audience and were equally forgettable.

The effort to construct the Persian Gulf War with the aesthetics and moral depth of *Top Gun* indicates not how little but how much the public's responses to the face of war can influence the conduct of it. When Americans saw the "face of the enemy," they were not indifferent to it; they became sympathetic to the tattered and exhausted Iraqi soldiers who surrendered in vast numbers, having been pulverized for days from the air. There was a public outcry when pictures were shown of the wreckage and burned bodies of the unarmed Iraqi soldiers who had tried to flee Kuwait and who were attacked by British and American planes flying over Mutla Ridge. The public response to these pictures is held in some quarters to have influenced the decision by President Bush to end the war, as some military strategists put it, "one day too soon"; a euphemistic phrase suggesting that Iraqi ground forces, and especially the Republican Guard, should have been annihilated; but Bush allowed political considerations to override military pragmatism.

The representation of the air war also masked the traditions of air combat itself. What was widely reported in Great Britain but not in the United States was that both British and American flyers indicated to their commanders that they did not wish to receive further orders to engage in the kind of annihilating attack they had accomplished over Mutla Ridge. All flyers are volunteers, officers, and highly trained. While the refusal of orders would constitute grounds for a court martial, the indication that they did not wish to receive further orders certainly carried considerable weight. It is worth speculating why this resistance was not covered in the American press.

There was a hue and cry in Great Britain against the government for seeming to try and pin on the pilots the lack of political will to carry the war to the annihilation of the enemy. That interesting question aside, the reluctance of pilots to engage in the bombing and strafing of a routed army points toward the nobler legacy of air combat, a legacy which, despite the effort to dilute it in Hollywood tales of hot-shot pilots, still carries a sense of moral restraint imposed upon fliers who—part of an elite military service conceived as engaged in civilized violence rather than impersonal mechanized warfare— actually see the enemy they must encounter, and so in some way actually know him as they gun him down.

EPILOGUE

Since this article was first published, the air power of the United States has been unleashed in a NATO offensive against Serbia, an effort to prevent the killing and forced removal of ethnic Albanians from the province of Kosovar. NATO officers used videotapes from attacking planes to prove during press briefings that pilots could not have seen or would have been unaware of the civilians who were about to be obliterated by a missile aimed at a bridge or other target; hence, the men, women, and children killed by American bombs were collateral damage—a moral exemption, the result of killing with one's fingers crossed.

The traditional morality linking what a warrior sees with the necessary measure of his humanity and constraint remains for the military leadership as a powerful signifier for the culture. Despite the evident desire to promote this romantic vision of the moral agency of the pilot, what determined the casualty rates was that missiles are necessarily fired while the target is out of sight of the plane, that missiles often do not make it to their targets and have to come down somewhere, and that the sites—such as bridges and office buildings—were regularly used by civilians. The justification that the pilot would have shown restraint had he seen civilians was used to legitimize a steady escalation of the targeting of civilian sites in urban areas while representing the pilot as a moral agent held hostage to an advanced technology. The bombing of the Chinese Embassy followed by profuse apologies made all the more credible to the American public the moral justification that any civilian losses were an accident.

The effort to circumvent or undermine the potential of televised coverage to arouse the American public to protest was further aided by the response from some prominent members of the intellectual left in the United States, who only a few weeks into the war were surprisingly calling for ground troops because the air war had, according to them, failed. Framed as a pragmatic argument favoring the rescue of Kosovar Albanians, the hue and cry was consequently not against the Serbian civilian casualties; presumably, had the bombing of urban targets brought Milosevic to his knees within, for instance, ten days, that would have been a satisfactory outcome for Clinton's critics.

An additional factor implicitly legitimizing the morality of waging war from the air against civilian targets was ironically the horrifying rampage at Columbine High School in Colorado, when two well-armed male adolescents went on a killing spree and then killed themselves. President Clinton, in his weekly radio address of May 15, 1999, took to the Bully Pulpit, urging the entertainment industry to consider the effects of glorifying violence. Noting that the typical American sees 40,000 dramatized murders by age 18, Clinton argued there is still too much violence on our nation's screens, large and small. He made the statements without any apparent self-consciousness about the very real violence and destruction filling the nation's small screens largely because of his own initiatives. This points less toward his near-legendary capacity to compartmentalize than it does to an underlying cultural duality which pits civilized restraint and the rational use of force against barbarian, unrestrained, irrational violence. The killers at Columbine are on the same side of this moral equation as the Serbian militias—acting without conscience or restraint, viciously killing an unarmed enemy on the ground. NATO was, logically, on the other side, demonstrating a reluctant, constrained, but necessary response to barbarism. Clinton was calling upon the entertainment industry to cease arousing barbarian instincts by glorifying violence, a position hence logically consistent with his decision to use air power against Milosevic.

There is no evading the need to come to grips with the morally difficult and inevitably contradictory terms by which the resort to violence is invested with cultural weight in the western world. The century ends as it began, with war in the Balkans; the significant difference is in the scope and the casualties, a consequence of military technology developed largely as a result of both World Wars and out of the desire to wage war without high casualty rates for ground forces. America's participation in World War I was legitimized on the grounds both that the security of the United States was threatened and that the civilian populations assaulted by the Germans required rescue and protection. Similar concerns about the stability of Europe and the need to protect Kosovar Albanians were used to justify the NATO air strikes. The cultural concern going into World War I was that the humanizing effects of guilt and fear would be lost in mechanized warfare, removing any constraints on the use of increasingly advanced technologies of destruction. It was a concern that has been justified, to a disconcerting extent. We end the century with the easy availability of weapons to children; and with a morality which bizarrely calls for distinctions between violence conducted with rational constraint against civilians and violence conducted out of irrational impulses. Both justifications are fueled by fantasies which encourage the belief that difficult problems can be solved without overly burdening one's conscience about a resort to violence, and by a love affair with the uneven power that comes from being on the operating end of a weapon.

NOTES

[1]   "This is just the way it was scheduled": *U.S. News and World Report* [staff], *Triumph Without Victory: The Unreported History of the Persian Gulf War* (New York: Times Books, Random House, 1992), 218. President Bush opened his January 18 press conference by cautioning against the "initial euphoria" and warning against becoming "overly euphoric." The mainstream press quickly adopted the word "euphoria" to describe the public mood. There was little polling evidence to indicate a general mood of "euphoria." Gallup polls taken during the weeks that followed the outbreak of war showed by the end of January a high level of favorable public response in the United States to such questions as whether the war would end quickly. The approval ratings for the actions of President Bush were also high. See: "American Opinion on Events in the Persian Gulf, January, 1991," *Gallup Report Monthly.* no. 304 (January, 1991) 2–17; "Public Backs President on Persian Gulf, But Many Still Have Nagging Doubts, January 11–13," *Gallup Report Monthly*, no. 304 (January 1991), 8–9.

[2]   Justin Lewis, Sut Jhally and Michael Morgan. *The Gulf War: A Study of the Media, Public Opinion, and Public Knowledge.* The Center for the Study of Communication. University of Massachusetts/Amherst. Document number: P-8.

[3]   Jean Baudrillard, "The Illusion of War," in *The Illusion of the End*, trans. Chris Turner. (Stanford, CA: Stanford University Press, 1994), 67; 1.

4   James F. Dunnigan and Austin Bay, *From Shield to Storm: High Tech Weapons, Military Strategy, and Coalition Warfare in the Persian Gulf*. (New York: William Morrow and Company, 1992), 165.

5   *U.S. News and World Report* [staff], p. 275; "B-52s accounted for not quite 2 percent of all sorties, but dropped nearly 30 percent of all bomb tonnage." Dunnigan and Bay, 155; on effects on Iraqi ground troops in Persian Gulf War, 206; 288; General Norman Schwarzkopf with Peter Petre, *It Doesn't Take A Hero* (New York: Bantam Books, 1992), 430; on missions of B-52s: 60 B-52 sorties were flown from Europe, dropping 1000 tons of bombs. Dunnigan and Bay, p. 166.

6   *U.S. News and World Report* [staff], p. 241.

7   Quoted in: John Milton Cooper, *The Warrior and the Priest: Woodrow Wilson and Theodore Roosevelt*. (Cambridge, Mass: Belknap Press of Harvard University Press, 1983), 310; See Woodrow Wilson, "prolegomenon" to peace note [circa November, 1916], in *The Papers of Woodrow Wilson*, ed. Arthur Link (Princeton, NJ: Princeton University Press, 1966, and following) vol. XL, 70–71.

8   Hilda Beatrice Hewlett, *Our Fighting Men*. (Kettering, GB: T. Beaty Hart, n.d.) 6.

9   Maurer Maurer, ed. *Col. Edgar S. Gorell, The Final Report and a Tactical History, Vol I of The U.S. Air Service in World War I*. 1921, 1948 (Washington, D.C.: United States Government Printing Office. 1978), 104–105.

10 See Clayton R. Koppes and Gregory D. Black, *Hollywood Goes to War: How Politics, Profits, and Propaganda Shaped World War II Movies* (Berkeley, CA: University of California Press, 1990), 78–80.

11 In one sequence, a Japanese plane crashes and the pilot emerges on fire from the burning wreckage. He is machine-gunned by one of the gunners for the "Mary Ann," who is standing on the ground not far from the burning wreckage, having witnessed the Japanese pilot gun down an American hanging in a parachute. The incident passes without a word of commentary. The "justification" for the killing is evidently taken for granted.

    It has often been noticed that the representation of the Germans in the war reflected the government's desire to distinguish the "Nazis" from the German people. The OWI wanted the same distinction to be made with regard to the Japanese, a desire made more difficult when the orders were issued to round up all Japanese-Americans and intern them. The regular use of the word "Jap" and the stereotype of the "Jap" as an animal, often a simian, has been understood as signifying the inherent racism of the American public. It is difficult to argue with this, except to point out that the aim of the OWI was to the contrary.

12 See Koppes and Black, *Hollywood Goes to War*, especially chs. 1–5. The OWI sought, usually successfully, to have America's participation in World War II represented in Hollywood films as a united effort that called for the collective will of Americans from all walks of life, regions, and backgrounds, an extension of New Deal liberal-

ism. The "bomber crew" is thus a much more useful model for the preferred national imagery of World War II than fighter pilots flying off to undertake individual feats of daring. *Air Force* brings together men of differing backgrounds, classes, ethnic background, age, and region—but not race—and depicts them as melding into a unified team that meets all adversities.

[13]   Walter Lippman, *Public Opinion* (1922; New York, NY: Free Press, MacMillan, 1965), 9.

Oppression, Guns, and Social Justice in *Battleship Potemkin* and *1900*

Anver Saloojee

POWER AND EMPOWERMENT

Both *Battleship Potemkin* (1925) and *1900* (1976) need to be understood in the context of socio-economic crises, the power of ruling elites, power relations between the elites and the masses, and the empowerment of the dispossessed and the marginalized in society. Power can be defined as the ability to get someone to do something they would not ordinarily do. This can be accomplished by the use of force, or by the threat of the use of force. In most democratic societies, the rule of law and the threat of the use of force by the police and the paramilitary is sufficient to secure compliance by the majority of citizens. In authoritarian societies governed by repressive regimes, the government has largely lost its credibility and legitimacy and therefore has to rely on force to secure compliance with its rule. Tsarist Russia and fascist Italy were two such societies where the state relied heavily on the military to rule, especially in times of socio-economic and political crises.

Empowerment can be defined as the ability of an individual or group to take control of their circumstances in order to develop their talents and capacities free from threats and intimidation. This is a developmental conception of power where the dispossessed, the powerless, are able to use power to change their social and material circumstances. In a situation of socio-political and economic crisis of the kind Russia faced in 1905 and Italy faced after the great depression, those who had the power were willing to exercise it over others even if that resulted in extreme oppression and death. Then, we may ask, in situations of crisis, when the repressive arm of the state is willing to secure the continued existence of repression and rule, is the "gun" the great leveler between contending classes? Can the "gun" empower the oppressed to fight tyranny? Can a legitimate, albeit limited, claim be made for the justifiable use of the gun to overthrow tyranny by empowering the oppressed to confront the might of the state? These are the central questions that both Eisenstein and Bertolucci explore in their respective films.

BATTLESHIP POTEMKIN

For Eisenstein, in *Battleship Potemkin,* the gun is the embodiment of early bourgeois rule stripped of its veneer of civility, while at the same time it enables the oppressed to seize control over their circumstances and secure a limited victory against the Tsarist forces. For Bertolucci in *1900,* the government's use of the gun symbolized its failure to secure its hegemony in post-World War One Italy: when empowered forces actually make use of their weaponry, their ability to maintain control through threat vanishes. The gun was symbolic of fascist rule, while at the same time it enabled the Italian resistance movement as well as the allies to fight against, and secure victory against, fascism.

Eisenstein began and completed *Battleship Potemkin* in 1925. The film is structured in five acts, and its composition is about the unity of the particular and the general, and about pathos:[1]

Act I: Men and Maggots
Act II: Drama on the Quarterdeck
Act III: Appeal from the Dead
Act IV: The Odessa Steps
Act V: Meeting the Squadron

Despite the use of a multitude of symbols in the film, it is the gun, embodied in the central anthropomorphized character of the film—the battleship—that is the dominant symbol. The ship's most prominent features, indeed, were huge guns and cannons mounted on deck expressly signifying the might and power of the Tsarist state. Once their presence is established, they assume omnipresence.

In Act I, the ship's crew are served soup contaminated with maggots. This sets the stage for the repression/rebellion duality that runs through the film. The crew refuses to eat the soup, and is ordered onto the deck by the officers. Approximately twenty rebels are isolated and covered by a tarpaulin. The captain agrees to have them shot to death. Eisenstein posits an interesting resolution to the seamen's direct challenge to authoritarian rule: use of the gun. However, the gun is wielded by human subjects who can be appealed to on ideological grounds of class solidarity. Shooting is a matter of conviction. Vokoulintchouk, one of the leaders of the rebellion on the ship, urges the riflemen to consider who they are going to fire upon ("Brothers, who are you going to shoot?"), and provides an alternative ("Come on, brothers, take up arms against these beasts"). The marines join the rebels, and together they secure control of the battleship. Officers are thrown overboard, but the rebels sustain an important loss—Vokoulintchouk is shot and killed: an officer pursues him and shoots him as he climbs onto a yardarm; he drops into the sea. That night, his body is taken ashore to Odessa and he becomes a martyr. The people of Odessa who had initiated their own rebellion against Tsarist rule begin converging on the harbor to pay their respects to the sailor and express their solidarity with the rebels. In the first half of the film, Eisenstein establishes two important themes: Class solidarity; and the legitimate right of the oppressed to use arms against those who have oppressed them.

These are themes he returns to in each of the remaining acts and they beg a much larger question, namely what conditions, if any, justify the use of arms? This is not a question Eisenstein confronts, for he asserts the right of the oppressed to bear arms in order to liberate themselves. But it is a question that troubled leaders of anti-colonial and social protest movements, such as Mahatma Ghandi in India and Martin Luther King in the United States, who offered *satyagraha* and peaceful civil disobedience as effective alternatives to armed confrontation.

If the use of the gun in Act I ignites a city against tyranny, the seizure of guns from the armory by the crew on the battleship in Act II signals that the momentum of power has shifted to the oppressed. Act III is Vokoulintchouk's appeal from the dead to his brothers to take up arms in revenge of his death—the commencement of the antithetical action. And Act IV is the epicenter of the film; the ultimate expression of *mise-en-scène,* and synthesis of the graphic and the expressive.[2] A resolution of the antagonism between Tsarist rulers and those oppressed by them is required; the scene at the Odessa steps which provides it compelled critics at the Brussels world's fair to declare *Battleship Potemkin* "the best film ever made." Here are exemplified both (a) the unity of the particular (the rebellion by the sailors and the citizens of Odessa) and the general (the 1905 Russian Revolution); and (b) pathos. Eisenstein uses structural and compositional movement to achieve audience participation and identification, and to heighten both emotional intensity (audience horror at the unprovoked massacre) and intellectual awareness (recognition of the legitimacy of the battleship guns being turned on the symbols of tyranny). Eisenstein acknowledges that this was consciously contrived and achieved through a number of means.[3]

The first part of the steps scene has an almost festive quality about it. The citizens of Odessa come to see and meet the heroes of the rebellion on board the battleship. Through a number of close-up shots, Eisenstein creates audience identification with individual citizens of Odessa. This mood is broken with the now famous title, "SUDDENLY," and Eisenstein introduces a close-up of a female student whose head is jerking violently as though by some force from behind. She is being shot (and being shot being shot). But what appears as a single filmic shot is in fact a series of four, brilliantly edited to break the festive mood and introduce the terror of the gun in the hands of the soldiers; in each shot the student's head is in a slightly different position. It is in the power of the gun—that is to say, the gun user—to fragment human action in a killing exactly in the way that Eisenstein here fragments the student's action by his editing. So his montage is itself a kind of "shooting."

The soldiers march rhythmically down the steps and begin firing into the crowd. Medium shots of the marching soldiers are cross-cut with long shots of the terrified crowd fleeing, and the rhythmic marching of soldiers is followed by static shots of soldiers firing on the defenseless citizens. The momentum of the crowd is broken into three cross-cutting lines of action. The first centers on a schoolteacher huddling with a group. The second focuses on a mother whose child has been shot. The third involves a mother with a baby in a carriage. The first two lines reverse the flow of action. The schoolteacher leads her group up the steps, appealing in vain to the soldiers to stop the massacre, and the mother carries her son up the stairs to confront the soldiers and is shot. The third line once again reverses the flow of action. The mother with the baby carriage is shot and the carriage bounds uncontrollably down the steps, amplifying the descent of the crowd. As the carriage gains momentum, Cossacks are shown attempting to divert the crowd, and Eisenstein uses a series of close-ups to once again alter pace and tempo. The schoolteacher's face is intercut with the carriage, and it is not clear that she is watching its descent. The carriage is up-ended, and a Cossack is shown slashing with his saber. The close-up of the Cossack gets closer, and the object of his attack becomes clear—we see the schoolteacher with her eye slashed out.

In the closing scene of Act IV, the massacre at the steps is replaced by the guns of the *Potemkin* trained on the military headquarters. The guns of the many are replaced by one gun. For the audience, psychologically, horror and terror are replaced with relief and a sense of social justice. As the cannons of the ship turn, Eisenstein utilizes a series of short shots to isolate the gestures of three cupid statues adorning a theater very close to the steps, using careful editing to suggest that they are in fact in flight from the impending explosions from the ship. After the blasts, Eisenstein uses three short shots to create the impression of a sculptured lion leaping to its feet. Reflecting on this symbolic pictorial expression, Eisenstein later commented that "the marble lion leaps up, surrounded by the thunder of *Potemkin's* guns firing in protest against the blood bath on the Odessa steps."[4] Once again, Eisenstein uses technique (isolation and intercutting of movement) to achieve his objective, grasping the audience intellectually and emotionally and shaking it into the realization of the depth of Tsarist oppression while simultaneously evoking sympathy for the oppressed. The very stones rise up.

Eisenstein was very critical of Dziga Vertov's theory of film, in which montage was a technique used to make "essentially-static shots simulate movement,"[5] not unlike the technique of rapidly flipping through a sequence of still images to obtain a simple sense of them moving in an animated fashion. For Eisenstein, the montage was more than a simulative technique; it was intended to "create" a movement that was not only kinetic but dynamic, not only physical but also political. The images used in the cutting were often disparate—like thesis and anti-thesis—and the rapid movement between them was synthetical in the sense that a meaning was created quite beyond the simple content of either original image. This is the nexus between the theory of the dialectic and his theory of film. It was purposeful in the extreme, and it is what made him a "political revolutionary filmmaker *par excellence.*"[6] Eisenstein was entirely conscious of remaking and reinterpreting reality via film composition. The latter involved the shot and its composition, and *mise-en-scène,* which Eisenstein saw as "a conscious and active remaking . . . of reality, not so much reality in general, but every single event and each specific fact."[7] *Mise-en-scène,* further, is:

> the graphic projection of the character of an event. In its parts, as much as in their combination, it is a graphic flourish in space. It is like handwriting on paper, or the impressions of feet made on a sandy path. It is so in all its pleni-

tude and incompleteness. . . . Character appears through action in movements (here we include in "action" words, voice, etc.). The path of movement is mise-en-scène.[8]

Mise-en-scène is about the depiction of reality through the fusion of the graphic and the expressive.[9] It involves using the isolating frame of the camera to take a social situation apart into fragments; and the technique of film editing to join fragments in such a way as to make a representation of a new "situation": reconstruction based on deconstruction. Eisenstein saw a political and a social event as a whole that was composed of several parts, which when separated and reassembled would impart new, perhaps contradictory, meanings and understanding. Deconstruction and reconstruction through montage are about revealing to audiences what is beneath the social surface, shaking the preconceived notions of audiences, replacing or at the very least challenging their reality with a coherently constructed alternative.

The act of seeing (by the audience), of imparting meaning (in the film) is mediated by what the director does—the shot and its framing. According to O'Pray, paradoxically, the idea that reality is a social construction, and as such indeterminable as meaning, rests on the highly-determined construction of the shot, and, most importantly, on the spectator seeing it as *"construction."*[10] The depiction of the constantly changing nature of social reality in film is, for Eisenstein, a function of the relationship between a director's political ideology and his theory of film:

> [Montage is the] destruction of the indefinite and neutral, existing 'in itself,' no matter whether it be an event or a phenomenon, and its reassembly in accordance with the idea dictated by attitude to this event or phenomenon, an attitude which, in turn, is determined by my ideology, my outlook, that is to say, our outlook. It is the moment that a living dynamic image takes the place of passive reproduction.[11]

For Eisenstein, therefore, the "shot" makes sense only when linked to other "shots" in a montage with purposeful intent; and film is made in "montage pieces, each of which provokes a certain association, the sum of which amounts to a composite complex of emotional feelings."[12] In *Battleship Potemkin*, Eisenstein carefully and deliberately constructs "shots" and creates montages that are informed by his ideology and his sense of social justice as well as by his desire to provoke a "composite complex of emotional feelings" among members of the audience.

Given that in any society the military, paramilitary and police forces are the only ones that have the legal right to use force, the audience is appalled when the military is deployed against its own citizenry in an indiscriminate fashion. Eisenstein skillfully leads the audience to the next quantum leap—the acceptance of revolutionary counterviolence which destroys property, not persons. The guns of the battleship are used to stop the massacre; the threat to the audience is thereby ended.

Transference and identification lead to a qualitatively new state—pathos. The audience accepts the gun as the symbol of simultaneous repression and liberation. If those wielding the gun are capable of massacring innocent civilians, then the guns of the *Potemkin* can justifiably be used to stop the senseless slaughter. Eisenstein does not use pathos in the traditional sense of "audience appeasement and conciliation," rather he has another purpose in mind—active audience participation and identification: "Pathos is what forces the viewer to jump out of his seat. It is what forces him to flee from his place. It is what forces him to clap, to cry out. . . . To be besides oneself is unavoidably also a transition to something else, to something different in quality, to something opposite to what preceded it."[13] Two options are open to the audience: they can be thoroughly repulsed by the gun and reject all forms of violence (leading to pacifism), or they can be seduced by the gun and accept its other possibilities (legitimate revolutionary counterviolence). If the first scenario prevails, then *Battleship Potemkin* ranks as the first anti-war film and *Gallipoli* (1981) walks in its wake. If the second scenario prevails, then *Battleship Potemkin* ranks as the first film to sanction the use of force to secure liberation from oppression.

The scene at the Odessa steps, therefore, is structured to bring the audience to the precipice and challenge it to make a leap to recognize the justness of revolutionary counterviolence. Pathos forces the audience to acutely and actively relive historical moments, to choose between the "many guns of the many soldiers" and the "one gun" of the rebels. Members of the audience are even forced to think about whether they can justify their choice, or whether they can justify not making a choice at all.

Interestingly, in his attempt to "create an artistic reality charged with a sense of immediate reality" in order that the audience experience the film as "bald fact," Eisenstein played loose with history. Hundreds of people were killed in the Odessa uprisings, but not all on the steps. As Eisenstein notes, the steps scene "was born in the instant of immediate contact." It was the very movement of the steps that gave birth to the idea of the scene, and that with its "'flight' aroused the fantasy of the director to a new 'spiraling.'"[14] The Odessa steps scene was not originally scripted; it was spontaneous and was born on location.

The continuous class struggle and the class-based usage of guns in *Battleship Potemkin* is highlighted by Eisenstein's typage, the use of an individual to signify a general character type. The officers on the deck of the battleship, with their refined features and sense of dress and decorum, represent the ruling classes, while the ship's rebels represent the oppressed. The purpose of typage is to move from the particular to the general, enabling Eisenstein to blend actors with non-actors, and the audience to step outside of the immediate action depicted on screen and focus on the broader context of the struggle between classes as represented by the types. Thus, when the gun is used by the characters representing the forces of repression, one set of emotions is unleashed, while an entirely different but nonetheless equally-orchestrated set of emotions is unleashed when the revolutionaries turn the ship's guns on the army barracks and on the other non-human symbols of the Tsar.

For Eisenstein, therefore, the gun is the common currency of the Tsarists and the sailors who fight against them. And the power of the gun is therefore linked to those he has cast in symbolic terms as representatives of rebellion or Tsarist rule. This gun symbolism finds its most heightened expression in the dialectical montage capturing the Odessa steps scene.

1900

The English title of Bertolucci's movie *1900* is a misnomer, because the Italian "Novocento" refers to the nineteen-*hundreds*. The film begins and ends on the day of Italy's liberation from fascism, April 25, 1945, and it chronicles Italy's history from 1900 (when Olmo and Alfredo, the two protagonists, are born) to the spring of 1945. Pre-World War II Italy was characterized by political instability, a huge and increasing national debt, rampant inflation, high unemployment, and a massive uprising in 1918 that was quashed but that only intensified the political instability of the country. It was in this period of national disillusionment that the nascent fascist movement of Mussolini was supported and harnessed (at least initially) by the landowners of the Po valley to combat the increasingly militant rural laborers. Bertolucci captures these political, social and economic forces in *1900*.

1900 can be understood on a number of levels. It can be seen as a simple allegory; as a Manichean parable; or as a fusion of contradictory elements (what Eisenstein called the juxtaposition of thesis and antithesis) that has a dramatic impact on the audience. Bertolucci expresses this fusion as the joining of: form and content; politics and art; Hollywood money and radical politics; big-name actors with peasants; spontaneity and structure; individual personalities and typage; and fiction and documentary.

Bertolucci structures the film in four segments/seasons. Olmo Dalco (Gérard Depardieu), the representative/symbol of the Italian peasantry, and Alfredo Berlinghieri (Robert De Niro), the representative of the Italian landed gentry, experience their childhood in the summer. Their relationship of mutual dependence, friendship and class antagonism is still nascent, but it is beginning to develop. Summer draws to a close when Olmo marries Anita Foschi (Stefania Sandrelli), a militant schoolteacher, and Alfredo marries Ada Fiastri Paulhan (Dominique Sanda), an urbane bourgeoise woman who prefers to remain "blind" to the atrocities committed by the fascists. But summer really ends when the peasants increasingly challenge the power of the landlords, who look to the fascist "black shirts" to quell the peasant uprising. Autumn signals the arrival of the fascists.

The landlords, says Bertolucci, feared the militancy of the peasants and thus "created fascism. In a sequence in the first part, for instance, a group of landlords and hunters meet, not by accident, in a church, and it is here, also not by chance, that the fascist squad receives its first financial support."[15] Like Eisenstein, Bertolucci was signifying what he saw as the relationship between the forces of repression and the Church (see the portrayal of the sycophantic priest on the deck of the *Potemkin* when the captain gives the orders to shoot the rebellious sailors). The relationship between fascism and the Roman Catholic Church was cemented in the Lateran Agreement (signed in 1929), which turned Italy into a confessional state.

One of the two most moving and memorable scenes in the film comes at the end of Autumn. Some of Anita's students—old men—are burned to death when the fascists led by Attila (Donald Sutherland) set fire to the People's Center. Their funeral procession in the village square signals the triumph of barbarism, fascism and violence. By winter, Attila has become the archetypical fascist and his friends have ascended to the throne. Here, the gun plays a seminal role. It is the power of the gun unleashed by the fascists that represses and massacres the peasants who resist fascist rule. The peasants had confronted the guns of the army before the birth of fascism and had succeeded in large measure because of the courage of women who used their bodies to block the path of the soldiers on horseback. This time, however, the fascist army is brutal.

The gun is also significant since the fascists use it to frame Olmo and drive him into the underground, where he joins the partisan forces aiming to liberate the peasants from the grip of fascism. With the arrival of spring comes that liberation and the most controversial scene in the film. The peasants take Alfredo prisoner and seize control of his estate. Olmo returns from hiding, and the partisans and the peasants make a common cause. A sign on one of the farm buildings reads "Ende," signifying the formal end of the film.

But the film has not ended; spontaneity takes over. Bertolucci allows the non-actor peasant cast members to take control of the film—as he believes they did in history, now portraying the peasants as protagonists and allowing Olmo and Alfredo to recede into the background (reduced as both are to "types" in the Eisensteinian sense). The peasants, with encouragement from the director, take charge of the film. Their creativity "became a real cultural proposal opposite to the basic culture of the rest of the movie. In the last half-hour, there is the illusion of revolution, and I think it is the very best part of the movie."[16] The peasants celebrate; they unfurl red flags long buried, posters of Stalin appear, symbols of the Italian Communist Party abound, and they sing, dance and eat. The celebration ironically ends when a partisan unit appears and asks them to turn in their weapons; the guns that liberated them are now appropriated.

Like Eisenstein, Bertolucci justifies revolutionary counterviolence because of its noble purpose (liberation from oppression). The audience is repeatedly subjected to the horrors and the atrocities committed by the fascists, for example, the shooting of the peasants in the town square; the brutal murder of landlords who opposed fascist rule; the rape and killing of a child in a cave by a number of Black Shirts. The destruction of fascism by any means, therefore, is a welcomed relief; there is an ideological justification for the use of the gun.

The liberation the peasants experience is real and utopian, real in the sense that it is liberation from fascism and utopian in the sense that the peasants really believed that socialism had arrived. As Bertolucci says: "Spring, the last season of the film, corresponds to Liberation Day, April 25, 1945. Liberation Day: liberation not only from Nazi fascism, but from all forms of exploitation. That's how I tried to show the 25th of April, as a moment of victory and also a moment in the peasants' dream. On Liberation Day, the peasants enact the utopia of revolution."[17] The duality of reality and utopia is captured when the peasants say, with a tinge of irony, "The landlord is dead, but we won't kill him because he is the living proof that he is dead." Fascism was defeated, but capitalism survived. The peasants are left with a fleeting sense of euphoria. This is the second ending of the film.

A third ending comes on the heels of this scene of spontaneity, when the individual protagonists reappear. Olmo and Alfredo are depicted as old men who continue to fight with each other (representing the continuation of the class struggle after liberation), until Alfredo places himself on the train tracks to commit suicide. As Bertolucci notes, "This is the moment when the boss understands that there is nothing else that he can do to change what's going on. The bourgeoisie is self-destructive . . . What happens next? The train about to run over Alfredo is the children's train, the grown-up Alfredo becomes the boy Alfredo, and Olmo is on the train."[18] The train was for Bertolucci what the battleship was for Eisenstein. Both were instruments of change; both represented the ultimate empowerment of the dispossessed, the oppressed and the exploited; both symbolized new beginnings.

CONCLUSION

Both Eisenstein and Bertolucci unashamedly championed the cause of socialism. Both depicted the plight of the oppressed. Both used the film medium to skillfully manipulate the audience by way of creating pathos. Both put the dialectic to tremendous use in their respective films to get the audience emotionally and intellectually involved as active participants who question the conditions under which the use of guns can be justified. Given their preoccupations and the contexts they sought to depict, it would not be fair to suggest that they ought to have been occupied with a question that genuinely plagues us in the 1990s, "Should guns be banned?" Such a question would not have even entered their minds because it would not have been self-evident to them that the presence of weapons in the hands of an oppressed citizenry—rather than only in the possession of a controlling State—was a social problem. For Eisenstein, the reality from the Russian people's point of view—and for Bertolucci, from the Italian peasants'—was powerlessness, which can be seen as a state of being in which guns, and all other technological ways to power, have already been banned. The power of the oppressor derives from his capacity to use his weapons to oppress the masses through the maintenance of a general state of threat. The corollary of this, that both Eisenstein and Bertolucci posit, therefore, is that the empowerment of the oppressed, to begin to take control of their material circumstances and end their oppression, must, of necessity, involve using their numbers, and using tools and machines, including the gun. Anything less than that is asking the oppressed to either voluntarily commit suicide (as they challenge the powerful), or to acquiesce in their continued oppression.

NOTES

[1] Sergei Eisenstein, *The Battleship Potemkin* (London, Faber and Faber, 1989), 7.

[2] Arun Khopkar, "Graphic Flourish: Aspects of the Art of *Mise-en-scène*," in Ian Christie and Richard Taylor, eds., *Eisenstein Rediscovered* (London: Routledge, 1993), 152.

[3] "The Realist Manifesto," cited by Vladimir Petric, *The Man with the Movie Camera* (Cambridge: Cambridge University Press, 1987), 5.

4   Eisenstein, cited by David Bordwell, *The Cinema of Eisenstein* (Cambridge, MA: Harvard University Press, 1993), 77.

5   Eisenstein cited by Petric, *Man,* 49.

6   Michael O'Pray, "The Frame and Montage in Eisenstein's Later Aesthetics," in Christie and Taylor, *Eisenstein,* 211.

7   Eisenstein cited by Petric, *Man,* 49.

8   Eisenstein, cited by Khopkar, "Aspects," 152.

9   Khopkar, "Aspects," 152.

10   O'Pray, "Frame," 214.

11   Eisenstein, cited by O'Pray, "Frame," 214.

12   Eisenstein, cited by Bordwell, *Cinema,* 72.

13   Eisenstein, cited by Bordwell, *Cinema,* 193.

14   Eisenstein, cited by Standish Dyer Lawder, "Eisenstein and Constructivism," in P. Adams Sitney, *The Essential Cinema, Vol. I* (New York: New York University Press, 1975), 72.

15   Bertolucci interviewed by G. Di Bernardo, "Red Flags and American Dollars," an interview with Bertolucci (n.p., n.d.).

16   Bertolucci interview with Di Bernardo.

17   Bertolucci interviewed by F. Di Vico F. & R. Degni, "The Poetry of Class Struggle," an interview with Bertolucci (n.p., n.d.).

18   Bertolucci interview with Di Vico and Degni.

Mighty Morphin' Four-Year-Olds: Heroes and Gunplay at Preschool

Ellen Seiter

Media and toys permeate the world of young children. Popular characters—and their weapons—are introduced into classrooms through play, through show and tell, and through the use of videotape in the classroom/day care centers—a practice that has become more widespread and more frequent over the last two decades. Day care centers have now become, in fact, a target of marketers who have more trouble locating children than they did thirty or forty years ago because children today spend more time in institutionalized settings at earlier ages, less time at home, and less time with broadcast TV.

Action/adventure stories featuring superhero characters and the various weapons deployed in their fight to save the world from villains form a big part of children's media worlds. Because popular media have penetrated the preschool and day care center, women who care for small children in these settings are on the front lines of the problems around socialization and violence, and of media literacy and education.

Since the outbreak of school shootings in the United States, most notably and especially those in Littleton, Colorado, a new wave of alarmism over media violence informs discussions of schools and socialization by journalists and politicians. From the mainstream press to the local PTA newsletter, public handwringing over childhood socialization and violence is everywhere.

My research has investigated what preschool teachers and caregivers think about children's experiences with media, through interviews, and observations of children's classroom play that references mass media and marketing. Let me begin by sharing some of the teachers' feelings about violence and children's media.

Head Start teacher:

> In the past couple of years, with some programs that have come on, the spillover into the classroom has been horrific. One in particular is *Power*

Rangers. This fall because out of 17 I had 11 boys—we finally had to talk about it in the classroom. And in my classroom there's never guns. We don't pretend guns. That's my personal thing. I always explain to them what your rules are at home that's fine. And I talk to them about it so that they understand that you know guns hurt and guns kill, or they kill animals. They are used for hunting. I just don't like them used for play. That's my personal bias. I don't put it on them that it's good or bad, you know. But that's, I won't, that isn't allowed in my room.

Teacher at a Fundamentalist church nursery:

I think they used to have Halloween parties until this certain person had a child in preschool and she had it changed that year. (On the grounds that Halloween is a pagan holiday.) They still wanted to have a party but they had a cowboy-cowgirl. They said that was really hard, too, because the cowboys wanted to bring their guns, and they couldn't have guns, so we just changed it back this year.

Montessori teacher:

I've seen this with some of the boys with guns, too. They are dying for the guns, so sometimes I just tell the parents, Let them earn some money and let them go buy a simple gun, and you might find it goes away. And it often does. With males, it's just as bad. They're perpetuating the macho, and the violence, and all the things that separate and make them not human beings as a whole but keeping this going. Advertising's probably as bad as anything, more so perhaps than the programming itself, especially with the marketing to teenagers. It's awful.

[Our policy is] no weapons. They can't even shoot with their fingers. That's how strict we are in this school. We don't allow any of this kind of stuff. They have a Lego work bench and they may make them and I just say, No weapons. And they accept it. We don't have any problems with this. Maybe once every few weeks, I'll have someone over there making a gun. And then, they know me well enough, they'll say, Oh, it's not a gun, it's a ladder or a chair! Or turn it the other way. I always say that this is in the school. It's up to your parents to decide what you can do at home. And then they understand that quite well. And I'm not proclaiming all their values for them. When you teach children for three years, the classroom culture is perpetuated by the oldest children, so the kids just know this. It's just like osmosis or something. I don't even tell them these things most of the time. An older child will come along and say, You know, you can't make guns in this school. You can't do that. And they'll say, Oh, OK, OK. Thanks for telling me.

There is broader general consensus around the harmfulness of toy guns than most adults realize. In the small midwestern city in the U.S. where this research was carried out, every school or day care center I contacted had a no-weapons policy. Nearly all teachers we interviewed, however, believed their school or classroom was somewhat unique for banning toy weapons. Toys 'R' Us responded to protests and boycotts in the early 1990s by banning toy guns from its shelves and the toy industry has responded by modifying weapons. These days it can be rather difficult to find toy guns that shoot bullets. On television, cartoonists have replaced six-shooters—in a move explicitly designed by program creators to appease parents—with elaborate ray guns (starting with the Ghostbusters and their vacuum back-pack shooters), flying objects; "Eastern" weaponry, and combination animal/vehicle/weapons, as with Power Ranger Zords.

Societal concern about guns and violent death has led to a special categorization of toy weapons as impermissible for fantasy—a recent development in the history of childhood. Research on young children's understandings of television that claims children have difficulty distinguishing fantasy from reality has reinforced adults' anxiety over gunplay. Thus gunplay has increasingly been singled out as beyond the pale.

Overall, it would be fair to say that all those interviewed in my study, from those doing family day care in their own home to those employed by the corporate chain Kindercare, were concerned about the effects on children of screen violence. It is significant, however, that the teachers most unfamiliar with television estimated its effects to be the greatest and most derogatory—and tended to report that children do not speak with them about TV. Adults were most worried about media that they were unfamiliar with. Teachers who watched the most TV were the least worried and tended to believe, and give anecdotes to support, children's ability to distinguish TV and reality. Teachers more familiar with *X-Men* (1992) and *Mighty Morphin' Power Rangers* (1993) thought of effects as less negative; and also reported having more conversations with children about the media.[1] It was extremely common for female teachers to be completely unfamiliar with the television programs or video games that the boys loved and were themselves so expert in re-creating. Frequently teachers claimed never to have seen a single episode of *Power Rangers*, for example—and yet seem absolutely certain of its deleterious effect on children.

Teachers in our study reported high levels of gender segregation in their classrooms and on their playgrounds. Children's play with television and film references reinforces this: with girls tending to play games based on Disney film characters—Princess Jasmine from *Aladdin* (1992); Beauty from *Beauty and the Beast* (1991); Ariel from *The Little Mermaid* (1989)—films usually familiar to the teachers. Though these licensed characters seem to be new, the plots girls generated tend to be highly similar to traditional forms of "playing house." The teachers rarely complained about girls' play: it was seen as unproblematic, except for its reinforcement of narcissism, and girls often played secretly, out of adults' earshot. Physical fighting and fake gunplay were nonexistent in the melodramatic stories girls preferred.

Boys, on the other hand, tended to focus on superhero shows such as *Power Rangers* and *X-Men*. Their fan interest in these forms was frequently identified as a problem: boys' media play was deemed obsessive by many teachers, who worried that boys were so locked in these action adventure worlds from film/TV and video games that they were incapable of conversing about anything else. Most of boys' playground games involved (imagined) weaponry, in open violation of school rules. Teachers defined boys' play as disruptive: kids' martial arts moves tended to knock over chairs or leave other children hurt. Thus not only were weapons (lasers, nunchucks, zords, etc.) banned—some schools banned all mention of the TV and film superheroes.

Against this background, I turn now to a project designed by one of the schools I studied as an intervention into the effects of screen violence.[2] These teachers decided that rather than battle with children over the presence of superheroes at school, they would invite the superheroes in. A Visiting Artist in the School grant was secured to help children learn how to draw their own superheroes. These drawings would, it was hoped, lead to stories about the superheroes, and then a collaborative script for a play the class could stage as a whole.

From the beginning, when the teachers first asked the group at circle time to define superheroes, themes of violence were uppermost on the children's and the teachers' minds. Everyone knew that superheroes were a subject usually objected to by teachers, and that the boys would be the authorities on this particular subject. (No girls participated in this discussion, for example.)

TEACHER: Tell me a little bit about a superhero, what is a superhero?

Z.: ... they rescue people, they're supposed to rescue people ...

TEACHER: Why do they do that? How do they rescue people? Who are some superheroes that you can think of in your mind?

J.: They're cartoons.

Z.: They're comics.

TEACHER: Am I a superhero? Cause I help people sometimes, when they're hanging from the monkey bars and they're like "Help" and I go save them. Does that make me a superhero?

CHILDREN IN CHORUS: Noooooo!

TEACHER: What is a superhero?

D.: Like Superman.

TEACHER: And who else?

R.: That's a cartoon and Spiderman's a cartoon.

TEACHER: Are there only two superheroes?

J.: Power Rangers.

Z.: I thought those were too violent.

TEACHER: Tell me the ones that you think are violent. First of all what does violent mean?

Z.: Too much killing and fighting.

TEACHER: So you say the Power Rangers are violent and who else?

J.: Superman.

TEACHER: Superman is violent?

Z.: He kills bad guys . . .

D.: No, he kills monsters . . .

Z.: Well, Power Rangers not Superman . . .

D.: But they also kill Putties (Power Ranger villains) and they also kill big bugs. *(He gets up and excitedly demonstrates kicks—and one of the teachers pulls him back to sitting in her lap.)*

TEACHER: All right, well, I have some more questions. Can you think of other superheroes that are violent besides the Power Rangers?

J.: *Double Dragons.*

TEACHER: Is that on TV or—

J.: Yeah.

TEACHER: . . . or is it a book?

J.: It used to be on TV.

TEACHER: Say it again? *(J. is silent.)* So what do they do? Did you ever watch it? No?

J. *(defensive)*: I don't know. How am I supposed to know? I didn't see the movie.

TEACHER: Did you ever watch it?

J.: NO . . .

TEACHER: Now let's hear about the superheroes that you don't think are violent.

Silence

TEACHER: So do superheroes—do they ever die?

Z.: Not really.

TEACHER: What happens if they got shot at?

Z.: They still don't. They have special heavy duty costumes . . .

This discussion focused early on about superheroes as violent. It is characterized by a wariness on the part of most of the children, who know more than they are willing to say. The boy identified as J, for example, seemed reluctant to participate and to admit to TV watching, as evidenced by his introduction of *Double Dragon* (1993) and then retreated from admission of any knowledge about it.

Immediately afterwards, children were directed to an art activity where paper, pens, crayons and special markers were provided and kids encouraged to create their own superheroes. Here the teachers' enthusiastic message to the kids was: Make your own superhero! Do anything you want! Tell us your own story about them! Let your imaginations run wild. After the drawing phase, children were interviewed about their drawings and encouraged to make stories about their characters.

The adults hoped to get sweet, innocent stories that were unfettered by the drive to sell toys and videos and candy, that portrayed just heroes who "used their words"—as preschool children are so often admonished to do—instead of violence, and offered positive role models for girls and children of color.

Instead, they got drawings of popular superheroes such as Batman, Spiderman, and others. They got white male superheroes. And they got heroes who were very quick to kick, kill, and shoot. From the girls they got princesses and kitties and glitter superheroes—creations that the boys did not recognize as belonging to the genre at all. Once a boy leaned over to look at a girl's drawing and complained: "That's not a superhero! Superheroes are not like that!" But he was sternly corrected, saying the girl could do anything she wanted to do. Here, a miscommunication arises where the boy is accurately reporting his knowledge of the genre, but is told he is wrong because he is being unsupportive of a classmate.

The violence in the boys' stories really worried the teachers, and seemed utterly unsuitable for transforming into a class play:

> I was with my brother Matthew and we were making a snowman at my house. The superheroes came in and they killed my brothers and my father. The superhero was mad about the candy. A blow pop. It was cherry. The superhero said "it's bad candy." And we said "it's good candy." I opened it, and I put it in my mouth, and bit it, and the superhero cried.

> The superhero saw a big spider that was bigger than a meteor. So he flew up and he went into the spider's mouth. The spider choked and he threw up and the superhero jumped out. He put his foot up and flew up. Then he saw some Putties kicking trees. And the superhero threw one of them on his back and another one into a tree. and he spun out of control and stopped before he could explode. A bunch of putties were kicking but he made friends with them by giving them chocolate cupcakes.

> Tokoman shoots rays that hurt. Different Tokomens shoot different colors. This one shoots blue. Everytime it gets a ray it gets bigger.

One study of boys' and girls' stories at four years of age found that the girls and boys had different forms of imagination, different images of social life, and different ways of coming to grips with reality.[3] The boys' stories tended to be characterized by violence, disruption and disorder. They were never set in the home, relied on fighting and destruction, were chaotic and anarchic, and use startling and disruptive imagery. It is interesting to note that such characteristics might be applied to the entire genre of action/adventure film and television—and most media forms which prominently feature guns.

Now that school shootings have captured headlines, it is going to be imperative to engage more fully in a discussion of distinctions between fantasies of violence and domination that fall within the norm of kids exposed to popular culture and the kinds of fantasies that are indicative of deeply disturbed boys contemplating violent acts and deeply engaged with fascist, racist or misogynist ideologies. The wave of shooting sprees by children and teens makes it all the more necessary to assert the difference between these levels of fantasy, rather than promote a blanket censorship of all violence or weapon-related play.

The boys' stories also evidenced a great deal of concern with changing colors: their casting of heroes and villains replicated the racial stereotyping that is also conventional to the genre. In one conversation over a drawing, for example, a boy explained:

BOY: I'm making micros.

TEACHER: Is that a kind of superhero?

BOY: Yeah, they're like adventure heroes.

TEACHER: What kinds of adventures?

BOY: They take adventures to find bad guys and fight them.

TEACHER: Hmmm, how do they find a bad guy?

BOY: When I find one.

TEACHER: How do you know somebody's a bad guy?

BOY: When they're different colors.

TEACHER: I never thought about that . . . what kind of colors do the bad guys have?

BOY: I haven't drawn them yet so I haven't figured out yet.

This boy was Anglo and normally very articulate, but the teacher found the racist undertones too disturbing to pursue any further in their conversation.

The girls produced stories that pleased the teachers: orderly, moral and family based. The girls' stories evidence traces of film and television influences, too, but they draw from a different set of genres and stories.

The Diamond superhero family has a ship. They have a sparkle ship with purple sails. They are taking an adventure to the Sugar Plum Fairy's castle. They're going to visit the Sugar Plum Fairy to ask her for some of her bags of sugar. They're going for kids. And then the ship crashed on their way back into the blue whale. The whale accidentally ate them.

The superheroes saved a kid out of a fire. They flew in the window of the house and flew back out. They saved the teacher. She had a baby in her stomach and they had to get her the nurse. They flew her to the nurse and took her to the door. The baby came out and they went home. Everyone was fine.

In an interview over her drawing of two superheroes, one girl explained:

GIRL: They always are sisters and they never die.

TEACHER: Are they superheroes?

GIRL: Yeah.

TEACHER: What kind of superpowers do they have?

GIRL: They save people all the time.

TEACHER: So babies can go save people?

GIRL: Yeah only if they're really really good at it.

TEACHER: If the babies are good at saving people?

GIRL *(nods unconvincingly then adds)*: Only if they're really good.

TEACHER: Oh they only save really good people.

GIRL: Yeah.

Girls were also capable of telling violent weapon-filled stories, but their characters were still enmeshed in family relationships:

> The pink superhero always kills a bad guy that has a knife. She kicks him and puts him away. The little sister superhero always hates the bad guy and kicks him like her big sister. She got a knife and killed him. The sister has knives and the baby has knives, too. Theresa the Mom has a knife and killed the bad guy. The Dad has a knife, too, he kills the bad guy. He hits them.

Stories such as these shocked and dismayed the teachers, who began to wonder if they had gotten into more than they could handle in the classroom. At the next circle time, the teachers asked the children to adjust their stories so that their characters would follow the school rules: no weapons, no one should get hurt. After that, many boys lost interest in the process. One boy started creating characters like "Poo-Poo Man," and refusing to share his pictures with the teacher. Through a process of backtracking and editing, the teacher went back over the children's stories (which had been translated into storyboard form). She asked the children for compromises, for ways of telling the same story without the violence. But it turned out to be very difficult to tell good action stories without bad guys, without supernatural elements, and without "magical agents"—usually weapons.

In the end, the teachers settled on a story that was an amalgam of several children's different stories. They allowed some disguised weaponry, such as shooting magic force fields from their fingers, and introduced violent threat through natural disasters (meteors and volcanic eruptions)—thus depersonalizing evil. Here is the text of the superhero play staged by the class:

Once upon a time a girl named Spike went to the store. She was at the window and she saw some superheroes. They were flying. Then Spike saw a robber . . . then the superheroes came in the window . . . and they talked to the robber. And the superheroes went back in the air. Then the ground started to shake. It was a volcano. The volcano erupted. Then the superheroes saved the store. They got a thousand camels and a thousand horses and pulled the store and the teacher away.

The teacher was on a field trip with the kids and the kids were about to get hurt by the volcano. Then the superheroes put a force field out around the kids and the teacher . . . and then after that the volcano blew up and it left a big hole in the roof of the store. Then the superheroes put an invisible force field that was like magic with their fingers around the whole earth because a meteor was about to hit it. And the meteor bounced off the force field, hit the superheroes in the head, and was destroyed.

By the day of the performance, however, teachers had to drag many of the boys to participate. What had begun as sometimes secretive playground fun with taboo characters had become an organized event. The teachers wanted something creative, different from TV, but in many ways they simply exchanged one form of TV imitation for another, in that this plot strongly resembled the *Magic School Bus* (1994) episode which had been shown to the children that same month.

CONCLUSIONS

What can we learn from the Superhero Project about tackling these issues with young children? Why would we want to keep trying? Education scholar Anne Haas Dyson has studied the use of superhero stories (*X-Men*, *Power Rangers*, and the like) in literacy education at a racially integrated, third-grade classroom in Oakland, California. Dyson articulates the position in favor of teachers' openness to popular culture in the classroom this way.

. . . a curriculum must be undergirded by a belief that meaning is found, not in artifacts themselves, but in the social events through which those artifacts are produced and used. Children have agency in the construction of their own imaginations—not unlimited, unstructured agency, but, nonetheless, agency: they appropriate cultural material to participate in and explore their worlds, especially through narrative play and story. Their attraction to particular media programs and films suggests that they find in that material compelling and powerful images. If official curricula make no space for this agency, then schools risk reinforcing societal divisions in children's orientation to each other, to cultural art forms, and to school itself.[4]

Television is cheap, easy, plentiful, and children love to watch it. It is also pathologized—often unreasonably—by those with the most invested in status distinctions. Dyson's work suggests that if superheroes are brought into the classroom in a more open way they can help build literacy skills, boost the store of children's knowledge, and provide a language for talking about conflicts related to gender and race dynamics, rather than suppressing them.

In the Superhero Project, there were complex dynamics of race, class, generation and gender underlying the conversations about media. White female teachers interacted with boys who were avid fans of the genre and were Japanese, African American, Puerto Rican, Korean. Talking about superheroes can lead into discussions of the ways villainy is racialized in action adventure stories—as in the discussion with the Anglo boy about bad guys who were "different colors." Among themselves, the boys often used such story conventions to interact, despite language barriers or mutual suspicions. With the teachers, the boys sometimes used discussions of superheroes to express hostile feelings about being under control. In one of the discussions the African American boy who mentioned *Double Dragon* told the teacher that if superheroes came to school they would be bigger in stature than she, wouldn't need to learn anything from teachers, and could do whatever he wanted.

Superheroes represent an area of knowledge where boys are usually more expert than their female teachers. This requires sensitivity to the dilemma of the child knowing a lot about a subject normally considered taboo by his adult caretakers. The primary flaw with this project was that superheroes were not really welcome in the classroom because they were considered objectionable by the teachers: so they were invited in but rapidly censured.

The teachers had hoped to get girls involved, but throughout the discussions girls were silent. When the boys objected that superheroes were not the way girls were drawing them, a peculiar conflict emerged. When the boys accurately reproduced genre rules (including gender stereotyping), the teachers discredited their knowledge. In fact, the boys understood superheroes and the conventions of the genre better than teachers. This is one of the issues that must be appreciated for its unusual reversal of roles in the classroom whenever media literacy projects are embarked upon.

I worry that in the wake of the Littleton massacre, projects such as this one will no longer be funded. Many teachers will decide that the safest route is to avoid explicit discussions of popular culture forms and fantasies that include violence or the fascination with weapons and guns. Teachers and parents around the United States and Canada who do tackle these issues will of necessity need to educate students about mental illness, depression and psychoses. In the long run, serious psychoses are, after all, more significant factors in producing murderers than any amount of media violence.

That curriculum is for public health experts to develop. Media critics can help promote a curriculum that targets racial and gender stereotyping in action/adventure genres. Such lessons are needed now more than ever.

Superheroes should not be banned from school and children should not be shamed for their interest in them. Children find superheroes very compelling and powerful. Their attraction to them can't be dismissed as brainwashing. There is a lot of genuine imagination and exploration going on in the way kids use superheroes in play and storytelling.

Superheroes on TV are especially popular with low income children and children of color—despite the racial stereotyping. Teachers need to think of ways to capitalize on children's love of superheroes by drawing them into writing activities. The stereotyping in the programs should be openly discussed and debated. TV is not going away: it is completely embedded in everyday life.[5] Even children whose parents ban TV find out about TV characters and play the games on the playground. It's much more realistic to discuss and learn about TV than to avoid it.

When thinking about violence, weapons and children's media, it is important to remember that children were hitting, shoving, pushing and fighting on playgrounds long before *Power Rangers*. Children have angry, violent fantasies, and rebellious feelings towards their adult caretakers with or without TV. Let's be sure we don't portray TV as the root of all evil. It's easy to blame the media for society's failures. However, superhero violence provides a very poor explanatory system for real life violence. Media effects pale by comparison with poverty, child abuse, the proliferation of guns, inadequate health care (including mental health for parents), neglect, and substance abuse. Let's keep this in mind as we begin to think in new ways about how to make best use of the popular culture surrounding our children.

NOTES

[1]   Ellen Seiter, *Television and New Media Audiences* (Oxford: Oxford University Press, forthcoming 1999).

[2]   The Superhero Project was made possible by a grant from the Indiana Arts Council. I wish to thank Katy Pastel, Laura Ballard and Bobbie Spencer for their leadership on this project and their generous assistance to me.

[3]   Angeliki Nicolopoulou, Barbara Scales, and Jeff Weintraub, "Gender Differences and Symbolic Imagination in the Stories of Four-Year-Olds," in Anne Dyson and Celia Genishi, eds., *The Need for Story: Cultural Diversity in Classroom and Community* (Urbana, IL: National Council of Teachers of English, 1994), 102–123.

[4]   Anne Haas Dyson, *Writing Superheroes: Contemporary Childhood, Popular Culture and Classroom Literacy* (New York: Teachers' College Press, 1997), 181.

[5]   Ellen Seiter, *Sold Separately: Children and Parents in Consumer Culture* (New Brunswick NJ: Rutgers University Press, 1993).

The Wonderful, Horrible Films of Paul Verhoeven

Dan Streible

Can a contemporary Hollywood movie traffic in both Nazi iconography and fascistic philosophy and still pass as harmless entertainment, noted only for its great special effects and its use of more rounds of ammunition than any film in history? And is the presence of "men with guns" a required signifier for a film either to encourage a fascist point of view or to be symptomatic of a culture listing to the right?

Such questions were raised in 1997 with the well-hyped release of Paul Verhoeven's $100 million adaptation of Robert A. Heinlein's 1959 "classic" science fiction novel *Starship Troopers*.[1] All of the films Verhoeven has directed since his arrival in Hollywood have generated controversy. His work has alarmed cultural guardians with its extraordinary levels of gruesome violence (*Robocop* [1987], *Total Recall* [1990]) and graphic sexual exhibition (*Basic Instinct* [1992], *Showgirls* [1995]). Comparatively, however, *Starship Troopers* received only a modicum of critical chastisement. This despite the fact that—in addition to the gory, flesh-ripping gunplay—the film offers up what its producers called a "fascist utopia."[2] Its top-gun, teenage warrior-heroes are showcased in a glossy display, steeped in Nazi aesthetics. They embrace a rousing militarism that deems democracy a failure and a martial State a success. Our young S.S. Troopers casually but willfully endorse the ideals of the Federation that teaches them "violence is the supreme authority." In short, under Verhoeven's helm, the position affirmed by all of the principal characters fails to differentiate itself sufficiently from, say, the ideology espoused by a certain well-known mustachioed orator captured on film in Nuremberg in September of 1934. A major studio release that doesn't just allude to, but looks, talks, and walks like Leni Riefenstahl's *Triumph of the Will* (1935)?

The release of *Starship Troopers* prompts a renegotiation of the critical debate around the issue of incipient fascism in contemporary Hollywood cinema. The film also represents a distressing shift in the ability of Paul Verhoeven to intervene from within the system as a potent postmodernist making blockbusters that knowingly ridicule the violent, action extravaganza mentality. Rather than critiquing such projects, *Starship Troopers* falls into a political incoherence that potentially enables viewers to entertain the idea of a fascistic military state as a viable future. While the machine gun and other instruments of firepower are fetishized in the imagery of this high-tech movie, men with guns do not necessarily rule the day. The "Morita"[3] rifles the troopers wield against hostile alien insects allow them to display a degree of bravado and power on the battlefield, but their guns do not win the war. In a cinematic age in which Texas-sized meteorites bombard the earth, guns ultimately become a symbol of impotence rather than power. However, in *Starship Troopers* this decline of the gun's dominion does not indicate a failing of the future warrior State. Rather, the film suggests that power lingers on even when weaponry fails, deriving from the lens of a camera rather than the barrel of a gun. The power of fascist force comes less from its military superiority than from its ability to captivate minds with its commanding, monumental imagery, its corporative ability to create group-think.

Given the troubling political implications of *Starship Troopers*, I'd like to examine how such a film came to be, how it was positioned for reception and how it was received. My conclusions are based on an examination of movie trade journals, promotional materials, journalistic reviews, and on-line discussions—both critical and fan-based. As secondary resources, I consider *Starship Troopers* in the light of what critical film studies have previously suggested about cinema and fascism. The key text remains Susan Sontag's 1974 essay "Fascinating Fascism," which sought to define the aesthetic markers that abetted fascist, or at least Nazi, art as evident in the work of Leni Riefenstahl.[4]

Also important is the way in which Verhoeven figures into the symptomatic readings of key films from Reagan-era Hollywood, particularly readings by critics such as Robin Wood, Michael Ryan, Douglas Kellner, David Denby, Susan Jeffords, Stephen Prince and others. They have noted how both patently conservative films (*Red Dawn* [1984], *Rambo* [1985], *Conan the Barbarian* [1981], *Predator* [1987]) and mainstream fantasies (the *Star Wars* [1977-1983], *Rocky* [1976-1985], and *Indiana Jones* [1981-1989] series) revealed tendencies that had disturbing parallels with fascist culture. "Vengeful patriotism, worship of the male torso," "military spectacle" and weapons of overkill were making U.S. commercial cinema into a showcase for what J. Hoberman called in 1985 "The Fascist Guns in the West."[5] In the decade following, Hollywood continued in a similar vein, with big-budget spectacles ranging from Bruce Willis action pictures to jingoistic sci-fi shootouts like *Independence Day* (1996). Yet cries of fascism diminished in critical circles. This was also a period when Verhoeven directed his acclaimed *Robocop* (1987) and the dense, complex *Total Recall* (1990)—two conspicuous blockbusters that retained big guns and special effects while seeming to subvert the political inflections of the genre.

Given this context, the contradictions of *Starship Troopers* require explanation. How did a Hollywood film with such in-your-face fascist imagery appear at a time when, judging from prevailing trends in critical discourse, quasi-fascist tendencies in popular cinema had diminished? And does not the film undo Verhoeven's previous reputation as a thoughtful if audacious social commentator?

We must begin by reading *Starship Troopers* as part of the "wonderful, horrible" films of Paul Verhoeven. I appropriate the title of Ray Müller's insightful documentary film about Leni Riefenstahl because as an enigma Verhoeven seems parallel to her: an *auteur* full of self-contradiction whose work invites polarizing analyses, an artist who avows provocative artistic creation while disavowing political intention or social responsibility.[6] In the 1990s, Verhoeven became a *bête noire*, a director whose horrible excesses pushed the limits of MPAA-approved violence and sex. Yet his films remained wonderful enough—in box office terms and in stylistic distinctiveness—to keep him on the major studios' A-list. In the 1980s, he also was lauded by analysts of pop culture politics. Retaining the edge of his Dutch films, Verhoeven was credited with critiquing the retrograde aspects of the Hollywood action blockbuster by making ultraviolent, effects-laden fantasies that ridiculed the conservative, militaristic ethos of Rambo and his cohort. If Sylvester Stallone could blow away his enemy with force of arms, Verhoeven would paint a world in which everyone was subject to gunfire. Like the Dutch masters of old, he put the anatomies of corpses on display. But his bodies were ripped by disorderly bullets, not scientifically vivisected by surgeons.

Stephen Prince's perceptive book *Visions of Empire*[7] epitomizes the critical valorization of Verhoeven. Prince discusses the director's work as part of a "dystopia cycle" that countered the conservative trend in '80s Hollywood. Arguing that dystopic films confront issues of political exploitation, corporate control and resistance to police-state coercion, he says such ideas "receive their most intelligent and deliberate working out" in Verhoeven's *Robocop* and *Total Recall*, the cycle's "two most outstanding exemplars." Prince calls the former a "grim indictment of Reagan policies" that is nothing less than "a thinking person's action film whose politics are left of center." Like other admirers of the movie, he interprets its satirical humor as granting viewers "the Brechtian distance necessary to see ties between their world and the film's future." While *Total Recall* is a more compromised critique, it remains a "cautionary fable" that becomes "one of the subtlest but most critical imaginative transformations of the political referents of the Reagan period." Arnold Schwarzenegger's proletarian hero of the future is a rebellious freedom fighter who overthrows a villainous corporate state (headed, as in *Robocop*, by a perfectly evil boss played by Ronny Cox). In Prince's estimation, "one feels that Verhoeven would have gone much farther" in his political critique if not for the constraints of commercial production.[8]

Verhoeven's earliest cinematic credentials seem solidly anti-fascist. After learning filmmaking in the Dutch military (like Heinlein, he was a Navy man), he made *Mussert* (1968), a documentary about the head of the Netherlands Fascist Party during World War II. *Soldier of Orange* (1979), which led Steven Spielberg to invite Verhoeven to Hollywood, is his historical drama about Dutch resistance fighters who take on Nazi collaborators. Far from lionizing fascistic ideals of order, monumentalism, virile posing and perfect bodies, Verhoeven's Dutch films undermine such values. His down-and-dirty seventies films are more at home with the work of the "degenerate" artists condemned by the Nazis; irreverent, messy and vulgar, they also demonstrate sympathy for the outsider. The bohemian sculptor in *Turkish Delight* (1971), the gay writer in *The 4th Man* (1979), and the disenchanted motorcycle riders of *Spetters* (1980) are a far cry from the cardboard supersoldiers of *Starship Troopers*.[9]

Yet his futuristic war extravaganza was consistent with a turn Verhoeven took when he came to Hollywood. The Americanized Verhoeven has taken up guns with a vengeance, and he has consistently used these high-caliber weapons to inflict grisly destruction upon the human body. The violence of what at first seems to be formulaic action escalates into deliberately unsettling presentations of blood, splatter and viscera. Since *Robocop*, his films, marked by their excessive splashy spectacle and intense action, each contain set pieces calculated to outrage middle-class sensibilities. Many turn disturbingly comical in tone. In *Robocop*, we see police officer Murphy (Peter Weller) tortured by drug dealers who make a game of shooting off his hands and arms. After he is resurrected as a cyborg, his first turn in crimefighting is to use his laser-accurate pistol to shoot a would-be rapist in the genitals. In *Total Recall*, the rebel hero fights off a series of machine-gun assaults, memorably using a human corpse as a bullet-absorbing shield. *Basic Instinct*'s infamous opening features an explicit sex scene that culminates with an icepick murder at orgasm; its astonishing finale features Detective Mike Curran (Michael Douglas) shooting his psychiatrist girlfriend Doctor Beth Garner (Jeanne Tripplehorn) at point-blank range. In *Starship Troopers*, a young enlistee, Djana'D (Tami-Adrian George) accidentally shoots off the head of her comrade Breckinridge (Eric Bruskotter) during a training exercise; Lt. Rasczak (Michael Ironside) uses a Morita on one of his own wounded soldiers, Sgt. Gillespie (Curnal Achilles Aulisio) proclaiming, "I expect anyone here to do the same for me"; and throughout, Johnny Rico (Casper Van Dien) uses his Tactical Nuclear Launcher (available at this writing in children's toy stores) to blast the really big tanker bugs into lime green slime.

Starship Troopers' deliberate flirtation with fascism and its monstrous carnage of combat, therefore, might be understood as just another wrinkle in the Verhoeven career: ironic deployment of dizzying violence, cold characters, outrageous political philosophy and allusion to *Triumph of the Will*—all merely for the sake of provocation. However, this excursion into the postmodern politics of irony differs from its predecessors. Its irony is so "blank" that it can invite readings as a text that seems neo-Nazi itself.

In the broadest sense, this special-effects fantasy is merely a part of the post-*Star Wars* "cinema of oppressive spectacle" of which so many critics (liberal, conservative, humanist) have complained. David Mamet, for example, spells it out in a lesson on screenwriting.

> We, as the audience, are much better off with a sign that says "A BLASTED HEATH" than with all the brilliant cinematography in the world. To say "brilliant cinematography" is to say, "He made the trains run on time."
> Witness the rather fascistic trend in cinema in the last decade.
>
> Q. How'd you like the movie?
>
> A. Fantastic cinematography.

Yeah, but so what? Hitler had fantastic cinematography. The question we have ceased to ask is "What is the brilliant . . . cinematography in *aid* of?"[10]

As cultural historian Russell Berman argues in his analysis of fascist form, *Triumph of the Will* exemplifies the "fascist privileging of sight and visual representation" because fascism "transforms the world into a visual object . . . the spectacular landscape of industry and war."[11] Thomas Elsaesser points out in his assessment of Nazi-era commercial cinema, however, that this matter can be over-stressed. To take this Frankfurt School view is "to propose that *all* popular cinema is potentially fascistic, if by this we mean illusionist . . . using affect and emotion to overpower reason."[12] Clearly, both *Triumph* and *Troopers* stand to abet fascist politics with their visual objectification of masses, their overwhelming cinematography. But to lump them together with *Brazil* (1985), *Metropolis* (1926), *2001: A Space Odyssey* (1968), *Contact* (1997), or *Apocalypse Now* (1979) is to lose their more particular political meanings.

A discernment of fascist tendencies in recent cinema also occurs in Robin Wood's reading of Hollywood from Vietnam to Reagan. Wood identifies "Fear of Fascism" as part of a Spielberg-Lucas "syndrome": the potential for America to become a totalitarian state, for the individualist American hero to become indistinguishable from the fascist one, for the weak-minded to be taken over by a Vader-ian Force. Although George Lucas' well-known reference to *Triumph of the Will* is more discrete than Verhoeven's, Wood suggests that its presence in *Star Wars* is more than just a joke. The thrill of the Jedi military victory and the spectacle of triumphant troops assembled at the movie's conclusion resonate with authoritarian overtones. He also reminds us that, historically, fascist cultures did not feed on overtly political propaganda films but on light entertainment that reinforced certain conceptions of the body, national identity, family, etc. Rocky Balboa and Indiana Jones are not protagonists in fascist films, but would be at home in a fascist popular culture.[13]

Starship Troopers puts fascist ideas on the table more explicitly than the Spielberg-Lucas films. Indiana Jones still knows a Nazi when he sees one. And he opposes them unambiguously. On a manifest level, these films don't encourage an understanding of a Nazi enemy—however cartoonish—as anything other than Other. Verhoeven's futuristic fantasy treads on this dangerous ground by reversing this, inviting us to identify with the fascist protagonist.

To be more historically precise, we can define fascism as a political and social system marked by authoritarian rule, military force, intense nationalism, expansionist conquest, demand for racial purity, the rhetoric of "new order," supremacy of the State, and obedience to a charismatic leader (the one element absent from *ST*). It values martial discipline, sacrifice, surrender of individual will to social order, glory in combat and death, youthfulness and a cult of the body *without* eroticism. None of these alone is unique to fascist philosophy and I am not suggesting that Verhoeven is advocating them. But in bringing Heinlein's novel to the screen, he creates a cinematic space where they are allowed to play amid a riot of Nazi *mise-en-scène*.

Starship Troopers combines Heinlein's sci-fi war story with an Aaron Spelling-styled teen love triangle. Four friends are graduating from a high school in a futuristic Buenos Aires that looks suspiciously like a Los Angeles suburb. All enlist in Federal Service: our dumb-jock hero, Johnny Rico, does it for his brainy-beautiful girlfriend Carmen Ibañez (Denise Richards), who goes to Flight Academy. Nerdy best friend Carl Jenkins (Neil Patrick Harris) goes into military intelligence, while smart-jock Dizzy Flores (Dina Meyer) gives up her career as a pro football quarterback to follow her beloved Johnny into the Mobile Infantry. Johnny is about to quit boot camp when the Giant Bugs drop a meteor on Buenos Aires, killing millions. Johnny's platoon of gung-ho roughnecks are led into battle by their high school civics teacher, Mr. Rasczak. The battle for planet Klendathu is a fiasco, as the troopers with their World War II-style machine guns prove to be no match for the deadly giant arachnids. A second battle ends in victory, thanks to Rico and Diz's sharpshooting and our hero's cowboy tactics with mini-nukes. The comrades-in-arms celebrate by having sex, Johnny finally giving in when the eugenically-minded Moral Philosopher Lt. Rasczak instructs him to procreate.

Finally comes an apparent suicide mission to Planet P, home of the giant Brain Bug. In a scene reminiscent of John Wayne's *The Alamo* (1960), we watch from inside the barricaded fort as millions of bugs swarm over the fortress walls. Diz and Rasczak die gruesome but heroic deaths, impaled by insect claws, before Carmen's fleet arrives to save Johnny. During a second attack, Carmen is captured and about to have her skull sucked dry by the Brain Bug when Lt. Rico saves the day. We end irresolutely, as Colonel Carl appears—dressed in full Goebbels regalia. He mindmelds with the captured Brain Bug and, with a cruel smile, reports "It's afraid!" Thousands of uniformed troopers, looking ever so much like an army of ants, mindlessly cheer the fear in their enemy ("Fascist art glorifies surrender, it exalts mindlessness," Sontag observes[14]).

As the absurdity of the plot reveals, Verhoeven's film is highly ironic and often satirical (Heinlein's high-minded patriotism having vanished), but what is this irony in *aid* of? In whose army do these soldiers march (an army whose sergeants insist "Your weapon is more important than you are!")? While Verhoeven's adaptation undermines Heinlein's right-wing homily, it fails on three fronts. *Starship Troopers* wallows too deeply in Nazi iconography, enjoying its "fascinating fascism"; it presents a narrative in which a fascist future works, with no suggestion of resistance or alternatives; and, most egregiously, it targets an audience of teens and children, offering them the possibility of making a positive identification with the film's young fascist heroes.

Asked about the Nazi aesthetics, screenwriter Ed Neumeier said simply, "The Germans made the best-looking stuff. Art directors love it." Verhoeven added, "I just wanted to play with these [Nazi images] in an artistic way." The film's opening, a recruitment ad, "is taken from *Triumph of the Will* ... When the soldiers look at the camera and say, 'I'm doing my part!' that's from Riefenstahl. We copied it. It's wink-wink Riefenstahl."

Neumeier's script begins and ends with the mocking description, "Proud YOUNG PEOPLE in uniform, the bloom of human evolution." In casting, Verhoeven tries to have things both ways, playing with fascist aesthetics to subvert them, but managing to privilege a racial type. This is most apparent in the lead role. Heinlein's Juan "Johnnie" Rico was a Tagalog-speaking Filipino *cum* Federation (read: American) citizen-soldier. The movie Johnny and his Spanish-surnamed girlfriends are supposed to be Argentinian (because this is where Perón harbored old Nazis?). But the actors in these roles are quite white. The soldiers in Rico's platoon reference the WWII combat film's generic melting pot, updated for a multicultural future. But even the characters bearing Jewish, Polish, Japanese and African American names have the same fair, too-pretty, idealized faces.

Even Verhoeven's nod to a gender-neutral military fails to undercut the fascist ideal. These full-blooded men and women shower together without sexual attraction, conjuring up the fascist cult of the body as an instrument of combat rather than eros. As in Riefenstahl's film, showering together demonstrates Spartan camaraderie. In the other notable scene of bodily display, Johnny's hairless torso is flogged in the public square, taking the scars that mark him as a true warrior. Again, Sontag's litany of fascist motifs is borne out: the "choreographed display of bodies," "physical perfection of beauty," "virile posing," the "endurance of pain," the "exhibition of physical skill and courage."[15]

As *Starship Troopers* overindulges its Nazi imagery, it does so in a narrative universe where a fascistic mentality operates without disruption. The rules are laid out for us in Mr. Rasczak's valedictory lecture on History and Moral Philosophy. As others have observed, this scene in which a teacher inspires wartime enlistment takes the anti-war *All Quiet on the Western Front* (1930) and stands it on its head.[16] The one-armed veteran explains to his class why military forces had to impose this new world order after too much democracy led to chaos. Things "work" because only those who have done State service are enfranchised. Veteran soldier-citizens are licensed to reproduce. Mere "civilians" lack "civic virtue" and cannot vote. Force is the supreme authority. The rabidly anti-intellectual, antibourgeois side of fascist philosophy is projected onto the only civilian characters in the film, Johnny's rich parents (Lenore Kasdorf and Christopher Curry). They discourage their son from becoming cannon fodder and insist he go to Harvard. Their soft liberalism earns them a spot on the Bug Meteor's fatality list—weak naïfs, like the people of Hiroshima, says Rasczak.

Accepting his teaching unproblematically, all sign up for military service. Comradeship replaces family. Youth are socialized into these values via the greatest of inculcation devices: football. As star athletes, Diz and Johnny become the leaders in battle. But when Johnny and friends adopt this fascistic ideal, at what point does the viewer decide to go along for the ride? Verhoeven does try to subvert the Federation's ideology by replicating the satirical framing device used in his earlier films. Just as *Robocop* intercuts scenes of mock news bulletins (showing a Reagan-figure accidentally zapped by his own Star Wars weapons), *Troopers* features a running propaganda broadcast. This "FedNet" is viewed in an interactive Web-TV format. An "Official Voice" presents vignettes about how and why to fight the insect menace and invites viewers to watch further with the refrain, "Would you like to know *more* . . . ?"

Does this lend sufficient critical distance? Perhaps for adult viewers, the excess, absurdity, irony, and satire make it clear this is no endorsement of a fascist future. But the conventionally character-driven plot remains in place with some expectation that viewers will identify with the hero's strivings. Unless one is willing to root for the horrific, scabrous bugs, the film offers no points of entry other than the wonderful, horrible protagonist. Verhoeven is consistently anti-humanist, but his film is confused about what it wants to articulate about fascism.

In the promotional book, *The Making of Starship Troopers*, Verhoeven speaks directly about this subject. At times, he hints at sympathy with Heinlein's philosophy, calling it "benign fascism." When pushed to defend himself, he avers his film is "subversive," decidedly *not* fascist. But in between, he is as contradictory as his film. He will say only that a Pat Buchanan-like cryptofascism in the U.S. in the 1990s is "interesting," rather than alarming or wrong-headed. When the FedNet's official voice repeatedly asks "Would you like to know *more*?" Verhoeven maintains his film is asking its audience to consider the nature of such a world.

> [I'm] not saying that *ST*'s society is wrong because of that resemblance [to the Third Reich]. . . . These references say, "Here it is. This futuristic society works on this level well—and it fights the giant insects *very well*. Look and decide. The judgment is yours."[17]

What audience, then, does *Starship Troopers* address and recruit? If it were only Heinlein readers (including all U.S. Marines, who are required to read *ST*),[18] there might be less reason for concern. Most of the author's fans rejected the movie as a disservice to the book. Verhoeven's coldness and bad taste also turned off many film reviewers. Those who were ready to give him the benefit of the doubt sometimes addressed the f-word head on, particularly *The Washington Post*, in a series of sharp critiques. But more typical were puff pieces on the film's brilliant cinematography and cheerleading reviews, such as one the *Detroit Free Press* headlined with "*Starship Troopers* Sucks Out Our Brains—and It Feels Great."[19] However, we must deal with the fact that idealized Brechtian spectators and historically knowledgeable postmodernists were not the film's main patrons. The *Troopers* audience (both actual and constructed) was largely "juvenile," to use the somewhat dated industry term.

If critical perspective and sophistication are required to read subversive irony, then what interpretive position is left for those too inexperienced to be discerning? Verhoeven's film was heavily promoted to teen and pre-teen audiences, with television ads on kids' cable, interactive cyberspace games, an official comic book adaptation, trading cards, a CD-ROM, a soundtrack album, and Toys R Us action figures and weapons ("for ages 4 and up"), not to mention the Disney imprimatur. The film's "Restricted" rating was problematic enough (as a *New York Post* stunt proved, showing 12-year-olds able to buy tickets).[20] But even if the gore and sex were absent, what sense might children make out of watching, desiring or identifying with Johnny Rico? Again using a random sampling of on-line teen chats as an indicator, I found that many reacted to eye-candy as they might with other films: "This film rocks"; "Johnny is awesome"; "Diz is one hot babe" ("Fantastic cinematography!"). With *Trooper* characters as representatives of a fascist utopia, what will these same viewers think when confronted with other fascistic principles? Hitler addressed his youth; Heinlein wrote his book as juvenile literature. Is Verhoeven juvenile enough for today's ten-somethings? Is not this starship fantasy—with its shiny patriots exterminating an alien enemy—the type of entertainment in which the fascist soul would take pleasure? As with Hitler loving Fritz Lang's *Metropolis* for all the wrong reasons, the artist's subversive intentions cease to matter if the film lends aid and comfort to the enemy.

When Verhoeven, frustrated by criticism, yells to the press, "I am not a fascist! I'm a Democrat!"[21] I believe him. He is right; *Starship Troopers* is not a fascist film. Nonetheless, a film sprung from a democratic spirit shouldn't be so difficult to separate from a fascist one. Verhoeven need not become a propagandist in the malevolent manner of Goebbels or even in the transparently didactic and proselytizing manner of Heinlein to speak clearly. His filmic portrait of human societies as ugly, harsh and depraved might have been redeemed by just a scrap of hope, by reference to an alternative. For all their depravity, *Robocop* and *Total Recall* at least center on protagonists searching for their human identity, fighting against corrupt corporate states. But with no Ronny Cox villain to deride, the Big Bug picture lacks a target. Incoherence, not irony, is the postmodern trait that best demarcates this film. With *Starship Troopers*, this incoherence becomes nihilistic, leaving the unfortunate residue of fascist-inspired images to resonate in ways that still matter.

If there is a way to read this war story in a less distressing way, it stems from the film's own construction of impotence. Despite all the gun-toting and the firing of 300,000-plus rounds of ammunition, the disciplined, devoted, clean, lean warriors of the Mobile Infantry remain no match for the intimidating space insects. An assault rifle might have been a macho problem-solver for John Rambo, but Johnny Rico proves inferior to the arachnids below him and the mind-managers above him. As we learn in the final scene, the only hope the Federation has for beating the bugs is a new breakthrough in telepathic mindreading. Carl, Johnny's Goebbels-inspired friend, has become the officer in charge of psychic research. He has (possibly) remotely controlled the foot soldier's thoughts with "psi-orders" during the final rescue mission. Able to siphon intelligence from the captured Brain Bug, the Federation's military can now out-think its enemy. Of course, mind control—mass trance through propaganda and ritual—is also a fascist weapon par excellence.

In this sense, the film's visual display shares the calculated effect of Nazi spectacles of order. Perhaps the most chilling image comes in the final scene, where thousands of young troopers jubilantly cheer the conquered enemy's fear. The pageant of bodies massed in uniform, framed in a long shot, renders a sensation not unlike that of Riefenstahl's *Triumph of the Will*. The reverberant, throaty roar with which they erupt adds to the effect, echoing "Sieg Heils" heard in the Nuremberg stadium.

Verhoeven's films certainly problematize the politics of issues like gun violence, militarism, and corporate corruption, but we might wish that this imagemaker's vision were clearer and more articulate—especially when playing with fascism. Rather than resorting to a nihilistic response to the political present, one might recall the clarity of singer Woody Guthrie. "This machine kills fascists," he scrawled across his guitar. Paul Verhoeven and Hollywood in general don't have to make the cinematic equivalent of "This Land Is Your Land" to signal what position they take on the possibilities of a fascist utopia. But neither do they need to produce films as ideologically muddled as *Starship Troopers*. Perhaps, as Mamet, Berman and a host of cultural critics have contended, there is something almost inherently fascistic and controlling in this machine of cinema that "transforms the world into a visual object." Not all pictures and narratives are endowed with the same political meanings and historical referents, however. Contemporary filmmakers like Verhoeven, aware of a contested cinematic past, would do well to consider more carefully which side they arm for the future.

NOTES

1   This essay relies in part upon the author's interview and classroom discussion with Paul Verhoeven, University of Wisconsin-Oshkosh, November 3, 1995.

2   Michael Wilmington, "Bug Wars," *Chicago Tribune* (November 7, 1997), A7.

3   According to screenwriter Ed Neumeier, the fictional Morita (a "futuristic-looking assault shotgun") was jokingly named after "a then-current Sony executive." Paul M. Sammon, *The Making of Starship Troopers* (New York: Boulevard Books, 1997), 73.

4   Susan Sontag, "Fascinating Fascism," in *Under the Sign of Saturn* (New York: Vintage, 1980), 73–105. See also James Hay, *Popular Film Culture in Fascist Italy* (Bloomington: Indiana University Press, 1987), Marcia Landy, *Fascism in Film: The Italian Commercial Cinema, 1931-1943* (Princeton, NJ: Princeton University Press, 1986), Thomas Elsaesser, "Hollywood Berlin," *Sight and Sound* (January 1998), 14–17.

5   J. Hoberman, "The Fascist Guns in the West," *American Film* (March 1986), 42–44. Hoberman cites David Denby's 1985 critique in *New York* magazine as specifically using the fascist label for *Rambo: First Blood, Part II, Red Dawn* and other films of that season. See Robin Wood, *Hollywood from Vietnam to Reagan* (New York: Columbia University Press, 1986); Michael Ryan and Douglas Kellner, *Camera Politica: The Politics and Ideology of Contemporary Hollywood Film* (Bloomington: Indiana University Press, 1988); Susan Jeffords, *The Remasculinization of America: Gender and the Vietnam War* (Bloomington: Indiana University Press, 1989); Stephen Prince, *Visions of Empire: Political Imagery in Contemporary American Film* (New York: Praeger, 1992).

6   *The Wonderful, Horrible Life of Leni Riefenstahl [Die Macht der Bilder: Leni Reifenstahl]* (Ray Müller, 1993).

7   New York: Praeger, 1992.

8   Prince, *Visions,* 171–84.

9   A comprehensive guide to the director's career is Rob van Scheers, *Paul Verhoeven* (London: Faber and Faber, 1997).

10   David Mamet, *Writing in Restaurants* (New York: Vintage, 1986), 16.

11   Russell A. Berman, "Written Across Their Faces: Leni Riefenstahl, Ernst Jünger, and Fascist Modernism," in *Modern Culture and Critical Theory: Art, Politics, and the Legacy of the Frankfurt School* (Madison: University of Wisconsin Press, 1988), 99.

12   Elsaesser, "Berlin," 14.

13   Robin Wood, "Papering the Cracks: Fantasy and Ideology in the Reagan Era," in John Belton, ed., *Movies and Mass Culture* (New Brunswick, NJ: Rutgers University Press, 1996), 211-13.

14   Sontag, "Fascism," 91.

15   Sontag, "Fascism," 86.

16   Stephen Hunter's stinging critique of the movie points this out. His review was by far the most trenchant immediate analysis of the film's fascist core. "Goosestepping at the Movies," *The Washington Post* (November 11, 1997), D1.

17   Sammon, *Making*, 138-39.

18   Kent Mitchell, "Movies Corps Values: 'Trooper' on Reading List," *Atlanta Constitution* (November 7, 1997), 22.

19   Hunter, "Goosestepping," D1; Stephen Hunter, "Ooze and Aahs: Why Disgusting, Slimy Movies are Hard not to Watch," *The Washington Post* (December 9, 1997), D1; Rita Kempley, "Starship Troopers," *The Washington Post* (November 7, 1997), D1; Terry Lawson, "*Starship Troopers* Sucks Out Our Brains—and It Feels Great," *Detroit Free Press* (November 7, 1997).

20   "Despite 'R' Rating, Kids Sneak into Troopers," Reuters/Variety wire report from America Online, November 1997. Sony executives, apparently trying to justify disappointing sales, sent a letter to exhibitors (citing the *New York Post* story) advising them to check for moviegoers under seventeen who were supposedly sneaking into *Starship Troopers* after buying tickets to other films.

21   Sontag, "Fascism," 95; Benjamin Svetkey, "The Reich Stuff: Nazi References and Fascist Images Creep Among the Bugs in *Starship Troopers*," *Entertainment Weekly* (November 21, 1997), 9.

Do you have a permit for that?: The Gun as a Metaphor for the Transformation of G.I. Jane into G.I. Dick

Lauren R. Tucker with Alan R. Fried

G.I. Jane (1997) tells us that gender is mind over matter. Yet, the film's argument obscures very real contradictions within feminist discourse in the 1990s—contradictions that often work to sustain the dominant gender constructions that the feminist movement ostensibly works to dismantle. At issue is whether a woman must adopt male-centered cultural values and mores in order to gain access to the societal power previously reserved for the male elite within the military industrial complex, where masculine authority is symbolized by the destructive power associated with weaponry.[1] Throughout the world, access to the destructive capability held by the armies of most nations represents social power that is as ideological as it is material. Those with access to these tools, men, have had the power to dominate and control others through force. Hence, the power of the gun has become routinely associated with male domination and control within society; it has become a metaphor and a definitive indicator of masculine authority. *G.I. Jane* explores society's political and cultural anxieties regarding full integration of women into the military, and, most importantly, full participation in combat units—the key to advancement within the military establishment.

Ultimately, *G.I. Jane* depicts its hero, Lieutenant Jordan O'Neil (Demi Moore), as a feminist success story. This essay analyzes *G.I. Jane* within the political and social climate surrounding the film's release on August 22, 1997 and identifies specific discursive features within the film that work to define the transformation of Lt. O'Neil as a social and political success. Selected as a test case, O'Neil makes history as the first woman allowed to train for the Navy SEALs, the military's most demanding commando unit. Central to the plot is O'Neil's desire and the desire of Lillian DeHaven (Anne Bancroft), senior member of the Senate Arms Committee and O'Neil's sponsor, to breach the single largest barrier to women's advancement in the military establishment—exclusion from operational experience. Chosen for her courage, skills and unflappable nature, O'Neil is determined to "gut it out" in spite of a grueling training routine and unimaginable physical and emotional abuse. To the surprise of the Navy command, her classmates and her sponsor, O'Neil repeatedly succeeds where 60 percent of her male counterparts fail.

G.I. Jane employs discursive strategies that are informed by specific discourses about the nature of gender difference and gender relations within the context of the male-dominated military establishment. The film was released in a political and social climate characterized by gender conflict within the armed services and military colleges.[2] During this period, women within the military described the culture as abusive, sexist and hostile. College-bound women seeking to attend the Virginia Military Institute and The Citadel—at the time, the only remaining all-male public military colleges in the United States—argued that gender-based admission policies are illegal. (They violate the 14th Amendment guarantee to equal protection.) Having lost the fight to keep their all-male status, these institutions soon found themselves faced with the same challenges to fully integrate women into the culture of military life that, for the last decade, have plagued the larger military establishment.

At the heart of this debate lies the question of whether women, in order to gain access to the power previously reserved for and by men, must become psychologically and culturally "male." This debate takes place between the narrow confines of feminist arguments that construct gender as a state of mind and arguments that define it as a state of being. Jean Bethke Elshtain identifies these two positions as "sex neutrality" and "sex polarity," respectively.[3] She argues that competition between these positions has historically defined the exchange between pro-feminist and anti-feminist discourses. Ironically, these positions serve to reinforce "the values of male-dominated, individualistic society" by focusing on what Elshtain calls a "turnover in personnel" rather than advocating a systemic change that would value the feminine qualities tied to gender difference:[4]

> Women bureaucrats for male bureaucrats, women corporate executives for male corporate executives, women generals for male generals, and all the rest.[5]

Ironically, or maybe not so ironically, *G.I. Jane* articulates this conundrum within feminist discourse through the familiar framework of the male-centered, military rite-of-passage drama. As a sub-genre of both war and male coming-of-age films, the military rite of passage embodies the ancient traditions of tribal folklore. These stories tell of the transformation of a boy into a man as he leaves his home and mother to go off to the wild to confront his fears and lose his innocence. His successful return paves the way for his entrance into the world of power and privilege reserved for the adult males of the tribe. The central characteristic of these stories is that they are about the least-likely survivor. The lead character must be unlikely, because the young male who experiences this tale must identify with the legendary hero and draw strength from his achievement. With this saga as their talisman, the adolescent males of the tribe go forth to confront their own transformation.

Films about military service have served as the modern equivalent to the rite-of-passage folktale. These films often highlight the indicators of the transformation process, the process in which a young boy becomes a military man. These indicators, both physical and cultural, traditionally include the move away from the bosom of the family, submission to the depersonalizing hair-cut, the issuance of the uniform, the subjection to a battery of psychological and medical exams, the endurance of the grueling physical training, and confrontations with hard-nosed drill sergeants. These steps symbolically deconstruct the recruit's adolescent identity so that his transformation into a new man can be effected. The catalyst for this transformation is often an incident that endangers the group physically, emotionally or both. Through perseverance and a resurgence of the recruit's heretofore obscured personal identity, the recruit rediscovers his unique talents to express himself as an individual and as a member of the unit.

The military as a male-centered rite of passage works to inscribe on the recruit a construction of manliness defined in opposition to the female physiology and feminine cultural indicators. So the tradition of military culture leaves very little, if any, symbolic space for the construction of female participation in the military establishment:

> As a male preserve, it [military service] also simplified the matter of identity—perhaps overly so—by institutionalised distancing not only from women but from "feminine traits." The hardihood of military life further protected male friendship from the insinuations of homosexuality.[6]

The key reward for completing the rite of passage is the social authority to dominate nature and control the surrounding environment. Within Western culture, nature is most often defined in feminine terms, while the destructive power of weapons and war are routinely associated with masculinity.[7] The male-centered military establishment offers men access to the authority embodied by its virtual monopoly on destructive technology and weapons. This connection between masculine authority and the destructive power of the military has been inscribed within the culture:

> Militarism as a way of thinking and responding to problems begins at an early age, socialized into the behaviour of small children through their relationships in the home and violent messages in the media. Boys learn to resolve conflict through force, domination and control. Girls, taught that they belong to the weaker sex, learn the arts of compromise, accommodation and submission.[8]

Throughout the history of this genre, masculine authority has been routinely linked with the dominance of First World industrial societies, specifically the United States and Britain. The end of the Cold War and the 1991 U.S. military action against Iraq have fueled social anxieties about the growing militarization of Third World countries. These anxieties and resultant discourses have informed much of popular culture during this decade. For example, *Navy Seals* (1990), like *G.I. Jane*, pits the high-tech skill of Navy commandos against the seemingly technologically and politically immature Arabs. In these films, Third World countries, especially Arab ones, are constructed as untamed forces of nature that have insupportable claims to the power represented by their arsenals.

Circumscribed by this discursive climate, the transformation of Lt. Jordan O'Neil occurs on three levels—political, physical, and cultural. Throughout the process, O'Neil exchanges her feminine identity for access to the masculine authority promised as her reward for her passage to "manhood." Despite its feminist overtones, and like a great deal of putatively representative cultural material produced in Hollywood, *G.I. Jane's* militaristic rite-of-passage structure defines O'Neil's experience in terms of the individualistic, male-centered cultural values of the military rather than portraying her transformation as a political and cultural response to the military's systemic sexist attitude toward women. Hence, *G.I. Jane* obscures our ability to make sense of O'Neil's success outside the terms set by the dominant masculine values, mores and power dynamics articulated by the military-industrial complex.

The opening scenes in the film emphasize O'Neil's subordinate position within the institutionalized structure of the military establishment. She is a political pawn, and her destiny is subject to the vagaries of political horse-trading between Senator Lillian DeHaven and Navy Secretary-elect Hayes (Daniel von Bargen), who needs the senator's support for confirmation. DeHaven and Hayes depict the political face of the military establishment. These characters voice the public policy debate about what the senator calls "the seemingly incontrovertible," sexist attitude toward women in the Navy.

DeHaven is pure Texas good ol' boy. Despite her feminist posturing, she has been transformed by the male-dominated political system before she is introduced to the audience. Her interest in forcing the issue of full integration of women in the military is not about women's rights but about the maintenance of her political viability in her home state of Texas, where the Department of Defense is planning several base closings. Hence, her feminist rhetoric is nothing more than political maneuver.

Likewise, the Defense Department officers are willing to go along to get along, as long as they control the terms on which women are allowed to participate in operations units. In exchange for DeHaven's support for Hayes' confirmation, the Defense Department proposes a full integration plan in which a series of test cases will determine the viability of women's participation in combat operations. The Defense Department hopes to beat the senator at her own game, and the choice of the elite Navy SEALs for the first case is intended to assure their success. Within this context, O'Neil is readied for sacrifice to the political expediencies of both Capitol Hill and the military.

The film's construction of O'Neil's workplace and domestic relations also underscores her subordinate social position. As a Navy Intelligence officer, her intellectual abilities are obscured by the refusal of her male superiors to take her initiative seriously. When a Navy commando unit loses communication with Intel headquarters, O'Neil's acumen and level-headed response to the crisis saves her male superiors from making a mistake that might have cost the lives of the unit. Instead of being praised for her ability, she is chastised for venturing beyond her support role.

This rebuke is articulated by O'Neil's boyfriend Royce (Jason Beghe), who outranks her as a commander despite the fact that they both entered the Navy during the same month. The tension between O'Neil and Royce symbolizes the complexity of the sexual politics of gender relations in the military. The film makes it obvious that the romantic relationship between the higher ranking male officer and his female subordinate is a clandestine one, a relationship the military defines as inappropriate. Yet, despite its taboo status, O'Neil's relationship with what Senator DeHaven calls a "solvent heterosexual" is a necessary, if not sufficient, condition for her acceptance as a test case. Throughout the selection process, DeHaven makes a special point of dismissing candidates whom she thinks are too masculine in appearance. According to the senator, these are not the type of female faces people want to see on the cover of *Newsweek*, and they suggest masculinity that can only be read as indicative of female homosexuality, a lifestyle prohibited by military policy. According to DeHaven, O'Neil appears to be "top drawer with silk stockings inside," but she warns the lieutenant, "I don't want this thing blowin' up in our faces if you happen to be battin' for the other side." Ultimately, O'Neil's identity as an able naval officer is subordinate to her female, heterosexual identity as defined by the institutionalized, male-centered values of the military establishment.

O'Neil begins her transformation when she starts to view herself against Royce's expectations and social position. While she claims not to want to be the "poster child" of the women's movement, she expresses to Royce her frustration that the Navy has denied her the same opportunities for advancement that he has enjoyed. Royce's lack of empathy and support for her aspirations parallels the institutional attitude of the military establishment (though he is cuddling her in a soapy bathtub when he expresses his position), and moves her to accept Senator DeHaven's sponsorship. This decisive moment initiates her transformation as she leaves Royce to go off to "war" with and among the Navy SEALs. The turnover in personnel commences when Royce is left to tend the hearth and home.

Upon her arrival at Cataland Naval Base, O'Neil is immediately defined by and within the base culture by her sex, not her character. Her introductory interview with Captain Salem, the base commander (Scott Wilson), is entirely focused on her awkward presence as a woman in a man's world. O'Neil attempts to diminish Salem's discomfort by immediately agreeing to cut her long hair and conform to the masculine culture of the base. She earnestly tries to dispel the notion that she is inherently different from her male classmates, and she requests that she receive no special treatment. However, Salem's quick dismissal of her request marks O'Neil as an unwanted intruder in his all-male domain: "We're not trying to change your sex, Lieutenant. You have a separate head. A separate bed."

Her intruder status is further developed when she first encounters the rest of her all-male training class in the cafeteria. Cat-calls, wolf-whistles and sexual innuendo greet O'Neil as she enters the mess hall, and the audience's attention is once again drawn to her "femaleness." The male recruits take up the debate about whether women should be fully integrated into combat units that initiated the film. O'Neil's feminine identity is constructed as "the problem," a problem that the military should have avoided. Her femininity is viewed as the single characteristic that makes her unfit for the elite world of combined reconnaissance work. In a moment of irony, a recruit suggests that O'Neil's gender may have given her an unfair advantage as he outlines his own use of social privilege to gain a spot in the class.

Look, I don't know what she did to get in here. I hate to speculate, but I know I petitioned for two years to get into this program; that's two years of letter writing, two years of pulling strings, and now I finally get here and it's gone coed! Elite combat unit! Whose ingenious idea was that?

At first, O'Neil seems reluctant to forsake the physical and cultural indicators of her feminine identity as she progresses through what the SEALs call the "evolutions" of the training program. Despite the obstacle posed by her long hair, she does not cut it before her first training exercise, her earlier comment to Captain Salem notwithstanding. Command Master Chief Urgayle's (Viggo Mortensen) characterization of the recruits as being "harder than the average man to even get into this program" seems ironic juxtaposed with O'Neil's constant rearrangement of her long hair during the course of the first evolution. O'Neil continues to exhibit the female indicators of sharing, cooperation and nurturing that defined her identity before she began the program. Throughout the first evolution, we find O'Neil asking about the well-being of her fellow classmates after a grueling training session on the beach. Having had little food and even less sleep, she and her classmates are locked in a hot room and are ordered to write a 500-word essay on why they love the Navy. Despite the extreme hostility she has endured from her male colleagues, she surreptitiously shares a muffin, squirreled away during dinner, with a fellow classmate.

However, during the obstacle course she realizes the heavy price of maintaining her feminine qualities within the military culture. Before the exercise, she is ordered to use the "female aids" found throughout the course. Her objections to using the aids fall on deaf ears, and she decides that rather than rely on the aids she will depend on the cooperation of her teammates.

But her best efforts to bond with her team are thwarted when they abandon her to fend for herself. When her team approaches the retaining wall obstacle, she gamely helps each member of the team over the wall. Yet, the last teammate over the wall refuses to assist her. To get over the obstacle, O'Neil is forced to use the "female aid" she disdained, in this case portable steps which help her to climb over the wall without assistance. Ultimately, her scramble to catch up to her team results in her triggering a tripwire and causing the symbolic death of the entire class. This incident crystallizes her image as "the problem."

O'Neil is one of the last to finish the obstacle course, but she is shocked to find out that her recorded time was better than many of the recruits who finished before her. She is told that the military's policy of "gender norming" for all women in physical training accounts for this discrepancy. Ironically, gender norming only serves to define O'Neil as an abnormality in a male world. She realizes it is not her, but the system, that constructs her as an outsider within the masculine culture of the Navy SEALs. Consequently, O'Neil takes an "if you can't beat 'em, join 'em" attitude, and her resolve to jettison her feminine traits begins her personal "evolution."

O'Neil's transformation is initially signaled by the loss of specific physical indicators of her femaleness, one of the most overt of which is her long hair. In a dramatic scene, she slowly and carefully cuts off her hair without the aid of the briefly-absent barber. Her intense personal training routine results in the loss of her period, and her body starts to take on a harder, more masculine look. In these sequences, the film constructs O'Neil's assimilation into the male world of the Navy SEALs as her personal choice.

These physical processes are accompanied by her adoption of masculine cultural traits. Throughout the earlier part of the film, O'Neil's expressiveness is an important symbol of her femininity. However, as she evolves into her masculinized identity, her speech becomes more clipped, her speaking style more laconic. When her doctor (Lucinda Jenney) asks why she is pursuing Navy SEAL training, O'Neil abandons her earlier rationale of career advancement for the male-centered objective of gaining destructive power. O'Neil asks the doctor whether she puts this same question to the male recruits:

DOCTOR: As a matter of fact, yes, I do ask them.

O'NEIL: And what do they say?

DOCTOR: "'Cause I get to blow shit up."

O'NEIL: Well, there you go.

The adoption of this masculine mentality is crucial to O'Neil's assimilation process, a point that is underscored by the story told by the only African American recruit in the class. The film constructs the African American recruit as a recent outsider who has successfully assimilated into the previously all-white world of the U.S. Navy. He tells of his grandfather's wish to "be a Navy man" and defend his country during World War II. However, the defense of country wasn't as important as his desire to access the authority and destructive power reserved for white men:

[He] wanted to fire them big guns off them big-ass battleships. Navy says to him, "No, you can only do one thing on them battleships, son, and that's *cook*."

The pivotal point in O'Neil's transformation is bracketed by scenes in which O'Neil and her fellow recruits are required to assemble a machine gun within a specific time limit. This sequence represents a bridge in O'Neil's evolution from a feminine "think tank" soldier to a masculine weapon of destruction. At the beginning of the sequence, she is unable to reassemble the weapon within the time limit and is outshone by one of the most sexist recruits in her class. The following scenes include dramatic footage of her personal fitness routine, symbolizing her determination to become "one of the guys." The sequence ends with her success at assembling the gun faster than any of her fellow recruits. As the instructor rewards her with a "well done," the reassembly of the gun operates as a metaphor for O'Neil's "accomplishment" in reconstructing her gender identity to fit within the terms established by the masculine culture of the military.

From this point in the film until the end, O'Neil begins to win the respect of her fellow recruits, her commanding officers and the politicians who set her up to fail. Her construction of the gun coincides with her (re)construction of herself, her physique, her demeanor and her mentality, into a new image—the techno-male. She, too, has the power to dominate and control others through force.

The final step of Jordan O'Neil's transformation requires that she and her fellow recruits psychologically accept her new identity. She is chosen to lead a team of her class-mates in a reconnaissance and evacuation simulation. In accordance with the military rite-of-passage structure, the newly-minted male must test the integrity of his manhood against the expectations of his fellows. The team's capture and imprisonment by Master Chief Urgayle and his assistants sets the stage for the climactic conflict between Urgayle and O'Neil. Urgayle subjects O'Neil to extreme emotional and physical abuse in full view of her classmates. Throughout this sequence, Urgayle tests the psychological mettle of his male recruits as much as the physical and emotional strength of O'Neil.

When the Master Chief begins to simulate a brutal rape of O'Neil, the psychological tide begins to turn for O'Neil and her fellow recruits. O'Neil's visceral response results in a battle royale with Urgayle. The audience is given the sense that Urgayle has higher motives that just teaching O'Neil how brutal combat can be for women. Urgayle explains his behavior to the male recruits by saying he is trying to save their lives and the life of O'Neil by showing them just how vulnerable units with female team members will be. But despite a game effort, O'Neil is thrown to the ground in defeat. Her fellow teammates turn their backs on Urgayle who tells O'Neil to "seek life elsewhere." Down, but not out, O'Neil tells the Master Chief, "Suck my dick!" As she basks in the cheers and acceptance of her fellow recruits, O'Neil's transformation into a rugged, individualistic techno-male is complete.

She and her fellow recruits have made the mental leap needed to accept her new male identity. Yet, the feasibility of her accomplishment is questioned by Urgayle who tells one of his assistants, "She's not the problem; *we* are." Ironically, Urgayle appears to be the only male within the unit that understands that it is not O'Neil but the system that must change if women are to be successfully integrated into combat units.

Her recent transformation is first challenged by the system in the political arena. Despite her recent success, the political horse-trading between Senator DeHaven and the military that resulted in O'Neil's placement in the SEALs program comes back to haunt her. The Department of Defense, concerned about O'Neil's success, threatens to close sev-eral Texas military bases if DeHaven doesn't find a way to guarantee O'Neil's withdrawal from the training program. O'Neil's successful transformation into a techno-male becomes her Achilles heel when she finds her friendship with the base's female doctor has been interpreted as a lesbian affair.

This incident is pivotal to understanding how O'Neil's transformation affects the sexual politics surrounding her. Her relationships with other women can only be inter-preted within the context of the dominant male, heterosexual culture that structures the military industrial complex. Her transformation into a male places her outside intimate female relations that are not sexual in nature. She is forced to withdraw from the program, but is reinstated after she threatens to expose the truth about the political maneuvering underlying her appointment to the SEAL program.

The final sequence of the film is characterized by O'Neil's introduction to the masculine authority that had been denied to her as a woman. Master Chief Urgayle and his recruits are diverted from their final training exercise to aid in extricating American troops from the Libyan desert in a real-life operation. O'Neil accompanies Urgayle on a scouting mission, and they encounter a small group of Libyan soldiers. When O'Neil moves closer to the unit in order to take stock of the "enemy," a Libyan soldier comes too close for comfort. Finally, she has the opportunity to use her hard-won destructive power and eliminate the threat. Rather than trust in O'Neil's ability to use the power that she has been given effectively, however, Urgayle takes it upon himself to shoot the Libyan. And this paternalism has a price. The Master Chief is critically wounded when his shooting of the Libyan soldier brings attention to the presence of the unit. O'Neil risks her own life to save Urgayle and the mission, and in doing so finds herself once again in the position of nurturer and caretaker.

Despite efforts to the contrary, the story of *G.I. Jane* does not tell of the success of feminism. O'Neil's transformation from woman to man can be viewed as a process of the abandonment of her primary, feminine identity, the adoption of a male identity and her symbolic merger with the destructive power of military technology. In the first two phases, she exchanges her femininity for access to social power and the cultural indicators of leadership and dominance. In the final phase, she becomes one with the weapon that would apparently reify her position in the male-dominated hierarchy. The depiction of the transformation works simultaneously as a modern retelling of rite-of-passage folklore; in this case, the boy is replaced by a small, boyish woman who wants to achieve the acceptance of a tribe of powerful men. Paradoxically, it also makes a statement in the current debate about the role of women in the military. O'Neil's story dramatizes the difficulties that women must face in this situation, and in so doing, actually obscures the question of how the military must adapt to its new female recruits.

Much popular debate revolves around the first two phases of the process of abandonment of femininity and adoption of male cultural indicators. This exchange encapsulates the phony argument that women want to be regarded as either sexually neutral or substitute men. In *G.I. Jane,* the argument is framed in an innovative way. Through the abandonment of her primary, feminine identity, O'Neil engages in social exchange. This is an example of the "personnel turnover" referred to by Elshtain. The film's narrative works to transform O'Neil both physically and mentally into the only type of female that can succeed within the existing culture and certainly the only kind that can succeed within the social structure of the military establishment.

The structure of the film's argument, overly simplistic and rationalizing the view that women cannot compete, is distinguished for its employment of the rite of passage as a metaphor for the process of becoming a man and for the extreme nature of the protagonist's transformation. Other films have shown women in power as suit-wearing dictators or even as cigar-chomping, loud and brassy political bulls; this is the first time that a woman, in a moment extreme, actually declares she has male genitalia. Within the framework of the rite-of-passage genre, the loss of femininity is constructed as the loss of innocence.

189

There is something still humanizing about O'Neil's travails. The audience empathizes with her struggle and applauds her success. While G.I. Jane appears to be a feminist hero who shows that a woman can win at even the roughest man's game, one is left with many questions to ponder. Could *any* woman succeed in the male arena? Or does this woman, who has engaged the forces of hell on their own terms, somehow possess powers that uniquely qualify her for membership in the SEALs? On the battlefield, will she act like a warrior—and kill more of the enemy—or act like a nurturer and save the lives of her fellows? Ultimately, does G.I. Jane's adaptation and her adoption of male codes represent true feminist success? There surely must be more to feminism—and to life—than this.

NOTES

[1] J. Vickers, *Women and War* (New Jersey: Zed Books, 1993).

[2] "The Citadel's Culture of Abuse," *New York Times* (January 14, 1997), A14. J. B. Elshtain, "Cultural Conundrums and Gender: America's Present Past," in I. Angus and S. Jhally, eds., *Cultural Politics in Contemporary America* (New York: Routledge, 1989), 123-134; C. Burke, "Dames at Sea," *The New Republic,* Vol. 207 (August 17, 1992), 16+; C. Sanger, "Will VMI be Used Against Us?" *Ms.* Vol. 7 (November/December, 1996), 24-25; B. Hewitt, "Conduct Unbecoming," *People Weekly* 47 (1997), 40-43.

[3] Elshtain, "Conundrums," 124.

[4] Elshtain, "Conundrums," 128.

[5] Elshtain, "Conundrums," 128.

[6] D. J. Mrozek, "The habit of victory, the American military and the cult of manliness," in J. A. Mangan and J. Walvin, eds., *Manliness and Morality* (New York, St. Martin's Press, 1987), 222.

[7] Elshtain, "Conundrums," 128.

[8] J. Vickers, *Women,* 43.

This Is for Fighting, This Is for Fun: Camerawork and Gunplay in Reality-Based Crime Shows

Fred Turner

Several years ago, I interviewed a Vietnam veteran named Brian Winhover. He had survived three tours of combat duty, but when he tried to tell me how he felt when he was under fire, it took him a while to find the words. Eventually he said, "[you could] call me a piece of ice.... You couldn't impregnate me with anything."[1] At first I was taken aback—I hadn't expected a word like "impregnate" to crop up in a war story—but the more we talked, the clearer the psychology of his combat experience became. Winhover had lived out all the confusions embedded in the ubiquitous boot camp chant, "This is my rifle, this [penis] is my gun. One is for killing, one is for fun."[2] Killing could be sex, the chant implied, and sex of a very particular kind. For Winhover, as for generations of soldiers before and since, to be a man, to belong to the unit, was to penetrate; to fail at those tasks, to be an enemy to the unit, was to be penetrated like a woman or a homosexual "bottom." The battlefield was a site of sexualized conflict, one at which it was Winhover's duty to assert his difference from the enemy by proving it "feminine." This Winhover did with aplomb: by his own description, he became a mechanical, rifle-like creature in Vietnam, hard and numb. He dedicated his days in the field to killing, to trying to penetrate the bodies of enemy soldiers, to trying to "impregnate" the enemy with his weapon. In short, he became the perfect soldier.

Winhover came home in 1969, yet the psychosexual dynamics that characterized his combat experiences remain very much alive. In fact, they are a defining feature of the now ten-year-old American television genre of "reality-based" crime programs. In these highly popular and resilient shows, viewers encounter a world much like the one Winhover saw in Vietnam, a world in which heavily armed, uniformed men move among impoverished civilians, trying to sort guerrilla-like criminals from the population. They also encounter the psychosexual economy of that realm. In boot camp, Winhover's drill sergeants trained him to confuse his penis and his rifle and thus to take a physical pleasure in being a soldier. In the far less coercive world of television, and toward a similar end, reality-based crime programs urge viewers to confuse the guns of the police with the cameras through which they see events. Just as military training has long sought to break down the psychic barriers between killing and sex in the minds of its soldiers, so the visual styles of these programs work to intermingle the processes of seeing and shooting, of knowing and arresting, and of consuming goods and upholding the law. As the producers of reality-based crime programming acknowledge, these shows aim not to be *watched*, but to be *experienced*.[3] With the full support and cooperation of the police themselves, the cameramen of reality-based crime programs invite viewers—both male and female—to feel the highly sexualized, hyper-masculine power of the state within their sedentary bodies.[4]

They extend this invitation by carefully equating their own cameras with the guns of the policemen and bounty hunters the cameras depict. After watching ten episodes of each of four of the most popular reality-based crime shows in the United States—*Cops* (1989), *Bounty Hunters* (1996), *America's Most Wanted* (1988), and *LAPD: Life on the Beat* (1995)—I've noticed that guns most frequently appear onscreen in three contexts: as weapons aimed at suspects, as holstered emblems of police authority, and, in advertising trailers especially, as explicit echoes of the cinematic six-shooter. These three incarnations correspond to three televisual devices common to the real-life crime genre: hand-held camera work, computer graphics, and intertextuality. Like aimed pistols, hand-held video cameras grant the viewer a policeman's power to pursue and arrest the suspect, albeit visually. Like holstered weapons, computer graphics make visible an omnipresent power—in this case, the power of TV producers, cooperating state authorities, and the viewer to embed potentially disruptive criminal activity in a body of knowledge. Finally, as symbols manipulated by TV producers, guns link the local realm of the arrest scene to the mythology of the American frontier. In these ways, guns and cameras work together to transform real-life crime programs into a sort of visual boot camp for the TV audience, one in which viewers are subtly coerced into taking pleasure in the feminization and domination of the poor and of people of color by a well-armed, fun-craving masculinized state.

The link between cameras and guns naturally precedes the advent of real-life crime programming (consider the phrase "shooting a movie"), just as the link between weapons and penises preceded the Vietnam War. Yet, in the four programs I will focus on, producers put extraordinary effort into maintaining and naturalizing the gun-camera analogy.

This is true despite the fact that each show features its own unique aesthetics. *Cops* and *Bounty Hunters*, for instance, offer seemingly raw (though in fact heavily edited) video-verité accounts of pursuit and capture. Each half-hour episode of *Cops* follows the exploits of police in a single American city, and includes between three and five sequences of police officers in action.[5] These are preceded by a video-montage title sequence which depicts some of the most dramatic moments from footage already gathered in that city, accompanied by the show's now-infamous reggae theme song ("*Bad boys, bad boys—What'cha gonna do when they come for you?"*). Each action sequence opens with a shot of the policeman centrally involved—a shot in which the officer frequently describes his motives for joining the force—and proceeds to show him responding to a radio call.[6] It then depicts the officer pursuing and usually capturing a suspect and concludes with that officer or one of his colleagues commenting laconically on the events that have just unfolded. *Bounty Hunters* follows a similar pattern. Each half-hour episode focuses on the work of one or two teams of bail enforcement agents and includes two to four sequences in which they discuss how to find and capture a particular bail jumper, pursue that person, arrest him, and bring him to jail.[7]

LAPD and *America's Most Wanted* feature a more varied menu of police activities and a correspondingly wider range of televisual devices. As its name suggests, *LAPD* attends exclusively to the activities of the Los Angeles Police Department. In addition to depicting pursuits and arrests, this half-hour show focuses considerable attention on the gathering of evidence. It also often has detectives recount the circumstances of unsolved crimes and ask the viewer for leads. At the end of many episodes, Los Angeles Mayor Richard Riordan appears on screen to encourage those with an interest in law enforcement to sign up for the force.

America's Most Wanted similarly encourages viewer participation. Hosted by John Walsh, an actor whose son Adam was murdered, the program's hour-long episodes tend to eschew capture sequences in order to introduce an average of three to five unsolved crimes or missing criminals, sometimes through re-enactments, and then ask viewers to assist in bringing the "bad guys" to justice. If they should spot one of these fugitives among their neighbors or can offer other leads, viewers are instructed to call "1-800-CRIMETV." Periodically, the program's producers present updates in which they show viewers how their calls have led to the arrest of fugitives from previous episodes.

With the exception of *America's Most Wanted*, then, each of these programs regularly features several sequences in which law enforcement officials pursue and capture suspects. These pursuits normally culminate in an arrest vignette. In one common form, this vignette depicts a group of policemen or bounty hunters bursting into a house, guns drawn, tackling an often half-naked suspect, and throwing him to the ground. In another form, it consists of a group of officers pointing their pistols at a suspect some feet away, forcing him or her to lie on the ground, face down, and then creeping closer until they loom over the suspect's prone figure. In a third, the arrest vignette features officers fingering their weapons while forcing a suspect to bend forward over the hood of a police cruiser, legs spread in preparation for an imminent frisking (itself often depicted as well).

Monotonously styled and frequently repeated, these vignettes are the equivalents of the "money shot" or "cum shot" in a porn movie: they are moments at which the full masculine potency of the leading character is revealed. These moments differ slightly from their pornographic equivalents, though, in the forms of pleasure they offer. In the conventional, heterosexual cum shot, the camera closes in strategically on the hard body and erect penis of the male performer. It thus offers the viewer at least two possible pleasures: of watching a powerful male control a female and of imagining himself as that male. The cameras of reality-based crime shows, on the other hand, go several steps further in enforcing an identification between the viewer and the protagonist (in this case, a police officer). Repeatedly, cameramen seek out not just the point of view of the officers, but points of view suggested by their *weapons*. In police cars on the way to crime scenes, camera operators record the dashboard and radio from the waist-level vantage point of a gun belt. At the moment of capture, they point their lenses down at prone suspects like pistols. When those lenses zoom in on key parts of a suspect's body—a pocket, a scarred chest, and, especially often, the buttocks (a place where a weapon or drugs might be hidden and where the suspect might be penetrated sexually)—they draw the viewer toward the suspect along the trajectory of an imaginary bullet. Unlike their counterparts in heterosexual pornography, the cameramen of reality-based crime shows will not simply let their viewers watch. Rather, by conflating camera and pistol, they demand that the viewer personally experience the power of penetration embodied in the weapons of the officers of the state.[8]

This power is highly sexualized, but only in a limited sense. As in much heterosexual pornography, the twinned phallic weapons of camera and gun are used here in order to humiliate and subjugate rather than excite a feminized Other. The pleasure on offer is not a fantasy of congress, but a fantasy of control. And what needs to be controlled is the sexualized agency of the "enemy"—in this case, the poor and people of color. Sometimes, this agency is represented by a weapon, or at least the possibility of one. Virtually every arrest vignette features a police pat-down of a suspect for knives and guns, a search conducted as though the almost-always impoverished suspect could actually have the same access to weapons that the police themselves have. In this way, reality-based crime shows imply that the agency of the "enemy" may be masculine—that is, that it may be able to "penetrate" the bodies of the police on the screen (and by implication, of police and viewers in the off-screen world as well).

More often though (and sometimes simultaneously), these programs suggest that the agency of suspects and their friends and families is symbolically female. When police arrive at a crime scene, cameras quickly record any signs of difference between the police and the citizenry. They peer over the uniformed shoulders of the police and zoom in on unkempt hair, scars and bruises, and tattoos. Likewise, when cameramen follow officers into a home, they focus on disorder, on piles of dishes, unwashed children, unmade beds. In contrast to the officers—who stand erect and uniformed, their bodies often hard with muscles or body armor—the suspects are depicted as unruly, messy, corpulent and disorderly. They are "soft" where the officers are "hard." Often upset, they appear "hysterical" where the officers appear commanding and "rational." In these ways, producers imply that the poor are not only undisciplined individuals, but stereotypically feminine as well. Producers here do much the same psychological work as Army drill sergeants: faced with the symbolically masculine potential of those whom they've defined as antagonists to assault policemen and viewer alike, to "penetrate" them so to speak, they assist viewers in labelling these antagonists not as "men," but as "women" who must themselves be symbolically penetrated by the forces of the state. Like Army recruits, viewers are invited to join the masculine community of these forces and to take pleasure in the domination of a feminized enemy.

That feminized enemy, however, constantly threatens to devour its masculine counterpart. Even weaponless, the poor are dangerous: in episode after episode, the sexualized entropy of their lives threatens to overwhelm the orderly police. And while this is true for all such suspects, it is especially so for people of color. In keeping with centuries-old American stereotypes, both male and female African Americans are often depicted as having uncontrollable libidos. In an episode of *Cops* set in Kansas City, Kansas, for instance, several white officers pull up to a disturbance in the middle of the night. At the edges of the light cast by the camera team, we can see black figures running here and there, like escaped slaves in some 19th-century plantation owner's nightmare. Then, a large African American woman rushes to the center of the frame, wielding a pipe. She points out a young black man and accuses him of lifting up her teenage daughter's shirt in front of her. The policemen chase, tackle and arrest the young man, who is clearly intoxicated. Later, a policeman explains: "A lot of the people we deal with out here are on what we call 'water'—that's marijuana dipped in formaldehyde. That gentleman obviously was, trying to have sex with a young girl in front of the child's mother. Now it's time to do a lot of paperwork and move on to the next one."[9] The implied alignment of forces is clear: young black men run wild in the streets looking for sex; young white men work to preserve a chaste world of order and reason. White men work with their minds on "paperwork," whereas young black men are out of their minds on "water."

This episode of *Cops* presents a fairly extreme example, but the principles at work within it run throughout reality-based crime programming. By depicting the poor and people of color as symbolically female, producers of real-life crime programs remind viewers of the pleasures of aligning themselves with a dominant and symbolically male state. Nor are these pleasures merely intellectual: when producers force viewers to look down (and sometimes, seemingly, *out of*) the barrels of police guns, they invite viewers to feel those weapons as extensions of their own bodies.

Alongside this form of camerawork, however, these programs also feature an abundance of computer-generated graphics. At the outset of each arrest sequence on *LAPD*, for instance, an icon appears on the screen, looking much as it might in a Windows computer interface, giving the title of the segment. Subsequent icons introduce the officers involved, describe the type of crime under consideration, and even present a map of the area the officers routinely patrol. *America's Most Wanted* regularly features a graphic drawing of a target zone into which the images of criminals are drawn as if dragged and clicked by a mouse across a screen. It also presents surveillance photographs from stores and banks, photographs which producers manipulate on screen as if they were digitized images on a home computer. Even the comparatively low-tech *Cops* and *Bounty Hunters* present onscreen tags at the start of each segment identifying the time, city, crime at hand, and officer in pursuit.

On one hand, these graphics are the products of a larger change in television style. As television critic John Caldwell has noted, the 1980s saw a shift across the medium "from programs based on rhetorical discourse to ones structured around the concepts of pictorial and stylistic embellishment."[10] Having come into being at the end of the decade, the reality-based crime genre reflects this shift. On the other hand, however, I think we can read the uses of computer graphics as an extension of an already-established conflation of gun, camera and masculine agency. In much the way that holstered pistols signal an omnipresent power to contain a given situation, so too do computer graphics seem to surround and neutralize dangerous individuals without necessarily assaulting them directly. When the computer *does* assault a suspect, it acts as a pistol might: by tearing apart the body. With the click of an off-screen mouse, producers reduce people to mug shots; that is, they eliminate their bodies and surround the faces that remain with statistics and icons. They take all that is dangerous and original in the criminal and embed it in the seemingly safe, rational world of information. In other words, they dam the flow of "water" with "paperwork."[11]

Computer graphics thus extend the camera/gun analogy in two ways: first, by fragmenting the bodies of suspects, they recall the pistol's ability to violate the boundaries of a human body; secondly, by surrounding the suspect with information, they suggest the power of the police to surround and arrest any individual—a power assured on the scene by weapons. These same visual techniques also work to normalize police activities by linking them to other, seemingly unrelated practices. Drag-and-click graphics, for instance, suggest a link between the pursuit of criminals on television and the pursuit of information on home computers. The penetrating style of camerawork that offers viewers a chance to look through the eyes of a weapon echoes the point of view available in many video and computer games and in broadcast news accounts of contemporary military actions (most notably the Gulf War, in which Americans delighted in being able to see through the eyes of "smart" bombs).

Extensive use of statistics and of overhead helicopter shots even suggests a resemblance between the televised monitoring of crime and the televised monitoring of sports such as baseball. This is not to say that viewers confuse crime, war and baseball in any conscious sense, but rather to note that to the extent that real-life crime programs share a visual style with other activities, they may also be able to borrow the perceived legitimacy of those activities. That is, to the extent that the viewer watches war or crime on TV as he watches baseball—from high above, from the heights reserved for the owners of luxury boxes, or, in the case of war, from the aerial vantage points usually reserved for government authorities—he may well be inclined to feel that war and the pursuit of criminals are naturally right and rule-bound in the manner of a sport.

Nor are such linkages confined to the predominantly masculine domains of the battlefield, the baseball diamond, or the video game. Real-life crime programs are shown in a highly commercial context and for the purpose of selling ad time, and in many ways, the structure of pursuit and arrest—a structure controlled in the material field through the use of weapons and in the televisual field through the use of cameras and computer graphics—mirrors that of the pursuit and acquisition of consumer goods. With each new crime, the viewer joins the police or the bounty hunters in a process of revealing a need to make an acquisition (in this case, of a suspect), of identifying the target for acquisition, of capturing that target, and finally, of taking that target "home" to jail. In real-life crime programming, the sexualized landscape of crime and its containment soon overlaps the commercial landscape of desire and its satisfaction, and producers know this.

To take one particularly glaring example, the Sam Adams Brewing Company advertises its beer (in California, at least) on *Bounty Hunters.* Their ad features a man drinking a beer who sees another man steal a woman's purse. The beer drinker flicks a bottle cap at the suspect's head and knocks him out cold, thus saving the day—and thus suggesting that the buying of beer and the capturing of suspects might each represent the exercise of a masculine agency.

That agency does not belong to the viewer alone, however, nor even to the law enforcement officials on the TV screen; it belongs to the American nation. In the same way that boot camp taught Brian Winhover not only to be a killer, but to be an American soldier, reality-based crime programs teach their viewers to feel not only the power of individual men within themselves, but the masculine power of the state itself. They do this by referring constantly to the Old West of American myth. The opening of *Bounty Hunters,* for instance, features four men wearing black vests or long range coats with silver badges on their chests. Scruffy, macho, they carry pistols and a rifle. "When the West was won," explains the voice-over, "bounty hunters helped to create law and order. In 1873, federal law gave them the power to enter residences and cross state lines in pursuit of bail jumpers. Today, modern bounty hunters continue to use that power to return fugitives to justice. Their motto: *You can run, but you can't hide."*

With such references, the America of today, like the Vietnam of yesterday and the Wild West before it, becomes a landscape in which to act out a national drama of justice. In this landscape, the gun symbolizes the link between past and present, and with it the link between the righteousness of American laws and the masculinity of their enforcers. By means of its conflation with the camera, the gun offers viewers a chance to walk alongside the bounty hunters, to undertake a mission on behalf of the nation, a mission to penetrate the dank, dark regions of American society, to "see" the suspect there, to "know" his crimes and thereby to humiliate him. In the slums of the twentieth century, as on the prairies of the nineteenth, those whom the government has identified as wanton and uncivilized "can run, but they can't hide."

But why should Americans and Canadians want to "see" criminals in the first place? And how is it that enough Americans and Canadians want to watch these shows that they should appear, in first-run and serialized episodes, twice a day, every day of the week, in a number of major North American media markets?

In part, the answer is economic: reality-based crime programs typically cost between $150,000 and $250,000 per episode to produce, while a typical news magazine program might cost between $250,000 and $400,000.[12] Primetime dramas and action adventure programs usually run between $900,000 and $1 million per episode.[13] Thus, even before they take the often substantial revenues from syndication into account, producers know that they need not attract either huge audiences or high-budget advertisements to turn a profit. Moreover, because viewers often perceive these shows as resembling news, producers see them as effective programs with which to lead into and out of the local evening news or with which to counter-program against other genres, such as sitcoms.[14]

Yet, I think these shows remain popular for more historical reasons as well. The first reality-based crime programs, *America's Most Wanted* and *Cops*, emerged in 1988 and 1989 respectively. These years fall toward the end of a nearly decade-long period in which first the Reagan administration and then the Bush administration sought to marginalize the poor and people of color. Under Reagan, this process took the form of cuts in aid to the poor, including $6.8 billion from the food stamp budget and $5.2 billion from child nutritional services between 1981 and 1987.[15] During the Bush administration, this process gained particular momentum as part of the "War on Drugs"—a war started under Reagan. In 1989, for instance, drug czar William Bennett implemented the National Drug Control Strategy. Even as it acknowledged that "the typical cocaine user is white, male, a high school graduate employed full time and living in a small metropolitan area or suburb," the Bennett plan devoted some 70% of its resources to law enforcement and focused most of its attention on the inner cities—areas inhabited predominantly by people of color and areas in which full-time employment outside the drug trade can often be hard to find.[16] As Michael Omi and Howard Winant have pointed out, these policies have been accompanied by "a regressive redistribution of income and a decline in real wages [across the country], a significant shift to the ideological right in terms of public discourse, and an increase in the use of coercion on the part of the state."[17] This broader process in turn, they argue, has resulted in the creation of an impoverished, disproportionately dark-skinned Third World inside the United States.

In that sense, then, reality-based crime shows represent the propaganda arm of a multi-tiered American state. Produced with the active assistance of local police departments (and at times national forces such as the F.B.I.), they serve as an ideological reservoir from which politicians and citizens alike can draw justifications of oppressive actions. This is particularly true of *LAPD: Life on the Beat*, a program first aired in 1995, two years after the Los Angeles Riots. As historian Mike Davis has pointed out, the Los Angeles Police Department considered South Central Los Angeles an internal Vietnam throughout the late 1980s. It thought of African American housing projects as "strategic hamlets" and regularly launched "search-and-destroy" missions in the area.[18] The 1992 riots exposed this process on live television. It should be no surprise, then, that the Los Angeles Police Department was eager to join MGM Television in producing a new series about its activities. As Chief of Police Willie L. Williams told a reporter in 1994, "For some time, the Los Angeles Police Department has been searching for a forum that would allow the public to see firsthand the dedication and selfless efforts of the men and women of the L.A.P.D. as they go about serving our community. The reality-based television series *L.A.P.D.* is a window through which the viewer will be able to see the truth of department activities."[19]

Yet despite their obvious propaganda function, we must be careful not to read reality-based crime programs only in the light of the services they provide to the state or to the television industry. We need to acknowledge the ways in which these programs deliberately confuse and intermingle several struggles, including the struggle of the state to justify its policies, the struggle of men and women at times to affirm and at times to tear down systems of racial and sexual distinction, and the struggle of people throughout our society to manage their economic and social anxieties.

We should also continue to examine the ways in which visual technologies and styles translate these sometimes abstract struggles into felt experiences of the body. As Kevin Robins and Les Levidow have written, "War converts fear and anxiety into perceptions of external threat; it then mobilizes defenses against alien and thing-like enemies. In this process, new image and vision technologies can play a central role."[20] Over the last two decades, the American government has fought a low-intensity war on the poor. For generations, American society has been plagued by persistent conflicts over racial and gender boundaries. By equating guns and cameras and by sexualizing the work of each, reality-based crime shows not only define the poor and people of color as external threats to their viewers, but engage viewers in a process of defining the poor and people of color as alien and thing-like. As in the military, the "good guys" are "men like us," men who take pleasure in being well-equipped, so to speak, and "hard." The "bad guys" are (symbolically) women or perhaps homosexual males, creatures who deserve to be penetrated and who indeed *must be penetrated* if their threat to the heterosexual male social order is to be contained. In the world of reality-based crime programs, as formerly on the battlefields of Southeast Asia, to be a good American is to be impregnable.

NOTES

1 Fred Turner, *Echoes of Combat: The Vietnam War In American Memory* (New York: Anchor Books, 1996), 76. Brian Winhover is a pseudonym for a veteran who requested anonymity.

2 *Ibid.*

3 As John Langley, co-creator of *Cops*, puts it, "What we try to do is capture the experience of being a cop. We put the viewers as close to being a cop as possible, to let them experience what a cop experiences. My ideal segment would have no cuts. We have very few cuts as it is. We try to be as pure as possible and take viewers through the experience from beginning to end." (Quoted in Cynthia Littleton, "True Blue: John Langley helped set the tone for the reality genre with 'Cops'," *Broadcasting & Cable* [May 20, 1996], 26).

4 Ratings have consistently shown that men and women watch reality-based crime programs in similar numbers. For example, a summary of the February, 1997 Nielsen ratings for *LAPD: Life on the Beat* broadcast on KUSI, San Diego, California, shows that in the Monday–Friday 5:30–6:00 PM time slot, an average of 9,000 females and 15,000 males between the ages of 25 and 54 watched the show. Another local station, KNSD, reports similar figures for February, 1996: an average of 7,000 females and 9,000 males

watched the show when it was broadcast Monday through Friday from 3:00 to 3:30 PM (Source: Tapscan, Inc.). The broad appeal of these programs is widely recognized by both producers and advertisers. As Cynthia Littleton has noted, the "broad-based demographics" of these shows have made them very popular with merchants selling such staples as frozen foods (Cynthia Littleton, "Reality Television: Keeping the heat on," *Broadcasting & Cable* [May 20, 1996], 25). For a discussion of the economics of reality-based crime programs, see "Special Report: Reality's Widening Role in the Real World of TV," *Broadcasting & Cable* (April 12, 1993), 24–38.

5 With one glaring exception: In 1989, *Cops* broadcast a one-hour special on Russian police.

6 And it is almost always a "him"—female police officers appear rarely in these programs.

7 Bail jumpers do include women of course, but on *Bounty Hunters*, males outnumber females approximately 2 to 1.

8 We need to note that the stimulation on offer brings violence and power together in a highly structured way: the viewer is never allowed to see through the "enemy's" weapons and is never allowed to look back at the officers at work. Much as boot camp limits the range of relationships open to a new recruit, and thus makes it easier and more pleasurable for him to give himself over to membership in the platoon, so the camerawork in these shows limits the range of identifications open to the viewer and makes it easier for him to enjoy an imaginary allegiance with the police.

In this respect, the camera style of reality-based crime television differs from that used most often in television news reporting. While reality-based crime shows work hard to position the viewer within the onscreen action, television news accounts tend to present that action in ways that allow the viewer to retain a greater emotional distance from the events depicted. Even in the network reporting of the deeply disturbing shootings in Littleton Colorado, Atlanta Georgia, and Forth Worth Texas, which filled television screens during the spring, summer, and autumn of 1999, news teams' camerawork rarely allowed viewers to approach the events from the point of view of an individual policeman. Cameras circled overhead in helicopters and moved in close among mourners, but in each case, the techniques of news reporting urged viewers to remain voyeurs. They brought viewers close to the action, but never structured the viewer's point of view in such a way as to demand that he or she see events through the eyes of a participant onscreen.

9 *Cops*, Kansas City, KS; Broadcast XETV, Ch.6, January 17, 1998.

10 John Caldwell, *Televisuality: Style, Crisis, And Authority in American Television* (New Brunswick, NJ: Rutgers University Press, 1995), 233.

11 I'm drawing here on concepts outlined by Klaus Theweleit in *Male Fantasies, Volume 1: Women, Floods, Bodies, History* (Minneapolis, MN: University of Minnesota Press, 1987). For the Freikorps soldiers Theweleit studied, as I believe for the policemen here, the labeling of an enemy as feminine and the generation of masculinized

response to that enemy occur simultaneously. One metaphor which participants have used to describe this process, Theweleit notes, is one of damming a flood.

12 Mike Freeman, "The economics of first-run reality," *Broadcasting & Cable* (April 12, 1993), 35.

13 Caldwell, *Televisuality*, 289.

14 According to Greg Meidel, president of syndication for Twentieth Television, "All our research says that viewers closely identify *Cops*' content with that of similar sorts of law enforcement coverage on newscasts locally. That's why [*Cops*] has been so compatible as a lead-in or lead-out from local news programming. It looks, feels and tastes like a first-run news program." (Quoted in Mike Freeman, "Ratings are reality for off-net," *Broadcasting & Cable* [April 12, 1993], 32.) For a lengthy discussion of reality-based crime shows and programming tactics, see Cynthia Littleton, "Reality matures into 'utility' player," *Broadcasting & Cable* (May 20, 1996).

15 Michael Z. Letwin, "Report from the Front Line—The Bennett Plan: Street-Level Drug Enforcement in New York City and the Legalization Debate," *Hofstra Law Review,* Vol. 18, No. 4 (Spring), 810; cited in Robin Andersen, *Consumer Culture and TV Programming* (Boulder, CO: Westview Press, 1995), 184.

16 Office of National Drug Control Policy 1989, 4; Quoted in Andersen, *Consumer Culture*, 182.

17 Michael Omi and Howard Winant, "The L.A. Race Riot and U.S. Politics" in Robert Gooding-Williams, ed., *Reading Rodney King/Reading Urban Uprising* (New York and London: Routledge, 1993), 108.

18 Mike Davis, *City of Quartz* (New York: Vintage, 1990), 268 and 244; Quoted in Caldwell, *Televisuality*, 311.

19 Quoted in David Tobenkin, "MGM Television follows 'LAPD' into syndication," *Broadcasting & Cable* (August 19, 1994), 20.

20 Kevin Robins and Les Levidow, "Soldier, Cyborg, Citizen," in James Brook and Iain A. Boal, eds., *Resisting The Virtual Life: The Culture and Politics of Information* (San Francisco: City Lights Books, 1995), 106.

The Gun as Star and the "U.N.C.L.E. Special"

Cynthia W. Walker

Viewers over thirty-five years old probably remember the television series *The Man From U.N.C.L.E.* Younger ones have probably never even heard of it. Judged too violent for wider syndication in the 1970s, the series languished in the MGM Library vaults for years.[1] A reunion telefilm, *The Return of the Man From U.N.C.L.E.: The Fifteen Years Later Affair*, aired on CBS in 1983. Afterward, the series surfaced briefly for short runs on The Christian Broadcasting Network (CBN) and a few PBS stations in the U.S. Midwest. In 1992, Turner Entertainment, which had acquired the MGM Library, released 44 of the 105 episodes on video cassette. Today, the series can be seen only sporadically on the TNT cable network, usually at five a.m. EST following wrestling.

For a few years in the mid-1960s, however, *The Man From U.N.C.L.E.* was a pop culture phenomenon, one of the hottest shows on television, particularly for teens and college students. From September, 1964, to January, 1968, viewers followed the adventures of a pair of secret agents: a suave American named Napoleon Solo (Robert Vaughn) teamed with an enigmatic Russian named Illya Kuryakin (David McCallum). The two worked for a mythical top-secret, technologically advanced, multi-national security organization called The United Network Command for Law Enforcement (U.N.C.L.E.). Each week, U.N.C.L.E.'s craggy spymaster, Alexander Waverly (Leo G. Carroll) would send his agents out to do battle against various international criminals and megalomaniacs bent on world domination. During the course of each mission, Solo and Kuryakin would meet an "innocent," an average person such as a homemaker, a film student, or a schoolteacher on vacation, who was inevitably caught up in the action. Both the naive innocents and the exotic, larger-than-life villains were portrayed by famous guest stars.

The Man From U.N.C.L.E. arrived during what Spigel and Curtin call the "classical" era of television.[2] During this period, Hollywood began to supercede New York as a television production center, and control over programming content passed from the sponsors

---

to the three major networks. Although the late 1950s and early 1960s saw the development of genre formulas and standardized narrative patterns, there was also a certain amount of innovation as well.[3]

Hoping to attract the widest audience possible, the networks began to rely on small independent production companies with proven track records to create hit shows that were fresher, breezier, more sophisticated, and had broader appeal. One of these companies was Norman Felton's Arena Productions, an in-house independent company of MGM. Arena had produced a string of hits for NBC, including the very popular medical series *Dr. Kildare* (1961). Because of their successes, executive producer Norman Felton and producer/writer Sam Rolfe (who was also the co-creator of *Have Gun Will Travel* [CBS, 1957–63]) were allowed a certain amount of creative leeway in developing *U.N.C.L.E.*

The result was a uniquely stylish show that appealed to a broad audience on many levels and in countries all over the world. A circa-1966 writer's guide for the series observed that for youngsters, *U.N.C.L.E.* was "simply an exciting adventure," but for more discerning adults, it could also be considered a spoof, a satire, and even "a sly commentary on our manners and morals."[4] *U.N.C.L.E.'s* success extended around the globe. It was telecast in sixty countries. Eight feature-length films were made from two-part episodes and profitably released in North America and Europe.[5] Everywhere they went for publicity tours, the two principal actors—and particularly McCallum—were mobbed like rock stars. Even the Beatles requested to meet them.[6]

"Nothing quite like *The Man From U.N.C.L.E.* has ever happened to television," *TV Guide* announced, dubbing the show "the mystic cult of millions."[7] "*U.N.C.L.E.* was very definitely the first television series to inspire a fandom-like reaction," observes Craig Henderson, a longtime editor of several fan newsletters; "*Star Trek* (1966) was the second, which is well worth remembering."[8]

That during *The Man From U.N.C.L.E.'s* most successful seasons fan letters poured in at the rate of ten thousand per week, wasn't surprising. However, that at least five hundred of that number were addressed not to the principal actors or to the guest stars, but to the unique gun the agents carried called the "U.N.C.L.E. Special," certainly was.[9]

The Man From U.N.C.L.E. series has often been called television's answer to James Bond, the agents projecting a concerned, caring, business-like image (they dressed in suits and ties, even when stomping through jungles or scaling the Matterhorn) and an absolute dedication to their work consistent with the socially-minded doctors, lawyers and other "professional" television characters so prevalent during that period. It took Ian Fleming's "sex, snobbery, and sadism" formula for romantic spy thrillers, domesticated it, and wedded it to elements found in more traditional television series.[10] In the pilot episode, called "The Vulcan Affair," Solo enlisted the aid of a so-called "ordinary housewife," PTA member and mother of two (played by Pat Crowley), to help him trap an evil industrialist who had once been the housewife's college sweetheart. The effect was as if James Bond had appeared in an episode of *Leave It to Beaver* (1957), dragging away June Cleaver to aid him.

Since Bond had his own distinctive weapon—first a .25 Beretta, later a Walther PPK—it was inevitable that Napoleon Solo would have one, too. However, unlike the Bond guns, both of which existed in real life, the U.N.C.L.E. Special would be a fiction, a clever construction that combined the physical appearance of an actual weapon with the capabilities of an imaginary one.

The Man From U.N.C.L.E. pilot (called *Solo* at the time) was shot in late November, 1963, using generic spy-type guns, like Lugers and various .45 automatic pistols. However, discussions about providing Napoleon Solo with a specialized, distinctive gun began soon after. Stanley Weston, who'd handled the toy licensing rights for another MGM property produced by Felton, *Dr. Kildare*, was now hired to do the same for *The Man From U.N.C.L.E.* Despite Disney's aggressive marketing of its properties since the 1930s, the toy licensing business at mid-century was still in an embryonic stage.[11] Weston, who was also involved in developing the toy phenomenon G.I. Joe, had particularly good instincts. After viewing the *Solo* pilot in February, 1964, Weston wrote a letter to Felton expressing excitement over the show's merchandising potential. A self-proclaimed admirer of Ian Fleming's James Bond, Weston made a list of 35 suggestions for emblem designs and spy gadgets that could be exploited for marketing purposes. Eventually, by the end of *U.N.C.L.E.*'s network run, the volume of tie-in items would be in the hundreds, ranking second only to *Batman's* (1966) during the entire decade of the 1960s.[12]

Among Weston's original suggestions was a proposal for a distinctive gun à la Bond that should feature a silencer. "Also, from our viewpoint," Weston added, "it would be great if Solo uses a machine gun from time to time."[13]

Felton and Sam Rolfe, the series' developer and first season producer, had also been giving thought to an *U.N.C.L.E.* gun. "I wanted one gun capable of shooting single shots or rapid-fire automatic shots," Rolfe observed in a *TV Guide* interview, "with sound or silently. I also wanted sleep-inducing darts, explosive bullets and just bullets, and a gun that could convert to a long-range rifle."[14] In addition, the gun would have to be concealed from time to time, either on an agent's person or broken down and hidden in an attaché case.[15] Of course, an actual gun with all these capabilities simply did not exist. It had to be built and, to give the illusion of reality, it was decided to use an existing gun as the foundation.[16] Since Weston had by now involved Ideal Toy Corporation, the problem was turned over to independent toy inventor Reuben Klamer and his staff at Toylab studios. The Toylab designers developed a "breakaway" gun based on the 1934 7.65 German Mauser pistol. By adding various attachments, including a shoulder stock, a longer, screw-on barrel, a silencer, scope, and extended magazine clip, the Mauser handgun could be converted to look like a spidery, futuristic state-of-the-art weapon.[17]

By the time the *U.N.C.L.E.* gun was ready in early June of 1964, the *Solo* pilot had been sold to NBC. With the name changed to *The Man From U.N.C.L.E.*, the series was already under production. But the gun that arrived on the set was not greeted favorably by the production crew. Not only did it photograph poorly—the small Mauser pistol seemed overwhelmed by the attachments—but it jammed constantly and wouldn't shoot. Prop masters Bob Murdock and Arnold Goode borrowed several Walther P-38 automatics from the *Combat!* (1962) television series set, which was filming nearby, and found this gun more to their liking.

During the next month, the *U.N.C.L.E.* prop crew developed a second U.N.C.L.E. Special, closely modeled on the original Mauser version, but now based on a P-38. For dramatic effect, the gun was modified to fire full-auto like a machine gun. Although the attachments looked impressive, they were nonfunctional. Indeed, the screw threads on the extended barrel made it impossible for the gun to shoot anything but blanks.[18] Also for cosmetic purposes, a magazine clip was created by taping two eight-shot clips together with duct tape.

The two versions of the U.N.C.L.E. Special were similar enough in appearance that even when the episodes were aired out of order of their production, it was difficult to tell that one had replaced the other. Eventually, the crew created six U.N.C.L.E. Specials at a cost of approximately $1,500 per gun, but only two had a full array of attachments. In recognition of their work creating unusual props, Murdock, Goode, and their assistant, Bill Graham, were nominated for a special Emmy in 1966. A few months earlier, they were also visited on the set by investigators from the Treasury Department, who subsequently fined MGM $2,000 for manufacturing automatic weapons without a license.[19]

Toylab continued to develop a plastic toy version for Ideal, dubbed "The Napoleon Solo Gun," that actually looked more like a standard .45 automatic than either the Mauser model or the Walther P-38. Selling for $4.99, the Napoleon Solo Gun Set (the pistol complete with attachments, badge and I.D. card) had an advance sale of $600,000 and was expected to sell over 2 million sets even before it was on the market.[20] When David McCallum's popularity skyrocketed, the Napoleon Solo gun was followed by an Illya Kuryakin Gun Set. The Kuryakin gun was also designed by Toylab, but was never actually seen on the series. Later, there was also a toy version of the villain's gun, the Thrush rifle, and several other *U.N.C.L.E.* gun sets, including one carried in an attaché case.

To protect its investment, Ideal nagged the producers to use the U.N.C.L.E. Special— preferably fully assembled— whenever possible. In a 1965 letter to William Reese, Ideal's Director of Sale Promotion, *U.N.C.L.E.*'s Associate Producer George Lehr diplomatically explained that "We do make every effort to include the gun where logically and physically possible," but that it was "impractical" many times to use the gun fully assembled. Lehr provided Reese with a list of scheduled gun appearances (both assembled and unassembled) and promised to keep Ideal abreast of developments.[21]

Over the course of its three-and-a-half-season run on network television, *The Man From U.N.C.L.E.* occupied five different time periods and was helmed by five different producers. As a result, the series lurched wildly, from straight adventure to humorous high adventure to satiric broad comedy to near-camp and finally back to serious adventure. These fluctuations in style and mood were echoed by the constantly changing role the U.N.C.L.E. Special played within the narrative.

Before, during, and a little past the show's first season, the customized gun occupied a conspicuous place of honor in the *U.N.C.L.E.* universe. Even before the show went on the air, it was featured prominently in publicity photographs, often fully assembled. In the introductory prologue that opened the first few episodes, the gun is assembled by Illya Kuryakin. Later, in the famous shattered-glass opening, it appears in Solo's hand. When the two stars traveled on promotional tours to boost the show's early sluggish ratings, the

U.N.C.L.E. Special, disassembled and stashed in publicist Chuck Painter's suitcase, went with them.[22]

Despite the involvement of the Ideal Toy Corporation, the gun's visibility was not merely a savvy effort at merchandising. Indeed, Ideal did not begin to market the plastic replicas until well into the show's second season, and a factory fire kept many units of the toy versions from reaching store shelves until after Christmas 1965.[23] Rather, the creators of *The Man From U.N.C.L.E.*—Sam Rolfe, in particular—saw the U.N.C.L.E. Special as an instantly recognizable symbol which would sum up the concept for the entire series.

It is ironic, really, that the Walther P-38 ended up, rather accidentally, as the foundation for *U.N.C.L.E.*'s distinctive weapon of choice. Mike Wetherell, an *U.N.C.L.E.* fan who now works within the motion picture industry, calls the P-38 a "dark character's gun," not one usually used by movie good guys.[24] Observes gun expert Jerry Ahern, "The P-38, only after the Luger and the Broomhandle Mauser, is as exotic and menacing-looking a pistol as they come."[25]

Nevertheless, Rolfe thought the P-38's negative image could be used to good advantage. Three years before *U.N.C.L.E.*, he wrote a television pilot in which the adventurer hero was a literal reincarnation of King Arthur.[26] In the script, which was never produced, Rolfe also armed his protagonist with a Walther P-38 which he described as "a wicked little memento of German ingenuity . . . which [gives] devastating and compact fire power to a single man."

Clearly, Rolfe, who also created *Have Gun Will Travel*'s chivalrous, black-suited gunslinger, Paladin, was fascinated by the concept of a latter-day knight errant. Solo and Kuryakin were not really spies, but world policemen, roaming the globe as international peace-keepers. Unlike Bond, they did not represent a particular country or political interest, but were supposed to protect and defend all nations, regardless of size or political system. The U.N.C.L.E. Special was meant to be a modern Excalibur, a deadly, potentially evil weapon, employed in the service of Good. Like the agents who wielded it, the Special was slim, sleek, and sophisticated, but also extremely powerful and highly versatile. Assembled, it supposedly could pick off a target, long-range, like a rifle, or, switched to full-auto, mow an enemy down with devastating rapid-fire power. Or, it could simply put someone to sleep with a tranquilizer dart.

This latter capability was apparently the contribution of Executive Producer Norman Felton. It may have been conceived in cynical anticipation of doing battle with the network over the show's potentially violent content. More likely, however, judging by the various inter-office memos, it was the result of Felton's genuine concern over *U.N.C.L.E.*'s youthful audience. "We don't kill anyone any more with the *U.N.C.L.E.* gun," Felton explained to *TV Guide*. "We just put them to sleep. And afterwards they're better off. They're nicer to their wives and kids after being hit with one of Mr. Solo's darts. The Thrush gun, of course, kills."[27] This was clearly wishful thinking on Felton's part. A few episodes in the first season did occasionally include the use of sleep darts, their impact signaled by a sound-effects "thup" inserted during post-production.

At the time of the filming of one such episode, Felton even sent a memo to then-producer Sam Rolfe requesting a scene in which Waverly would declare that *U.N.C.L.E.* would now be using sleep darts exclusively. "Now that we are moving into a new [earlier] time period," Felton wrote, "we should reinforce it so that young and old among the viewers know that we abhor killing, and in our *Man From U.N.C.L.E.* series, use sleep darts, which are not fatal but have the temporary effect of putting the victim to sleep."[28] However, no such scene was ever filmed and the use of the sleep darts actually decreased during the ensuing seasons. Nevertheless, nearly every article that appeared on the gun, from those in specialized magazines to those in the popular press, inaccurately reported that it was used by the agents mainly to shoot sleep darts. The impression created, that *U.N.C.L.E.* agents generally put their opponents to sleep rather than kill them, persists in accounts of the series to this day.[29]

Still, violence was always an issue with *The Man From U.N.C.L.E.*, both for the producers and for the NBC network. During the first season, when episodes averaged only one to three fatalities and few were deliberately or directly caused by the agents themselves, Felton felt justified in protesting against the network's concern. "In the hundreds of letters which pour in," he pointed out to executive Robert Wood, then at NBC, "we have yet to receive one criticizing us in terms of 'brutality' or 'shocking action.' Indeed, the mail all reflects favorably on the 'land of unreality' and the derring-do."[30] However, after producer Sam Rolfe left the show, to be replaced by David Victor, Mort Abrahams and Boris Ingster, the body count began to rise. For example, in "The King of Diamonds Affair," an episode filmed in January, 1966, and aired that March, a dozen characters die, including an entire group of eight villains dispatched by a cannon in the climax.

Ironically, as deaths increased, appearances by the U.N.C.L.E. Special decreased. Bombs, exotic devices, and "evil" guns like the Thrush rifle were used by both good guys and bad to dispatch each other. By the beginning of the third season, while bodies continued to pile up, the U.N.C.L.E. Special itself practically disappeared from view.

Network concerns and the success of the campy *Batman* series on rival ABC prompted *The Man From U.N.C.L.E.* to take yet another stylistic turn. In 1967, during the second half of the third season, gun battles and serious confrontations were replaced by what George Gerbner calls "happy violence"—long, elaborately choreographed brawls and silly, Keystone Cops-like car chases.[31] The body count dropped to zero, but in this atmosphere, the U.N.C.L.E. Special still had no useful place. Whether it was used to shoot bullets or sleep darts, the U.N.C.L.E. Special would have ended any brawl or chase before it began.

In the spring of 1965, discussions began about creating an *U.N.C.L.E.* spin-off series featuring a woman agent. No American hour-long action/adventure series had ever starred a woman, however, and Felton himself was dubious that it would work for *U.N.C.L.E.* "I was personally interested in developing a television series featuring women," he recalled years later, "but I did not believe, at the time, that a series with a woman in physical combat, which we often had in *U.N.C.L.E.*, would be acceptable or logical."[32]

Felton had reason to be nervous. The NBC Broadcast Standards Department was particularly vigilant in reviewing action scenes involving female characters. For example, a department review of "The Take Me To Your Leader Affair," a 1966 episode of *The Man*

From U.N.C.L.E., advised "caution on the blow which momentarily fells Coco [guest star Nancy Sinatra], since violent treatment of women is a sensitive area."[33]

In the end, economics won out. Even if *The Girl From U.N.C.L.E.* (1966) ran only a season (as, indeed, it did), it would be enough to fill out *U.N.C.L.E.*'s future syndication package.[34] A pilot, "The Moonglow Affair," was shot at the end of November, 1965, and aired as an episode of *Man* the following February. It starred Mary Ann Mobley as a very young April Dancer, fresh out of training school, teamed with a middle-aged agent named Mark Slate, played by Norman Fell. NBC was pleased with the 45 percent share the episode earned, but not with the cast. When *The Girl From U.N.C.L.E.* premiered in Fall, 1966, Stefanie Powers starred as a more accomplished, athletic April Dancer, teamed with Noel Harrison as a younger—and British—Mark Slate.

As with *The Man From U.N.C.L.E.*, Stanley Weston was once more hired to coordinate the merchandising effort. Even before the pilot aired, Erwin Benkoe, Director of Product Development for Ideal, suggested a line of "girl spy items," including a cosmetic bottle with a hidden radio, a mascara box with a secret camera, and a "pearl-handled derringer" made in "very feminine colors inlaid with a couple of rhinestones." Benkoe also discussed a compact that was actually a gun, but noted it would not fire caps, since "we do not believe that this will suit little girls."[35] But *The Girl From U.N.C.L.E.* did not last long enough for any girlish spy toys to even make it to store shelves. Except for a doll and a Halloween costume, most of the line of tie-in toys was eventually scrapped.[36]

As Felton predicted, trouble began almost immediately. Two weeks after the first episode of *The Girl From U.N.C.L.E.* aired, Felton sent a note to *Girl*'s producer, Douglas Benton, pointing out that "some New York reviewers commented adversely in terms of violence, or as one put it, 'sadism.'" He requested that Benton review all episodes to "make sure we don't have any offensive actions." Benton agreed and promised that "we'll watch it."[37]

Since *The Girl From U.N.C.L.E.* aired on Tuesdays at 7:30 p.m., and was aimed at younger audiences, the solution was to substitute humor for action. Jeopardy in the stories was almost always cartoonish, even surreal. For example, in "The Petit Prix Affair," a car chase is staged with go-carts. In "The Carpathian Caper," April and Mark are almost cooked to death in a giant toaster.

Although the U.N.C.L.E. Special appeared in Dancer's purse in the pilot and was subsequently featured in publicity shots with Powers and Harrison, the customized gun was largely absent from the series. Slate used it once fully assembled. Dancer never used it, even in pistol form, at all. Her regular weapon was a communicator/gun that looked like a transistor radio and shot only sleep darts.

George Lehr, who served as associate producer for both *U.N.C.L.E.* shows, says that neither of the two stars was comfortable handling the U.N.C.L.E. Special. "It was a large, bulky gun and Noel's hands were even smaller than Stefanie's," remembers Lehr. "And both of them were anti-violence. We said, 'Wait a minute: you're in the wrong show.' You can't just use your sense of humor to protect yourself in the face of threat. So we came to some compromises."[38]

Competing with *Daktari* (1966) on CBS, *The Girl From U.N.C.L.E.*'s share of the audience averaged in the mid-20s and never rose above 30 percent.[39] It was canceled after one season.

In the fourth and last season of *The Man From U.N.C.L.E.*, the U.N.C.L.E. Special made a comeback of sorts. It appeared more often and was shown, fully assembled, in three episodes.

In order to bolster *Man's* plummeting ratings, Felton had hired a very young producer, Anthony Spinner, to oversee the series. Spinner was supposed to restore the balance of action and humor and return the series to the more serious tone of the first season. By all accounts, he overshot his goal. Now, it was Felton who wrote constant memos to Spinner cautioning against the use of violence. "Let's watch out that we don't let our agents be shown as cold-blooded," Felton warned in one memo.[40] In another, he suggested the introduction of an "electric stunner" to the agent's arsenal, a device that would give an assailant a mild shock and thus cut short any hand-to-hand combat.[41] Although Spinner felt that motivated violence was necessary to keep the series dramatic and believable, he tried to comply.[42] The use of sleep darts occurred occasionally, brawls were kept short, and body counts seesawed. For example, in "The J for Judas Affair," there were nine deaths; in "The Maze Affair," no one died at all.

By the end of the year, the question of violence was academic. In January, 1968, *The Man From U.N.C.L.E.* was canceled and replaced by *Rowan and Martin's Laugh-In*. In the early 1970s, all six U.N.C.L.E. Specials, along with other series props, were sold at the widely publicized MGM auction. Five are currently owned by fans.

The next appearance of the U.N.C.L.E. Special came in 1983, in the TV movie *The Return of The Man From U.N.C.L.E.: The Fifteen Years Later Affair*. Special effects designer and *U.N.C.L.E.* fan Robert Short was hired to create a new, updated Special. With a limited budget and only two weeks to complete the work, Short managed to design only one gun based on a Heckler and Koch P-7. This Special was more modern and compact, but with the added attachments, the silhouette was similar to the original.[43] The gun was carried by Robert Vaughn as an older Solo during the action climax, but received no particular introduction or emphasis. Indeed, in a scene in which *U.N.C.L.E.*'s current female armorer outfits Solo and Kuryakin for their mission, Solo asks, "What happened to the special U.N.C.L.E. guns we used to carry?" The young woman replies, "They're in the special U.N.C.L.E. wing of the Smithsonian."

Arriving as it did, between President John F. Kennedy's "New Frontier" and the turbulent years of protest, *The Man From U.N.C.L.E.* series attempted to reconcile a number of contradictory, cross-cultural currents. The cozy conservatism of the 1950s was being challenged by a new, more radical culture—the so-called "Counter culture." New voices, younger voices, previously marginalized voices, were demanding to be heard. The public vocabulary expanded to include terms like "Civil Rights," "New Left," "peace movement," "generation gap," "turn-on/drop out," "flower power," "Pop Art," and "liberated woman."

In order to appeal to the largest audience possible, even escapist fantasies like *The Man From U.N.C.L.E.* tried to accommodate both cultures, attempting to be all things to all generations. For example, while *U.N.C.L.E.* included a good deal of violence and gunplay, its producers struggled to present the heroes as moral role models for younger audiences. The show featured a Russian spy, but left his political affiliation ambiguous, thus side-stepping the Cold War. Its sister series offered a woman as an action/adventure hero, but then refused to allow her to act unladylike.

The *U.N.C.L.E.* formula mixed reality with fantasy; the mundane with the exotic; political intrigue with campy humor; adult appeal with comic-book excitement; knowing irony with an almost utopian optimism. The U.N.C.L.E. Special, which was an actual licensed weapon, an expensive special effect, and a prototype invented by a toy designer, remains a perfect metaphor for the internal contradictions of the series, and an icon of the era as well.

Perhaps that's why it is in such demand as a collectible today. The Ideal Napoleon Solo Gun Set, which originally sold for $4.99, is worth $600 in the original box. One of the actual P-38 Specials from the series is also currently for sale. The asking price is $15,000.[44]

NOTES

[1] John Heitland, *The Man From U.N.C.L.E. Book: The Behind the Scenes Story of a Television Classic* (New York: St. Martin's Press, 1987). See also Jon E. Lewis and Penny Stempel, *Cult TV: The Essential Critical Guide* (London: Pavilion, 1996).

[2] Lynn Spigel and Michael Curtin, introduction to *The Revolution Wasn't Televised: Sixties Television and Social Conflict* (New York: Routledge, 1997), 1–18.

[3] Mark Alvey, "The Independents: Rethinking the Television Studio System," in Spigel and Curtin, *The Revolution Wasn't Televised*, 139–158.

[4] *The Man From U.N.C.L.E. Information for Writers* (circa mid-1967), 3. Norman Felton Collection, University of Iowa Library, Iowa City, Iowa.

[5] Cynthia W. Walker, "*The Man From U.N.C.L.E./The Girl From U.N.C.L.E.*," entry in Horace Newcomb, ed., *Encyclopedia of Television* (Chicago: Fitzroy Dearborn, 1997), 988–990.

[6] Robert Vaughn, interview by author, tape recording, February 14, 1997. Also mentioned in Heitland, *The Man From U.N.C.L.E. Book*.

[7] Leslie Raddatz, "The Mystic Cult of Millions: The People from U.N.C.L.E.," *TV Guide* (March 19, 1966), 15–18.

[8] Craig Henderson, private e-mail to author, April 17, 1996.

[9] Joel Cymrot, "The Cat With the Gat From U.N.C.L.E.," *Gun World* (May 1965), 24, 26–27. See also "What a Weapon for a One Man Army!" *TV Guide* (February 6, 1965), 12–14.

[10] Walker, *Encyclopedia of Television*, 988–990. See also the "Spy Programs" entry, 1562–1565, by the same author.

[11] G. Wayne Miller, *Toy Wars* (New York: Times Books, 1998).

12   Brian Paquette and Paul Howley, introduction to *The Toys From U.N.C.L.E.: Memorabilia and Collectors Guide* (Worchester, MA: Entertainment Publishing, 1990), 6-8.

13   Stanley A. Weston, letter to Norman Felton, February 19, 1964, Norman Felton Collection.

14   "What a Weapon," 14.

15   Cymrot, "The Cat with the Gat."

16   Heitland, *Man Book,* 150.

17   Rick Polizzi, Fred Schaefer and W. Stevenson, "Those Crazy Toys From *The Man From U.N.C.L.E.*," *Spin Again* (Summer 1992), 14-20.

18   Although the conception and development of the U.N.C.L.E. Special gun has been discussed a number of times over the years, Jon Heitland, who interviewed members of the original prop crew for his book, gives the most detailed and in-depth account of what happened with the gun on the set. See *Man Book*, 150-155.

19   Heitland, *Man Book,* 153.

20   Paquette and Howley, *Toys,* 8.

21   George Lehr, assistant to the producer, letter to William Reese, director of sales promotion, Ideal Toy Corporation, November 3, 1965, Norman Felton Collection.

22   Heitland, *Man Book,* 45.

23   Polizzi, et al., "Those Crazy Toys," 16.

24   Mike Wetherell, telephone interview with author, May 8, 1998.

25   Jerry Ahern, "The U.N.C.L.E. Gun," *Petersen's Handguns* (March 1989), 85.

26   Sam Rolfe, "The Quest for the King," pilot episode for unproduced television series, *The Dragons and St. George.* Unpublished manuscript, Sam Rolfe Collection, American Heritage Center, University of Wyoming, Laramie.

27   "What a Weapon," 14.

28   Norman Felton, memo to Sam Rolfe, December 4, 1964, Norman Felton Collection.

29   For example, see W. Stevenson Bacon, "Crazy Gadgets of *The Man From U.N.C.L.E.*," *Popular Science* (December 1965), 46-47, 186. Also, Robert Anderson, *The U.N.C.L.E. Tribute Book* (Las Vegas, NV: Pioneer Books, 1994).

30   Norman Felton, letter to Robert Wood, December 29, 1964, Norman Felton Collection. Felton reiterated his objections to Grant Tinker, then a vice president of NBC, in a slightly less formal letter dated the same day. Felton warned Tinker that "we are in danger of knocking the props out of *The Man From U.N.C.L.E.* series if we are forced to pull back any more in terms of action."

31   George Gerbner, "Television Violence: The Art of Asking the Wrong Question," *The World and I* 9, No. 7, 385-397.

32   Norman Felton, letter to Karen Vik Eustis, October 2, 1982, Norman Felton Collection. Eustis was a graduate student at UCLA who was doing research for a paper on spy dramas of the mid- to late 1960s.

33   Jean Messerschmidt, NBC Broadcast Standards Department, report on "The Flying Saucer Affair," [later renamed "The Take Me To Your Leader Affair"], October 12, 1966, Norman Felton Collection.

34   Felton, letter to Eustis, October 2, 1982, Norman Felton Collection.

35   Erwin Benkoe, director of product development, Ideal Toy Corporation, letter to Stanley A. Weston, October 25, 1965.

36   See Polizzi, et al., "Those Crazy Toys," 20, for *The Girl From U.N.C.L.E.* toys that were developed but never sold; Paquette and Howley, *Toys,* for the *Girl* items that did make it to store shelves.

37   Norman Felton, memo to Douglas Benton, September 28, 1966, Norman Felton Collection. Felton sent a follow-up memo on violence in *The Girl From U.N.C.L.E.* on October 28, 1966, to which Benton responded with a short note of agreement (no date).

38   George Lehr, telephone interview with author, April 13, 1998.

39   Stanley Birnbaum, report to John B. Burns, both of MGM Research, May 2, 1967, Norman Felton Collection.

40   Norman Felton, memo to director Tony Spinner, July 7, 1967, Norman Felton Collection.

41   Felton, memo to Spinner, August 23, 1967, Norman Felton Collection.

42   Spinner, memos to Felton, June 30, 1967, and August 16, 1967, Norman Felton Collection.

43   Walter L. Rickell, "Magical Movie Guns," *Guns* (August 1983), 34-35.

44   Thank you to Robert McGowan and the Special Collections and Manuscripts staff of the University of Iowa Library, Iowa City; Carol Bowers, assistant archivist at the American Heritage Center, University of Wyoming Library, Laramie; and George Lehr. Also thank you to Jon Heitland, Mike Wetherell, Sue Cole, Craig Henderson, James McMahon, William Koenig, Marc Douglas, Steve L'Italien, David Munsey, Diana Karge, Patti Ellis, Linda White, Alexandra Haropulos, and the rest of the *U.N.C.L.E.* fan community for assistance in preparing this article.

Life Against Death: A Lecture on Gregg Araki's *The Doom Generation*

Robin Wood

Y ou will have noticed that this film is so little regarded that nobody has bothered to bring out a screen version in the correct format, so you get these ridiculously cropped images all the time, which suggest that Araki doesn't know how to frame a shot. The laser disc, by the way, is just as bad, so don't write off to the States for it; I did.

I talked a little before about Araki's career.[1] I want, first of all, to contextualize this film by means of reference points, points of comparison. One that Araki himself brings up in the interview I mentioned[2] is Larry Clark's *Kids* (1995). Araki himself, I think without false modesty, but also without any conceit and absolutely reasonably, compares his own film to *Kids* very favorably. Another point of comparison, of course, is the work of Quentin Tarantino, because Tarantino is always who we immediately think of when we think of violence in film today. In fact, the first time I saw this film in a public theatre, I had a public confrontation with a gentleman who was walking out just ahead of me who was declaiming loudly to his wife, "They shouldn't allow films like that outside film school. It's all the fault of Tarantino," so I informed him that Araki was making films sometime before Tarantino began, and that Tarantino has shown himself quite incapable so far of making a film of this level of passion and intelligence. He didn't look very pleased, but he shut up.

What I wanted to say about any comparison to *Kids* is very simple; it is an interesting film, and I think everybody probably agrees that it is also a very unpleasant and very unhealthy film. Clark seems to regard his "kids" with a kind of desire, a simultaneous desire, fascination and disgust, the three not making a very palatable combination; they are simply objects *out there*. Araki, it seems to me, identifies passionately with his young people; he himself talks about his own romanticism, that he is above all a romantic, and I think this is very clear.

With Tarantino, the comparison rests on the use of violence in the film. Araki, it seems to me, defines responses to violence very precisely. In this film, it is possible to distinguish three quite different uses of violence, three different types of violence: comic violence, pathetic violence, and horrific violence. The first of those, comic violence, is exclusively associated with aggression by outsiders: the Korean storekeeper (Dustin Nguyen) who believes that shoplifters should be executed (and obviously means it), and the three people who attempt to lay claim to Amy (Rose McGowan) in the film who all inform her that if they can't have her, they would rather have her dead than not at all. The aggressive violence activating Xavier's (Johnathon Schaech) violence is always in retaliation; he never initiates violence, and his violent acts are always in the interests of saving his two young friends, whose protector and lover he is on the way to becoming.

Pathetic violence is evident in the wonderful scene with the dog, which is a crucial moment in the film I think, where the three leading characters suddenly respond to the horror of being responsible for the death of an innocent, the dog being associated with a kind of innocence that all these other characters obviously don't possess. A moment when the film comes to a pause in its violent onrush takes place over the dog's grave, when they have momentarily stopped their flight to nowhere to bury the animal that they inadvertently killed.

The horrific violence obviously occurs during the climactic bloodbath, to which I shall return.

Of these types of violence, only the first, the comic violence, in any way resembles that of Tarantino. But in Araki, it seems to me it is very carefully placed within the other modes of violence that are shown. I see here an absolute sureness of tone; nothing in the film is like the totally uncertain tone of, for example, the torture of Bruce Willis in *Pulp Fiction* (1994), which is disturbing for all the wrong reasons, disturbing because we feel that Tarantino means it to be funny.

These are by way of preliminaries to place the film in the context of cinema today. Why do I consider this one of the important films—American films in any case—of the 90s? This will need a detour.

There is a book that has, I think, long been out of fashion, but had an enormous following at one time and a good deal of influence, a book called *Life Against Death* by Norman O. Brown, subtitled *The Psychoanalytic Meaning of History*. The thesis of the book is that since the beginning of human history, man—or humankind, if you like—defined, following Freud, as "the neurotic animal," has been engaged in a struggle between death impulses and life impulses on every level, on the level of international politics, the level of national politics, the level of the social, the level of the personal, the level of the conscious, the level of the unconscious; and, Brown claimed (this is back in the '60s), that the decisive phase of that struggle had been reached in our own time with the invention of weapons of universal destruction that made the triumph of the death forces a terrifying possibility. Today, of course, everything has gotten much worse, and we must add to the nuclear threat pollution, the devastation of our planet's natural resources, the depletion of the ozone layer, the melting of the ice caps, the greenhouse effect and so on, and the weird weather that we see all around us daily nowadays.

Scientists vary in their estimates of how much longer humankind can sustain itself if the present escalation of what is commonly called "progress" cannot be arrested and quickly, but the general prognosis is not at all encouraging. Estimates I have seen range from 50 years to a couple of hundred. Nor is the realization very encouraging that such an arrest would involve no less than the overthrow throughout the world of capitalism and patriarchy, which is not exactly an easy task; it's the only task, it seems, that can possibly now save the future of human life on the planet.

On the level of the individual, the struggle is between the forces of repression and the drive toward liberation. Brown defines liberation in terms of the overthrow of all forms of domination, and in terms of what he calls the "resurrection of the body" (he is a bit fond of quasi-religious terminology from time to time). What he means by the "resurrection of the body" is the infant's discovery of delight in all the body's parts and all the body's functions, the total rejection of disgust and shame over bodily functions, over sexuality in all its forms. This in turn would lead to the freeing of human sexuality from all the constraints that our forms of social organization impose upon it: possessiveness; monogamy; the family, as we know it; the rejection of all taboos on sexual freedom and its many varieties of expression.

I think it is very unlikely—of course, it is not impossible—that Araki has read Norman O. Brown's book, yet *The Doom Generation* is the closest work I know to a full dramatization of Brown's thesis.

Let us start with the world that the film creates. We are given no date, and so we have a choice, I think. We can see it as a film set in the near future, possibly the year 2000, the year of supposed Apocalypse and the new millenium, or we can see it as a kind of surrealist heightening of today's reality, especially for young people. Anyway, one can obviously say that the film is set at the tail-end of the decline of western civilization. The scenes through which the characters travel are very eloquent: wrecked cars; clouds of pollution hanging over everything; barren landscapes—the pollution and detritus of so-called "advanced" capitalism. This is linked to all the signs in the film: Apocalypse defined as hell, the coming of hell on earth; "Welcome to Hell" are the first words we read. Within this world, Araki presents his alienated young people, confronted by a world in which no one of real intelligence or sensitivity could possibly wish to live, hence the flight to "nowhere"; they know, I think, that they have nowhere to go, that there can be no goal.

This brings me to a slightly controversial question, which is the relationship between, or the difference between, nihilism and pessimism. People called this film nihilistic, and Araki gets very angry about this, since it is not nihilistic at all; it is pessimistic. It is obviously deeply pessimistic as to the future of our world, of our own civilization, and the possibilities of growth it offers. The point is that nihilism means literally "a belief in nothing." Araki is claiming that he believes *very strongly* in certain things: in his characters; in their impulses; in their lives; in the life within them; in their longing for something, something that perhaps can never be reached and can never even be defined. This makes the film far from nihilistic. The truly nihilist directors of our time, I would say, are David Lynch and, possibly, Tarantino.

What we are confronted with throughout the film are questions of property and our own possessiveness, as embodied in the store owner who is willing to shoot anybody who shoplifts, so intense and extreme is his desire to preserve his property; and the possessiveness of the people who claim Amy as their longlost lover, two men and one woman, in the course of the film, their possessiveness taking the form of preferring her dead to not being able to own her. These, of course, are presented in a cartoon-like exaggerated (surrealistic, if you like) form, and reflect the drives of our culture with which we are all too familiar: our obsession with possession, especially the possession of other human beings; exerting control over other human beings; *owning* other human beings. What Araki shows us in the film—*what the main thrust of the film is*—is the three young people's progress towards a non-oppressive, unrepressed sexuality, necessary conditions for which are the casting off of all disgust over all kinds of bodily functions and parts of the body, and the casting off of possessiveness. By the end of the film the three have learned to share each other as equal lovers in a three-way relationship without jealousy, without possessiveness, and, finally, with the acceptance of bisexuality, crucial as the final stage. The moment at which the nice, wholesome, all-white American boys burst in with their flag and their swastikas is the moment when the two men are obviously on the verge of making love when Amy goes out to pee.

That whole scene in the barn is extraordinary, the scene at the end in which there is complete acceptance of a fully-shared relationship and the final moment of which is about to be shared between the two men as well as between the men and the woman. That culminates in what seems to be the most audacious political statement that anybody has ever dared to make in an American film: the clean-living, all-American boys unfurling the flag of the United States, pledging allegiance to it; the flag immediately juxtaposed to the swastika painted on the man's chest; playing the American national anthem on their ghetto-blaster as a prelude to stamping out the alternative young America that dares to liberate itself, dares to free itself from the rules, reimposing domination through killing. It is only in the final credits that we learn that the three characters' names are Xavier Red, Jordan White (James Duval) and Amy Blue, clearly Araki's alternative America stamped out by the moral American Right that is all-too-familiar at the present time.

I am not suggesting that Araki's films are without weaknesses, of which the most glaring, I think, consistently (though perhaps it is a little less offensive in this film than it is in his previous films) is his treatment of female characters. Amy is allowed a certain amount of autonomy and strength and force. She is very much shared between the two men, though; I don't think that she is ever quite given the kind of choice that they seem to have, especially Xavier, the "demon from hell."

In Araki's previous films, I think the treatment of women—he can't seem to identify with females—puts him in a very compromised position, although he has announced himself from the very beginning as a gay film maker. He *did* shock the gay community very recently, though, by announcing that he had fallen in love with a woman, and hopefully this is going to make a difference; perhaps he will be able to identify with women more closely after this.

I am especially glad to find what appears to be a very positive response to this film, because I think very highly of it indeed, and it has been so pushed aside and overlooked, and suffered a terrible critical reception; all the critics had to express how superior they were to it, how much more sophisticated and mature they were to it, and so on. Thank you very much.

* * *

Q: This could sound like it's a question framed as an attack, so I want to explicitly state that it's not, because I'm trying to get at something else. When you speak about this film, you give what anyone must see as an exceptionally articulate statement, and in doing that, you stand within a certain tradition of academic discourse, where people work at constructing, as best as they can, musical and harmonious articulate discourses like that one, and of course Brown does that very beautifully.

I'm quite touched by your comments, since I know the book you're referring to intimately. What troubles me about the film, though, is that this discourse you're producing is not in the film; these people talk in monosyllables if at all, and Amy's virtually catatonic most of the time. I'm not so much interested in saying this by way of critiquing your critique of the film, because I think that your critique is correct; what I'm interested in is the problem produced by Life Against Death *for this articulate discourse; I mean, what happens to the articulate discourse in this world of polymorphous, perverse sexuality?*

RW: You say the discourse is not articulated in the film? Well, I am afraid I think it is, very firmly. It is not articulated by any of the characters if you mean a sort of spoken dialogue, but it makes sense of the entire film; the entire filmic text is its articulation, not anything anybody says. It's realized in the body of the film, in the action, as the film moves absolutely logically, I think, to that devastating conclusion.

Q: I guess it would make sense too, then, that some of the more contrived and cliché moments of the film are the times at which it can be perceived as criticizing obsessiveness, such as the echoed hackneyed line, "If I can't have her, no one will."

RW: Yes, sure; it is a recurring gag, of course.

Q: Yeah, and even though it's absurd and silly, at the same time, its recurrence puts across that point of yours of that being central to the film.

RW: Another very obvious influence on Araki besides Howard Hawks and Jean-Luc Godard is the comic strip. Obviously, this film owes a great deal to the comic strip: its exaggeration, its parodistic qualities, the speed with which everything happens.

Q: I wonder if you can comment on the gun scene—that rather blatant one in which the convenience shop owner's head is blasted off by Xavier, and flies through the air and lands on the floor still talking. It's very outrageous and colorful and seems to be making some statement about gun use.

RW: I think Araki always loves to throw in a scene which is as wildly politically incorrect as he can make it. He does the same thing in *Totally Fucked Up* (1993). Here, the guy is defending his store with a gun and that's the gun that's used. Xavier doesn't have a gun. The point is that the violence originated with the other person. Xavier doesn't initiate violence, it's always the reaction to a provocation. It's always the other people who have the guns. Even though it's an extremely graphic and violent scene, there's a kind of innocence on Xavier's part.

I am really so sick of reading about guns everywhere, guns as the extension of the phallus: it's been done so much. I'm much more interested in the idea of civilization that's collapsing into extreme violence of any kind. The gun is the most convenient tool, the easiest to get hold of. Every family seems to have a gun in the United States, because of the ridiculous gun laws and the absence of any serious restriction. Obviously it's an extension of the phallus, everybody's known that for ages. Why say it again? If anybody wanted to listen they'd have listened a long time ago. None of these right wing idiots—who are gradually bringing about not only the end of civilization but the end of life on the planet—want to listen. In the U.S. at least, they appear to be a majority.

All the oppressive people in *The Doom Generation* initiate violence, with or without guns.

Q: Maybe Araki did *read Brown, since Brown was a Freudian psychoanalyst, and one of the final clips (pun intended) of the movie is of Jordan getting dismembered with hedge clippers, possibly playing off castration fear.*

RW: It is possible; I don't know. When we interviewed him, he didn't give the impression of having read a great deal of theoretical works. He gave the impression of knowing a lot about movies, and having a vast background in movies, fiction, and certainly in comic strips and pop and rock music; that is why I would be a little surprised if he has actually read *Life Against Death,* but I would love to ask him. If I ever meet him again, I shall ask him; he hadn't made this film when we interviewed him. He talked about it in the interview, and said how much he hoped it would be shown not only in film festivals, but also in shopping malls, because he wants to reach audiences of the same age as the characters in the film.

Of course, that's an aim that was completely defeated. The film was only shown in a few art-houses here and there. It may be reaching the public he wanted to reach on video, I suppose, now. It's obviously a very dangerous film from the point of view of the establishment, and could have a very dangerous, indeed revolutionary, effect on the right person—or on the wrong person, perhaps, depending on your political point of view.

Q: I'd like to respond to [the first] question: when I watch Araki's films, I feel that cinema is alive; there's tremendous love and energy in his films, and when I watch David Lynch's or Tarantino's, I feel that cinema's dead. The cinema of Eisenstein, Godard, Truffaut or Howard Hawks, I don't see it in a Tarantino or David Lynch movie.
RW: Lynch especially, I think.

Q: Yes, there's extreme cynicism there, a kind of fuck-you attitude; it's like, "Why go on?", whereas the lyricism and romanticism of someone like Araki makes me feel like the cinema's worth going to.

RW: Yes, I know, because there is a kind of passion there. Yes; I can't understand why anybody would want to make or be able to make a film like *Blue Velvet* (1986), because if that is how you feel, what is the point in doing anything or even trying to communicate or trying to speak? Why not either commit suicide or just retire quietly to a country cottage somewhere?

Q: I have difficulty with the scene with the dog, which I find a maudlin, sentimental scene; it's sentimental, it turned me against the characters. Where have I gone wrong?

RW: Well, I don't know; this may be simply a different way of reacting. I find it an extremely touching scene in the context of the rest of the film, which so totally, except between the three lovers in various ways, lacks tenderness, and is in a world that lacks tenderness. I find it touching that there would be this sudden remorse at causing an animal's death and a sudden feeling of caring for an innocent victim, unlike our lack of feeling for all the humans who Xavier shoots the heads and arms off of, who are all aggressive themselves, violent and murderers; I don't find that sentimental, myself.

Q: In one of the recent issues of CineAction, *it was mentioned that you either completed or are in the process of completing what was slated to be your final work of film criticism, and I am curious to hear what films, filmmakers or issues you find yourself drawn to in completing that work.*

RW: Well, if you are a reader of *CineAction,* you will have read quite substantial chunks of that book already, because all the things I wrote were written for the book, but I did publish them in *CineAction* as separate articles. It examines the treatment of sexual politics in a very wide range of narrative films, from the end of the sound era to the present and all around the world. In fact, it begins with *Sunrise* (1927) and ends with *The Doom Generation,* two representations of the love triangle.

Oddly enough, since I completed that book I am now starting work on another one, but I wouldn't call this one a book; the British Film Institute asked me if I would write what I would call a monograph or extended essay, around 20,000 words. I have arranged to do it on a very recent film that I love, *The Wings of the Dove* (1997), and to extend the whole thing into a long discussion of the enormous problems involved in adapting literary classics to film, so it is going to cover Dickens and Jane Austen and Henry James, and raise a whole lot of questions that I can't answer.

Q: It strikes me that there are a fair number of parallels between this film and Rebel Without A Cause *(1955); I was wondering if you have noted any such connections or similarities?*

RW: No, it hadn't occurred to me, but I think I already see what you mean; loose connections.

Q: You can see how Jordan could be—

RW: Sal Mineo, yes. But Xavier isn't a bit like James Dean . . . Extraordinary, I think, that actor, Johnathon Schaech. I've never seen such a naked expression of desire on a film actor's face, the way he looks especially at Jordan more than at Amy, despite the fact that Gregg Araki calls this "a heterosexual movie"; I don't think it is very heterosexual.

Johnathon Schaech, now, I don't know what he has been doing since. He played a small part in that innocuous Tom Hanks movie *That Thing You Do!* (1996), where he was one of the band, but that's about it. I hope we are going to see more of him; he's quite a presence.

221

Q: I was quite moved by what you had to say about the film, but I found myself feeling very sad during your comments, since I last heard you speak in the '70s when I was in film school at Northeastern, and it seems to me like I'm still hearing in a lot of film criticism what I would hear then, which is "This is a great film, but unfortunately the director hates women, or doesn't understand women, or isn't really interested in women." I don't know; I feel a great sense of despair, in that this has not really significantly changed.

RW: Yes; I think, in many ways, things have become worse. I don't know if it is much rarer now to get films centered on a really strong female character, where, even if she gets punished, we are entirely on her side; there used to be so many. All the great female stars of Hollywood filled that kind of role, and those films, it seemed to me, drew so much more attention to the ways in which women are oppressed. Today, on the surface, there's this sort of nice, cozy feeling that women are now liberated and emancipated, and they are all happy and have got all the things they want, so what have we got to say about this? Isn't it nice? Of course, you are absolutely right. All the evidence is to the contrary. I think Araki, to come back to that, has made a considerable stride forward with Amy in *The Doom Generation,* where the man and the woman have exactly equal prominence, I think.

No, I believe you. I think it is very sad, worse than sad. I think the worst part of it is that there are not enough films that can be read as actually foregrounding the ways in which women are still oppressed, at least not American films. You get this a lot in films from Asia, though, such as all these wonderful melodramas that are coming out, a direct line, I think, from the classic Hollywood melodramas—*Shanghai Triad* (1995) and *Temptress Moon* (1996), and other films. That is all gone, because the myth is that women are not oppressed anymore, so you can't make films about that, and on the other hand, there have not been that many strong, interesting, challenging roles for women.

What I find even sadder is that when two highly intelligent (I think) women, who also happen to be very close friends, get together to make a film, the result is *A Thousand Acres* (1997), which is an awful film. I thought, "My God; Jessica Lange and Michelle Pfeiffer together— they had been friends, they had always wanted to make a film together, this is their project, this is going to be wonderful." It is a lovely project, too, a feminist reworking of *King Lear,* a simply wonderful idea. It is so badly written and directed, though, and the plot is so clunkily constructed—a great opportunity missed.

Q: On that note, I was wondering what you thought about All Over Me *(1997), for example, in terms of its representation of young women, and in light of all this apparent despair on the subject.*

RW: Yes; I want to say that I have it in my private library, but I haven't got around to watching it. I will.

NOTES

[1]   The lecture was preceded by a brief overview of Araki's career.

[2]   In *CineAction* No. 35 (August 1994).

Playing with Words, Speaking with Guns: The Case of *Grosse Pointe Blank*

Steven Woodward

> "Where are all the good men dead,
> In the heart or in the head?"
>   Debi Newberry
>   in *Grosse Pointe Blank*

What is deeply unsettling about *Grosse Pointe Blank* (1997) is that it is a generically mixed film where words and guns, speaking and shooting, laughter and violence are yoked together, vying with each other for significance in the plot, dramatically represented as a battle for possession of Martin Blank's soul. Blank (John Cusack), the film's protagonist, is a baby-faced professional killer, a man who, ten years earlier, had wrenched himself out of a pedestrian suburban adolescence and transformed himself into a cold-blooded businessman who kills for a living. But as we see in this film, even the business of killing, in which people do violence dispassionately, is governed and directed by a formal language of contract terms and union agreements. Worn out by the mundanity of murder, Blank dreams about the adolescent world he has left behind, and most avidly, indeed, about his high school sweetheart Debi (Minnie Driver), whom, as perhaps his greatest crime, he had abandoned just hours before the prom. But now the time has come for the ten-year high school reunion, and when Blank returns he finds Debi miraculously preserved, so much so that she entrances him and he is faced with the difficulty of bringing professional life and dream life together. What is both surprising and disturbing about this film is that Martin—rather than coming to a cathartic collapse and release that could lead him to find emotional expression through language (Rhett Butler to Scarlett O'Hara, for instance: "Frankly, my dear, I don't give a damn!")—discovers that only his guns can really ly express the depth of his love. *Grosse Pointe Blank* adds a disturbing new romantic tone to screen violence, and a disturbing new destructive tone to screen romance.

Because this film is built so clearly on a division between two worlds, two ways of being, and indeed, two different filmic genres, the audience comes to expect that the resolution will involve a reversion to one world and the conventions of one genre. The character of Martin Blank is poised over the rupture between two radically different narrative modes: the action film and the melodrama. Crudely speaking, *Grosse Pointe Blank* starts as a boy film, modulates towards a girl film, but never really makes the switch completely. And that inconclusiveness is disruptive and disquieting. By playing with genre conventions and audience expectations, *Grosse Pointe Blank* becomes an extremely unstable text. Martin's gun plays a distinctive role in generating this instability, as we shall see.

Certainly, an incongruous mixture of jabber and cool-headed violence, and a combination of campy humor and hyper-real malevolence, are obvious from the first scene of the film, in which from a high window Martin Blank is eyeing a businessman stepping onto the sidewalk from a posh hotel. As with pinpoint accuracy and a single shot from a silenced telescoped rifle he executes a mountain-biking courier/assassin who is swooping down the street to kill this gentleman, his secretary, Marcella (Joan Cusack), is chirping into his headset about where to bank his contract payments and the invitation to the high school reunion. But Blank's economical shot does not save the target he was hired to protect. Another hired killer (whom we later discover as Blank's arch-competitor, Grocer, [Dan Aykroyd]), has been disguised as a hotel doorman, and now emerges from behind the target and his bodyguards to gun them down with his pair of silver revolvers, emptying the last shots gratuitously into the prostrate but twitching body of the businessman. Because this is the first scene in the film, it is impossible for us to take up a moral perspective on what we are witnessing. The cues we are given—Blank's cool-headed actions, the financial discussion with his secretary, the mention of the reunion, the numerous histrionically choreographed deaths, and Grocer's campy, almost play-cowboy style—do not in themselves add up to any obvious, generic situation. We have to defer a moral and emotional reaction to the scene because we do not know what is happening with enough certainty. And interestingly, this deferral continues throughout the film as we wait for the words which will explain the violence.

But our suspense is allied to a curious tension in Blank's character, built into the geography of the film and coded in its very title. "Grosse Pointe Blank" is, of course, an elaborate pun, a title which is in fact a melange of geography, character, and film history: *Grosse Pointe*, the wealthy white suburb of Detroit where Martin grew up, poised on the shores of Lake St. Clair, and remarkable for its racial exclusiveness; Martin *Blank*, the film's dubious protagonist with an uncertain past; *Point Blank* (1967), John Boorman's film in which a downtrodden criminal, Walker (Lee Marvin), returns from the dead for revenge; and, of course, *point-blank*, the terminology for a shooting at zero range, with its connotations of face-to-face confrontation and certain murder. So the title of the film points us toward both a play of language and a profusion or confusion of meaning. Is this film about point-blank murder or about normal social relations in a sleepy suburb called Grosse Pointe? These two themes may well be presumed to be exclusive before we see this film: Detroit, the urban nexus, a site of personal and corporate violence; safely removed from

Grosse Pointe, a suburban "retreat," site of family life and high school reunions, of isolation from the horrors of the inner city.

The two realms must dramatically merge after Blank accepts a contract for a hit in Grosse Pointe, and this coincidence provides the impetus for him to confront his past. By going to his high school reunion, he mixes the two worlds of radically different possibilities—brutal urban action and bucolic pastoral romance—and thereby confuses the film's genres. Boy film meets girl film; action film meets melodrama. Blank's world of cold-blooded killing makes no sense within the confines of Grosse Pointe, a world where violence is experienced only vicariously through video-game action. There is a radical difference between the bullyish violence threatened by the drunk and stoned classmate Beamer Bob (Michael Cudlitz) and the reflexive, deadly violence delivered by fellow-assassin Felix La PuBelle (Benny Urquidez). And when Martin announces to Debi, her father, and his high school peers that he is a professional killer, no one takes him seriously. Debi later confronts him about this: "You were joking. People joke about the horrible things they don't do. They don't do them, it's absurd!" But Martin *does* do them—trickling deadly poison down a string into a sleeping man's mouth—and that fact seems absurd within the placid calm of Grosse Pointe—of which, over and over, we see shots empty of disruptive traffic noise, free from congestion, and with plenty of empty sidewalks on which timid citizens can peacefully walk. That "absurdity" has a greater impact and implication than we might at first imagine; and to understand that, we have to examine not just the dramatic confusion, but also the generic confusion that's involved in *Grosse Pointe Blank*.

No doubt, for better or worse, guns and shooting have become naturalized parts of Hollywood storytelling, mundane genre indicators not particularly remarkable as threats. Guns are, indeed, *key* signifiers in the identification of genre organization. Mainstream cinema involves the organization of genre conventions into clearly defined and limited antinomies—guns/gunlessness, for example—that fulfill, condition, and occasionally defy or modify audience expectations. Within that cinema, guns have to fulfill a specific narrative function, but that function is pretty much limited by the conventions of the genre: so, for example, in a melodrama, a film structured primarily for a female viewing audience around the play of emotion and talk, a character can't—conventionally, at least—simply pull out a gun and go mad shooting people.[1]

In the melodrama, language is the medium of plot progression and resolution. Forms of violence, and most especially usages of the gun, are the vehicle for confrontation and catharsis in the action film—a genre aimed primarily, in the history of Hollywood film production, at males. "Action" films themselves fall into at least two main types. Most are either essays in hard-core brutality involving a narrative of good and evil resolved through physical aggression and domination (to name but three examples, *The Terminator* [1984], *Die Hard* [1988], and *Broken Arrow* [1996]); or crime/gangster films (*Scarface* [1983], say, or *GoodFellas* [1990]), where shooting is roughly continuous with the dimension of interaction the characters employ. Neither of these sub-genres, in their conventional form, typically challenge audience expectations with their violence. The hard-core hero must shoot to be good; the mafioso must shoot to survive—in neither case are we shocked to see the shooting. The moral elements of the action film ratio-nalize, and therefore excuse the violence, as long as the outcome is perceived to be just. And gangster violence, typically viewed from a point of relative detachment, can usually be voyeuristically enjoyed. Will Self has noted, "Around Scorsese's depictions of intra-gangster violence hangs the heavy scent of dog eating dog."[2] And this comment could apply to the majority of gangster films.

But in *Grosse Pointe Blank*, the justifying moral frame of the action film is absent, as we shall presently see. Without that frame, the gun sequences move us instantly into the realm of horror: our desire to witness violence and our filmic pleasure at seeing it hor-rify us (at ourselves) when that violence is not palliated by a sense of justice. We might like to hope that the horror of Martin's profession were balanced by the moral justice of his murders. And near the film's beginning, Martin does suggest that he has scruples, that he wouldn't, for example, sink a Greenpeace boat. But later in the film, he confesses to Debi that for most killers such ideological posturing is only a facade:

> It matters, of course, that you have something to hang onto. You know. A spe-cific ideology to defend, right? "Taming unchecked aggression," that was my personal favorite. Other guys like "live free or die," but you know, you get the idea. But that's all bullshit, and I know that. That's all bullshit. You do it because you were trained to do it, you were encouraged to do it and ultimately, you know, you . . . get to like it.

If Martin acknowledges that he has no committed ideological motive for his deeds, that he kills because he likes it, then both the audience and Debi can only excuse him if he undergoes some personal redemption, if he gives up his guns and recovers another self.

Nor does Blank possess the psychotic quirks of the gangster character that would allow us to detach ourselves from—and elevate ourselves above—him while vicariously enjoying his violence. Blank is an extraordinarily mundane character, plagued not by grandiose fantasies of guilt but by the middle-class businessman's entrepreneurial and personal ennui. He is both, like an action hero, a shooter; and, like a romantic lead in a melodrama, a vocalizer,[3] but neither his guns nor his words reveal any passion or moti-vation behind his actions. As he says to one of his victims, just before plugging him, "It's nothing personal."

And just as we do not know whether it is guns or words that matter most to Blank or are most revealing of his character, we are uncertain whether shooting or speaking will resolve the plot of the film. Within the conventions of the action/gangster film, it is the staccato stutter of gunfire that resolves the plot, not the careful modulations and negoti-ations of dialogue. Words involve negotiation of subject with subject and of subject with himself/herself. Shooting is the effacement of language, the end of negotiation. While in action films dialogue fills those long stretches between gunshots, it is never more than an artificial segue between one vital bloody moment and the next. (And with the new rapid-fire automatic and semi-automatic pistols, those stretches of expressionless talk are being compressed—see, for example, *True Lies* [1994] and *Heat* [1995]). With words, we maneuver into positions. With shots, we make our marks. Since there is seldom room for significant verbal negotiation in conventional action tales, dialogue does not really serve to resolve the plot, but merely to inform the audience of the situation and to prepare the scene for the all important shoot-out. Divorced from all physical and mental struggle, the shooter silences the world of language with the exclamation of the shot. The shot ends time and, therefore, ends language.

Further, within the action genre, the real-world gravity of the shot is sometimes replaced by a strictly filmic convention: struck bodies fly in all directions, literally as though they have no mass; or as though no social difficulties are posed by the deaths of the characters. In the rising action before the climax, in such a gravity-free environment, shooting and speaking need not be in opposition and may in fact become interchangeable. Characters use smart-alec one-liners rather like projectiles, and in place of bullets. They toy with their guns but spar with their words. In the eye of the action storm, we have time to observe and admire the dexterous handling of deadly weapons and the cool-headed wit of hero and villain. For a space, the smart comment, the pun and sarcastic jab serve as verbal equivalents of the shot. And this *playing* with guns— Arnold Schwarzenegger's face-off with David Patrick Kelly in *Commando* (1985), for example—and shooting with words—the teeter-totter Joe Pesci-Ray Liotta restaurant conversation in *GoodFellas* [1990]—are important elements of the highest-grossing action films (like the *Die Hard* series, the *Terminator* series, the *Lethal Weapon* series, and so on).

This kind of deferral cannot continue indefinitely. Nor can verbal wit alone provide the basis for resolution of the true action film. At some point towards the end of the film, violence will become malignant and explicit once more, and then, regardless of its size, he who plays most efficiently with his weapon wins the day. The apparent confusion of shooting and speaking in the action film is part of a larger, conventional cycle of preparation for, and anticipation of, shooting violence. At the close of the cycle, after the verbal shooting is done, the normative relation between men and guns is re-established, blood spills, and a moral is enforced.

But *Grosse Pointe Blank* is by no means a conventional action film. While so many recent action films are about a movement from speaking to shooting, from home life to violent action, *Grosse Pointe Blank* seems to move in the opposite direction. Though the shift from hit-man film to high school melodrama suggests that Martin will make a corresponding shift and, in the interests of winning Debi back, be converted from a shooter to a speaker, he is in fact not converted at all. If such a "redemption" did occur in the film, it would be figured in Martin's use of language, just as the establishment of his character in the first part of the film is figured in his use of the gun. This issue of language is supremely important in *Grosse Pointe Blank*. It is Blank's attempt to move from the contractual, dispassionate use of language to emotional engagement with himself and others through speech that provides the tension and the comedy of the film. For Blank and the other killers, language has taken on a restricted utility as a tool of evasion, a mask over the horrors of reality. When are Blank's words sincere? "I love you," he insistently calls to Debi as she runs from his hotel room after his brutal murder of a Venezuelan terrorist. "I'm a professional killer," he flatly tells friends and acquaintances who enquire about his work. "It's not me," he protests to Debi after stabbing a terrorist. Strictly speaking, all these pronouncements might be true. But language seems to remain impersonal for Blank, so that he must struggle to make talk, action, and personal belief coincide.

The film offers two linguistic mentors for Blank: Grocer and Dr. Oatman (Alan Arkin), a psychiatrist he sees regularly and to whom he resolutely refuses to acknowledge that he identifies with what he does for a living—"I don't wanna talk about work, 'cause I don't think necessarily what a person does for a living reflects what he is." Grocer wants to establish a hitman's union to avoid "embarrassing overlaps" in the contracts of the world's killers (such as that with which the film starts). Grocer is, by his very name, a purveyor of various goods for cash, an entrepreneur uncommitted to any single product, a supplier of the community's need. His bid for a union or club of professional killers involves an attempt both to formalize the contractual terms of the hit and to institutionalize the hierarchy of power among killers. But Blank is the descendant of the seamus or private dick, the wise-cracking film-noir detective now come squarely into the full light of day, and he naturally resists such repression of his own instincts and their corresponding pleasures. The presumably more wholesome Oatman is the psychotherapist who should be the mediator for Blank, guiding him through the spaces of his own psyche to make the essential connections for a healthy soul. Oatman's job is to establish a political accord among all the elements of Blank's psyche. But both Grocer and Oatman depend upon language in their negotiation with Blank, and, in both cases, the failure of language will presumably precipitate some violence. With Blank and Grocer, the immanence of violence is figured in the edgy dance they perform around each other whenever they meet, circling for advantageous position while their dialogue modulates between conventional, even gemütlich, politesse—"Good to see you!"—and outright threat—"I'm gonna get you!" With Blank and Oatman, the violence is soft-spoken, figured in the patterns of session ritual and telephone calls. But paradoxically, it is the fear-stricken Oatman who struggles to repress his emotions and who finally explodes into physical violence, demolishing his answering machine while a terrified patient (Sarah DeVincentis) looks on.

Oatman's sessions don't ultimately help Blank. His recuperation requires not just mental journeying, but a physical journey, a quest, a return to the site of his past: to his high school and the sweetheart he dreams about; to his manic-depressive mother (Barbara Harris); to his family home. And while Martin hopes the voyage will help him recover his suppressed emotional life, the audience hopes to find in the Wonderland of Grosse Pointe some rationale for his apathetic behavior.

But Grosse Pointe is smooth and unrevealing, a utopian blot. When Blank's secretary, Marcella, is trying to convince him to go to the reunion he challenges her: "Why are you so interested in my high school reunion?" Marcella simply replies, "I just find it amusing that you came from somewhere." But the somewhere turns out to be a nowhere. This is no *Big Chill*: Martin's high school classmates do not reawaken or reveal anything about him. Blank's father has apparently drunk himself to an early grave. His mother, confined to a mental hospital, seems to have only a lascivious interest in her son. And his child-hood home has been converted into the ultimate banality, an Ultimart convenience store which is the scene of Felix La PuBelle's attempt to eradicate Martin: after a spectacular shootout, it is blown up by a plastic explosive Felix stashes in the microwave. Martin's past turns out to be no less a *blank* than he is, all its qualities being either erased or unreadable. Only Debi provides a trace, a lead to Martin's dormant emotional life.

The confrontation between Debi and Martin demonstrates their different uses of language. In perhaps one of the most telling scenes in this regard, a kind of trial sequence, Debi and Martin sit in the DJ booth at WGPM, microphones before their mouths, every word they project at one another broadcast to an unseen audience-jury. Debi asks about Martin's ten-year absence, "What happened, Mr. Blank?" Martin's response is completely inadequate: "I don't know. I could venture a guess, but I think it would sound like a rationalization, some sort of a cop-out. I thought coming home, see-ing some friends, and I thought maybe seeing you, of course, would be the most impor-tant part of the equation. That didn't come out right." One belligerent listener, Nathaniel (Pat O'Neill), phones in to comment: "I don't hear any real remorse." Whenever Martin responds to Debi's direct questions, he hurries and stutters. But with her final ques-tion—"Do you have any deeply personal responses you want to share with our listen-ers?"—he is reduced to a silently mouthed "No." He can be smug, he can be smart, he can be funny, he can be cute; but Martin is incapable of saying anything that really matters. Words don't "come out right."

Trying to justify to Debi the fact that he gets paid for being a killer, Blank explains: "When I left [Grosse Pointe] I joined the army, and when I took the service exam, my psych profile fit a certain moral flexibility." This "moral flexibility" makes him a psy-chopath in Debi's eyes. But Martin desperately counters this: "No, no, no. A psychopath kills for no reason. I kill for money. It's a job." Of course, the psychopath does have a rea-son to kill, though it's an emotionally quirky, irrational, unpredictable reason. Therefore, Martin's purely pragmatic reason for killing renders him even less human than the psy-chopath. His killings are self-indulgent—as he admits, "You get to like it after a while"—not attached to any personal emotion or social morality. And what Debi calls psychotic, the audience interprets, from one step further removed, as black humor, a way of enact-ing or, at least, naming the possibilities that we do not or cannot act out: "People joke about the horrible things they don't do." But Martin does not joke, he enacts.

If Martin is to be restored, if his soul is to be filled, we would expect the moment to come at the reunion. Here, in the company of his prom date, among old classmates living statistically normal lives, underneath banners that proclaim that "The future is UNWRIT-TEN," Martin has a chance to rewrite his life. And we are given several clues that Martin is, in fact, undergoing a renewal. Face to face with a former classmate's baby, Martin reverts to a spellbound amazement as he watches the expressions that cross the angelic face (for not even this is blank). And when he is confronted in the hallway by Beamer Bob, a former bully turned BMW salesman, we expect Martin to flatten him with a few adroit blows. But as Debi spies on the scene, Martin defuses the confrontation, mocking-ly encouraging Bob to turn his violence into the personal expression of poetry. It seems that Martin Blank, the character who has been described as an "altar boy with a gun,"[4] can recover some of his innocence simply by giving up the gun.

But the transition is not so uncomplicated, nor is it painless. Martin's personal history may not be inscribed in the placid text of his high school past, but he has written his autobiography with his violent acts and these represent malignant memories that both deform him and inevitably provoke retaliation. Before Martin left for the reunion, he stood before the mirror, loading his gun and reciting Dr. Oatman's little mantra, "This is me breathing." Shooting is as irrepressible as breathing, both natural and necessary. Not surprisingly, then, when Felix La PuBelle appears at Martin's locker, just after the poetic pacification of Beamer Bob, Martin quickly recovers his killer instincts, exchanging grapples and punches. But the death blow is not delivered with gun or with punch. In a parody of the idea of verbal communication, of writing his own future, Martin dispatches La PuBelle, stabbing his jugular with an insurance salesman's pen. And when Blank and Grocer finally battle it out, man to man, in Debi's house, their guns seem powerless to harm each other. The band of killers who have come for Debi's father and the federal agents who want to trap and kill Blank are mowed down with bullets (except for one who is finished off with a skillfully-wielded frying pan), but Grocer has to be felled with a TV set. These symbolically charged, point-blank deaths by pen and TV set are, in fact, the most shocking and visceral in the film. And paradoxically, it is from the *blank* glass of the TV screen that Blank receives the gravest of his injuries—stigmata on his hands.

It takes a freak chance, a queer Oedipal twist of the script, to give the film the gloss of a happy ending. The man Martin Blank is supposed to assassinate in Grosse Pointe turns out to be Debi's father. And by identifying with him, by protecting rather than killing him, Martin is finally able to prove the depth of his love to Debi. Not surprisingly, it is at this point, where his shooting has some personal relevance to him, that he becomes verbally eloquent. The climactic shootout is in full force. And in this virtual *flagrante delicto*, Martin finally explains his ten-year absence: "I was sitting there alone on prom night, in that goddamn rented tuxedo, and the whole night flashed before my eyes and I realized finally, and for the first time, that I wanted to kill somebody." The future was, apparently, all too clearly written for Martin—the entirely predictable professional life, the serenity of long-established love, homogenized suburban living, and choice reduced to a decision between BMW or Saab—and the only way to escape it was through the symbolically liberating power of murder.

Somewhere between the bullets and blows that follow, and a few words offered through the bathroom door, Debi finally accepts Martin for what he is. As the two drive out of town together, perhaps in parody of that perpetual American motif of lighting out for the territories, Debi has the last lines of the film, delivered over the shot: "Some people say forgive and forget. Ah, I don't know. I say forget about forgiving, and just accept. And . . . get the hell out of town." But if Debi and Martin are driving, honeymoon-fashion, along the banks of the lake out of town, they are in fact going nowhere. For by mixing words and guns, melodramatic dialogue and sincere shooting, the film has confused the geography of genres—the suburban house, site of melodrama, with the urban turf, site of the typical action film. And Grosse Pointe, far from simple neutral space through which characters can move to a conclusion, is in fact contaminated—not just by the violence which has been performed there, but by repression in general.

If *Grosse Pointe Blank* really tries to cross the great divide, to make words matter and guns mute, then it ultimately fails. For all of Martin Blank's efforts to get in touch with a reality through words—the reality of his childhood and youth by attending his high school reunion, the reality of his love for his abandoned high school sweetheart, the reality of his inner emotional life through Dr. Oatman—fail. This is a film about confrontations that language fails to resolve. And here it must be this way, because violence is the end of language, where the mute visceral reality of the body—its vulnerability—becomes the only point. Words are just tricks, limitations, instructions about when to fire: ultimately irrelevancies. Guns are the point of the film—its central narrative dimension. But given this, what can be done with the language, the words, that surround the pistol-talk, pressing in upon the stretches of silence between shots (and which disappear almost completely at the film's ending)? If Blank longs to cross over into a world where words mean what they say, as material and effective as bullets, he must be disappointed because the constricting walls of the male-centered action genre won't break.

Perhaps because of the complex implications of the film, critics remain divided, even with themselves, on the issue of Blank's redemption. Stanley Kauffman is at once sardonic and outraged: "This picture is a sunburst, a bright and breezy romantic comedy," and "All the shootings . . . are presented in the tone of a Tropicana commercial. The picture is ludicrous, not funny; disgusting, not smart."[5] But Jill Gerston, reviewing in the *New York Times*, wrote: "The film's violence couldn't be so nasty or gory as to turn off audiences, and Martin Blank (Mr. Cusack), the burned-out assassin, couldn't be a cold-blooded psychopath incapable of redemption."[6]

Cusack himself has referred to the film as "deeply subversive." The inconsistencies evident in critics' responses to the film are certainly a sign of its subversive structure in which generic expectations are defied by narrative ironies. In the end, the language of the film may be what it is, not for the protagonist to resolve his spiritual malaise, but for the scriptwriters to play with: "Grocer," the type of person one may become under the urban corporate stresses that construct places like Grosse Pointe. "Gross," the high school adjective which serves as universal comment on the trivial, the objectionable, the hideous, and the terrifying, at once. "Grosse Pointe," the sour suburban setting from which any vital teenager would long to escape.

NOTES

[1]   An exceptionally interesting play with this exact genre convention, involving guns, "madness," and melodrama, is to be found in Douglas Sirk's *Written on the Wind* (1956).

2 Will Self, "The American Vice," *Screen Violence*, ed. Karl French (London: Bloomsbury, 1996), 74.

3 It is worth noting that Cusack had played both romantic and action leads before contracting to do this film.

4 Peter Travers, "*Grosse Pointe Blank*," *Rolling Stone* 759 (May 1, 1997), 57.

5 "Disneyland and Elsewhere," *The New Republic* Vol. 216 No. 19 (May 12, 1997), 26–27.

6 "Murder: With Laughs on the Side," *New York Times* (May 11, 1997), 23.

Afterword

Murray Pomerance

Popular culture has put a face of spectacle and bravura on guns and gun use, to be sure—a face that has come to seem mawkish, irredeemably crass, and perverse in a world where within a period of eight months, children shoot at other children with military weapons in public schools in Alberta and Colorado; a would-be assassin stakes out a daycare center; a disgruntled day-trader commits a frenzied attack on his family and on brokerage clerks in Atlanta; and an unemployed man shouting anti-religious slogans guns down teenagers praying in Texas. But it is easy enough to forget, in the face of gruesome realities that seem pitted *against* Hollywood imagery, that Hollywood, too, is an address where guns can be bought and used.

Like the bullet-eaten bodies of *Grosse Pointe Blank, Dawn Patrol, Broken Arrow, The Doom Generation, G.I. Jane, The Virginian, Due South, The Peacemaker, Thelma and Louise, Juice, Blue Steel, The Man From U.N.C.L.E., Starship Troopers, LAPD: Life on the Beat, Battleship Potemkin, Bulworth* and the many other cultural artifacts explored in this volume, the history of motion pictures has itself been a bullet-torn corpus—or at least bullet-pocked, a dance of targets and targeters, both on and off the screen. As for television, that noticeably lower *monde*,[1] though it has in general shown itself, over the past ten years, politically sensitive enough to have a little less to do with bullet wounds than with gun flashing—prime-time police dramas and space epics notwithstanding—its own history, going back to *The Cisco Kid* (1950), *Gunsmoke* (1955), *Have Gun Will Travel* (1957), *The Rifleman* (1958), and *The Untouchables* (1959) is similarly one in which gun use has been as notable out of the narrative context as in. It could be argued, indeed, that the transformation of shooting into a noteworthy, staged, melodramatic and crisis-provoking activity in everyday life has been accomplished through the agency of the mass media and the framing techniques of pop culture. Because shooting was designed to be looked at it has become, in many ways, especially visible, even an icon of visibility and showmanship, like the huge cinema razed to the ground during the Blitz by errant anti-aircraft guns in London in a terrifying but wondrous scene in *Things to Come* (1936): it is photographed—shot—with a wide-angle lens and grows even huger to our eyes as it is hit and crumbles, a monster bloated with visibility.

We can gloss the shot-filled history of film and television easily enough by touching upon only a few incidents and images of notable off-stage gunfire in and around Hollywood, only isolated cases drawn from a bullet-riddled, and often riddling, history of community and production violence. The most recent of many gunny public extravaganzas focused on the May 28, 1998 murder by gunshot of Phil Hartman, a satiric comedian, at the hands of his apparently unbemused wife. Not long before, Bill Cosby's son Ennis was gunned down on the shoulder of the San Diego Freeway. Tupac Shakur was mowed down in Las Vegas September 7, 1996 not long after rapping about his allegiance to his "girlfriend"—his favorite pistol; Biggie Smalls was shot outside the Petersen Automobile Museum in L.A. March 9, 1997. Hervé Villechaize, a star of the prime time series *Fantasy Island* (1978), died by self-inflicted gunshot wounds on September 4, 1993 in North Hollywood; as, in other locations in the movie colony, did actors Dennis Tait in January 1993 and Brian Keith in June 1997, director Donald Cammell in April 1996, and producer David Begelman in August 1995. Sometimes the machine of movie-making itself seemed malevolently to pull the trigger: at CBS Studios October 12, 1984, while shooting *Cover Up* (1984), a young actor named Jon-Eric Hexum playfully pointed at his head and then triggered a stunt gun that turned out to be loaded. In a similar misplay, Brandon Lee was killed at Carolco Studios March 31, 1993 during the shooting of *The Crow* (1994). Fame and public celebrity, not quite a movie machine but surely part of one, indisputably inspired the shooting (in an elegant New York neighborhood) of John Lennon, the star of *How I Won the War* (1967), in December 1980; and the attempt by John Hinckley— singing praises of Jodie Foster, star of at least two gun-centered feature films, *Taxi Driver* (1976) and *The Silence of the Lambs* (1991)—upon the life of Ronald Reagan, then President of the United States but earlier—and at least as memorably—the star of *Murder in the Air* (1940), *This Is the Army* (1943), and *The Killers* (1964).

But since early in the century life in Hollywood has been rich with deaths—usually suicides—by the gun: Kenneth Anger alone lists Ross Alexander, Pedro Armendariz, "Red" Barry, Paul Bern, Herman Bing, Clyde Bruckman, Wilfred Buckland, James Cardwell, Arthur Edmund Carew, Lester Cuneo, Karl Dane, Bob Duncan, Tom Forman, Claude Gillingwater, Jonathan Hale, Bobby Harron, Jose Alex Havier, George Hill, Nelson McDowell, John Mitchell, Bert Moorhouse, George Reeves, Walter Slezak, Mary Wiggins, and Gig Young, in his *Hollywood Babylon II*, a quirky saga devoted to relishing the seamy underbelly of an industry devoted to producing "shots" and yet shot through itself with weapons and tensions and itchy trigger fingers.

Of course, legion have been the stagings and crises of gun use onscreen, jumping the gaps between genres and developing in a continuous line since the very beginnings of film and television. Scientists, mad and rational; soldiers, honorable and mercenary; intellectuals, hardboiled and effete; questing lonely men and women; tycoons and destitutes; even children carry guns, point them, pull their triggers in a wide range of entertainment contexts only some of which have logical or historical connections with shooting (such as Alan Bridges's *The Shooting Party* [1984]). In the form of a gratuitous, bloated, pirates' cannon, we can see the gun powering the plot of Disney's animated fantasy *Peter Pan* (1953) just as it does in his *Old Yeller* (1957), which ends with a signal—and, for children, profoundly disturbing—rifle shot aimed at a beloved, now rabid, dog. We can observe (and celebrate), in Truffaut's sparkling *The Bride Wore Black* (1967), a female serial killer (Jeanne Moreau) taking pot-shots at males with a rifle from a high window; or be released by Maria Schneider's gunshot as sexual culmination and liberation in Bertolucci's *Last Tango in Paris* (1973). The character and quality of guns is charming in itself: we can be astonished by the gigantic *Guns of Navarone* (1961), tickled by the bizarre pink laser-snorting guns of *Mars Attacks* (1996), revolted by the brazen, thundering, merciless guns in *GoodFellas* (1990), chilled by the obese shotguns of *Donnie Brasco* (1997), which seem to shoot blood. In *Men in Black* (1997), guns can be a source of delirious pleasure, squirting cobalt blue goo, blinding illumination, even wit.

Wit, indeed, has infected gun narratives and the gunner parody is becoming a new staple of production. Harold Ramis's *Analyze This* (1999) explores the possibility that a mafia hitman (Robert De Niro) has developed a debilitating (and hilarious) neurosis. *Mickey Blue Eyes* (Kelly Makin, 1999) spoofs Mafia shootist sagas, placing the unlikely Hugh Grant in the company of the once-mortifying but now comedic James Caan and the bulb-nosed (and, in contemporary mafia films, virtually omnipresent) Joe Viterelli. Interestingly enough, both of these films contain virtually the same scene of a rabid nocturnal riverside gunfight and in each film the trained, experienced killer (De Niro; Caan) hides in terror of being shot. The viewer doesn't know whether to sympathize or explode with laughter; but either way, in viewing we are made to feel powerful and safe, not threatened with victimization through violence.

The gun typically marks the hero and the villain—James Bond's PPK, for example, or Shane's weathered Colt on one side; and the Imperial Death Star "projector" in *Star Wars* (1977) or the Jackal's take-down armature in *The Day of the Jackal* (1973) on the other. There are women's guns, such as the shrunken sweet little object Peter Lorre was typically made to hold; and long heavy armatures of masculinity: we see them in the hands of Clint Eastwood (who growls, if only in *Unforgiven* [1992], "Any man that don't want to get killed better clear on out the back!"), of John Wayne, of Gary Cooper. In *The Maltese Falcon* (1941), virtually every character has a gun (of idiosyncratic size and appearance); and sometimes, as in Hitchcock's *Marnie* (1964), the weapon turns up in the hand of a character so psychically or existentially wounded that shooting is almost impossible. Hitchcock, of course, has explored gun use from almost every angle, reaching an apotheosis of sorts in *Rear Window* (1954), where the gun is loaded with flashbulbs; and in the cantata scene of *The Man Who Knew Too Much* (1956), where the gun becomes a camera. Even improbable, guns are significant: in Frank Oz's comedic spoof, *What About Bob?* (1991), a neurotic psychiatrist keeps a hunting rifle over his mantlepiece, insinuating even into the Hippocratic profession at least the dream of blowing irritating folks away. Just as guns can be definitive and blunt in narrative use, they can be subtle and riddling:

Antonioni's *Blow Up* (1966) is structured like a crystal configured upon a narrative space occupied by a gun, at once profoundly visible and exegetically silent, hidden in the greenery of a tranquil park; and his *The Passenger* (1975) tells the story of a civilized journalist who trades identities with a dead stranger, only to learn that he now apparently makes his living by arming a revolution. Guns and gun-holding can be innocent: see the fast food scene of *Falling Down* (1993). And for all their lethality, guns can be hilarious: in Charles Jones's *Rabbit of Seville* (1949) and other cartoons starring Elmer Fudd, the hunting rifle is a token of immortal quest—instantly, and hilariously, conjuring the ineffable "wabbit" who is impossible to kill. Guns resurface as emblems of human impotence—antiphalluses—in the 1950s sci-fi horror genre, massed but utterly inutile against alien invasion threat: in *Invaders from Mars* (1953), gun users themselves are neurologically neutralized; in *The Day the Earth Stood Still* (1951) and *The War of the Worlds* (1953), as in countless other films of the same time, big military guns find alien hardware impregnable.

Guns and gun use, at any rate, are notably present *outside* the conventional police, cowboy, adventure, and *noir* genres which normally embed them, though we should look at those genres. Gun use in police films and television cop shows has become both sophisticated and unrestrained since the days of *The Public Enemy* (1931) and *Dragnet* (1951). If we look at *Die Hard* (1988), *Hard Boiled* (1992), *The Fugitive* (1993), *Seven* (1995), and *The Negotiator* (1998), for only recent examples of police stories, we find the earlier constrained and self-conscious, indeed moralistic, gun use of Nicholas Ray's socially critical police films, *They Live By Night* (1948), *On Dangerous Ground* (1951), and *Rebel Without a Cause* (1955), now become a febrile and nauseating dance of wanton destruction. The same is true if we follow even so shooty a Western as *The Magnificent Seven* (1960) forward to the limits of *Unforgiven*. What we now call the "adventure" film used to be the "swashbuckler" or the "heroic biography." But Douglas Fairbanks's colorful swordplay in *The Black Pirate* (1926), Leslie Howard's articulate and passionate speechifying in *The Scarlet Pimpernel* (1934), and even the loyal—if military-industrial—heroism of James Stewart in, say, *Strategic Air Command* (1955), become the cynical but marksmanly bullying of Schwarzenegger in films like *Total Recall* (1990) or *Eraser* (1996); the canny and strategic coldness of Kurt Russell in Carpenter's *Escape . . .* films (1981–1996); the pathology of Dennis Hopper in *Waterworld* (1995); the cold cunning cruelty of Harrison Ford in *Raiders of the Lost Ark* (1981), *Star Wars, Air Force One* (1997), or *Patriot Games* (1992); or the mechanical alienation of Sean Penn in *Casualties of War* (1989). As for *noir*, we need only notice the wide gulf between the poetry of Jules Dassin's *Night and the City* (1950) and the wholesale sadism of Curtis Hanson's *L.A. Confidential* (1997) to learn that gunplay has grown from a logical aspect of the representational strategy through which characters once were created, into a *character itself*.

The gangster saga, once embodied in the noble bloodbaths of Coppola, De Palma and Scorsese has been transformed by the graphic hunger of Raimi and the adolescent anthropology of Singleton into a commonplace background, a kind of scenic tone, in which shooting is a linguistic form. Christopher Walken's performance in Ferrara's *The Funeral* (1996) is a striking example of the relation between aphasia and firepower. In very contemporary cinematic ganglands, while explosions are still used for dramatic punctuation (a notable case being Scorsese's *Casino* [1995]) it is increasingly typical to see the wholesale destruction of human life and property—the diminishing of a social scene into an array of tatters through the agency of high-powered automatic gunfire, as in the bizarre opening sequence of *Darkman* (1990), where a villain removes a wooden leg to uncache the lethal weapon, then bounces merrily on the other while his colleague pulverizes a small army of henchmen.

But the gunshot is a natural artifact of screen tellings and in some important ways, therefore, elemental to visual narrative. Like the touch of lips, the lighting of a cigarette, the carnal body lock, and the interrogation, the pointing and use of a gun is a simple means whereby disparate elements in a story can be connected on the screen. The gun, the eye of the gun holder taking aim, the sound of the shot, the visual indication of the wound, all sew together in a diegetic space what could otherwise be alienated fragments of imagery. As the story flows from "point" to "point" it can be shown as a series of jumps: from lips to lips, from flame to cigarette, from body to body, from question to answer, from muzzle to wound. But gunshots invoke technology more elaborately than these other connectives; punctuate more rhythmically; are instantaneous in effect, and so more modern. That so many visual genres—both filmic and televisual—are sprung from styles of gunplay, then, seems unsurprising; because regardless of the specific momentary effect upon the audience in any case, the gun is always a magnificent way for a character to get another character's attention; the gun use is always a pathway from one key narrative spot to another. Melville's *Le Samouraï* (1967) demonstrates this; as does the female showdown in *Johnny Guitar* (1954).

A great many of the writers in this volume address with considerable detail of focus the role played by guns and gunning in the movement of peoples toward frontiers. Guns assist in appropriation, in domination, in cultural definition and control, and therefore in the making of both empowerment and powerlessness. In this particular sense, the critical study of popular cultural materials is an aid to the further understanding of the history of cultural development. Yet not every act of cultural representation is a faithful imaging of society; and as we see by reading closely here, many are the persons and classes in everyday life who are systematically exaggerated, overarmed, brutalized and rendered brutal by producers in the quest for ever more saleable cultural product. The world we live in is, then, *not* mirrored by *True Lies* (1994) (which title somehow fails to give over this point); or by *Speed* (1994), *Basic Instinct* (1992), *The Man Who Shot Liberty Valance* (1962), *The X-Files* (1993), or thousands of other entertainment vehicles which depend for their simulation of "reality" on eager and articulate use of guns.

As Bart Tare (John Dall) learned in Joseph H. Lewis's *Gun Crazy* (1950), guns are entrancing, perhaps only because like the camera, or like fascinated human beings, they are so insistent, so demanding, so focused, and so true; or perhaps because, as so many have argued, like the one-eyed snake they are so loaded. But regardless, the awakening and saddening fact that guns—phallic, military-industrial, conglomerate, bourgeois, genrebound, politically incorrect, or otherwise—are key astringents in media mindwash does not make movie gunplay less appealing to the part of us that dreams confrontational dreams, that seeks the moral resolution of a showdown between the forces we cast—in whatever limited cultural system which is our world—as good and evil. For my own part, I am still enchanted and hurled into a dream that has an inner, sweet truth when I recall Jack Palance creeping with a slinky gait and shining holster in *Shane* (1953); Bogey, grimacing with distaste, shooting Major Strasser in *Casablanca* (1942); Robert Mitchum serenely staring down the barrel of his long rifle at strangely beautiful Johnny Depp in *Dead Man* (1995).

And I can still remember with fondness, and a chill, my own quite real—which is to say, non-diegetic—childhood adoration of The Lone Ranger. He came, in the person of Clayton Moore, to ride his horse Silver in the hockey rink of my hometown, once many years ago. They had piled the surface of the place with rich loam, and the horse raced in with him astride, the straps of his chilling black mask aflutter behind him in the spotlight glare. Silver, I remember, was huge, and magnificent, and The Lone Ranger rode him better than ever he had done on TV. When the night was done I stood with my father outside at the curb, and watched the Ranger get into a maroon Cadillac with a horse-trailer attached, still wearing that silver-blue costume, and the white hat, and the mask. He opened his window and smiled at me and put something in my hand, and rode off down Cannon Street. I looked down—all this is true—and saw my very own silver bullet.

NOTE

[1]   People who make movies did not, on the average evening, have dinner with people who make television," Joan Didion wrote in *After Henry* (New York: Simon and Schuster, 1992), "People who make television had most of the money, but people who make movies still had most of the status."

Index of Films and Television Shows Cited

Brooklyn South (1997), Pearson
Bulworth (Warren Beatty, 1998), Fuchs, Pomerance
Casablanca (Michael Curtiz, 1942), Pomerance
Casino (Martin Scorsese, 1995), Pomerance
Casualties of War (Brian De Palma, 1989), Pomerance
Cisco Kid, The (1950), Pomerance
Clockers (Spike Lee, 1996), Fuchs
Clockwork Orange, A (Stanley Kubrick, 1971), Miller
Combat! (1962), Walker
Conan the Barbarian (Paul Verhoeven, 1981), Streible
Conspiracy Theory (Richard Donner, 1997), Hunter
Contact (Robert Zemeckis, 1997), Streible
Cops (1989), Sakeris, Turner
Copycat (Jon Amiel, 1995), Dole
Cover Up (1984), Pomerance
Crow, The (Alex Proyas, 1994), Pomerance

Daktari (1966), Walker
Darkman (Sam Raimi, 1990), Pomerance
Dawn Patrol (Howard Hawks, 1930), Pomerance, Robertson
Dawn Patrol (Edmund Goulding, 1938), Robertson
Day of the Jackal (Fred Zinnemann, 1973), Pomerance
Day the Earth Stood Still, The (Robert Wise, 1951), Pomerance
Dead Man (Jim Jarmusch, 1995), Pomerance
Dead Pool, The (Buddy Van Horn, 1988), Pearson
Die Hard (John McTiernan, 1988), Dole, Pomerance, Woodward
Dirty Harry (Don Siegel, 1971), Pearson
Dr. Kildare (1961), Walker
Donnie Brasco (Mike Newell, 1997), Pomerance
Doom Generation, The (Gregg Araki, 1995), Pomerance, Sakeris, Wood
Double Dragon (James Yukich, 1993), Seiter
Dragnet (1951), Miller, Pomerance
Due South (1994), Pearson, Pomerance, Sakeris

Eraser (Chuck Russell, 1996), Pomerance
Escape from ... (series: John Carpenter, 1981–96), Pomerance
E.T. (Steven Spielberg, 1982), Forman
Eternal Jew, The (George Roland, 1933), Farrell

Face/Off (John Woo, 1997), Sakeris
Falling Down (Joel Schumacher, 1992), Forman, Pomerance
Fantasy Island (1978), Pomerance

Fargo (Joel Coen, 1996), Dole, Miller
Fatal Beauty (Tom Holland, 1987), Dole
Femme Nikita, La (Luc Besson, 1990), Miller
4th Man, The (Paul Verhoeven, 1979), Streible
Frankenstein (James Whale, 1931), Farrell
Fugitive, The (Andrew Davis, 1993), Pomerance
Full Metal Jacket (Stanley Kubrick, 1996), Miller, Pomerance
Funeral, The (Abel Ferrara, 1996), Pomerance

Gallipoli (Peter Weir, 1981), Saloojee
Gang That Couldn't Shoot Straight, The (James Goldstone, 1971), Forman
G.I. Jane (Ridley Scott, 1997), Dole, Pomerance, Sakeris, Tucker-Fried
Girl From U.N.C.L.E., The (1966), Walker
Godfather, The (Francis Ford Coppola, 1972), Miller
Gone With the Wind (Victor Fleming, 1939), Fiedler
GoodFellas (Martin Scorcese, 1993), Pomerance, Woodward
Grosse Pointe Blank (George Armitage, 1997), Pomerance, Sakeris, Woodward
Gun Crazy (Joseph H. Lewis, 1950), Pomerance
Gunfighter, The (Henry King, 1950), Cooke
Guns of Navarone, The (J. Lee Thompson, 1961), Pomerance
Gunsmoke (1955), Pomerance

Hamish Macbeth (1995), Pearson
Hard-Boiled (John Woo, 1992), Pomerance
Have Gun Will Travel (1957), Pomerance, Walker
Hearts and Minds (Peter Davis, 1974), Streible
Hill Street Blues (1981), Pearson
Homicide: Life on the Street (1993), Pearson
How I Won the War (Richard Lester, 1967), Pomerance

I Got the Hook Up (Michael Martin, 1998), Fuchs
If . . . (Lindsay Anderson, 1968), Miller
I'm Bout It (Moon Jones & Master P, 1996), Fuchs
Impulse (Sondra Locke, 1990), Dole
Incident on Long Island (1998), Fiedler
Independence Day (Roland Emmerich, 1996), Hunter, Streible
Indiana Jones (series: 1981–1989), Streible
Innocent Blood (John Landis, 1992), Farrell
Invaders from Mars (William Cameron Menzies, 1953), Pomerance

Jackal, The (Michael Caton-Jones, 1997), Hunter
Johnny Guitar (Nicholas Ray, 1954), Pomerance
Juice (Ernest Dickerson, 1992), Forman, Fuchs, Pomerance

Karate Kid (John G. Avildsen, 1984), Miller
Kids (Larry Clark, 1995), Wood
Killers, The (Don Siegel, 1964), Pomerance

L.A. Confidential (Curtis Hanson, 1997), Pomerance
LAPD: Life on the Beat (1996), Pomerance, Turner
Last Tango in Paris (Bernardo Bertolucci, 1973), Miller, Pomerance, Saloojee
Law and Order (1990), Pearson
Leave It To Beaver (1957), Walker
Lethal Weapon (Richard Donner, 1987), Dole, Hart & Patrick, Woodward
Little Caesar (Mervyn Le Roy, 1931), Miller
Little Mermaid, The (Ron Clements & John Musker, 1989), Seiter
Long Kiss Goodnight, The (Renny Harlin, 1996), Dole, Hunter

Magic School Bus, The (1994), Seiter
Magnificent Seven, The (John Sturges, 1960), Pomerance
Making of an American Citizen, The (Alice Guy Blache, 1912), Farrell
Maltese Falcon, The (John Huston, 1941), Pomerance
Man From U.N.C.L.E., The (1964), Pomerance, Sakeris, Walker
Man of the West (Anthony Mann, 1958), Cooke
Man Who Knew Too Much, The (Alfred Hitchcock, 1956), Pomerance
Man Who Shot Liberty Vallance, The (John Ford, 1962), Pomerance
Marnie (Alfred Hitchcock, 1964), Pomerance
Mars Attacks! (Tim Burton, 1996), Pomerance
Matrix, The (Andy and Larry Wachowski, 1999), Miller
Men In Black (Barry Sonnenfeld, 1997), Farrell, Hunter, Miller, Pomerance, Sakeris
Menace II Society (Albert & Allen Hughes, 1993), Fuchs, Miller
Metropolis (Fritz Lang, 1926), Streible
Mickey Blue Eyes (Kelly Makin, 1999), Pomerance
Mighty Morphin Power Rangers (1993), Miller, Seiter
MP: Da Last Don (Master P, 1998), Fuchs
Mulan (Tony Bancroft & Barry Cook, 1998), Dole
Murder in the Air (Lewis Seiler, 1940), Pomerance
Mussert (Paul Verhoeven, 1968), Streible

Natural Born Killers (Oliver Stone, 1994), Farrell
Navy Seals (Lewis Teague, 1990), Tucker-Fried
Near Dark (Kathryn Bigelow, 1987), Farrell

Shanghai Triad (Yimou Zhang, 1995), Wood
Shooting Party, The (Alan Bridges, 1984), Pomerance
Shootist, The (Don Siegel, 1976), Cooke
Showgirls (Paul Verhoeven, 1995), Streible
Silence of the Lambs (Jonathan Demme, 1991), Dole, Pomerance, Sakeris
Sleeping With the Enemy (Joseph Ruben, 1991), Dole
Soldier of Orange (Paul Verhoeven, 1979), Streible
Speed (Jan de Bont, 1994), Pomerance
Spetters (Paul Verhoeven, 1980), Streible
Starship Troopers (Paul Verhoeven, 1997), Pomerance, Sakeris, Streible
Star Wars (George Lucas, 1977), Pomerance
Star Wars (series: George Lucas; Irvin Kershner; Richard Marquand, 1977–1983), Pomerance, Streible
Stepford Wives, The (Bryan Forbes, 1975), Farrell
Strapped (Forest Whitaker, 1993), Forman, Fuchs
Strategic Air Command (Anthony Mann, 1955), Pomerance
Streets Is Watching (Jay-Z, 1998), Fuchs
Sunrise (F.W. Murnau, 1927), Wood

Taxi Driver (Martin Scorsese, 1976), Pomerance
Temptress Moon (Kaige Chen, 1996), Wood
Terminator, The (James Cameron, 1984), Farrell, Forman, Woodward
Terminator 2 (James Cameron, 1991), Dole
Tetsuo II: Body Hammer (Shinya Tsukamoto, 1992), Cooke
That Thing You Do! (Tom Hanks, 1996), Wood
Thelma and Louise (Ridley Scott, 1991), Dole, Forman, Keating, Pomerance, Sakeris
They Live By Night (Nicholas Ray, 1948), Pomerance
Things to Come (William Cameron Menzies, 1936), Pomerance
This Is the Army (Michael Curtiz, 1943), Pomerance
Top Gun (Tony Scott, 1986), Robertson, Sakeris
Total Recall (Paul Verhoeven, 1990), Pomerance, Streible
Touched by an Angel (1994), Miller
Triumph of the Will (Leni Riefenstahl, 1934), Streible
True Lies (James Cameron, 1994), Pomerance
Turkish Delight (Paul Verhoeven, 1971), Streible
2001: A Space Odyssey (Stanley Kubrick, 1968), Streible

Unforgiven (Clint Eastwood, 1992), Pomerance
Untouchables, The (1959), Pomerance

V.I. Warshawski (Jeff Kanew, 1991), Dole
Videodrome (David Cronenberg, 1982), Cooke

Contributors

GRAYSON COOKE is a student of machinic thought in the Humanities doctoral program at Concordia University, Montreal.

CAROL DOLE is Chair of the English Department at Ursinus College in Pennsylvania, where she teaches both literature and film courses. Her most recent essay on film appears in *Jane Austen at the Movies* (University of Kentucky Press, 1998).

KIRBY FARRELL's latest book is *Post-Traumatic Culture: Injury and Interpretation in the '90s* (Johns Hopkins, 1998). He is Professor of English at the University of Massachusetts in Amherst, and the author of *Play Death and Heroism* and other books on Shakespeare as well as several novels.

LESLIE A. FIEDLER is Samuel Clemens Professor of English, and SUNY Distinguished Professor, at the State University of New York at Buffalo. His books include *An End to Innocence* (1955), *Love and Death in the American Novel* (1960), *The Return of the Vanishing American* (1968), *Being Busted* (1970), *The Stranger in Shakespeare* (1972), *Freaks: Myths and Images of the Secret Self* (1978), *What Was Literature* (1982), *Tyranny of the Normal* (1996) and eighteen others. He is currently writing about minstrels.

MURRAY FORMAN has done research and writing on popular music, urban youth subcultures, and media representations of minorities and has lectured in Communications and Cultural Studies. He teaches at Northeastern University in Boston. His book, *"The Hood Comes First": Race, Space and Place in Rap Music and Hiphop* is forthcoming from Wesleyan University Press.

ALAN R. FRIED is an Assistant Professor at the University of South Carolina. His research interests include the history of desegregation and the history of newspaper marketing.

CYNTHIA FUCHS teaches English, Film and Media Studies and African American Studies at George Mason University. She has written articles on Michael Jackson, the Artist, and queer punks, and is a regular reviewer for *Philadelphia City Paper* and *nitrateonline.com*.

GEORGE GERBNER is Bell Atlantic Professor of Telecommunication in the School of Communications and Theater at Temple University. *He is the author of Telling All the Stories: Collected Essays* (Peter Lang, forthcoming), *Invisible Crises: What Conglomerate Media Control Means for America and the World* (Westview, 1996), *The Global Media*

247

Debate: Its Rise, Fall and Renewal (Ablex, 1993), and *Triumph of the Image* (Westview, 1992) as well as Dean Emeritus of the Annenberg School for Communication.

JUDY HUNTER is Assistant Professor of English and Coordinator of the Language Centre at Ryerson Polytechnic University in Toronto. She teaches writing and English language courses. She has spoken and written on media heroes and gender in children's and adolescents' writing. Her research interests are language and literacy and social identity.

NICOLE MARIE KEATING is a doctoral candidate at the Annenberg School for Communication at the University of Pennsylvania. She is the co-producer of *Barbara's Dollhouse* (1996), a documentary which aired on PBS in Philadelphia; and is a contributor to the *Encyclopedia of Contemporary American Culture* (Routledge, forthcoming).

MARK CRISPIN MILLER is the author of *Boxed In: The Culture of TV* (Northwestern, 1988), and the editor of *Seeing Through Movies* (Pantheon, 1990). He is Professor of Media Studies at New York University and Director of the Project on Media Ownership. His *Mad Scientists* will be forthcoming from Norton.

WENDY PEARSON's publications include "Vanishing Acts II: Queer Reading(s) of Timothy Findley's *Headhunter* and *Not Wanted on the Voyage*" and "The Queer as Traitor, the Traitor as Queer: Denaturalizing Concepts of Nationhood, Species and Sexuality in Ursula Le Guin's *The Left Hand of Darkness* and Eleanor Arnason's *Ring of Swords*." She is currently in Australia, watching cop shows and writing a series of articles on science fiction and queer theory.

LINDA ROBERTSON is co-director of the Media and Society program, and a member of the Writing and Rhetoric program, at Hobart and William Smith Colleges. She has published on the rhetoric of economics (with William Waller) and appears in the *Elgar Companion to Feminist Economics* (forthcoming). She is working on a collection of essays on the cultural significance of Martha Stewart and on a monograph, *The Myth of Civilized Violence: The WWI Combat Pilot in American Culture.*

ANVER SALOOJEE is Professor in the Department of Politics and Public Administration at Ryerson Polytechnic University. He is the co-editor of *Creating Inclusive Post-Secondary Learning Environments* and a specialist in the areas of human rights policy and education equity.

ELLEN SEITER is Professor of Communication at the University of California, San Diego, the co-editor of *Remote Control: Television, Audiences and Cultural Power* (Routledge, 1989), and author of *Sold Separately: Children and Parents in Consumer Culture* (Rutgers, 1993) and *Television and New Media Audiences* (Oxford, 1999). She has published numerous articles on television, toys, children, audiences, and culture and has released a CD-ROM, *Hero TV* (Southmoon Press, 1999).

DAN STREIBLE teaches Film Studies at the University of South Carolina. He is the author of *Fight Pictures: A History of Prizefighting and Early Cinema* (Smithsonian Institution

Press) and is co-author, with Douglas Kellner, of *An Emile de Antonio Reader* (forthcoming from the University of Minnesota Press).

LAUREN R. TUCKER has published articles in *Journalism Quarterly, Critical Studies in Mass Communication, Journal of Broadcasting and Electronic Media,* and the *Howard Journal of Communication.* She is working in advertising in Chicago.

FRED TURNER is the author of *Echoes of Combat: The Vietnam War in American Memory* (Anchor Books, 1996) and a former journalist. He has taught Communication at Harvard University's John F. Kennedy School of Government and is currently teaching at the Massachusetts Institute of Technology. His features and reviews have appeared in *The Progressive, The Chicago Tribune Sunday Magazine,* and *The Boston Phoenix.*

CYNTHIA WALKER is a doctoral candidate in the School of Communication, Information and Library Studies at Rutgers University, and has taught film, television, scriptwriting, journalism and mass communication at Rutgers, New School University, and New Jersey City University. She has contributed several entries to the *Encyclopedia of Television,* edited by Horace Newcomb (Fitzroy Dearborn, 1997).

ROBIN WOOD is the author of *Hitchcock's Films Revisited, Hollywood From Vietnam to Reagan* and *Sexual Politics and Narrative Film: Classical Hollywood and Beyond* (all from Columbia University Press). He is at work on a monograph about *The Wings of the Dove* and a fourth novel. He is the author of numerous studies of filmmakers, including Antonioni, Chabrol, Bergman, Penn and Hawks.

STEVEN WOODWARD is completing a doctoral dissertation on the English writer Walter de la Mare at the University of Toronto. Formerly a student of film and photography, he has published an essay on the films of Krzysztof Kieslowski and is writing about both the recent films of Roman Polanski and killer girls. He teaches Children's Literature at Nipissing University in North Bay, ON.

MURRAY POMERANCE and JOHN SAKERIS are professors in the Department of Sociology at Ryerson Polytechnic University, Toronto, and co-editors of *Pictures of a Generation on Hold: Selected Papers* (1996). John Sakeris is writing about gender police in Hollywood flim. Murray Pomerance is also author of *The Complete Partitas* (Les Trois O, 1992–1995), and *Magia d'Amore* (Sun and Moon, 1999); and his "Finding Release: Storm Clouds and *The Man Who Knew Too Much* (1956)" appears in James Buhler, Caryl Flinn and David Neumeyer, eds., *Music and Cinema* (Wesleyan University Press, 2000). He is the editor of *Ladies and Gentlemen, Boys and Girls: Gender in Film at the End of the Twentieth Century* (forthcoming, State University of New York Press).

Index